STATE OF THE
WORLD
1997

Other Norton/Worldwatch Books
Lester R. Brown et al.

State of the World 1984	*State of the World 1993*
State of the World 1985	*State of the World 1994*
State of the World 1986	*State of the World 1995*
State of the World 1987	*State of the World 1996*
State of the World 1988	*Vital Signs 1992*
State of the World 1989	*Vital Signs 1993*
State of the World 1990	*Vital Signs 1994*
State of the World 1991	*Vital Signs 1995*
State of the World 1992	*Vital Signs 1996*

ENVIRONMENTAL ALERT SERIES

Lester R. Brown et al.
Saving the Planet

Alan Thein During
How Much is Enough?

Sandra Postel
Last Oasis

Lester R. Brown
Hal Kane
Full House

Christopher Flavin
Nicholas Lenssen
Power Surge

Lester R. Brown
Who Will Feed China?

Lester R. Brown
Tough Choices

Michael Renner
Fighting for Survival

STATE OF THE WORLD 1997

A Worldwatch Institute Report on Progress Toward a Sustainable Society

PROJECT DIRECTOR
Lester R. Brown

ASSOCIATE PROJECT DIRECTORS
Christopher Flavin
Hilary F. French

EDITOR
Linda Starke

CONTRIBUTING RESEARCHERS
Janet N. Abramovitz
Chris Bright
Lester R. Brown
Christopher Flavin
Hilary F. French
Gary Gardner
Anne Platt McGinn
Michael Renner
David Malin Roodman

W · W · NORTON & COMPANY

NEW YORK   LONDON

The text of this book is composed in ITC New Baskerville, with the display set in Caslon. Composition by
Peggy Miller Associates; manufacturing by the Haddon Craftsmen, Inc.

First Edition

ISBN 0-393-04008-9
ISBN 0-393-31569-X (pbk)

W. W. Norton & Company, Inc., 500 Fifth Avenue, New York, N.Y. 10110
http://www.wwnorton.com

W. W. Norton & Company Ltd., 10 Coptic Street, London WC1A IPU

1 2 3 4 5 6 7 8 9 0

This book is printed on recycled paper.

A SPECIAL TRIBUTE

The Worldwatch Institute has had the rare good fortune to be governed by an outstanding Board of Directors; their names appear on the preceding page. At the helm of this Board during the Institute's first 21 years was Orville L. Freeman. Whatever the Institute's achievements over the years, this Board and its quiet, behind-the-scenes direction under his leadership have played a key role.

During Orville Freeman's years as chairman, from 1974 through 1995, the Institute's staff grew from a meager dozen in the early years to 30 today. Worldwatch expanded its stable of publications, steadily increasing the number of languages, until now its work is published in some 30 languages. This period saw *State of the World*, launched in 1984, acquire a semi-official status, being used by government and corporate leaders alike.

Orville Freeman is one of the most remarkable public servants of the last half-century. A World War II veteran and three-term governor of the State of the Minnesota during the fifties, he placed John Kennedy's name in nomination for the presidency at the Democratic convention in Los Angeles in 1960. He served as Secretary of Agriculture from 1961 to 1969, one of three Kennedy cabinet appointees, along with Dean Rusk and Stewart Udall, to serve throughout the eight years of the Kennedy/Johnson administration. After leaving the Department, he served many years as the CEO of Business International.

My relationship with Orville Freeman goes back to the U.S. Department of Agriculture, where I served him as an advisor on international agricultural policy and later as Administrator of the department's technical assistance agency, the International Agricultural Development Service. Our official relationship quickly turned into a close personal one.

When we were launching the Institute in early 1974, it seemed only natural to turn to Orville Freeman as our first Board chairman. We could not have made a better choice. Somewhere there may have been a better relationship between the chairman of a board and the chief executive officer of an organization, but it is impossible for me to imagine it. It was this close personal tie that made the relationship between the Board and the Institute so supportive, constructive, and pleasant.

When Orville and his wife, Jane, decided in 1995 to return to Minnesota to be closer to family, and especially to their three grandchildren, he felt it was time to step down as chairman. He continues to serve on the Board, which is now headed by his very able successor, Hunter Lewis, the founder and president of Cambridge Associates, one of the country's premier financial consulting firms.

Hunter, other members of the Board, the current staff, and Institute alumni all join me in this expression of gratitude to Orville Freeman for helping to make the Worldwatch Institute the leading worldwide source of environmental policy analysis and information that it is today.

Lester R. Brown

Acknowledgments

As the variety and complexity of environmental issues has grown, Worldwatch Institute's need for talented, dedicated staff has increased with it. We have been lucky to find a unique array of committed individuals who understand the need to look beyond narrowly defined disciplines and to consider the interconnections in the global economy and environment that are making it impossible to solve problems in isolation.

This year we would like to start by acknowledging the fine work of the research staff, many of them new to the Institute, who worked with our senior researchers and research associates in preparing *State of the World 1997*. Cheri Sugal brings to Worldwatch an impressive background and knowledge of the emerging field of ecological economics, which helped her contribute to the preparation of Chapter 6. Molly O'Meara joined the Institute at mid-year, and worked under unusually tight deadlines on the research for Chapter 9 on the ozone issue. Her grasp of science and her work on methyl bromide proved particularly useful.

Jennifer Mitchell, also new to the Institute, brought her strong research skills and dedication to more chapters than anyone else—Chapters 4, 7, and 8. Seth Dunn joined the Institute near the end of the *State of the World* process, and pitched in with last-minute research (while finding time to run the New York City marathon).

We also were lucky to have several very talented interns at Worldwatch over the summer, all of them contributing vital research help. Kira Schmidt brought her extensive knowledge of U.N. environment processes to her skillful work on Chapter 1, April Bowling contributed strong analytical skills to Chapter 8, and John Tuxill brought his background in conservation biology to Chapter 5. We are grateful for their contributions to this year's book.

All this activity at the Institute is made possible by the generous support of various foundations. We are grateful to the United Nations Population Fund for specific funding for *State of the World*. In addition, we would like to thank the following for their support of the overall work of the Institute: the Carolyn, Nathan Cummings, Geraldine R. Dodge, Ford, George Gund, William and Flora Hewlett, W. Alton Jones, John D. and Catherine T. MacArthur, Andrew W. Mellon, Curtis and Edith Munson, Surdna, Turner, Wallace Genetic, and Weeden foundations; the Lynn R. and Karl E. Prickett, Rockefeller Brothers, and Wallace Global funds; The Pew Charitable Trusts; and Rockefeller Financial Services.

We continue to benefit from a dedicated support staff who are normally unsung. Lori Baldwin is now in charge of updating the Worldwatch Database Disk in addition to being our Librarian and webmaster. Laura Malinowski keeps researchers up to date on the week's news through clippings from more than 100 journals. And the publications office makes sure your orders get filled as quickly as possible, thanks to the hard work of Publications Sales Coordinator Millicent Johnson, Publications Assistant Joseph Gravely, and Receptionist Amy Warehime.

We have been pleased this year to welcome as Senior Vice President for Operations Bill Mansfield, who came to the Institute after many years as Deputy Executive Director in Nairobi at the U.N. Environment Programme. He is joined by our very able management team: Executive Assistant to the President and Computer Systems Administrator Reah Janise Kauffman, Assistant Treasurer Barbara Fallin, and Administrative Assistant to the Senior Vice President for Research Suzanne Clift. Reah Janise also provides valuable assistance with fundraising.

Our communications team includes several key people who by now are very experienced at getting the messages in all Worldwatch publications out to you: Director of Communications Jim Perry, Deputy Director Denise Byers Thomma, and Administrative Assistant Tara Patterson. Our award-winning magazine, *World Watch*, remains in the capable hands of Editor Ed Ayres; Associate Editor Chris Bright, who once again this year managed to also write a chapter for this volume; and Designers Liz Doherty and Jennifer Seher.

This year, for the first time, we have prepared *State of the World* using a desktop publishing program. Our thanks to Peggy Miller Associates for taking on this assignment, and to long-time editor Linda Starke for overseeing the production of the camera-ready copy as well as accommodating the schedules and writing styles of nine chapter authors. The index was again prepared by Ritch Pope of Dexter, Oregon.

Outside the Institute, we would like to thank the following generous individuals for their assistance and, in many cases,

their comments on early drafts of the chapters: Stephen Andersen, Gilbert Bankobeza, Richard Benedick, Charles Beretz, Norman Berg, Sally Bolger, T. Colin Campbell, Elizabeth Cook, Pierre Crosson, André de Moor, Corinna Gilfillan, Davidson Gwatkin, Douglas Koplow, Tom Land, Luc Martial, Pauline Midgley, Alan Miller, Norman Myers, Edward Parson, Sandra Postel, Madhava Sarma, Ronald Steenblik, Jason Weston, George Woodwell, Derek Yach, and John Young.

I would like to end the acknowledgments this year on a more personal note. Our vice president for administration, Blondeen Gravely, who has suffered from lupus for many years, went on long-term disability in early 1996. One of the original incorporators of the Institute, along with Erik Eckholm and myself, Blondeen was part of the core group around which the Institute has developed over the last 22 years.

For me, this interruption of our working relationship, which goes back more than 30 years to when we were both in the U.S. Department of Agriculture, is particularly painful. Shortly after Blondeen joined the department, while still in her teens, we began working together, united by a quiet bond of trust and mutual confidence that kept us together throughout our working careers.

In the early days of the Institute, Blondeen quickly assumed responsibility for the administrative side of things, leaving me and others free to concentrate on shaping the Institute's research program. It is with more than a little sadness that I have watched this interruption of the official part of our relationship. Not only are we at Worldwatch indebted to Blondeen, but so are those throughout the world who have benefited from the Institute's research.

Lester R. Brown

Contents

Worldwatch Database Disk

The data from all graphs and tables contained in this book, as well as from those in all other Worldwatch publications of the past two years, are available on disk for use with IBM-compatible or Macintosh computers. This includes data from the State of the World *and* Vital Signs *series of books,* Worldwatch Papers, World Watch *magazine, and the Environmental Alert series of books. The data are formatted for use with spreadsheet software compatible with Lotus 1-2-3 version 2, including all Lotus spreadsheets, Quattro Pro, Excel, SuperCalc, and many others. For IBM-compatibles, a 3 1/2 inch (high-density) disk is provided. Information on how to order the Worldwatch Database Disk can be found on the final page of this book.*

List of Tables and Figures

LIST OF TABLES

LIST OF FIGURES

Chapter 5. Tracking the Ecology of Climate Change

Chapter 6. Valuing Nature's Services

Chapter 8. Reforming Subsidies

Chapter 9. Learning from the Ozone Experience

Foreword

This fourteenth edition of *State of the World* coincides with two important milestones: the fifth anniversary of the Earth Summit in Rio de Janeiro in 1992 and the tenth anniversary of the 1987 Montreal Protocol to protect the earth's ozone layer. With these two landmarks in mind, 1997 seemed a particularly good year to review progress in addressing global environmental problems.

In this year's book, we look at the broad Rio environmental agenda, ranging from climate to biodiversity, with a wide-angle lens in Chapter 1—and then with a much tighter focus we look at the decade-long effort to protect the ozone layer in Chapter 9. The first chapter describes the broad failure so far to achieve an environmentally sustainable economy, while the last shows that when faced with a clear crisis, the world community is capable of swift and effective action.

Whether progress is viewed as a glass half empty or half full, the international environmental agenda is increasingly crowded as the decade draws to a close. Extreme climatic events such as the destructive tropical storms that ravaged North America and Asia in 1996 and the crop-withering heat wave that claimed 465 lives in Chicago in the summer of 1995 have heightened concern about the rising concentration of greenhouse gases in the atmosphere. Dangers to the natural world are seen in the thousands of species of amphibians, birds, and mammals now threatened with extinction.

In this year's book, we have assembled the latest information on these new environmental threats, and have also described some of the surprising and potentially dangerous connections between these problems. One chapter, for example, examines the far-reaching effects that climate change may have on natural ecosystems, while another shows how dependent humanity is on the "services" provided by those ecosystems—from the pollination of crops to the maintenance of safe water supplies.

On the principal threats addressed in Rio, including climate change and the loss of biodiversity, progress so far has been slow and inadequate. Yet we see many signs that the policy wheels have begun to turn, and remain optimistic that the complex international agreements signed in 1992 will soon bear fruit. As described in Chapter 9, experience in tackling the ozone problem has shown that with the concerted efforts of scientists, industry leaders, government officials, and citizen activists, a strong international agreement can lead to surprisingly rapid progress.

The first step to action is awareness, and on this front there are many signs of hope. From insurance companies to agribusiness firms, concern about environmental trends is rising. The banking community is beginning to worry about the sustainability of its investments. And the insurance industry has begun to cut back on its coverage in regions that are vulnerable to tropical storms, which it believes are becoming more frequent and powerful as a result of global climate change.

All these trends strengthen the interest in Worldwatch research products, not only *State of the World*, but also our second annual, *Vital Signs*, plus the Environmental Alert book series, Worldwatch Papers, and *World Watch* magazine. Mounting concern is also reflected in a sharp increase in invitations to address international conferences and to meet with corporate management teams and parliamentary groups.

In most countries, *State of the World* is handled by commercial publishers. But one of the more interesting exceptions is Sweden, where it is put out jointly by the Swedish Environmental Protection Agency and the Society for the Protection of Nature, that nation's oldest and largest environmental group. The Environmental Protection Agency used the launch of *State of the World 1996* as the occasion to organize a conference on agricultural sustainability in the Baltic region, inviting delegates from countries such as Poland, Estonia, and Russia. Among the speakers were Nicholai Vorontsov, former environment minister of the Soviet Union, and Andres Tarand, former prime minister of Estonia.

In late March, Romanian President Ion Iliescu convened a conference entitled "Workshop Worldwatch: Sustainable Development and International Cooperation," at which the Romanian edition of *State of the World* was launched. Some 120 invited participants attended from countries in the region, including the environment minister of Moravia, the head of the Institute of Hydropolitics in Istanbul, and the water minister of Croatia.

After a meeting in which we discussed the issues covered in *State of the World 1996*, U.K. Minister of Environment John Gummer ordered copies for distribution to other members of the cabinet. Norwegian Environment Minister Thorbjorn Berntsen presided at the launching of the Norwegian edition of *State of the World 1996*, calling it "the most important book in the world."

In many countries, committed individuals play an important role in ensuring publication of *State of the World*. Romanian President Iliescu launched the Romanian edition of *State of the World* when he was the head of a small publishing house, Editore Tehnica, a dozen years ago. In Italy, Gianfranco Bologna, Secretary General of the Italian World Wildlife Fund for Nature and a long-time friend and supporter of Worldwatch, will with this edition be editing his tenth Italian edition of *State of the World*.

It is this commitment by many individuals to building an environmentally sustainable global economy that makes it possible to publish *State of the World* in 27 languages. And strong interest in this topic on college and university campuses led in 1995 to the adoption of *State of the World* and other Worldwatch books in 1,027 courses in U.S. colleges and universities alone.

In recent years, the aid agencies of Norway and Denmark have invested in subscriptions of Worldwatch publications—*State of the World*, *Vital Signs*, the Worldwatch Papers, and the Worldwatch database disk—for key officials and individuals in developing countries where they provide assistance. In countries where information is scarce, they reason that a modest investment in the distribution of basic environmental information could substantially improve the quality of decision making. This year, the U.S. Agency for International Development is joining the two Nordic agencies in purchasing subscriptions for distribution in developing nations.

And in 1996, for the first time, a private company—the Ikari Corporation of Japan—invested $5,000 in subscriptions to Worldwatch publications for key individuals in countries in East and Southeast Asia.

We deeply appreciate the interest and support from every corner of the planet. It helps us retain our optimism that we will, indeed, one day succeed in reversing the degradation of the planet and creating an environmental sustainable global economy for our children.

If you have any comments or suggestions for improving *State of the World*, please let us know by letter, fax (202-296-7365), or e-mail (world watch@worldwatch.org). We also hope you will visit the Worldwatch Website at <http://www.worldwatch.org>.

Lester R. Brown
Christopher Flavin
Hilary French

Worldwatch Institute
1776 Massachusetts Ave., NW
Washington, DC 20036

December 1996

STATE OF THE
WORLD
1997

1

The Legacy of Rio

Christopher Flavin

Five years after the historic U.N. Conference on Environment and Development in Rio de Janeiro, the world is falling well short of achieving its central goal—an environmentally sustainable global economy. Since the Earth Summit in 1992, human numbers have grown by roughly 450 million, which exceeds the combined populations of the United States and Russia. Annual emissions of carbon, which produce carbon dioxide, the leading greenhouse gas, have climbed to a new high, altering the very composition of the atmosphere and the earth's heat balance.[1]

During these past five years, the earth's biological riches have also been rapidly and irreversibly diminished. Huge areas of old-growth forests have been degraded or cleared—in temperate as well as tropical regions—eliminating thousands of species of plants and animals. Biologically rich wetlands and coral reefs are suffering similar fates. Despite a surge in economic growth in

developing countries, an estimated 1.3 billion people are so poor that they cannot meet their basic needs for food or shelter.[2]

In its vast scope and ambitious record, the Earth Summit set a standard for itself that was almost certain to lead to disappointment. Of course, the failure to reverse in only five years trends that have been under way for decades is not surprising. Unfortunately, few governments have even begun the policy changes that will be needed to put the world on an environmentally sustainable path. Only a half-dozen countries, for example, have levied environmental taxes to discourage the unsustainable use of materials and energy. And many nations continue to subsidize clear-cutting of forests, inefficient energy and water use, and mining. (See Chapter 8.)

One of the signal accomplishments of Rio was the official linking of environment and development issues, including an explicit recognition that poverty itself is a driving force behind a large share of environmental degradation. Although many think of development in

---

Units of measure throughout this book are metric unless common usage dictates otherwise.

simple economic terms, it can be better thought of as an increase in the options available to people—for meeting their basic needs for food, shelter, and education, for example. As biological and cultural diversity are diminished, those options are reduced.

In the years since Rio, millions of poor people have fallen even further behind, and governments have been either unable or unwilling to provide an adequate safety net. In many countries, environmental and social problems are exacerbating ethnic tension, creating millions of refugees and sometimes leading to violent conflict. (See Chapter 7.) Yet most governments still pursue economic growth as an end in itself, neglecting the long-term sustainability of the course they chart. In many developing countries, rapid growth has led to a sharp deterioration in air and water quality in the nineties, and undermined the natural resources on which people depend.[3]

Five years is not long enough to judge Rio's full legacy, but one lesson is clear: Although substantial progress has been made on specific environmental problems, the world has so far failed to meet the broader challenge of integrating environmental strategies into economic policy. Until finance ministers, and even prime ministers, take these problems as seriously as environmental officials do, we will continue to undermine the natural resource base and ecosystems on which the human economy depends.

If the economy is to be put on a sustainable footing in the twenty-first century, it is unlikely to be the result of a top-down, centralized plan; the answer is more likely to lie in an eclectic mix of international agreements, sensible government policies, efficient use of private resources, and bold initiatives by grassroots organizations and local governments. In fact, Rio may have been a last hurrah for those who hope for vast "Marshall Plans" to solve world problems. National governments have generally failed to meet even the minimal financial commitments made in Rio. If the long-term viability of human society is to be assured, we all have to get involved.

THE ROAD FROM RIO

The broad goals of the Earth Summit were laid out in Agenda 21, the 40-chapter plan of action for achieving sustainable development that was signed by the leaders gathered in Rio. This landmark document concludes that "an environmental policy that focuses mainly on the conservation and protection of resources without consideration of the livelihoods of those who depend on the resources is unlikely to succeed."[4]

The goals included in Agenda 21 range from protecting wetlands and deserts to reducing air and water pollution, improving energy and agricultural technologies, managing toxic chemicals and radioactive wastes more effectively, and reducing the incidence of disease and malnutrition. By embracing a broad range of environmental and social aims, Agenda 21 reflects the scope of the challenges the world now faces. But its very ambition has weakened its effectiveness—by straining the limited capacities of governments and international agencies.[5]

The most important institution to emerge from the Earth Summit was the United Nations Commission on Sustainable Development (CSD), set up to review national implementation of Agenda 21 and to provide high-level coordination among various U.N. environment and development programs. At annual ministerial-level meetings in New York, the CSD has focused on a range of disparate environmental goals—from protecting mountains and grasslands to phasing lead out of gasoline and developing environmental indicators. The CSD has been a useful discussion forum and has launched some promising initiatives, including the Intergovernmental Panel on Forests, which is now meeting regularly to craft stronger efforts to protect the world's woodlands. The Commission lacks regulatory powers and a budget of its own, however, so it can only cajole other U.N. programs and agencies into taking its pronouncements seriously.[6]

Under Agenda 21, governments are required to prepare national sustainable development strategies. By 1996, 117 governments had formed national commissions to develop these strategies—most of them made up of a diverse array of industry and nongovernmental organization (NGO) representatives as well as government officials. Unfortunately, most reports prepared so far are broad, rhetorical, self-congratulatory documents that describe existing environment and development programs but do little to redirect them. Too many of the strategies treat environmental issues as separate concerns to be addressed by environment ministries rather than as problems that are woven into the very fabric of the world economy.[7]

Nevertheless, in the five years since the Earth Summit, the international community has begun to embrace the concept of sustainable development and to use that notion to shift the priorities of existing agencies and programs. Governments have also adopted a number of specific agreements, including guidelines for safety in biotechnology and an agreement to protect fish that straddle the boundaries of national waters. In addition, a new Desertification Convention has been negotiated and signed. The Basel Convention has been strengthened to ban many exports of hazardous wastes to developing countries, and a program of action for the protection of the marine environment from land-based

pollution has been adopted. Meanwhile, a treaty to control persistent organic pollutants is being negotiated.[8]

The speeches of the more than 100 world leaders at the Earth Summit were marked by bold rhetoric about the need to channel billions of dollars toward the new challenge of environmentally sustainable development. The Conference Secretariat, led by Canadian industrialist Maurice Strong, prepared a report concluding that developing countries alone would need to invest an additional $600 billion annually during the nineties to achieve Agenda 21's goals, and that $125 billion of this would need to be in the form of aid from industrial countries—more than double the total foreign aid being received by developing countries in the early nineties.[9]

The world has so far failed to meet the challenge of integrating environmental strategies into economic policy.

Very little new money has been forthcoming since Rio. To the contrary, the last five years have been marked by major economic and political changes that diverted attention away from the challenge of sustainable development. The end of the cold war has seen the collapse of economies throughout Central Europe, and has added nations such as Russia and Ukraine to the list of leading foreign aid recipients—a kind of negative "peace dividend."

During the nineties, economic and social pressures have made "rich" countries feel poor, leading them to cut back on domestic social programs and, in some cases, to slash their foreign aid commitments. In Agenda 21, these countries reaffirmed earlier promises to raise annual foreign aid contributions to 0.7

percent of their gross national products (GNP). Instead, overall assistance levels have fallen to their lowest level since 1973 and now average just 0.3 percent of GNP. The steepest falloff was in the United States, where official development assistance declined from $11.7 billion in 1992 to $7.3 billion in 1995; by then, Japan was providing twice as much development assistance as the United States.[10]

Similar cutbacks have undermined the budgets of agencies that many nations had been counting on to promote sustainable development, including the United Nations Environment Programme (UNEP) and the United Nations Development Programme (UNDP), which saw their annual budgets stagnate at $106 million and $1.4 billion respectively in 1995. (By way of comparison, a company must have revenues of $8.9 billion just to make the Fortune Global 500 list.) Effective U.N. programs such as the International Register of Potentially Toxic Chemicals and the Global Environment Monitoring System have been starved for funds, as have programs to help developing countries craft new environment and development strategies.[11]

The fastest progress is now occurring on issues that were first identified decades ago.

The one major financial initiative dedicated to the Rio agenda is the Global Environment Facility (GEF), a specialized fund managed by the World Bank, UNEP, and UNDP. Started in pilot form in 1991, the GEF was envisioned in Agenda 21 as a means to support developing-country projects that mitigate global environmental problems. Since Rio, the GEF has also become the interim funding arm of the climate and biodiversity conventions.[12]

Following these mandates, the GEF has provided support for several dozen worthwhile projects, including efforts to set up national parks, protect endangered species, and promote solar energy, energy efficiency, and other alternatives to fossil fuels. But it has been hampered by feuding member governments and by a management structure that is complex even by the byzantine standards of the United Nations. The $315 million approved for GEF funding in 1996 is actually slightly smaller than the $322 million approved in 1992.[13]

The World Bank, which loans roughly $20 billion to developing countries each year, has a far greater impact on environmental trends around the world. Since Rio, the Bank has strengthened its environmental review process and has withdrawn support from some high-profile environmental projects that critics denounced as wasteful or destructive, such as the Arun Dam in Nepal. James Wolfensohn, who became President of the 50-year-old Bank in 1995, has publicly embraced the challenge of sustainable development, a commitment that is backed up by a Vice-President for Environmentally Sustainable Development—Ismail Serageldin.[14]

These symbolic changes have highlighted a growing gulf between the new environmentally concerned senior management and the hundreds of task managers and country directors that wield the Bank's real power. These individuals remain focused on narrow financial goals, and so far the Bank has failed even to develop an adequate environmental screening process for their loans, according to internal assessments. Consequently, it continues to lend large sums for projects that add to global carbon emissions, destroy natural ecosystems, and undermine the livelihoods of poor people, say outside critics, while the broader vision of a more sustainable economy is largely ignored.[15]

The failure to fulfill the legacy of Rio during these past five years can be attributed in part to the inevitable time lags that mark any new policy initiatives—particularly at the international level. In fact, the fastest progress is now occurring on those issues that were first identified decades ago. In most industrial countries, for example, air and water pollution are now less severe than they were during the Stockholm Conference on the Human Environment in 1972. And many developing countries have begun to implement stringent air pollution laws and to phase lead out of gasoline. At the global level, efforts to end production of the chemicals that deplete the atmosphere's protective ozone layer are already well under way, and have led to a 76-percent reduction in the manufacture of the most damaging ones. (See Chapter 9.)[16]

In other areas, the world still seems to be moving in reverse. Lack of clean water, for example, has permitted a resurgence of infectious disease in many developing nations, while human and animal immune and reproductive systems are being disrupted by chlorine-based chemicals that have become ubiquitous in ecosystems. More seriously, three global problems still stand in the way of achieving a sustainable world: human-induced climate change, the loss of biodiversity, and expanding human population and consumption levels. As recognized in three separate agreements—the 1992 Framework Convention on Climate Change, the 1992 Convention on Biological Diversity, and the 1994 Population Plan of Action—a stable atmosphere, a rich biological world, and a steady human population are essential to humanity's future prospects. Failure to achieve these goals would complicate a range of other problems and lead to an almost inevitable decline in the human condition.[17]

Eight Environmental Heavyweights

In assessing progress on these three global issues since the Earth Summit, it is clear that all countries are not created equal. Global environmental trends are dominated by just a few nations. This chapter looks at eight countries—four industrial and four developing—that together account for 56 percent of the world's population, 59 percent of its economic output, 58 percent of its carbon emissions, and 53 percent of its forests. (See Table 1–1.) These eight environmental powers include the country with the largest population—China; the one with the largest economy and carbon emissions—the United States; and the nation that arguably claims the richest array of biodiversity—Brazil. Together with Germany, Japan, India, Indonesia, and Russia, these countries constitute what could be called the E8—eight nations that disproportionately shape global environmental trends.[18]

Even more than the Group of Seven (G7)—the industrial nations that have dominated the global economy since World War II—the E8 will help shape the future of the entire world. The political systems of the E8 range from communist to democratic, and their experience with capitalism varies from five years to two centuries. But in terms of environmental impact, these eight nations are in a league of their own. Their post-Rio record provides a revealing picture of the progress being made by the world as a whole.

The industrial countries in the E8 shape global trends in part because of their economic strength, their high levels of material consumption and social trend-setting, and their dominance of technology. The developing countries' influence, in contrast, is determined in part by their large populations, their

Table 1–1. Eight Environmental Heavyweights

Country	Share of World Population, 1996	Share of Gross World Product, 1994	Share of World Carbon Emissions, 1995	Share of World Forest Area, 1990	Share of World Flowering Plant Species, 1990[1]
			(percent)		
United States	5	26	23	6	8
Russia	3	2	7	21	9
Japan	2	17	5	0.7	2
Germany	1	8	4	0.3	1
China	21	2	13	4	12
India	17	1	4	2	6
Indonesia	4	0.7	1	3	8
Brazil	3	2	1	16	22
E8 Total	56	59	58	53	—

[1]Based on a total of 250,000 known species. Total could not be calculated due to overlap in species among countries.

SOURCES: Population Reference Bureau, "1996 World Population Data Sheet" (wallchart), Washington, D.C., 1996; World Bank, *World Bank Atlas 1996* (Washington, D.C: 1995); Christopher Flavin and Odil Tunali, *Climate of Hope: New Strategies for Stabilizing the World's Atmosphere,* Worldwatch Paper 130 (Washington, D.C.: Worldwatch Institute, June 1996); U.N. Food and Agriculture Organization, *Forest Resources Assessment 1990: Global Synthesis,* FAO Forestry Paper 124 (Rome: 1995); World Conservation Monitoring Centre, *Global Biodiversity: Status of the Earth's Living Resources* (London: Chapman & Hall, 1992).

rapid economic development, and their rich diversity of wildlife. Because these eight nations use such a large share of the world's resources and produce so much of its pollution, they have a disproportionate responsibility for crafting solutions to the problems identified in Rio.

The E8 nations are also major players at international economic and political fora, heavily influencing the policies of their neighbors and allies, and so are well positioned to lead the way to a more sustainable world. The G7 nations come together each year to discuss and take responsibility for global economic stability, but the E8 will have a far greater influence on the prospects of future generations. No such collection of countries can replace the important role played by global institutions such as the United Nations and its various agencies. Yet the E8 nations, if they choose, could become an important catalyst for action elsewhere—filling a vacuum that now seems to suck energy out of the sustainable development agenda.

During the cold war, the U.S. government provided leadership on a host of issues, including the environment. U.S. air and water quality laws were forerunners of those passed by other nations, and the United States helped establish UNEP in 1972 and formulate the landmark Montreal Protocol to protect the ozone layer in 1987. But U.S. leadership had faded by the time of the Earth Summit, when the government kept other leaders guessing as to whether President Bush would even show up. Since Rio, the United States has failed to ratify the Convention on Biodiversity or the Law of the Sea, clashed with allies over action to slow climate change, and slashed funding for many U.N. environmental programs.[19]

Other nations have stepped forward during the last five years to fill the leadership void. Germany, for example, has adopted some of the world's tightest environmental standards as well as innovative policies to reduce consumer packaging and harness renewable energy. As a pivotal member of the European Union, which is now attempting to speak with one voice on international environmental issues, Germany has also provided leadership at treaty negotiations—notably the Berlin climate conference in 1995, where it stitched together a consensus on a new round of commitments.[20]

Japan, on whom many hopes had been placed in Rio, has compiled an impressive record of domestic environmental progress, including substantial reductions in emissions of sulfur and nitrogen oxides. It has so far failed, however, to assert itself as a global environmental leader—and in fact is known for its resistance to international limits on whaling and on imports of tropical timber from old-growth forests.[21]

Russia, meanwhile, beset by economic and political chaos, has largely lost control of its ecological future. Vast areas of Siberia are being stripped of their natural riches, and belching smokestacks are only cleaned up when the factories beneath them go out of business. Scores of dangerous nuclear reactors continue to operate, while Russian industry still produces and uses chlorofluorocarbons (CFCs) in violation of international ozone agreements the government has signed. "What happened to Russia's green movement?" asked Mark Borozin, editor of *Green World,* an environmental newspaper in Moscow. "People now say, 'Give us bread, shelter and clothing—then we will think about the ecology.'"[22]

Although developing countries still lag behind in implementing and enforcing environmental laws, they have come a long way in understanding the seriousness of the threats. Prior to Rio, many Third World leaders believed they could afford to address only local environmental problems, but now they realize that global climate change and loss of biodiversity also threaten their development prospects. Rising seas, for example, could inundate large areas, displacing 140 million people in Bangladesh and China alone. Tropical and subtropical countries are also likely to see their agricultural harvests diminished by climate change, increasing the need for food imports. In addition, destruction of natural ecosystems may undermine supplies of fresh water, and limit potential revenues from "bioprospecting" and tourism.[23]

With such dangers in mind, and prodded by the Earth Summit agreements, many developing countries have taken steps to redirect development efforts. Among the E8, Brazil has tried with some success to slow deforestation of the Amazon, and, thanks in large measure to the efforts of its NGOs, has dramatically reduced its fertility rate. India, too, has strengthened its environmental efforts, and is an emerging world leader in renewable energy. At climate negotiations in Berlin in 1995, the Indian environment minister helped broker the final North-South bargain. Yet most developing countries still depend heavily on extractive industries; in many cases, the owners of those industries have kept the money flowing to these traditional sectors.[24]

China, which now has the world's third largest economy when measured in purchasing power parity terms, will be increasingly pivotal in any efforts to protect the global environment. As of 1995, China already consumed more coal, grain, and red meat than the United States did. It is the world's number two emitter of carbon, and its air pollution is affecting Japan and South Korea, as well as China itself. In response, China has crafted one of the most elaborate, ambitious national Agenda 21 plans. Still, the government has a relatively poor record of enforcing its environmental laws, and it remains to be seen whether the paper promises will be translated into policy changes.[25]

As this litany suggests, today's environmental geopolitics is marked by a "new world disorder" in which strong leadership is lacking and most countries have mixed records. Shifting alliances have marked recent negotiations on climate and biodiversity. It is time for the E8 countries to take more responsibility for strengthening existing agreements and forging new ones. By establishing informal links between their officials and bridging North-South differences that often impede negotiations, the E8 could catalyze action. A key challenge will be to focus on the common interests of all countries rather than on national interests; in the struggle for a sustainable world, the fates of rich and poor, of North and South, are inextricably linked.

STABILIZING THE CLIMATE

One of the centerpieces of the Earth Summit was the Framework Convention on Climate Change signed by the world leaders gathered in Rio. In the five years since, the urgency of the climate problem has grown, according to scientists. With the atmospheric concentration of carbon dioxide at its highest level in 150,000 years—and still increasing—the world is projected to face a rate of climate change in the next several decades that exceeds natural rates by a factor of 10. Scientists believe that the rapid climate change ahead is likely to be erratic, disruptive, and unpredictable. Local weather patterns may shift suddenly. The incidence of floods, droughts, fires, and heat outbreaks will probably increase as global temperatures rise.[26]

Between 1990 and 1995, annual fossil-fuel-related emissions of carbon, which produce carbon dioxide, rose by

113 million tons, reaching 6 billion tons in 1995. (See Figure 1–1.) They would have risen an additional 400–500 million tons if not for the collapse of fossil-fuel-dependent industries in Central and Eastern Europe. An estimated 1.6 billion tons of additional carbon are released annually from forest clearing, primarily in tropical regions. Emissions of CFCs, another important greenhouse gas, are falling sharply as a result of efforts to protect the ozone layer (see Chapter 9), while emissions of hydrofluorocarbons and methane—both potent greenhouse gases—are still increasing.[27]

Greenhouse gas emission levels vary widely among nations, as seen in figures for the E8. Per capita carbon emissions from fossil fuels range from 5.3 tons in the United States to 2.4 tons in Japan and 0.3 tons in India. (See Table 1–2.) This more-than-twentyfold range in emission rates reflects many differences, including stages of industrial development and personal life-styles and consumption levels. But even among countries at similar stages of economic development, the situation varies widely: per capita emissions in China are 75 percent higher than they are in Brazil,

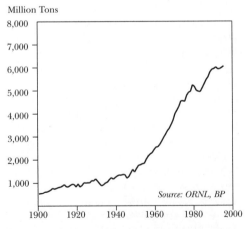

Figure 1–1. Global Carbon Emissions from Burning of Fossil Fuels, 1900–95

Table 1–2. Carbon Emissions from Burning of Fossil Fuels, E8 Countries, 1995

Country	Total Emissions	Share of World Carbon Emissions	Emissions Per Capita	Emissions Growth, 1990–95
	(million tons)	(percent)	(tons)	(percent)
United States	1,394	22.9	5.3	6.2
Russia	437	7.2	2.9	−27.7
Japan	302	5.0	2.4	8.7
Germany	234	3.8	2.9	−10.2
China	807	13.3	0.7	27.5
India	229	3.8	0.3	27.7
Indonesia	56	0.9	0.3	38.8
Brazil	62	1.0	0.4	19.8
E8 Total	3,521	57.9	0.9	—

SOURCES: Christopher Flavin and Odil Tunali, *Climate of Hope: New Strategies for Stabilizing the World's Atmosphere,* Worldwatch Paper 130 (Washington, D.C.: Worldwatch Institute, June 1996); Oak Ridge National Laboratory, *Trends 1993: A Compendium of Data on Global Change* (Oak Ridge, Tenn.: 1994); British Petroleum, *BP Statistical Review of World Energy* (London: Group Media & Publications, 1995).

for instance, while those in the United States are 120 percent higher than in Japan.[28]

Under the terms of the climate convention, all countries must prepare a full inventory of greenhouse gas emissions as well as a national climate plan. Only industrial countries, however, are required to hold their emissions of greenhouse gases at or below the 1990 level in the year 2000—a commitment likely to be missed by roughly half the countries. Among the E8, Germany and Russia will almost certainly make the year 2000 target, but the United States and Japan have fallen badly off track.[29]

Germany, Europe's leading producer of greenhouse gases and the fifth largest producer worldwide, has established a far tougher emissions target than required under the convention—carbon emissions in 2005 that are 25 percent below the 1990 level, a goal that reflects strong public concern about climate change as well as the fact that some reductions are coming easily as the energy-intensive industries of Germany's eastern states close down or switch from coal to gas. By 1995, German emissions were

already more than 10 percent below the 1990 level, and continuing to fall.[30]

The German climate plan includes incentives for improving the energy efficiency of buildings and a law that allows generators of "green" power to sell it to the utilities at a premium price. As a result of this law, Germany installed more wind turbines in 1995 than any other country. It also has high gasoline taxes, but in early 1996 backed down from a new energy tax initiative after industry leaders interceded with Chancellor Kohl. However, he used the threat of the tax to extract a commitment from major industries to cut carbon emissions 20 percent by 2005. Still, even German climate policy is plagued by contradictions, including a $5.3-billion annual coal subsidy that is only gradually being phased out. (See Chapter 8.) The government will need to end such subsidies and enact other reforms if it is to meet its own ambitious target.[31]

Russia, the third largest emitter of carbon, has done little to reduce emissions, hampered as it is by economic problems. Still, Russian carbon emissions in 1995 were already 28 percent below the 1990 level due to the collapse of many of the country's energy-intensive enterprises. As Russia develops a more efficient economic system, it is unlikely to ever emit as much carbon as it did at the peak. But it remains to be seen if the government will build the policy framework needed to achieve high levels of energy efficiency and develop carbon-free energy sources.[32]

The situation is not so encouraging in two other E8 countries. The United States, the world's leading producer of greenhouse gases, launched a Climate Change Action Plan in 1993 that includes 50 measures to promote energy efficiency, commercialize renewable energy technologies, and encourage tree planting. Two thirds of these are relatively weak voluntary programs that do not include the kind of firm industry commitments found in Germany's "voluntary" programs. By 1996, U.S. carbon emissions were already 6 percent above the 1990 level, and a projection by the U.S. Department of Energy indicates that without new policy initiatives, in 2000 these may exceed 1990 levels by a full 11 percent.[33]

The Convention on Climate Change risks becoming an empty vessel: strong on principle but desperately weak in implementation.

Japan, which has a reputation for energy efficiency and a commitment to developing new technologies, has had only limited success with its national climate program, which includes new energy standards, a program to promote solar-powered homes, and other initiatives. Japan's carbon emissions have surged by more than 8 percent since 1990—mainly spurred by increased driving and heavier reliance on central heat-

ing and air-conditioning in buildings. Government officials believe that strong additional measures will be required if Japan is to have any hope of returning to the 1990 level by the year 2000. Japan's task is made more difficult, however, by the fact that its per capita carbon emissions are already less than half the U.S. level.[34]

Carbon emissions have soared in developing countries in the first half of the nineties. Emissions rose 20 percent in Brazil between 1990 and 1995, 28 percent in China and India, and 39 percent in Indonesia. Growth in energy demand, which was restrained by high oil prices and economic stagnation in the eighties, is now surging. Such growth is hardly surprising, given that emissions per person in India and Indonesia are only one tenth the European level, while Brazil's are one seventh and China's one fourth as high. And in many developing countries, emissions are growing slower than the economy because light industries and services are developing faster than heavy manufacturing. In China—which is already the world's second largest carbon emitter—emissions grew at 5 percent a year in the early nineties, while economic growth averaged 10 percent.[35]

The climate convention recognizes developing countries' needs for improved housing and transportation, and so only requires them to adopt national climate plans, not to meet specific emission targets. So far, no national plans have been completed, but it is hoped these will help demonstrate a host of cost-effective means of reducing emissions, including energy efficiency and solar power projects supported by the GEF. Gradually, the economic efficacy of such efforts is being recognized by developing countries, and over time is likely to slow their emissions growth.[36]

Still, the overall record on climate policy to date is not encouraging. Unless additional policies are implemented, the

International Energy Agency projects, global emissions of carbon from fossil fuels will exceed 1990 levels by 17 percent in 2000 and 49 percent by 2010, reaching nearly 9 billion tons annually. The Framework Convention on Climate Change risks becoming an empty vessel: strong on principle but desperately weak in implementation.[37]

Treaty members recognized this shortcoming at the Second Conference of the Parties, which convened in Geneva in July 1996. The U.S. government abruptly abandoned its earlier opposition, and supported European calls for a legally binding protocol to limit emissions. The declaration issued in Geneva calls for such a protocol to be adopted at the third Conference of the Parties in Kyoto in December 1997. It is testimony to the lobbying skills of the fossil fuel industries that it has taken five years just to begin these discussions. If the climate convention is to finally become effective, these commitments will have to be strong ones, and will have to be accompanied by the kind of flexible implementation schemes and regular review procedures that allow the Montreal Protocol to be so effective. (See Chapter 9.)[38]

CONSERVING BIOLOGICAL WEALTH

Harvard biologist Edward O. Wilson calculates that the rich fabric of life that makes up the earth's ecosystems is now being ripped up at the rate of at least 50,000 species a year. Tropical rain forests and other natural ecosystems are being extinguished wholesale by expanding agriculture and human settlements and by water diversions and pollution. Globally, freshwater lakes and streams, coastal mangroves and coral reefs, and temperate rain forests are among the

biological systems most at risk. Three fourths of the world's bird species are declining, and nearly one fourth of the 4,600 species of mammals are threatened with extinction. Scientists are also concerned that rapid climate change in the coming decades could accelerate the already dangerously high rate of species loss. (See Chapter 5.)[39]

For the first time, a single species—*Homo sapiens*—has become a vast, destructive ecological force. The pressures can be seen in China, where 1.2 billion increasingly prosperous people have already put 15–20 percent of the country's species in danger of extinction. With 21 percent of the world's population, China has only 4 percent of the forested area, and growing demand for agricultural land and wood products has placed severe pressure on its remaining forests.[40]

Humanity has worked since the beginning of this century to conserve wildlife, and the land area set aside for protection has grown dramatically since mid-century—reaching nearly 1 billion hectares, equivalent to the entire land area of the United States. (See Figure 1–2.) Still, the Convention on Biological Diversity, opened for signature in 1992, provided the first comprehensive

Million Hectares

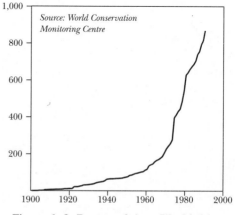

Source: World Conservation Monitoring Centre

Figure 1–2. Protected Area Worldwide, 1900–94

framework for conserving diversity across the globe. It recognizes the "intrinsic" value of biodiversity and seeks to preserve it, while encouraging "sustainable and equitable use" of those resources. (See Chapter 6.) By November 1996, 162 countries had ratified it, although the United States had not. Developing countries have strongly supported the treaty's assertion of their sovereign right to charge other nations that use their biological resources to manufacture drugs and other marketable products. The convention suffers, however, from a lack of targets, timetables, and enforcement mechanisms.[41]

The challenges facing the Convention on Biological Diversity can be seen clearly in the records of the eight environmental heavyweights, which together possess a sizable portion of the world's land area and biodiversity and which face a range of accelerating pressures on their natural ecosystems. (See Table 1–3.) Russia has the most extensive forest

area—21 percent of the world total—but Brazil is estimated to have the world's richest store of biodiversity, including an estimated 22 percent of the earth's flowering species. China also has a wealth of biological resources—12 percent of the flowering plants; India, Indonesia, Russia, and the United States are not far behind.[42]

At the first Conference of the Parties to the Convention on Biological Diversity, in 1994, Brazil's Deputy Minister for the Environment pledged "to conserve this national patrimony and to promote the sustainable utilization of its biological resources," and to "integrate the conservation and sustainable use of biological diversity into...forestry, fishing, and agriculture," including the promotion of ventures such as rubber tapping that sustainably use those resources. Since hosting the Rio Earth Summit, Brazil's government has sought to limit its earlier efforts to encourage road building and settlement schemes in the tropical

Table 1–3. Protected Areas and Threatened Species, E8 Countries, Nineties

Country	Land in Protected Areas, 1994[1]	Share of Land Area Protected	Threatened Plants[2]	Threatened Animals[3]
	(million hectares)	(percent)	(number)	
United States	130	13	1,845	281
Russia	71	4	127	59
Japan	3	7	704	79
Germany	9	26	16	11
China	58	6	343	153
India	14	4	1,256	137
Indonesia	19	10	281	242
Brazil	32	4	483	167
E8 Total	336	7	—	—

[1]Includes all protected areas (IUCN categories I–V), including totally protected areas and partially protected areas: totally protected areas are maintained in a natural state and are closed to extractive uses; partially protected areas can be managed for specific uses (such as recreation), and some extractive use is allowed. [2]Data for E8 total not presented due to overlap of threatened species in different countries. [3]Includes mammals, birds, reptiles, amphibians and fish; data for E8 total not presented due to overlap of same threatened species in different countries.
SOURCE: World Resources Institute, U.N. Environment Programme, U.N. Development Programme, and World Bank, *World Resources 1996–97* (New York: Oxford University Press, 1996).

forests of the Amazon Basin—which is arguably the world's greatest single concentration of biodiversity.[43]

Still, Brazil's efforts to conserve its rich biodiversity are marked by a wide gulf between promises and actions—a gap that is seen in most other biodiversity plans. Satellite monitoring indicates that the pace of deforestation in the Amazon actually increased 34 percent between 1991 and 1994. Responding to such concerns, the government has cracked down on illegal logging and has increased the share of property that landowners must preserve as forest from 50 percent to 80 percent.[44]

Indonesia is arguably the second most important country when it comes to biodiversity, and its wildlife is uniquely threatened. The official list of endangered species includes 126 birds, 63 mammals, and 21 reptiles. Although this nation has only a little more than 1 percent of the earth's land area, it has roughly 12 percent of the world's mammals, 16 percent of the reptiles and amphibians, and 17 percent of all birds. According to government estimates, Indonesia's species are being lost at a rate of one a day, driven by a large and politically influential logging industry as well as a human population that is expanding by some 3 million people each year. Crowded conditions on the island of Java have led the government to encourage migration to the biologically richer outer islands.[45]

At the second Conference of the Parties to the Convention on Biological Diversity, in Jakarta in 1995, Indonesia released a revised biodiversity plan. At its core is the setting aside of 16 million hectares (8 percent of Indonesia's land area) for protection. Additional areas, including coastal and marine resources, are being considered for inclusion. Local communities and NGOs, with their wealth of biological knowledge and dependence on nature, are to be actively involved in the biodiversity plan.[46]

The United States, which established the world's first national parks a century ago and enacted a landmark Endangered Species Act in 1973, has recently found its conservation efforts under assault by the timber, mining, and grazing industries. So far, their efforts to undermine the species act and other laws have been unsuccessful, but the budgets of the agencies that administer this legislation were slashed. The Clinton administration's attempts to protect the Everglades wetlands in Florida, the ancient forests of the Pacific Northwest, and other valuable wild areas may fare better in the Congress that came to office following national elections in November 1996.[47]

Russia, which stretches across 11 time zones from the Baltic Sea to the Pacific Ocean, still has vast areas of intact ecosystems—mainly boreal forests and sub-Arctic tundra found in Siberia. Although these ecosystems are not nearly as rich in biodiversity as those of tropical countries, they are a valuable resource, containing a vast store of carbon that, if released, would accelerate global warming. According to British environmental consultant Norman Myers, Siberia may now be losing 4 million hectares of forest annually—nearly twice the rate of deforestation in Brazil's Amazon. Some sections of Siberia have fallen victim to an uncontrolled timber rush as local and foreign companies race to export logs that can earn hard currency.[48]

Although the political system is teetering, Russian officials and scientists are valiantly trying to protect the country's forests. Russia has many trained ecologists and foresters, as well as a network of 89 protected areas called *zapovedniks* that were started in 1920, plus 29 national parks. Altogether these cover about 2 percent of Russia's vast landscape—equivalent to the entire territory of Germany. In response to the Convention on Biological Diversity, and with

GEF assistance, Russia has developed a new strategy that aims to improve monitoring of biodiversity, promote eco-tourism, and protect wildlife. In March 1995, President Yeltsin signed a federal law setting up a new category of regional parks and a new wildlife conservation law. Whether they will be effective in Russia's lawless "Wild East" is not yet clear.[49]

The Earth Summit and the efforts that flowed from it seem to have gone a long way toward convincing national political leaders that the long-term health of their people is inextricably linked to the rest of the biological world. And in late 1997, treaty members are planning to submit national plans for conserving and using indigenous biological resources sustainably. Still, the biodiversity convention is off to a slow start. If it is to become an effective instrument, it will have to develop a system of strong, enforceable national action plans. And in order to conserve biodiversity in the long run, we will need to slow growth in human numbers and reduce the poverty in the South and overconsumption in the North that drive people to clear land.

LIMITING HUMAN NUMBERS AND CONSUMPTION

The world had only 1.6 billion people when the current century began; by the time it ends, there will be more than 6 billion people on the planet—up 3.5 billion (58 percent) just since 1950. (See Figure 1–3.) Population growth is a driving force behind many environmental and social problems. With human numbers now growing at a near record pace of 88 million annually, slowing population growth is an urgent priority. In countries such as Bangladesh and Zaire, where the population is projected to

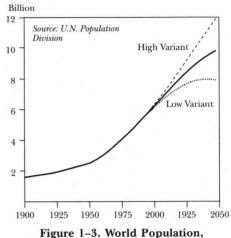

Figure 1–3. World Population, 1900–2050, Under Three Assumptions of Population Growth Rate

nearly double in the next two decades, this growth is threatening the social and ecological viability of whole nations.[50]

As much as the Earth Summit, the International Conference on Population and Development in Cairo in September 1994 was a watershed. The third in a series of U.N. population conferences that began in 1974, Cairo finally addressed the inextricable links among population growth, social inequity, material consumption, and environmental degradation. In the months leading up to the conference, traditional advocates of "population control" were challenged by a new coalition of women's and human rights groups that said improving the status and well-being of women and children should be the top priority. They noted that many women were alienated by programs that treat them as instruments of government family planners. In their view, sustainable development is as much a social concept as an environmental one.[51]

The plan of action produced in Cairo bridged this chasm by emphasizing the urgency of slowing population growth, particularly in poor countries, but also concluding that this goal is best accomplished by meeting urgent social needs. Recent studies show that unless these needs are met, fertility levels will likely remain high. The Cairo plan therefore calls for efforts to empower women, reduce poverty, and expand the availability of education, health care, and economic opportunity. The plan was a victory for the scores of NGOs that played a major role in shaping the final agreement. Many family planning programs, whether funded by governments, the United Nations, or private groups, have been overhauled and redirected to focus on raising the status of women. Already, some 31 countries have stabilized their populations. But the world has a long way to go if the extraordinary growth in human numbers that marked the twentieth century is to be halted in the twenty-first.[52]

The good news is that world population growth has slowed from a peak of 2.1 percent a year in the early sixties to 1.5 percent in 1996. Among the developing countries in the E8, India's average fertility has fallen by 41 percent since the sixties, Indonesia's has declined 46 percent, Brazil's by 55 percent, and

China's by 68 percent. In Brazil, 66 percent of married women use modern contraceptives, and in China, 83 percent of women do. (See Table 1–4.) This compares with figures of 75 percent in Germany and just 22 percent in Russia. Still, demographic momentum continues to push total numbers up at a near record pace; slowing that relentless growth remains a top concern.[53]

Indonesia is a leader in slowing population growth—in part because it has worked to improve the welfare of women. Its family planning program began in the seventies and from an early stage focused on village-level health care and education as well as the wide dissemination of contraceptives. The infant mortality rate fell from 133 infant deaths per 1,000 births in the early sixties to 57 in the 1990–94 period. By the early nineties, half the married women of reproductive age were using contraceptives. Since Cairo, Indonesia has strengthened the grassroots and community involvement aspects of its population program, expanded the availability of health care in remote rural areas, and vowed to continue lowering fertility rates.[54]

Table 1–4. Population and Social Trends, E8 Countries

Country	Population, 1996	Annual Growth Rate, 1990–95	Total Fertility Rate, 1990–95	Contraceptive Prevalence Rate, 1988–92	Maternal Mortality Ratio, 1987–91
	(million)	(percent)	(children per woman)	(percent)	(deaths per 100,000 live births)
United States	265	1.0	2.1	74	22
Russia	148	−0.1	1.5	22	75
Japan	126	0.3	1.5	64	18
Germany	82	0.6	1.3	75	22
China	1,218	1.1	2.0	83	95
India	950	1.9	3.8	43	570
Indonesia	201	1.6	2.9	50	650
Brazil	161	1.7	2.9	66	220
E8 Total	3,151	1.3	—	—	—

SOURCES: U.N. Population Division, *World Population Prospects: The 1994 Revision* (New York: United Nations, 1995); U.N. Population Division, *Abortion Policies: A Global Review* (New York: 1995).

Latin American countries have also had some success in slowing population growth, including Brazil, where the annual growth rate went from 2.8 percent a year in the sixties to 1.5 percent in the nineties. Brazil's demographic transition appears to stem from the pressures of urbanization, the spread of mass communications, and efforts by local governments, community groups, and women's organizations to organize health care and family planning. Their work has been supported by generous assistance from international organizations such as the United Nations Population Fund. This allowed a dramatic reduction of fertility despite the opposition of the Catholic Church and the absence of national population targets and programs.[55]

Population growth cannot be adequately considered without reference to the resource consumption levels of individual nations.

China has experienced one of the world's fastest demographic transitions: its fertility rate fell from nearly 6 births per woman in the sixties to 1.9 in 1995—slightly below the replacement level of 2.0 found in the United States. Remarkably, this sharp drop has occurred in a still mainly rural population with relatively low income levels. China's aggressive efforts to slow population growth were driven by concern about the country's density—roughly a billion people squeezed into an area the size of the eastern United States.[56]

This desperation led China to adopt national population targets and coercive family planning programs in which women were not permitted to have more than two children—and in some cases just one. Not only were these women forced to use contraceptives, but often abortions were required in the event of unauthorized pregnancies. Female infanticide has also been reported among families whose only child was a girl. Both in Cairo and at the 1994 women's conference in Beijing, China faced growing pressure to develop a more humane approach. Some governments cut back on funding for China's family planning programs over concern about such abuses. In response, China issued a White Paper on Family Planning in 1995 that urges couples to choose "freely and responsibly the number and spacing of their children." Still, China's population program remains coercive, and few international family planners consider it a model.[57]

Among industrial countries, population presents a different kind of problem. The United States, Germany, and Japan already have fertility rates near or below the replacement level; in Russia, rising death rates and falling birth rates have caused the population to decline by several million since 1990. In the United States, the population is growing by nearly 1 percent each year, but almost half the increase is from immigration. A more important population issue for these nations is their support of family planning programs in developing countries, which exceeds $1 billion annually. Although Western Europe and Japan increased such support after Cairo, U.S. support plummeted from $582 million in 1995 to $76 million in 1996. Unless these programs are maintained or strengthened, the goals of the Cairo conference cannot be achieved.[58]

Moreover, population growth cannot be adequately considered without reference to the resource consumption levels of individual nations. Roughly 1.5 billion people in the world's consumer class—who drive automobiles, own refrigerators and televisions, and shop in malls—consume the bulk of the world's fossil fuels, metals, wood products, and grain. A newborn in the United States requires more than twice as much grain and 10 times as much oil as a child born in Brazil or Indonesia—and produces far more pollution. In fact, a simple calculation shows that the annual increase in the U.S. population of 2.6 million people puts more pressure on the world's resources than do the 17 million people added in India each year.[59]

Unless industrial countries develop less resource-intensive life-styles and less-polluting technologies, it will be impossible to develop a sustainable world economy—whether the world's population ultimately stabilizes at 12, 10, or even 8 billion people. Detailed studies undertaken by the Wuppertal Institute in Germany conclude that by using resources more productively, it will be possible in the coming decades to reduce energy and material consumption levels in industrial countries by a factor of four while actually improving the standard of living. And because industrial countries are the model that developing countries tend to follow, the decisions they make about life-styles and technologies could be decisive for the world as a whole.[60]

RIO PLUS FIVE... AND COUNTING

In June 1997, the General Assembly of the United Nations will convene on the fifth anniversary of the Earth Summit to review progress and consider next steps. It may be an awkward gathering: member nations are far behind in their contributions to the United Nations, foreign aid is stagnating, and trade disputes are exacerbating international tensions. Moreover, the diplomats who assemble in New York will be confronted with their failure to meet the financial commitments made in Rio or to effectively implement the major conventions signed there. Independent reviews by NGOs and the press are likely to sharpen the spotlight.

From the perspective of 1997, should Rio be seen as a nineties Woodstock for environmentalists, or perhaps as a successful media event that did little to meet the challenges of creating a sustainable world? Though the pace of change has been frustratingly slow so far, and disappointments abound, a purely negative verdict would be too harsh, and certainly premature. It is already clear that the Earth Summit set in motion historical processes that will bear fruit for decades to come.

The expansion in public awareness that flowed from Rio—through the world's newspapers and over its airwaves—has done much to forge the political basis for action at every level. Dozens of smaller institutions, from local governments to grassroots development organizations, have been empowered by the spirit of Rio. Since 1992, some 1,500 cities in 51 countries have crafted local Agenda 21s. Many of these are more substantive than the plans crafted by national governments, as they are aimed at achieving practical goals such as improved public transportation and recycling.[61]

The spirit of Rio has also energized the efforts of private citizens to protect the environment and promote human development. Some 20,000 individuals from outside government participated in the Earth Summit in 1992, and many U.N. treaty processes since then have been opened to the participation of NGOs that provide ideas as well as pressure for change. Bangladesh has more than 1,000 NGOs, and India has tens of thousands, thanks to the support of religious organizations and tax incentives. In Brazil, Amazonian Indians and rubber tappers have organized to protect their forests from would-be ranchers and miners. Although each of these initiatives may by itself seem inconsequential, together they are making a difference.[62]

The mid-nineties are also marked by a growing role for private businesses and financial institutions in world affairs as trade barriers are removed and industries privatized, including electric power, telecommunications, railways, and even roads. In many cases, the rise of the market has accelerated the degradation of natural resources—particularly in timber and mining—and increased pollution. But it has also accelerated the transfer of more environmentally benign technologies. China is now the world leader in manufacturing energy-efficient compact fluorescent light bulbs, while India has developed the world's second largest market for wind turbines—a market that barely existed in 1992.[63]

The surge in economic growth in much of the developing world has reinforced the urgency of putting the world economy on a sustainable path.

The flow of private capital from industrial to developing countries has soared from $18 billion in 1987 to $225 billion in 1996, according to preliminary estimates by the Institute of International Finance. This is four times the $55 billion of official bilateral and multilateral capital that moved from North to South in 1995—although most of the private flow is channeled to a half-dozen booming economies. One of the highest priorities is redirecting these private funds. Among the tools available are reduced subsidies to extractive industries, taxes on pollution, and international environmental investment criteria, particularly for projects that are backed by the World Bank's International Finance Corporation or by bilateral export credit banks. Aid agencies will also need to consider an accelerated shift away from road and dam building and toward greater support for education, health care, public transportation, and other development priorities.[64]

Opportunities abound for profitable investments in more environmentally benign products and processes, ranging from solar power to ozone-friendly refrigerators, sustainable forestry projects, integrated pest management systems, and chlorine-free paper mills. Numerous green investment funds have been mobilized in recent years to let individuals and institutions match their investments with their social concerns. Another financing mechanism, pioneered by Bangladesh's Grameen Bank and now used by scores of similar institutions, provides financial backing for hundreds of tiny local enterprises that supply goods and services to the urban and rural poor.[65]

As consumer demand has grown, many businesses have revamped their manufacturing processes or developed new environmentally sustainable products. Paul Hawken, a successful California business executive, noted in his 1993 book *The Ecology of Commerce:* "We have reached an unsettling and portentous turning point in industrial civilization....Business people must either dedicate themselves to transforming commerce to a restorative undertaking, or march society to the undertaker."[66]

In response to such calls, many business leaders now point out that rapid advances in electronics, materials science, and biotechnology offer important solutions to environmental problems. Although there are still many business groups that vociferously oppose and lobby against environmental progress, their messages now compete with more progressive voices, such as the World Business Council for Sustainable Development or the 60 insurance companies that gathered at the climate parley in Geneva in July 1996 to urge "early, substantial reductions in greenhouse gas emissions."[67]

Environmental solutions no longer come in the form of a simple top-down plan or government mandate. In the future, substantive, practical solutions will require the concerted efforts of a host of "stakeholders" from across society. Still, governments and international organizations remain crucial—though often as catalysts and motivators of change rather than as implementers. For example, ozone-friendly refrigerators would not be a profitable business today if governments had not made CFC production illegal in industrial countries, and India's wind power industry would not have taken off if renewable energy tax credits had not been introduced and trade barriers lowered in the early nineties.[68]

Even with these successes, the surge in economic growth—and the accompanying boom in automobile sales, home building, and electricity use—sweeping much of the developing world in the nineties has reinforced the urgency of putting the world economy on a more sustainable path. Ironically, it may be China, India, and other developing nations that finally force the United States and other industrial countries to come to terms with the environmental unsustainability of their own economic systems.

The eight environmental heavyweights could be crucial in taking these next steps. Just as the G7 now gets together annually to forge a consensus on economic issues that can be forwarded to the various international organizations they belong to, so could the E8 become a major catalytic force. These nations could play a particularly strong role in bridging North-South differences. The current list of permanent members of the U.N. Security Council reflects the lineup of Great Powers circa 1945. As the world community looks to modernize the United Nations, a new list of permanent members—made up of the E8, plus one African nation—would make sense.

A model of the new alliance can be seen in the way the United States, China, India, and Germany have been major players at recent climate negotiations, working to reach a consensus between industrial and developing nations. And U.S. Secretary of State Warren Christopher launched an important initiative in 1996 to integrate environmental concerns into U.S. diplomatic operations around the world. This is the kind of reorganization of foreign and economic ministries that is necessary if the members of the E8 are to assert themselves as environmental leaders. Among the priorities the E8 will have to face up to are strengthening the conventions on climate and biological diversity—following the model of the ozone agreements of the eighties, which went gradually from empty vessels to tough, legally binding, effective agreements. (See Chapter 9.)[69]

Over the past century, in developing a vast, high-technology civilization, humanity has created a set of ecological dilemmas the likes of which our ancestors could not have imagined. It took only a century to get into this fix, and we have less than another century to get out of it. With that perspective in mind, the Rio Earth Summit and the international agreements it led to can be seen as a critical step toward turning around unsustainable trends such as the heat-

ing of the atmosphere, the wholesale
elimination of the web of life, and the
rapid growth in our own numbers. Still,
humanity is only at the beginning of a
long road. Unless the pace of progress
accelerates soon, we may be too late.

2

Facing the Prospect of Food Scarcity

Lester R. Brown

During the late spring and early summer of 1996, world wheat and corn prices set record highs. Wheat traded at over $7 a bushel, more than double the price in early 1995. In mid-July, corn traded at an all-time price of $5.54 a bushel, also more than twice the level of a year earlier.[1]

These startlingly high prices were the result of production falling behind demand. During the nineties, the growth in world grain production has slowed dramatically, while demand has continued to climb, driven by the addition of nearly 90 million people a year and an unprecedented rise in affluence in Asia, led by China. Part of this widening gap has been filled in recent years by drawing down carryover stocks—the amount left in the world's grain bins at the start of each new harvest. By 1996, these had fallen to 50 days of consumption, the lowest level on record.[2]

This chapter is adapted from *Tough Choices: Facing the Challenge of Food Scarcity* (New York: W.W. Norton & Company, 1996).

Several trends are converging to create scarcity and raise prices. With all oceanic fisheries being fished at or beyond capacity, growth in the oceanic fish catch came to a halt in 1989. For the first time in history, farmers can no longer count on getting any help from fishers in expanding the food supply. Yet there is little new cropland to bring under the plow (see Chapter 3), and a growing scarcity of fresh water for irrigation. In many countries, efforts to raise land productivity are handicapped by the physiological inability of existing varieties of grain to use more fertilizer than is already being applied.[3]

In addition, farmers who have always had to cope with the vagaries of weather may now be dealing with climate change. The 11 warmest years since recordkeeping began in 1866 have all occurred since 1979. In fact, the three warmest years took place during the nineties, with 1995 topping the list. Unfortunately for farmers and consumers, crop-withering heat waves like those that shrank harvests in 1995 across the United States, Canada, several

European countries, the Ukraine, and Russia could become even more frequent and intense if atmospheric carbon dioxide (CO_2) levels continue to build.[4]

At the same time that the growth in grain production is slowing, the growth in demand is accelerating. In addition to trying to feed nearly 90 million more people each year, farmers now face a record rise in affluence in Asia—home to more than half the world's people. A large share of Asia's 3.1 billion people are moving up the food chain, eating more pork, poultry, beef, and eggs and drinking more beer, all of which are grain-intensive products.[5]

FOOD SECURITY TRENDS

All the basic indicators of food security—grain production per person, seafood catch per person, carryover stocks of grain, seafood prices, and grain prices—signal a tightening situation during the nineties. This development can be seen most clearly with the oceanic fish catch.

The amount of fish caught in the world's oceans grew from 19 million tons in 1950 to 88 million tons in 1988, an increase of 4.6-fold. During this period, the catch per person worldwide climbed from just under 8 kilograms to 17 kilograms, more than doubling. But since 1988 the oceanic catch has fluctuated around 88 million tons.. As a result, the catch per person has started to decline, falling some 9 percent since 1988 as population has continued to grow.[6]

The period from 1950 to 1988 witnessed both remarkable advances in technology and an impressive growth in the investment in fishing trawlers and factory processing ships, which enabled the exploitation of fisheries in the most remote corners of the planet. At 88 mil-

lion tons, the oceanic catch of seafood exceeded the combined production of beef and mutton on the world's rangelands. Seafood became an important source of animal protein, particularly for people living in island countries and in continental countries with long coastlines—augmenting diets otherwise dominated by starchy staples such as rice, corn, wheat, cassava, and other tropical root crops.[7]

Historically, the principal determinant of the size of the fish catch has been the investment in fishing capacity: spending more on fishing trawlers increased the harvest. But with fisheries being pushed to their sustainable-yield limits, this approach just leads to overfishing, stock depletion, and a decline in catch. The traditional economic determinant of the size of the catch is being replaced by an environmental determinant—the sustainable yield of fisheries.

While growth in the harvest from the oceans has come to a halt, growth in the harvest from the land has continued during the nineties, but at a much slower rate than during the preceding decades. From 1950 to 1990, the world grain harvest increased from 631 million tons to 1,780 million tons, nearly tripling. This was a remarkable period in history, one in which rapidly growing demand driven by record growth in both population and incomes stimulated production increases as farmers drew on a huge backlog of technology developed during the preceding century. Since 1990, however, the growth in the grain harvest has slowed dramatically. After expanding 182 percent from 1950 to 1990, the harvest has increased only 3 percent between 1990 and 1996. (See Figure 2–1.) Signs of a slowdown in growth in grain production were already evident in the late eighties as the grain harvest per person fell from the all-time high of 346 kilograms in 1984 to 336 kilograms in 1990, a drop of 3 percent. By 1996, the harvest per

Million Tons

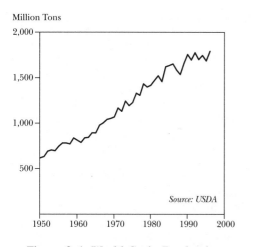

Figure 2–1. World Grain Production, 1950–96

Kilograms

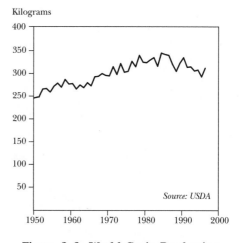

Figure 2–2. World Grain Production Per Person, 1950–96

person had fallen to 313 kilograms, declining an additional 7 percent. (See Figure 2–2.)[8]

With this loss of momentum in the growth in the world grain harvest since 1990, it comes as no surprise that world grain stocks during the nineties have dropped to their lowest level ever. The bumper harvest of 1990 boosted carry–over stocks for 1991 to 342 million tons. But during the six years since then they have dropped to 240 million tons—a mere 50 days of consumption. (See Figure 2–3.)[9]

In response to the tightening grain situation, in 1996 the United States released for production the remaining land held out under commodity set-aside programs. Yet even with this additional land, there will be little rebuilding of stocks from the 1996 harvest.[10]

In some ways, carryover stocks of grain are the most sensitive indicator of food security. Stocks that will provide at least 70 days of world consumption are needed for even a minimal level of food security. Whenever they fall below 60 days, prices become highly volatile. With the margin of security so thin, grain prices fluctuate with each weather re-

port. When carry–over stocks of grain dropped to 55 days of consumption in 1973, for example, world grain prices doubled. When they reached the new low of 50 days of consumption in 1996, the world price of wheat and corn—the two leading grains in terms of quantity produced—again more than doubled.[11]

Another factor affecting future world food security is the share of current food production that is based on the unsustainable use of land and water. For example, a small fraction of the world's cropland is so highly erodible that it cannot sustain cultivation over the long term. A few countries have attempted to calculate the share of their harvest in this category. In Kazakstan, a wheat-exporting country, for instance, the Institute of Soil Management estimates that its grainland area will be reduced by one fourth or more when the rapidly eroding land now under cultivation is eventually abandoned as its productivity falls.[12]

A similar situation exists with irrigation water use. For example, the U.S. Department of Agriculture reports that 21 percent of U.S. irrigated cropland is being watered by drawing down underground aquifers. In northern China, the

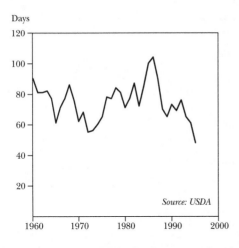

Figure 2–3. World Grain Carryover Stocks as Days of Consumption,1961–96

limited information that is available suggests that farmers may depend even more on overpumping. No one knows precisely what share of the world grain harvest is based on the unsustainable use of land and water, but the inevitable abandonment of eroding cropland and the depletion of aquifers both threaten future food security.[13]

So do rising atmospheric levels of greenhouse gases, which are linked to higher temperatures and more extreme weather events, including droughts, floods, crop-withering heat waves, and more powerful, more destructive storms. If the earth's average temperature continues to rise over the next 15 years at the same rate it has during the last 15, more intense crop-withering heat waves—like those that lowered world harvests in 1988 and 1995—could take an even heavier toll on future grain harvests. The experience in 1988 shows that intense heat and drought can totally eliminate the exportable surplus of grain in the United States, the world's breadbasket. If that were to happen at a time when grain stocks were already depleted, as they are now, it would drive the price of grain off the charts, creating chaos in world markets.[14]

Given the slowdown in the growth of the oceanic fish catch and the world grain harvest, meeting the food needs of the nearly 90 million people being added each year is now achieved in part by reducing consumption among those already here. If the sustainable-yield limits of the oceans have been reached, the only way to arrest the decline in the per capita fish catch and the accompanying rise in seafood prices is to stabilize world population size. And while there are still innumerable opportunities for expanding the world grain harvest, it is becoming difficult to sustain rapid growth. Unfortunately, as described in the remainder of this chapter, the situation is likely to get worse before it gets better.[15]

LAND AND WATER SCARCITY

As the world's population, now approaching 5.8 billion, continues to expand, both the area of cropland and the amount of fresh water per person are shrinking, threatening to drop below the level needed to provide minimal levels of food security. Over time, farmers have used ingenious methods to expand the area used to produce crops. These included irrigation, terracing, drainage, fallowing, and even, for the Dutch, reclaiming land from the sea. Terracing let farmers cultivate steeply sloping land on a sustainable basis, quite literally enabling them to farm the mountains as well as the plains. Drainage of wetlands opened fertile bottomlands for cultivation. Alternate-year fallowing to accumulate moisture helped farmers extend cropping into semiarid regions.[16]

By mid-century, the frontiers of agricultural settlement had largely disappeared, contributing to a dramatic slowdown in the growth in area planted to grain, the source of half of human caloric intake consumed directly and a substantial share of the remainder consumed indirectly in the form of meat, milk, and eggs. (See also Chapter 3 for a discussion of the loss of cropland.) Between 1950 and 1981, the grain area increased from 587 million hectares to 732 million hectares, a gain of nearly 25 percent. But part of the expansion was on land that was subject to severe soil erosion by wind or water, much of it in the former Soviet Union. The peak Soviet grain area of 123 million hectares in 1979 shrank to 91 million hectares in 1995, declining almost every year during this 18-year stretch, as falling productivity forced the abandonment of marginal, often heavily eroded, land.[17]

In the United States, a more formal effort was made to rescue the highly erodible land that was plowed in response to the high grain prices of the mid-seventies. In 1985, Congress, with the strong support of environmental groups, passed the Conservation Reserve Program, an initiative designed to retire much of this land by paying farmers to return it to grass before it became wasteland. By 1990, some 14 million hectares had been set aside under long-term contracts.[18]

In addition to soil erosion, another leading source of cropland loss is industrialization, a trend that is strongest in countries already densely populated when rapid industrialization gets under way. The subsequent changes claim large amounts of land for the construction of factories and warehouses, as does the evolution of an automobile-centered transportation system.

Indeed, one of the leading potential cropland claimants in Asia, particularly in China and India, is the automobile. In 1995, China had only 2 million cars—barely 1 percent of the U.S. fleet. An increase to 22 million cars by 2010, as now projected, would lead to land being paved for a national network of high-

ways and roads and for streets, parking lots, and service stations on a scale that will inevitably take a severe toll on the country's scarce cropland.[19]

India, too, will be sacrificing cropland to the automobile, trading the prestige of car ownership by a few for the food security of the many. In fiscal 1996, the Indian automobile industry expanded by an estimated 26 percent, with further gains in prospect as the world's major automobile manufacturers flock to the country.[20]

In addition to the conversion of grainland to nonfarm uses, substantial areas are converted to other crops, such as oilseeds, fruits, and vegetables, as industrialization progresses and incomes rise. From 1950 to 1995, the world's soybean harvest climbed from 17 million to 123 million tons, a sevenfold gain, as the demand for cooking oil and for protein supplements for livestock and poultry feed soared. With farmers unable to raise rapidly yields per hectare of this leguminous crop with its own nitrogen supply, the land in soybeans increased from 14 million hectares in 1950 to 62 million hectares in 1995, with growth coming largely from the shift of grainland to soybeans.[21]

All of these economic forces have been at work in Japan, South Korea, and Taiwan, which have lost nearly half their grainland area since it peaked around 1960. As Asia industrializes, the construction of factories, roads, parking lots, and new cities is eating into the remaining productive cropland. In more affluent regions, land is also being claimed by shopping centers, tennis courts, golf courses, and private villas. In China's rapidly industrializing Guangdong Province, an estimated 40 golf courses have been built in the newly affluent Pearl River delta region alone. In 1995, concern about the effect on food production of this wholesale loss of cropland led the Guangdong Land Bureau to cancel the construction of all golf courses planned but not yet completed.[22]

China has experienced a particularly rapid loss of cropland in the southern coastal provinces, such as Guangdong, where much of the rice crop is produced. A combination of rapid industrialization and conversion of cropland to other nonfarm uses has taken such a heavy toll of China's riceland that it has more than offset the rise in land productivity, preventing any gains in the rice harvest during the nineties.[23]

The expanding demand for water is draining some of the world's major rivers dry before they reach the sea.

Other Asian countries, including Indonesia, Vietnam, Thailand, Malaysia, and India, are also facing heavy losses. To make matters worse, industrialization is claiming some of the region's best cropland. For example, land now occupied by factories in southern China was just a few years ago producing two or three crops of rice per year. This is some of the most productive cropland not only in China, but in the world.

Despite frequent claims about vast opportunities for expanding the earth's cultivated area, the chances to do so with food prices that the world's poor can afford are in fact quite limited. With a doubling of grain prices, some marginal land, such as the cerrado (dry plain) in eastern Brazil, might be profitably cultivated. But in this particular case, the plowing of the cerrado is unlikely to do little more than help meet rapidly growing local demand. Brazil, now the largest grain importer in the western hemisphere, is facing a population increase of some 50 million by 2030 and a widespread rise in affluence that is boosting consumption of livestock products.

If it can become self-sufficient in grain, it will be doing well; it is unlikely to have much left over to export to densely populated countries such as Bangladesh, China, or Indonesia.[24]

Although in 1996 the United States returned to production all the remaining cropland idled under commodity programs, the European Union was still idling 10 percent of its cropland. If this were all planted to grain, it would boost the European grain harvest by roughly 18 million tons, enough to provide for eight months of world population growth. Beyond this, roughly half of the 14 million hectares in the U.S. Conservation Reserve Program could be returned to production and farmed sustainably, adding perhaps 28 million tons of additional grain, enough to cover world population growth for one year.[25]

The world grain harvested area expanded from 1950 until it peaked in 1981 but the growth was quite slow compared with that of population. As a result, the grainland area per person has been declining steadily since mid-century, shrinking from 0.23 hectares in 1950 to 0.12 hectares in 1995. After a point, if population growth continues, this shrinkage can override rises in land productivity, leading to a decline in grain produced per person.[26]

In addition to land scarcity, farmers are now facing water scarcity. The expanding demand for water is pushing beyond the sustainable yield of aquifers in many countries and is draining some of the world's major rivers dry before they reach the sea. As the demand for water for irrigation and for industrial and residential uses continues to expand, the competition between countryside and city for available water supplies intensifies. In some parts of the world, meeting growing urban needs is possible only by diverting water from irrigation.

One of the keys to the near tripling of the world grain harvest from 1950 to

1990 was a 2.5-fold expansion of irrigation, a development that extended agriculture into arid regions with little rainfall, intensified production in low-rainfall areas, and increased dry-season cropping in countries with monsoonal climates. It also accounts for part of the phenomenal growth in world fertilizer use since mid-century. Most of the world's rice and much of its wheat is produced on irrigated land.[27]

From the beginning of irrigation several thousand years ago until 1900, irrigated area expanded slowly, eventually covering some 40 million hectares. From 1900 to 1950, the pace picked up, and the total area more than doubled to 94 million hectares. But the big growth occurred from 1950 to 1993, when 154 million hectares were added, bringing the total to 248 million hectares. (See Figure 2–4.)[28]

During this period, a key threshold was crossed in 1979. From 1950 until then, irrigation expanded faster than population, increasing the irrigated area per person by nearly one third. This was closely associated with a worldwide rise in grain production per person of one

third. But since 1979, the growth in irrigation has fallen behind that of population, shrinking the irrigated area per person by some 7 percent. This trend, now well established, will undoubtedly continue as the demand for water presses ever more tightly against available supplies.[29]

The best conditions for irrigating with river water are found in Asia, which has some of the world's great rivers—the Indus, the Ganges, the Chang Jiang (Yangtze), the Huang He (Yellow), and the Brahmaputra. These originate at high elevations and travel long distances, providing numerous opportunities for dams and the diversion of water into networks of gravity-fed canals and ditches. As a result, some two thirds of the world's irrigated area is in Asia. China and India lead the world, with 50 million and 48 million hectares of irrigated land respectively.[30]

In monsoonal climates, where the wet season is followed by a long dry season with several months of little or no rain, irrigation holds the key to cropping intensity. Where temperatures permit year-round cropping, as they often do in such climates, irrigation allows the production of two or even three crops a year. In China, rapid irrigation expansion helped increase multiple cropping on all cropland from an average of 1.3 crops per hectare in 1950 to 1.5 in 1980.[31]

During the nineties, several trends are emerging to reduce irrigated area. Principal among these are the depletion of aquifers and the diversion of irrigation water to cities. Water tables are now falling in the major food-producing regions. This is most dramatic where irrigated agriculture depends on fossil water, such as in the southern Great Plains of the United States, Saudi Arabia, and Libya. As noted earlier, an estimated 21 percent of U.S. irrigated cropland is watered by the unsustainable practice of drawing down underground aquifers.[32]

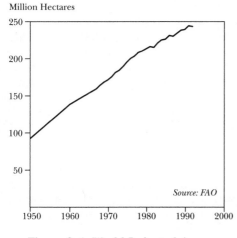

Million Hectares

Figure 2–4. World Irrigated Area, 1950–93

Source: FAO

In the U.S. Great Plains, farmers from South Dakota south through Nebraska, Kansas, eastern Colorado, Oklahoma, and the Texas panhandle greatly expanded irrigation from mid-century through 1980 by tapping the vast Ogallala aquifer. But this is essentially a fossil aquifer. Although in some locales it does receive a modest recharge from rainfall, most of the water in it was deposited there eons ago. Heavy reliance on the Ogallala is therefore ultimately unsustainable. In some of its more shallow southern reaches, it is already partly depleted. As a result, between 1982 and 1992 irrigated area in Texas shrank 11 percent, forcing farmers to return to traditional—and less productive—dryland farming. Irrigated area is also shrinking in Oklahoma, Kansas, and Colorado.[33]

The world's farmers face a steady shrinkage in both grainland and irrigation water per person.

In India, water tables are falling in several states, including the Punjab—the country's breadbasket. The double cropping of high-yielding, early-maturing wheat and rice there has dramatically boosted the overall grain harvest since the mid-sixties, but unfortunately it has pushed water use beyond the sustainable yield of the underlying aquifer. Water tables are also falling in parts of the semi-arid state of Rajasthan in India's northwest. As this happens, cities and towns drill deeper wells. Meanwhile, villagers without the capital to deepen their own wells are left high and dry, forced to abandon irrigated agriculture.[34]

In China, which is trying to feed 1.2 billion increasingly affluent consumers, much of the northern part of the country is a water-deficit region, satisfying part of its needs by overpumping aqui-

fers. Under Beijing, for example, the water table has dropped from 5 meters below ground level in 1950 to more than 50 meters.[35]

Professor Chen Yiyu, vice president of the Chinese Academy of Sciences, reports that under a large area of northern China the water table has fallen some 30 meters over the last two to three decades. He estimates that about 100 million people live in the affected area. At some point in the future, the aquifer will be depleted. Whether that is imminent or still some years away is not clear. But whenever it comes, it will reduce abruptly the supply of water for this population. Meeting residential and industrial needs for water may be possible only with a steep cutback in irrigation.[36]

The growing demand for water is putting excessive pressure on rivers as well as aquifers. The planet's great rivers are perpetually renewing, but in more populated regions, rivers have been dammed, diverted, and tapped until often there is little water left to continue on its way. In fact, many rivers now run dry before they reach the ocean.

China's great Huang He (Yellow River), which first failed to reach the sea in 1972, now runs dry each year and for progressively longer periods. In the late spring of 1996, it completely disappeared before it reached Shandong Province, the last one it travels through en route to the Yellow Sea. For the farmers of Shandong, who produce one fifth of China's wheat and one seventh of its corn and who depend on the river for half their irrigation water, this was not good news.[37]

At the same time, the major river in the southwestern United States—the Colorado—now disappears into the Arizona desert, rarely reaching the Gulf of California. And in central Asia, the Amu Dar'ya is often drained dry by Turkmen and Uzbek cotton farmers before it reaches the Aral Sea, thus contributing not only to the sea's gradual disappearance but also to the collapse of the 44,000 ton-per-year fishery it once supported.[38]

The world may have entered a new era during the nineties, one in which overall irrigated area no longer increases. A few irrigation projects are still coming on stream here and there around the world, including one in Turkey that is systematically tapping the remaining unused potential in the Tigris and Euphrates Rivers. Vietnam is planning to expand its irrigated area by tapping the waters of the Mekong. But gains from new projects such as these may be offset by losses elsewhere from aquifer depletion and the diversion of water to cities.[39]

David Seckler, Director General of the International Irrigation Management Institute, believes the losses may now be exceeding the gains, leading to a shrinkage of world irrigated area. If this is happening, as seems likely, then the irrigation water supply per person—which has declined slowly for some years—will fall even faster. Arresting the reduction in water availability per person may now depend more on stabilizing population than on anything else that policymakers can do.[40]

The bottom line is that the world's farmers face a steady shrinkage in both grainland and irrigation water per person. Their ability to offset the drop in grainland per person has relied heavily on using ever greater amounts of fertilizer, but now this, too, is becoming more difficult.

THE FERTILIZER FACTOR

The discovery in 1847 by German agricultural chemist Justus von Liebig that all the nutrients that plants remove from the soil could be restored in mineral form set the stage for the eventual emergence of the modern fertilizer industry. It was not until the middle of this century, when the frontiers of agricultural settlement had largely disappeared, that the use of fertilizer emerged as the key to raising land productivity and thus to expanding the world's food supply.[41]

Once fertilizer use began to increase and yields started to rise in response, the growth in fertilizer use became one of the most predictable of all global economic indicators. Between 1950 and 1989, fertilizer use went from 14 million tons to 146 million tons, a tenfold increase. (See Figure 2–5.) After 1989, usage began to decline. In many countries, farmers discovered that the amount of fertilizer they were applying was exceeding the physiological capacity of existing crop varieties to absorb and use nutrients. In the United States, Western Europe, the former Soviet Union, and Japan, usage had reached the level where additional fertilizer had little effect on yields. Fertilizer use by U.S. farmers was actually roughly one tenth less in the mid-nineties than it was in the early eighties. In part, this was because farm-

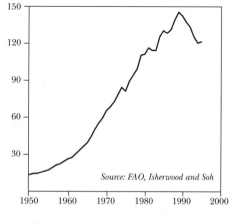

Million Tons

Source: FAO, Isherwood and Soh

Figure 2–5. World Fertilizer Use, 1950–95

ers were using more precise soil tests to determine the nutrient needs of their crops.[42]

In the Soviet Union, where fertilizer use had soared far beyond the level that could be used profitably, the economic reforms of 1988 triggered a dramatic decline in use. Among other things, they moved fertilizer prices toward world market levels—far higher than they were under the centrally planned economic system prevailing before 1988. In addition, as the nineties unfolded, the disruption associated with both economic reform and the breakup of the Soviet Union led to a severe depression, sharply reducing food prices and further weakening the demand for fertilizer.[43]

Most of the technologies used to boost output since mid-century have actually been designed to facilitate the use of more fertilizer. For example, irrigation raises yields largely by increasing the amount of fertilizer that can be used. Similarly, the higher yielding varieties produce more because they are capable of converting heavier applications of fertilizer into higher yields.

At one time, the level of fertilizer use was largely related to the level of economic development in a country. Today, however, differences in fertilizer use are largely the result of moisture availability. It makes little difference whether the moisture comes from rainfall or from irrigation, so long as it is abundant. Western Europe is generally well watered, and therefore able to use large amounts of fertilizer per hectare. In North America, fertilizer use rates vary widely according to rainfall: farmers in the midwestern Corn Belt, with its relatively generous rainfall, use vast amounts of fertilizer, while those in the western plains, producing dryland wheat, use only a fraction as much. In Asia, a combination of irrigation and rainfall lead to heavy fertilizer use in most of the region. The two continents that are mostly arid and semiarid, Africa and Australia, use relatively little fertilizer.[44]

As the world grainland area per person shrank steadily after mid-century, the world's farmers steadily raised fertilizer use. (See Figure 2–6.) From 1950 to 1990, the formula of combining ever higher yielding varieties with more and more fertilizer was remarkably successful in boosting output. It led to a near tripling of the world grain harvest over four decades. But since 1990, this approach has not worked too well in many countries. As production has lagged, grain consumption per person in the world has dropped and grain stocks have fallen even more precipitously.[45]

The world now faces an unprecedented challenge. The old formula that was so remarkably successful in expanding the world's food supply is no longer working very well, and there is no new one to take its place. The ability of the world's political leaders to come up with alternative ways of balancing food supply and population will help determine the kind of world the next generation will live in.

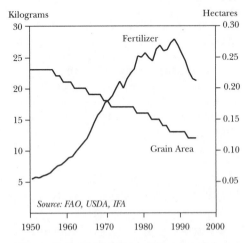

Figure 2–6. World Grain Harvested Area and Fertilizer Use Per Person, 1950–95

THE CARRYING CAPACITY QUESTION

Recent food production and population growth trends underline the urgency of reassessing the earth's population carrying capacity. For example, as noted earlier, growth in the world fish catch came to a halt as fishing fleets pushed against the sustainable yield of oceanic fisheries. Using round numbers, a catch of 100 million tons and a world population of 5 billion would provide 20 kilograms of seafood per person a year. If the population expands to 10 billion people, then this same catch will provide only 10 kilograms per person. Our generation, the one now in positions of leadership, has benefited from a doubling in the seafood catch per person during our lifetimes. In stark contrast, today's children will see their seafood consumption over a comparable period cut nearly in half. They face the prospect of far higher seafood prices than any we have experienced.

Carrying capacity calculations for land-based food production are much simpler now that the frontiers of agricultural settlement have largely disappeared. With little prospect for substantially expanding cropland area, the key determinant of the earth's carrying capacity is land productivity. From 1950 to 1990, the world's farmers raised land productivity at an unprecedented rate. Grain yield per hectare went from 1.06 tons in 1950 to 2.54 tons in 1990—a gain of 140 percent, or roughly 2.3 percent a year. (See Figure 2–7.) This enabled the world's farmers to feed a population that had more than doubled during this four-decade span.[46]

After 1990, the rise in land productivity slowed dramatically, increasing only 3 percent from 1990 to 1996. This rise of 0.5 percent each year is less than one third of the 1.6 percent annual

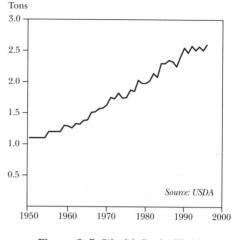

Figure 2–7. World Grain Yield Per Hectare, 1950–96

growth in population during this period. In the absence of a dramatic technological breakthrough that will restore a rapid rise in cropland productivity—a discovery comparable to that of fertilizer—the world will soon face some unprecedented belt-tightening.[47]

Trends in individual countries help illustrate this dramatic slowdown in the rise in land productivity. In Japan, for example, which was the first country to launch a sustainable rise in the productivity of its cropland, rice yield per hectare has not increased at all since 1984. After a century of raising productivity, Japan's farmers have run out of new technologies that will dramatically boost rice yields.[48]

A quick look at trends in the two major food-producing countries, the United States and China, is illuminating. For the United States, big gains in land productivity came in the fifties and sixties as land productivity rose by an average of 3.7 percent a year. (See Table 2–1.) Then during the seventies it dropped by roughly half, to 1.9 percent. During the eighties it fell to 1.0, again by roughly half. If it declines further during the nineties, it will be well below the U.S.

State of the World 1997

Table 2–1. United States: Grain Yield Per Hectare, 1950–90

Year	Annual Yield Per Hectare[1]	Increase by Decade	Annual Gain by Decade
	(tons)	(percent)	(percent)
1950	1.65		
1960	2.40	+ 45	+ 3.8
1970	3.43	+ 43	+ 3.6
1980	4.13	+ 20	+ 1.9
1990	4.56	+ 10	+ 1.0

[1]Each number shown here is actually a three-year average centering on the decadal year shown in order to minimize the effect of weather fluctuations.

SOURCE: Based on U.S Department of Agriculture (USDA), "World Grain Database" (unpublished printout), Washington, D.C., 1991; USDA, "Production, Supply, and Distribution" (electronic database), Washington, D.C., February 1996.

rate of population growth. With little new land to plow in the United States, a rise in land productivity that is slower than population growth will make future expansion of grain exports difficult.[49]

For China, the productivity of land climbed by 2.7 percent a year from 1950 to 1977, largely because of a remarkable growth in irrigation. The key, however, to the record land productivity gains in China after 1977 was the economic reforms launched in 1978. Between 1977 and 1984, grain yield per hectare climbed from 2.11 tons to 3.41 tons, an annual growth of more than 7 percent. (See Table 2–2.) This extraordinary rise in land productivity helped boost China's grain production above that of the United States and set the stage for the rapid growth in production of livestock, particularly pork.

The key to the rapid growth during this seven-year span was a near tripling of fertilizer use as Chinese agriculture was restructured, replacing the huge, collectivized production teams with the family responsibility system, which allocated land to individual families. Many Chinese leaders assumed that the new market-oriented economic system would sustain continuing rapid growth indefinitely, failing to realize that this was

largely a one-time gain. Once fertilizer application rates rose to levels similar to or higher than those in the United States and other agriculturally advanced countries, the annual rise in land productivity slowed dramatically, averaging only 1.6 percent from 1984 to 1995.[50]

Feeding the nearly 90 million people added to the world each year now depends almost entirely on raising land productivity. The number of people the earth can support depends, of course, on their level of consumption. The average American requires 800 kilograms of grain a year, the great bulk of it consumed indirectly in the form of beef, pork, poultry, eggs, milk, cheese, yogurt, and ice cream. The average Indian, in contrast, gets by with 200 kilograms of grain a year, almost all of it consumed directly. The world's healthiest people are not those who choose to follow an American-type diet, heavy in fat-rich livestock products, or those who consume an Indian diet, wholly dominated by a single starchy staple such as rice. It is those who live at an intermediate position, using perhaps 400 kilograms of grain, the so-called Mediterranean diet. (See Chapter 4.)[51]

If the world's farmers can push the grain harvest up from the estimated 1.82

**Table 2–2. China: Grain Yield Per Hectare,
Selected Years, 1950–95**

Year	Annual Yield Per Hectare	Increase by Period	Annual Gain by Period
	(tons)	(percent)	(percent)
1950	1.04		
1977	2.11	+ 103	+ 2.7
1984	3.41	+ 62	+ 7.1
1995	4.06	+ 19	+ 1.6

SOURCE: Based on U.S Department of Agriculture (USDA), "World Grain Database" (unpublished print-out), Washington, D.C., 1991; USDA, "Production, Supply, and Distribution" (electronic database), Washington, D.C., February 1996.

billion tons of 1996 to 2 billion tons, that would be enough grain to support 2.5 billion Americans or 10 billion Indians. In weighing the options between improving diets or feeding a larger population, people in various countries will have to decide whether they prefer a diet resembling that of the average Indian, the average American, or something in between. With a diet of 400 kilograms of grain per person, roughly what Italians eat each year, 2 billion tons of grain would support 5 billion people.[52]

If the oceanic fish catch is no longer expanding and the rise in land productivity has dropped below 1 percent per year, how can the world's food production systems support a population expanding at a projected 1.5 percent a year? This is the key carrying capacity question facing national political leaders today.[53]

FOOD SECURITY: THE NEXT GENERATION

The growth in food production is slowing while the growth in demand, driven by both population growth and rising affluence, continues strong. The politics of surpluses that dominated the world food economy during the half-century following World War II is being replaced by a politics of scarcity.

Not only is the growth in production slowing, but in Asia rising affluence is rivaling population growth as a source of additional demand for food. When Western Europe entered its period of rapid modernization after World War II, creating a modern consumer economy and boosting consumption of grainfed livestock products, it had 280 million people. North America, which was going through the same rapid rise at the same time, had 160 million people. To-day, Asia—the region from Pakistan east through Japan—has 3.1 billion people, more than half the world's population. Excluding Japan, the economy of this region grew by some 8 percent a year from 1991 to 1995, much faster than the growth achieved by either Western Europe or North America. There is no historical precedent for so many people moving up the food chain so fast.[54]

Economic growth in the region is led by China, whose economy grew by two thirds between 1990 and 1995. Given a population growth of just over 1 percent a year, this means that on average incomes for 1.2 billion people went up by 60 percent in only five years. Much of this additional income is translating into demand for more livestock products. During this five-year period, China's grain consumption increased by 40 million tons. Of this total, 33 million tons were consumed as feed and 7 million tons as food.[55]

Farmers who have always had to deal with variations in weather now face the prospect of rising temperatures as well.

China is not alone in moving up the food chain. In India, the broiler industry is growing by 15 percent a year, doubling every five years. And milk consumption is rising. The broiler industry in Indonesia, a country of 200 million people, is growing at a comparable rate. Feedgrain use is now climbing throughout Asia: in China, India, Indonesia, Malaysia, Pakistan, the Philippines, South Korea, Thailand, and Vietnam.[56]

This record rise in affluence for such a huge segment of humanity helps explain why world surpluses are being replaced by scarcity. Asia's grain imports have increased from some 6 million tons in 1950 to more than 90 million tons in 1995. Some Asian countries, including Japan, South Korea, and Taiwan, now import more than 70 percent of all the grain they consume. Asia is becoming industrially strong, but agriculturally vulnerable.[57]

This vulnerability is underlined by importing countries' dependence for nearly half of all grain imports on the United States, which controls a larger share of grain exports than the Saudis do of oil. This is risky because the U.S. harvest varies widely from year to year, depending on temperature and rainfall.

Farmers who have always had to deal with variations in weather now face the prospect of rising temperatures as well. Increasingly intense heat waves, such as those that decimated the 1988 U.S. grain harvest and dropped production below consumption for the first time in history and those that shrank grain harvests in northern industrial countries in 1995, could lead to wide swings in the world grain harvest in the years ahead.[58]

In 1994, grain prices started to rise in China, climbing by nearly 60 percent as demand expanded faster than production. In an effort to check this potentially destabilizing price rise, China turned to the outside world for massive imports of grain, which in turn triggered an increase in world grain prices. As this happened, exporting countries were tempted to impose restrictions or even outright embargoes in order to control food prices at home.[59]

In the spring of 1995, Vietnam embargoed exports of rice for some months simply because so much rice had moved across its northern border into China, where rice prices were much higher, that it created potentially unmanageable inflationary pressures. In December 1995, the European Union imposed an export tax on wheat of $32 a ton in order to dampen the rise in bread prices within Europe. In January 1996 it did the same thing for barley, its principal feedgrain, because barley prices had nearly doubled, driving up prices of livestock products.[60]

Over much of the last half-century, aid was an important source of food for needy countries, whether it was the war-torn nations of Europe in the late forties or Africa in the mid-nineties. But from fiscal year 1993 to fiscal year 1996, the international budget for food aid has been cut in half—dropping the amount of grain available from roughly 15.2 million tons to 7.6 million. With donor countries facing fiscal stringencies, political support for food aid is weakening. In a world of surpluses, the argument of "killing two birds with one stone" by simultaneously reducing the surpluses and providing food assistance appealed strongly to political leaders in donor countries. But in a world of scarcity, where providing food aid will raise domestic food prices, it will become more difficult to justify such assistance.[61]

In this new world of scarcity, countries would do well to devise agricultural and population strategies that would permit them to avoid excessive dependence on imported food. The assumptions underlying population and agricultural policies during an age of surpluses need to be reassessed as the world moves into an age of scarcity.

RESPONDING TO THE CHALLENGE

At the root of many of these difficult problems is population growth. Many countries with grain deficits at present are expected to have even larger deficits by 2030. For example, in the Middle East, the 1995 population of 243 million is projected to increase to 544 million by 2030, forcing this water-short region to depend on imports for most of its grain.[62]

The population of the northern tier of countries in Africa—from Morocco through Egypt, an area already facing acute water scarcity—is projected to grow from 136 million in 1995 to 239 million by 2030. Even now, each of the countries in the region imports one third to half or more of its grain.[63]

The projected growth in sub-Saharan Africa is even more staggering, going from 585 million in 1995 to 1.45 billion in 2030. With thin soils and a limited potential for irrigation development,

Africa seems destined to become a massive importer of grain, assuming the grain is available and that countries in the region can afford it.[64]

To the east, Asia's imports, growing by leaps and bounds, will continue to increase. China, already turning to the outside world for massive quantities of grain, may need to import some 200 million tons by 2030, an amount equal to current world exports.[65]

India's population, likely to pass 1 billion in 1999, is projected to hit 1.45 billion in 2030. Already facing widespread groundwater depletion, it will likely be importing heavily. Pakistan, now pushing against the limits of its water resources, is projected to increase its population from 132 million in 1995 to 312 million in 2030.[66]

As Mexico, with a 1995 population of 94 million, moves to 150 million in the year 2030, its current grain deficit is projected to be much larger—again because it is pushing against the limits of water supplies. Brazil, a country with one of the poorest agricultural land endowments of any major country and already the largest grain importer in the western hemisphere, is facing an increase from 161 million people in 1995 to 210 million in 2030.[67]

Many countries sense that they will need to import more grain, and all seem to assume that the United States will be able to cover their needs. But with little new land left to plow in the United States, this may not be easy. If the rise in land productivity continues to slow, dropping below population growth, expansion of exports will be difficult, if not impossible. At the same time, the export potential of both Canada and Australia is severely limited by rainfall. Argentina, which exports roughly 12 million tons of grain a year, might be able to double its exports if it plowed enough of its grassland, but cropping has already expanded onto highly erodible land. Even a doubling of Argentinean exports would cover world population growth for only five months.[68]

With the world demand for grain beginning to outrun the supply, and with the conditions that underlie this differential growth now strengthening, it is likely that real grain prices (after adjusting for inflation) will rise in the years ahead, reversing the historical trend of declining real prices that was so strong from mid-century through the early nineties. This challenges projections done by the U.N. Food and Agriculture Organization of continuing surpluses and declining real grain prices through the year 2010. The government of Japan, on the other hand, has done a set of global projections that indicates that wheat and rice prices could double by 2010—an assessment much more consistent with the prospect outlined here.[69]

A steep rise in grain prices could topple many governments in the Third World.

If prices rise in the future, how will they affect production and consumption? Historically, when grain prices climbed, production responded strongly. Farmers would bring more land under the plow. Unfortunately, the experience of the last several decades suggests that the opportunities for expanding the cropland area sustainably are limited.

In the past, farmers also responded to higher grain prices by investing more in developing water resources. When grain prices doubled in the seventies, investment in irrigation wells climbed, helping to expand production. But in the late nineties, investment in more irrigation wells in most food-producing regions of the world would simply accelerate the depletion of aquifers. Similarly,

in the seventies farmers could substantially expand fertilizer use as prices rose. But in much of the world, applying additional fertilizer during the nineties will have little effect on yields. As higher grain prices in the mid-seventies led to higher meat prices, the investment in fishing trawlers expanded, increasing the catch and alleviating the scarcity of animal protein. But investing in more fishing trawlers in the nineties will simply hasten the collapse of fisheries.

This is not to say there will be no production response to higher grain prices in the nineties. There will be. But it will be weak compared with earlier responses simply because economic determinants of production levels are being eclipsed by environmental constraints. Traditionally, the principal determinant of the amount of irrigation water pumped was the amount of investment in irrigation wells, but now it is more likely the sustainable yield of aquifers. Historically, the quantity of fertilizer applied was determined by the availability of capital to farmers, but today, it is more often the physiological limits of crop varieties to absorb nutrients. And in the past, the size of the fish catch was fixed largely by the amount of capital invested in fishing trawlers, whereas today it is the sustainable yield of fisheries that governs the size of the catch.

On the demand side, there will also be adjustments. The supply and demand of grain always balance in the marketplace, even in times of scarcity, but at a much higher price. The key question is, What will be the social and economic effects of these price rises? Those most affected obviously will be the poorer segments of the world population, specifically the 1.2 billion people who now live on $1 a day. For these individuals, who spend 70¢ of that dollar just for a minimal, subsistence-level diet, a doubling of grain prices could quickly become life-threatening. If grain prices rise uncontrollably in developing countries, people will hold their governments responsible, taking to the streets. A steep rise in grain prices could topple many governments in the Third World, leading to an unprecedented degree of political instability.[70]

The principal effect on the world's affluent may not be the higher food prices at the supermarket checkout counter, annoying though that could be, but rather the effect on the world economy of growing political instability in developing countries. This could directly affect the profits of multinational corporations, the performance of stock markets, and the earnings of pension funds. It is the indirect effects of food scarcity on the international economic system that will most likely affect the world's affluent.

The bottom line of this analysis is that whereas in the past the world has relied primarily on fishers and farmers to achieve a balance between food and people, it now depends more on family planners to achieve this goal. In a world where both the seafood catch and the grain harvest per person are declining, it may be time to reassess population policy. For example, in such a world, is there any moral justification for couples having more than two children, the number needed to replace themselves? If not, then political leaders everywhere should be urging couples to limit themselves to two surviving children.

If family planners are to assume the principal responsibility for balancing food and people, then they need more resources. The most urgent need is to fill the family planning gap, getting family planning services to the 120 million women, mostly in the Third World, who want to limit family size but lack access to the services needed to do so. At the same time, there is a need to invest heavily in the education of young females throughout the Third World. The social trend that correlates most closely with a shift to smaller families is the educational level of females. Simply stated, the more education women have, the fewer children they bear.[71]

Replacement of surpluses with scarcity also argues for a far heavier investment of both private and public funds in agriculture. This includes agricultural research, agricultural credit, agricultural extension, and soil and water conservation, to cite some of the more obvious ones.

But the distinguishing feature of food security for the next generation is that achieving it is no longer a matter of simply investing more in agriculture. Future food security now depends on changes in every major facet of our lives, including profound changes in reproductive behavior, family size, and population policy. Historically, food scarcity could be alleviated by simply investing more in agriculture and taking other actions within the domain of the Ministry of Agriculture. But now decisions made in the Ministry of Energy that will affect future climate stability may have as much effect on the food security of the next generation as those made in agricultural ministries.

The shift to scarcity will also affect land use policy. During the last half-century, when the world was plagued with farm surpluses and cropland was being idled, there seemed to be little need to worry about the conversion of cropland to nonfarm uses. But in a world of scarcity, this suddenly emerges as a central issue. (See also Chapter 3.) If the conversion of cropland to nonfarm uses such as industry, residences, and transportation, and to recreational uses, such as golf courses, continues without restriction, it will threaten the food security of the next generation. Already, a group of leading scientists in China has issued a White Paper challenging the decision to develop an auto-centered transport system, arguing that the country does not have enough land to both provide roads, highways, and parking lots and feed its people. Instead, they argue for a state-of-the-art rail passenger system augmented by bicycles.[72]

The only remaining reserve that can be tapped in a world food emergency is the grain used as feed.

Water, too, is being diverted to nonfarm uses. With water scarcity now constraining efforts to expand food production in many countries, the efficiency of water use is emerging as one of the keys to expanding food production. A shift to water markets, requiring users to pay the full cost of water, would lead to substantial investments in efficiency. The common practice of supplying water either free of charge or at a nominal cost to farmers and urban dwellers for residential use leads to water waste.[73]

In addition to protecting cropland from conversion to nonfarm uses, either through zoning or through a stiff tax on conversion, the loss of topsoil from soil and water erosion also needs to be addressed, since it too is a threat to the food security of the next generation. In an integrated world economy facing food scarcity, the loss of topsoil from erosion in any country affects food prices everywhere.

The shrinking backlog of unused agricultural technology suggests the need for a dramatic increase in agricultural research. Even if there is little prospect of a new technology that would bring a quantum jump in world food production, every new technology that would lead to even a small local expansion in food supply is a valuable one—and far more so now than in the past, when sur-

pluses reigned. Similarly, as grain prices rise, the return on investing in measures to reduce losses of grain in storage will also rise. New, synthetic materials that are designed for small-scale storage at the village level hold out the hope of reducing such losses.

The time may have come for national governments to begin assessing the merit of using cropland for the production of nonessential crops. For example, the 5 million hectares of cropland used to produce tobacco could produce 15 million tons of grain, enough to cover population growth for nearly seven months. The grain used in the United States for the production of ethanol as an automobile fuel is not essential and, if phased out, could provide an additional 10 million tons of grain for human consumption, enough to cover world population growth for nearly four months.[74]

Until recently, the world had three reserves it could call on in the event of a poor harvest: cropland idled under farm programs; surplus stocks of grain in storage; and the one third of the world grain harvest that is fed to livestock, poultry, and fish. As of early 1997, two of these reserves—the idled cropland and the surplus stocks—have largely disappeared. The only remaining reserve that can be tapped in a world food emergency is the grain used as feed. This is much more difficult to draw on. Higher prices, of course, will move the world's affluent down the food chain. But they also threaten the survival of the world's low-income consumers.

One way to restrict the rise in grain prices would be to ration the consumption of livestock products. Another approach, one much easier to administer, would be to tax the consumption of these products among the affluent, thus lowering the demand for grain. This would bring the price of grain below what it otherwise would be, with the price effect being influenced by the size of the tax. Unpopular though it would be, such a tax might be politically acceptable if it were the key to maintaining political stability in low-income countries.

If this analysis is at all close to the mark, then food scarcity is likely to emerge as the defining issue of the era now beginning, much as ideological conflict was the defining issue of the historical era that recently ended. National political leaders everywhere will be thoroughly challenged by the new demands placed on them by the prospect of growing food scarcity. Ensuring the food security of the next generation requires fundamental changes in population policy, energy policy, land use policy, water use policy, and, indeed, in the very definition of national security itself. Whether or not political leaders can respond quickly enough to avoid widespread political instability remains to be seen.

3

Preserving Global Cropland

Gary Gardner

Some 4,400 years ago, the city-states of ancient Sumer in modern-day Iraq faced an unsettling problem. Their farmland was gradually accumulating salt, the by-product of evaporating irrigation water. The salt steadily poisoned the rich soil, and over time harvests tapered off until many plots were entirely barren.[1]

Until this time, Sumerians had responded to farmland degradation and dwindling harvests by cultivating new land. But now they had reached the limits of agricultural expansion. Over the next three centuries, accumulating salts drove crop yields down more than 40 percent. The crippled production, combined with an ever-growing population, led to shrinking food reserves, which in turn reduced the ranks of soldiers, civil servants, and priests. By 1800 B.C., Sumerian agriculture had effectively collapsed, and this once glorious civilization faded into obscurity.[2]

The decline of ancient Sumer holds valuable lessons for today's policy-

An expanded version of this chapter appeared as Worldwatch Paper 131, *Shrinking Fields: Cropland Loss in a World of Eight Billion.*

makers, whose indifference to cropland allows it to be eroded to exhaustion or converted to nonfarm uses. Many nations now see their food supplies squeezed by the same pressures that afflicted the Sumerians: losses of cropland to degradation and urban expansion, the virtual end of agricultural expansion, and the growing demand for food. Especially in Asia, this combination of trends may soon threaten the food security of many nations as their dependence on imported food grows. And several emerging threats to cropland, especially loss of water for irrigation, are likely to worsen in coming decades.

The casual official attitude toward cropland loss and degradation is the remnant of a bygone era, when robust growth in yields provided grain surpluses year after year. In the sixties, seventies, and early eighties, rapid increases in grain yields outweighed the simultaneous losses of arable land. Since 1984, however, yield growth has slowed—dramatically so, in the nineties—and yield increases no longer fully compensate for the steady elimination of grainland.[3]

While yields could conceivably regain their strong rates of growth of past decades, banking on this is risky. Some of the components of the earlier surge in yields are now difficult to obtain, such as new irrigation water, or are dangerous to humans and ecosystems, such as pesticides. As a result, food supplies are likely to be tighter in coming decades than they were between 1950 and 1995. Indeed, as in ancient Sumer, sluggish productivity and loss of land are draining food reserves: global grain stocks have fallen in seven of the past nine years, hitting a record low in 1996. (See Chapter 2.)[4]

The double blow to food production—a shrinking supply of quality cropland and lethargic growth in yields—comes on the eve of the largest increase in food demand in human history. In 25 years, farmers will be asked to feed 7.9 billion people, 39 percent more than they do today. Nine of every 10 new births will occur in developing countries, where grain self-sufficiency fell from 96 percent in 1969–71 to 88 percent in 1993–95.[5]

In an era of tight food supplies, policymakers will soon realize that cropland is a vital national resource. They can then take a number of measures to stem the losses and protect the quality of the farmland that remains, as discussed later in this chapter. But the challenge is pressing. Future generations will urgently need the farmland that we have long treated as an expendable commodity.

TRENDS: FROM SURPLUS TO SCARCITY

Human efforts to produce ever-greater amounts of food reached a historic pinnacle in 1981. After thousands of years of expansion, the amount of grainland under cultivation worldwide peaked, topping 732 million hectares. Then between 1981 and 1995, the harvested grain area fell by 7.6 percent. A surge in grain prices prompted grain area to rebound in 1996, but it is still no larger than it was in 1974, covering 695 million hectares. From the perspective of land use, the period since 1981 marks a new agricultural era, in which increasing demand for grain is met on a generally contracting base of land. (See Figure 3–1.)[6]

This new era is the latest of three historical periods that highlight the changing role of land expansion in agriculture. In the 10,000 years that ended in the middle of this century, expansion of cultivated area was the chief tool for increasing food production. Cropland (which covers grainland and all other land for crops) increased as population did, from the first plots farmed on the Anatolian Plateau in what is now Turkey to the 1.4 billion hectares under production globally in 1955.[7]

After World War II, global population increased rapidly, prompting the search for other ways to increase output. Cropland expansion was now a minor source of growth in output with the exception of two initiatives—the Virgin Lands pro-

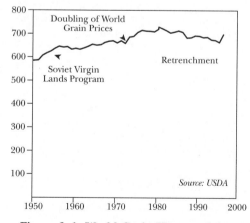

Figure 3–1. World Grain Harvested Area, 1950–96

gram in the Soviet Union in the mid to late fifties and the expansion prompted by the sharp run-up in grain prices in the mid-seventies. But yield increases accounted for nearly 80 percent of new output between 1950 and 1981. New crop varieties, pesticides, and increased use of fertilizer and irrigation made each hectare more fruitful. Yield increases for grains even outpaced population growth, raising production per person during this period. In essence, rising yields became a strikingly effective substitute for land expansion.[8]

In the current era, area expansion's contribution to new output has virtually ended. Except for a temporary increase in area in 1986 and the rebound of 1996, expansion has not been available to boost output. Indeed, as grain area has contracted, a startling change is apparent: for the first time ever, the entire burden of increased grain production rests on yields alone. Not only is area expansion unable to assist in raising output, but net shrinkage in cropped area is a drag on production, increasing the pressure on yields still further.

Falling grain prices may account for some of the contraction in grain area in this third period. Prices of the major grains fell nearly continuously in the eighties and early nineties, giving farmers incentive to switch to crops such as fruits and vegetables, whose prices rose in the same period. Then grain price increases rose more than 30 percent in 1995–96, which boosted grain area by some 2.5 percent. If maintained, the higher prices might provoke more crop shifting, and coax out any remaining idle land. But should demand for fruits, vegetables, and other nongrain products remain strong, the potential for switching this area back to grains would be limited.[9]

By relying on a single source of growth—rising yields—today's global agricultural system is more vulnerable to supply failures than when area expansion was an option. Hints of this vulnerability appeared early in this third era, as yield increases began to falter. In 1985, and in nearly every year since, grain yields have grown more slowly than global population—a reversal of the previous 35 years' experience.[10]

The vulnerability of global agriculture is best illustrated by using the trend in grainland per person. Grain area per capita shrank by 30 percent between 1950 and 1981, to 0.16 hectares—less than a quarter the size of a soccer field. (See Figure 3–2.) Massive famine was avoided only because of the robust yield growth. But by 1985, yield growth began to falter and production per person began to decline, ending a 34-year rising trend.[11]

Today, grain harvested area per person is 0.12 hectares—less than one sixth of a soccer field—and falling. Because yields no longer compensate for the continuing loss of land, a widening gap now separates the amount of food produced and the amount needed. This gap was closed between 1993 and 1995 by drawing down grain reserves, our global food

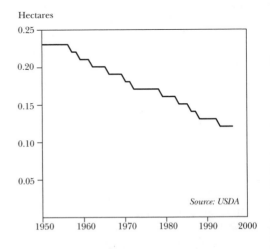

Figure 3–2. World Grain Harvested Area Per Person, 1950–96

savings account. (See Chapter 2.) The gap was also minimized by a decline in grain consumption per person in several regions, especially the former Soviet Union (due to a severe depression) and Africa (due to deepening poverty). Clearly, however, neither reserves nor depression nor deepening poverty are sustainable or desirable solutions for balancing supply and demand.[12]

Many argue that the gap between food needs and food availability will be closed by market forces, as growing food demand causes prices to rise. Cropland, they assert, will no longer be degraded or paved over once strong food demand makes land more valuable for crops than for other uses. The minimal incentive today for farmers to invest in soil conservation or to keep their land in farming is evidence, these observers argue, that farmland is not in short supply.

Markets are indeed often efficient in allocating scarce resources, but they are not perfect. To begin with, markets focus on the near-term, while societal and environmental needs often require a long-range perspective. Investors, for example, may be more interested in cropland's immediate development value than in its future value as farmland. Where this is true, the need for quality cropland two or three decades hence hardly registers in today's market transactions.

In addition, markets respond only to the needs of those who have money— the entrance ticket to any market. The food needs of the world's 800 million chronically hungry people are underrepresented in food markets. When this happens, the need for cropland is understated as well. Cropland is then undervalued in land markets, and is converted to other uses more readily than its true value would justify.[13]

Because markets are slow to recognize the dangers of soil degradation or the future need for food, and because they do not include the poorest, they are late in signaling the need to conserve soils and preserve farms. And the stock of land finally preserved may be less than necessary to meet food needs at affordable prices. As food prices rise, governments may feel strong pressure to subsidize food for their poorest citizens—outlays that might have been reduced or avoided if soils had been conserved and cropland preserved.

Governments can lessen the current era's pressure on yields by working ahead of markets to care for soils and preserve cropland today. With foresight and planning, a country's capacity to provide food abundantly and cheaply in the future can be maximized.

EXPANDING CITIES

For millennia, cities have expanded into neighboring fields and orchards as people needed more space for living, working, and playing. When land was plentiful, such expansion was easily accommodated: farmers simply moved on to new plots. But because little new land is available for cultivation in the world's most crowded regions, cropland losses from urban expansion are typically net losses.

Since many cities were founded in agricultural areas, urban expansion is an ongoing threat to farmland. More than half of all U.S. agricultural production, for example, comes from counties on the edge of expanding cities. Moreover, cropland near cities is often highly fertile. In the United States, just over 18 percent of all rural land is classified as prime farmland; but within 50 miles of the largest urban areas, 27 percent is prime. And because the paving over of agricultural land is rarely reversed, encroachment represents a permanent loss of a principal agricultural resource.[14]

The activities spurred by economic growth, including construction of factories, houses, and roads and the development of recreational areas, can take a greater or lesser toll on cropland, depending on how they are pursued. The U.S. model of suburban sprawl is especially costly to cropland. But even in crowded regions like Asia, where land is more highly valued, development paves over more cropland than is necessary. Failure to consider the cost to agriculture of a blind pursuit of industrialization has led to large losses of land around the world, most notably in Asia (excluding Japan), where economic growth has averaged more than 8 percent in each of the past four years.[15]

Consider the Indonesian island of Java, for instance, where urban and industrial growth is feverish. The U.S. Department of Agriculture estimates that urban expansion claimed 20,000 hectares of cropland there in 1994, an area large enough to supply rice to 330,000 Indonesians. The losses are part of an ongoing boom. Population in the urban agglomeration that encompasses Jakarta ballooned by 44 percent in the eighties, from 11.9 million to 17.1 million; office space in Jakarta multiplied by 19 times between 1978 and 1992. Housing development has been still more land-intensive. Between 1983 and 1992, approved requests for housing starts in just three cities in West Java—Bogor, Tangerang, and Bekasi—covered nearly 61,000 hectares. It is unclear what portion of this urban expansion came at agriculture's expense, but the share is likely to be quite high since Java is one of the most densely populated areas in the world, with little flat land to spare.[16]

Perhaps the greatest losses, however, are experienced in China, where economic growth has been measured in double digits each year since 1991. Data on losses of arable land there, though incomplete, are startling. George Brown,

a political scientist at the University of Missouri, analyzed official land use data and found that 6.5 million hectares of arable land—some 5 percent of the national total—were pulled from production in only six years, 1987 through 1992. (See Table 3–1.) Nearly two thirds of these losses are unexplained, possibly because their conversion to nonfarm uses was illegal. Of the explained losses, 40 percent involved expansion of infrastructure, industry, and housing. If the unexplained losses can be accounted for in the same way, 2.6 million hectares of land were surrendered to urbanization in just six years, an annual loss of 433,000 hectares.[17]

China also brought new land into production during the 1987–92 period, but the net losses were still considerable—some 3.87 million hectares. This area represents a drop of 15 million tons of grain, enough to feed 45 million Chinese. The net losses are also large compared with the country's remaining potential for expansion. Experts estimate that China can hope to expand its

Table 3–1. China: Gross Loss of Arable Land, 1987–92

Source of Loss	Area Lost	Share of China's Cropland
	(thousand hectares)	(percent)
Explained Losses	2,317	1.8
National Capital Construction	508	0.4
Township and Village Construction	240	0.2
Peasant House Building	184	0.1
Forest Expansion	833	0.6
Pasture Expansion	552	0.4
Unexplained Losses	4,239	3.3
Total	6,556	5.0

SOURCE: George P. Brown, "Arable Land Loss in Rural China," *Asian Survey*, October 1995.

cropped area by less than 8 percent (some 10 million hectares), and only at great expense. Continued losses at the 1987–92 rate would offset this expansion potential in just 15 years.[18]

While cropland loss to urban expansion is most critical in Asia, it is increasingly felt in other areas, even in land-rich countries. In the United States, where land is relatively abundant, some 168,000 hectares—the equivalent of two New York Cities—were paved over each year between 1982 and 1992. The loss jeopardizes much of U.S. fruit and vegetable production. A study by the American Farmland Trust mapped urban growth against prime and unique farmland to identify areas with the highest likelihood of loss. Rapid urbanization is under way in south Florida, California, and other areas that supply most of the nation's fruits and vegetables. In fact, the study found that more than 86 percent of U.S. fruit and 87 percent of vegetables are grown in rapidly urbanizing areas. Without cropland protection, the United States could be exporting much less produce in coming decades. Such exports accounted for 35 percent of the U.S. agricultural trade surplus in 1995.[19]

In the agricultural core of California, the Central Valley, a highly productive, 500-kilometer-long cornucopia supplies 8 percent of U.S. agricultural output (by value) on less than 1 percent of U.S. farmland. Indeed, 6 of the top 10 agricultural counties in the United States are found in the valley. But California is steadily losing agricultural land. Between 1984 and 1992, some 3 percent of its total cropped area was converted to urban or other nonfarm uses; more than a third of this was prime farmland. The trend is a long-standing one in California: Los Angeles County, an urban agglomeration of more than 9 million people, was the most productive agricultural county in the nation at the end of World War II. The Santa Clara Valley,

once acclaimed worldwide for its apricots, prunes, and other fruits, traded its orchards for industry, houses, and freeways—and is now known as Silicon Valley.[20]

Economic and urban growth also stimulate expansion of transportation infrastructure, which can devour cropland. The interests of motorists and farmers are increasingly at odds as roads and parking lots pave over farmland. Automobile ownership is surging in Latin America, Eastern Europe, and especially Asia. In China, domestic car production has been growing at more than 15 percent annually; the government plans to increase automobile output from 1.4 million units in 1994 to 3 million in 2000. In Vietnam, import quotas for cars were tripled in 1996, and sales of four-wheel vehicles are projected to increase sixfold between 1995 and 2000. Vehicle sales and registrations are surging in India, Indonesia, Malaysia, and Thailand as well. Around Asia, the shift to transportation systems that emphasize private automobiles is in full swing.[21]

In the United States, the equivalent of two New York Cities was paved over each year between 1982 and 1992.

In the seven Asian nations for which road data are available, paved area would need to expand by more than 4 million hectares to handle the increase in cars registered between 1989 and 1994 without increasing congestion. If these roads were built, and if three quarters of the area were taken from cropland, an area that could satisfy the grain needs of some 30 million people would be lost. The likelihood that a large share of the new road space would come from cropland is high, given the lack of spare land in Asia and the fact that roads and farming are most economical and function best on flat valley bottoms.[22]

Urbanization and rising prosperity also spark demand for recreational space. Golf, an increasingly popular, land-intensive pastime, is spreading rapidly in Asia. In Thailand, 160 golf courses were built between 1989 and 1994—one every 11 days. If construction followed the same pattern it did prior to 1988, two thirds of these were built on agricultural land. At 160–320 hectares each, the golf courses most likely displaced 17,000–34,000 hectares—an area that, if planted in grain, would have supported hundreds of thousands of people.[23]

In other Asian countries, golf's effect on agriculture is less well known, but the large number of new courses in densely populated countries is bound to take a toll on farmland. South Korea had 86 operating golf courses in 1993–94, but a further 200 were under construction and another 200 await approval. And in the early nineties, land-poor Japan—with 2,016 courses covering an area larger than metropolitan Tokyo—had 395 courses being built or with permits to begin construction.[24]

Urbanization is projected to continue at a brisk pace into the next century. By 2000, for the first time in human history, more than half the world will live in cities, making continued pressure on cropland likely. If land per urban resident in developing countries is estimated at 0.05 hectares, some 50 million hectares will be needed there for urban expansion by 2010.[25]

Not all of this area will be developed at the expense of cropland. But in crowded regions such as South Asia and East Asia, net farmland losses are likely to be quite high. In South Asia, for example, where the potential for cropland expansion is widely believed to be virtually nil, the urban population is projected to increase by some 420 million people between 1995 and 2010, imply-

ing an expansion in urban area of some 21 million hectares. This would inevitably lead to large losses of cropland.[26]

The continuing urbanization of China, home to more than one fifth of humanity, is expected to be especially striking. China's Vice Minister of Construction has asserted that the nation hopes to build close to 600 new cities by 2010, nearly doubling the 633 already in existence. If this prompts cropland losses to industry, infrastructure, and housing at the rate experienced between 1987 and 1993, about 6.5 million hectares—another 5 percent of China's agricultural land—would be lost from production by 2010, even as population there rises by some 14 percent.[27]

Projections of cropland loss from urban growth in California are worrying as well. At the 1984–92 rate of loss, the state will lose more than 393,000 hectares—nearly 10 percent of its cropland—over the next 25 years.[28]

DEGRADING OUR FUTURE

Nearly everywhere, the greatest threat to cropland comes not from a bulldozer but from a less visible and more diffuse source: land degradation. Around the world, agriculture has eroded, compacted, contaminated, salted, or waterlogged extensive tracts of cropland. And the damage continues almost unabated today. Because most of the degradation is unseen, the threat it poses is commonly underestimated. Yet the collapse of civilizations from the Sumerian 3,800 years ago to the Mayan in the ninth century—attributed in part to the loss of quality agricultural land—is testimony to the fundamental importance of soil health.[29]

The thin layer of earth called topsoil is essential to land's fertility. Typically only some 15 centimeters deep, topsoil is a rich medium containing organic matter, minerals, nutrients, insects, microbes, worms, and other elements needed to provide a nurturing environment for plants. Loss or disruption of this soil community through erosion or other forms of degradation impairs soil's fertility over time.

Data on the global extent of degradation and its toll on productivity, though sketchy, are worrisome. (See Table 3–2.) A landmark 1991 United Nations study estimated that 552 million hectares—equal to 38 percent of today's global cultivated area—had been damaged to some degree by agricultural mismanagement since World War II. And the report may understate the extent of the damage. A 1994 study of South Asia that compared the earlier findings with local studies estimated that soil damage extends to some 10 percent more area than the U.N. study indicated.[30]

In the worst cases, degradation has actually taken land out of production. In the U.N. study, soils described as "strongly" or "extremely" degraded—either beyond restoration or requiring major engineering work (such as terracing of hillsides) to restore their produc-

tivity—accounted for more than 15 percent of the world's damaged cropland. This lost area, some 86 million hectares, is roughly twice the size of Canada's cropped area. If it were producing grain at average yields for the nineties, it could feed some 775 million people. In an era of increasingly tight food supplies, this forfeiture of production capacity looms large. Yet degradation severe enough to pull land from production continues today, and may be on the increase: while annual losses between 1945 and 1990 averaged just under 2 million hectares, various sources suggest losses today of 5–10 million hectares each year.[31]

Most degraded land, however, is still in production, though much of it is less fertile than it used to be. Productivity losses to degradation have not been measured on a global scale, but some rough estimates have been made. Using likely productivity losses for each degradation category in the U.N. study, the approximate drop in output can be calculated. This exercise indicates that lightly and moderately degraded lands yielded on the order of 10 percent less in 1990 than they would have without degradation. When strongly and extremely degraded (nonproductive) lands are added in, the production loss from all degradation rises to more than 18 percent.[32]

Erosion, the most pervasive form of soil degradation (accounting for 84 percent of degraded areas in the U.N. study), robs the world of a natural inheritance that is formed at only a glacial pace. A typical hectare accumulates only 1 ton or so (a few millimeters) of new soil each year. Net erosion—the amount worn away from a hectare, less the amount that is washed or blown to it from a different hectare—is difficult to measure, but the higher rates of gross erosion are certainly many times greater than the rate of new formation. Reports of annual losses exceeding 100 tons per

Table 3–2. Share of Agricultural Land Degraded, by Region, 1945 to 1990

Continent	Share Degraded
	(percent)
Australia	16
Europe	25
North America	26
Asia	38
South America	45
Africa	65
Central America	74

SOURCE: L.R. Oldeman, International Soil Reference and Information Centre, Wageningen, Netherlands, personal communication, April 12, 1996.

hectare are common for individual plots, on sloping terrain in many developing nations.[33]

Erosion and poverty interact in a destructive cycle: erosion is often rooted in poverty and crowding, while poverty and crowding are often the fruit of erosion. The 1991 degradation study asserts that overgrazing, deforestation, agricultural mismanagement, and overharvesting of fuelwood—activities carried out disproportionately by poor people—account for 70 percent of the damage done to the world's soil. These problems, in turn, are often related to a skewed distribution of land. (See also Chapter 7.) Inadequate access to land pushes poor farmers onto small plots of marginal quality that they cultivate more intensively than the soil can bear or without the investments needed to use it sustainably.[34]

More than 11 percent of the world's cropland was identified in 1989 as "severely eroded."

Because the best valley land in much of the world was claimed long ago for agriculture or other purposes, more and more poor farmers are retreating to hillsides, an ecologically vulnerable topography because of the great potential for erosion. Some 160 million hectares of hillside land—more than 11 percent of the world's cropland—were identified in 1989 as "severely eroded" in areas as diverse as the highlands of Ethiopia, the uplands of the Andes and Himalayas, and the central highlands of Central America. With rising population densities, the threat to mountain plots has grown. In the Philippines, cultivated upland forest area increased from less than 10 percent of total cultivated area in 1960 to more than 30 percent in

1987.[35]

Another type of marginal agricultural land subject to increasing stress is farmland cut from tropical forests. Tropical soils are low in fertility, and can be cultivated successfully only with long fallow periods, typically 20–25 years. As land pressures increase, farmers are forced to cultivate fallowed land before it has completed its full rest period. In tropical regions of Africa and Southeast Asia, where fallow periods were once measured in decades, land is now idled for just a few years, not enough to recover fertility fully.[36]

The extent of pressure on marginal lands is difficult to quantify, but some approximations have been made. A 1989 study estimated that 370 million very poor people live in "low potential" rural areas—regions of low soil productivity that are probably environmentally sensitive. Another study asserts that 300 million people worldwide practice shifting cultivation, which depends on adequate fallowing. To the extent that areas with "low potential" and those subject to shifting cultivation are experiencing population pressures, the result is likely to be increased degradation.[37]

Salinization, another form of soil degradation, affects a much less extensive area. But because this damage is common on irrigated land—which is especially productive—salinization carries disproportionate importance. A 1995 study, drawing on national and global data from the eighties, estimated that 20 percent of the world's irrigated area suffers from this problem. Because the investments needed to flush salts from irrigated land are often not made, salinization severe enough to remove land from production claims an estimated 1.5–2.5 million hectares annually. And salinized land that remains in production often yields poorly, just as it did in ancient Sumer. In the Central Asian republics, for example, salinization is blamed for declining cotton yields: fields that produced 2.8 tons per hectare of cotton in the late seventies were yielding only 2.3 tons in the late eighties, even with increased use of fertilizer.[38]

Despite the adoption of conservation measures in some parts of the world, damage to land, especially from erosion, is still a serious problem on all continents. If the most severe degradation—which leads to cropland abandonment—continues at its 1945–90 rate, some 47 million hectares will be lost by 2020. Meanwhile, productivity on most of the remaining damaged lands will likely continue to decline. Such losses, which were manageable in a less crowded world, are no longer tolerable.[39]

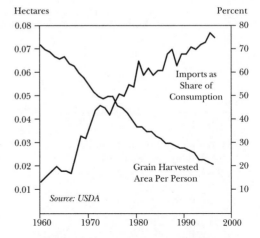

Figure 3–3. Grain Harvested Area Per Person and Imports as Share of Consumption, Japan, South Korea, and Taiwan, 1960–95

IMPORT DEPENDENCE: THE CASE OF ASIA

Ongoing cropland loss, if not counteracted by rising yields, eventually strips a country of the capacity to feed itself, sending it to global markets. Because cropland losses in Asia are especially severe, and because most Asian nations have little room for expansion, the continent is increasingly vulnerable to dependence on overseas suppliers for its staple foods. Indeed, the veteran Asian industrializing economies—Japan, South Korea, and Taiwan—have seen grain imports grow to more than 70 percent of consumption as grainland per person ratcheted downward over several decades. (See Figure 3–3.) As other countries attempt to repeat the veterans' industrial success, their import dependence may also surge—at a time when the international market for grain is increasingly unstable.[40]

The decline in per capita grain area and the rise in imports appear to march together in foreseeable ways. For the early industrializers, grain import levels became substantial—more than 20 percent of consumption—at roughly similar points: at 600 square meters of grain area per person for Japan (around 1950), 750 square meters for South Korea (in 1967), and 610 square meters for Taiwan (in 1967). (Grain area per person in Asia is so small that it is easier to express in square meters than in hectares; for reference, 600 square meters is 0.06 hectares.) For these three countries, the 600–750 square meter per person range constituted a sort of "import dependency threshold"—the point below which land loss began to translate into serious importing. If 600–700 square meters is used as today's threshold, the club of heavy grain importers in Asia is on the verge of expanding dramatically.[41]

Sorted on a land-per-person basis, a large group of Asian countries sits just above the threshold. (See Table 3–3.) By 2020, seven of these will drop to or below the threshold, joining the six already there. When this happens, the share of

**Table 3–3. Asian Countries Importing and Likely to Import
More Than 20 Percent of Grain Consumption by 2020**

Countries	Grain Harvested Area Per Person		Share of Asia's Population, 2020
	1995	2020[1]	2020
	(square meters)		(percent)
Already Below Import Dependency Threshold of 600–700 Square Meters Per Person			
Japan	190	180	3.0
Taiwan	210	180	0.6
South Korea	260	220	1.3
Malaysia	350	220	0.7
Sri Lanka	450	360	0.5
North Korea	530	410	0.7
Likely to Fall Below Import Dependency Threshold by 2020			
Indonesia	700	520	6.5
China	730	610	33.0
Bangladesh	830	510	4.9
Philippines	890	560	2.7
Pakistan	920	480	5.9
Laos	1,140	620	0.2
Afghanistan	1,150	490	1.2
Total			61.2

[1]Projected area conservatively assumes preservation of 1995 cropland area.
SOURCE: U.S. Department of Agriculture (USDA), Economic Research Service (ERS), "Production, Supply, and Distribution" (electronic database), Washington, D.C., May 10, 1996; U.S. Bureau of the Census, as published in Francis Urban and Ray Nightingale, *World Population by Country and Region, 1950–1990, with Projections to 2050* (Washington, D.C.: USDA, ERS, 1993).

the Asian population within or below this zone will skyrocket, from less than 7 percent today to more than 61 percent. Once India joins the importers, probably by 2030, more than 90 percent of Asians will likely rely on imports for 20 percent or more of their grain consumption. So within 35 years, roughly half the world could depend on foreign sources for at least 20 percent of their staple foods.[42]

The import dependency threshold is not fixed at one level for all countries and for all time. It could shift downward—postponing heavy reliance on imports—if a country increases farm productivity, or if it consumes less grain per person than Asia's three early industrializers did. Or it could move upward if consumption outpaces productivity—the current trend in many Asian countries. But it is sobering to note that the threshold has not moved below the level established by Japan nearly 50 years ago, in spite of the impressive productivity gains of the Green Revolution. Land area per person was higher in Malaysia, North Korea, South Korea, and Taiwan than in Japan when each country began to import heavily. The threshold seems to be relatively immobile because leaps in productivity have been largely offset by increases in consumption.[43]

The same offsetting forces are at work in many nations today. In China, for example, intensive use of irrigation and other technologies has raised productivity and kept substantial imports at bay: with a grain area of 730 square meters per person, China currently imports 6 percent of its grain needs. But consumption is increasing rapidly, counteracting a large share of the productivity gain and sending imports skyward. Between 1994 and 1995, China shifted from a grain exporter to the world's second largest grain importer. Likewise, Indonesia—which proudly achieved self-sufficiency in rice production in the mid-eighties—saw grain imports approach 20 percent in 1994 and 1995 as grain area dropped to 700 square meters per person and as consumption per person rose by 12 percent during the nineties.[44]

Whether productivity gains can offset growing consumption in coming decades is a major concern, especially as opportunities for irrigation expansion—a key to increased production—dry up. When Taiwan and South Korea reached 20 percent import dependence in 1967, nearly 60 percent of their cropland was highly productive irrigated land. Today, China irrigates the same share of its land, which largely accounts for its success in deferring heavy importing. But most other Asian countries irrigate less than 30 percent of their cropland, and prospects for expansion are dismal as dams and other irrigation infrastructure are increasingly expensive and socially and environmentally destructive. Because other sources of increased productivity—fertilizer and high-yielding crop varieties, for example—need generous applications of water to perform well, the limited potential to expand irrigation will work against lowering the import dependency threshold.[45]

The shift to import dependence would put many Asian nations in a vul-

nerable food supply position. Five suppliers—the United States, the European Union, Canada, Argentina, and Australia—account for some four fifths of the world's grain exports, a supply concentration that will likely translate into diplomatic leverage. Exporters will be tempted to flex their agricultural muscle to press for concessions on a range of diplomatic fronts, from trade disputes to treaty negotiations of all kinds. And if the top suppliers were to act in concert, their power would be quickly multiplied. The United States controls nearly half of world grain exports, but in combination with Canada and Europe, the share of control jumps to two thirds. Such a bloc could be threatening for nations importing more than a fifth of their grain needs.[46]

The United States, the European Union, Canada, Argentina, and Australia account of some four fifths of the world's grain exports.

Even good-faith suppliers, however, may not meet the full global demand for imports if production increases continue to slow. In the United States, for instance, grain yield increases have decelerated each decade since the fifties; by the nineties, they barely matched the growth in U.S. population. (See Chapter 2.) Continued sluggish growth in yields will leave little room for the United States to increase exports. Indeed, shipments from the five major grain-exporting nations have been flat in this decade because of the slowdown in production increases.[47]

Year-to-year fluctuations in grain suppliers' production could also threaten Asian grain imports. U.S. corn exports, which account for three quarters of the global total, have oscillated between 31 million and 60 million tons over the past decade, due to the uncertainties of rainfed production. In the sixties, seventies, and eighties, the impact of a bad production year could be cushioned by drawing down grain reserves or putting idled land back into production. Today, these backup options are largely unavailable. As noted earlier, reserves hit their lowest levels ever in 1995 and were not expected to recover in 1996, and land is no longer set aside in the United States (except for conservation purposes). With so little slack on the supply side, a bad production year—like 1988, when severe drought cut U.S. grain production by 27 percent and Canadian output by 31 percent—will be felt directly. As more nations depend on this supply, the prospects for meeting any one nation's grain needs will drop sharply.[48]

This raises some interesting ethical questions. Few African nations could compete with the major Asian countries in a bidding war for grain. Does Asia's impressive economic clout justify greater access to food? Or does Africa have a greater moral claim to grain exports because it uses grain more efficiently—for direct human consumption—while Asians feed much of their imported grain to livestock? And if efficient use is a moral issue, does the United States—with one of the world's highest levels of meat consumption per person—have a moral obligation to cut its grain consumption first?

Because of the uncertainties surrounding grain deliveries from the major suppliers, and because competition for a limited pool of exports is likely to increase in the future, countries that still have any operating latitude may want to think twice about developing a heavy dependence on imported grain. Avoiding this, however, requires preservation of agricultural resources, especially cropland.

A LAND-SCARCE WORLD

Given projected increases in population in coming decades, the amount of cropland per person will certainly continue to fall. If grain area stabilizes at 700 million hectares, the current area per person of 0.12 hectares will drop to 0.09 hectares by 2020 as global population climbs. But new threats to farmland—especially vanishing supplies of irrigation water—will put further pressure on the grainland base. Between 5 and 8 percent of global irrigated area, for example, depends on nonrenewable water or on renewable sources that are pumped faster than they are replenished. (See Chapter 2.) And in the western United States and parts of Asia, cities and the natural environment compete increasingly with farmers for water.[49]

These imminent pressures on farmland, and today's continuing losses, raise the question of the potential for sustainable expansion of agricultural area. Nowhere is that potential great, especially relative to the coming food demand. Indeed, major grain producers now acknowledge the error of past overextension of cropland, and are returning marginal farmland to more environmentally sustainable uses, such as grazing.

In the former Soviet Union, for example, land brought into cultivation in the 1954–62 Virgin Lands campaign is now being returned to pasture. The contraction is dramatic in Kazakstan, where harvested grain area has fallen 24 percent since the mid-eighties. With eroded soils and scant rainfall, the abandoned land had yielded only one fifth the world average for grains. Grainland area there is forecast to stabilize at some 13–16 million hectares—just half to two thirds of the mid-eighties peak area.[50]

In the United States, the Conservation Reserve Program (CRP) has removed from production some 14 million hectares of marginal land, an area roughly equal to the unsustainable expansion of the seventies, when grain prices doubled and the government exhorted farmers to plant "fencerow to fencerow." And 40,000 hectares now devoted to sugarcane in Florida's Everglades may be returned to natural wetlands under a 1996 plan designed to reverse the pollution of South Florida's water, which is contaminated by fertilizer and pesticide runoff, and which has caused vegetation changes in the Everglades ecosystem.[51]

In China, cropland lost to urban expansion grabs the headlines, but of the country's vanishing farmland, 60 percent was turned back to forest and pasture between 1987 and 1992. Farmers and officials recognized that these lands could be used more profitably for wood harvesting and meat production. In their natural state, they could also protect against erosion, retain water in their soils, and provide other important environmental services.[52]

For these nations, and for India and Europe as well—which all together supply two thirds of the world's grain—little potential for expansion exists. If Europe released for production the 10 percent of its cropland that was set aside in 1996, and if the United States were to reopen (and carefully farm) 7 million hectares of the least sensitive land set aside under the Conservation Reserve Program, some 11 million hectares would be added to the global stock of land, enough to feed 150 million people—just 20 months' worth of world population growth.[53]

In Africa and Latin America, the potential for expansion is greater, but not extensive. According to the U.N Food and Agriculture Organization (FAO), more than 70 percent of land with agricultural potential in sub-Saharan Africa

and Latin America is handicapped by unfavorable conditions such as steep slopes, poor drainage, and shallow soils. Low natural fertility affects 42 percent of the untapped soils in sub-Saharan Africa, and 46 percent in Latin America. Add to these poor natural conditions the lack of infrastructure and the institutional support needed for successful farming, and the plausibility of greatly increasing food supplies is doubtful.[54]

Low natural fertility affects 42 percent of the untapped soils in sub-Saharan Africa, and 46 percent in Latin America.

Brazil's attempt to colonize the Amazon region in the seventies is a clear demonstration of the difficulty of introducing farming to remote regions with poor soils. The Transamazon colonization scheme, announced in 1970, envisioned construction of a highway through the Amazon jungle that would open millions of hectares of forest for farming. The plan foresaw resettlement of a million families by 1980. But by 1978, only 7,600 families had been settled; turnover rates were high, as the scheme was plagued by lack of infrastructure, administrative difficulties, and, above all, poor soil fertility. Tropical soils like those in the Amazon are notoriously meager in nutrients, and can be farmed sustainably only with long fallow periods. In the late seventies, rice yields in the resettled areas were less than half the U.S. average, and well below the world average. Much of the land that could not sustain ongoing, intensive cultivation was converted to grazing land or abandoned; by 1980, the program was sharply curtailed.[55]

Even if farming were viable in the Amazon, the environmental cost of converting forests to fields would need to be considered. Tropical forests host a rich diversity of species that may hold the key to future advances in agriculture and medicine, for instance. Forests also store vast amounts of carbon, typically absorbing 20–50 times more than crops and pastures do; clearing them for agriculture triggers a huge net release of carbon, a greenhouse gas, into the atmosphere. Clearing tropical forests for agriculture typically entails high environmental costs and relatively little gain.[56]

In this context, some calculations of potential expansion are unrealistically optimistic. FAO, for example, estimates that 124 million hectares of harvested area are available for agricultural expansion in developing nations (except China) between 1990 and 2010, mainly in sub-Saharan Africa and Latin America. But this estimate is strictly a technical one that leaves aside the question of infrastructural and institutional capacity. It may also include forested area (their data cannot determine this), and much of the uncultivated area is of poor quality. The estimate depends, too, on an optimistic projection of irrigation expansion, at a time when irrigated area may have peaked.[57]

One possible source of land that may already be counted in the FAO figure is underused land on large haciendas in Latin America. Data from some nations suggest that land is used less intensely as landholdings get larger. In Brazil in 1980, for example, the share of land fallowed by the largest landholders was 11 times greater than the share fallowed by the small ones. These data are insufficient to determine the degree of underuse on large farms—this would require knowledge of specific land characteristics. And, of course, the smallest farms may be cultivated too intensively. But the large differences in intensity of use suggest that the scope for more intensive cultivation is indeed great.[58]

Whatever the potential for future expansion, the world will need all the land it can sustainably farm—along with steady yield increases—to meet the coming global food demand. Population growth alone will require a 50-percent increase in food production by 2030. The need for extra food will grow still further if rising incomes in developing countries continue to spur an increase in demand for livestock products, oilseeds, fruits, and vegetables.[59]

Future cropland needs will depend on the level of food demand and on future yield trends—neither of which can be predicted with confidence. Although yields may be re-energized in the future, yield growth could well be offset by rising consumption per person as Asian economies continue to surge, and as the former Soviet republics emerge from their depression.

With sluggish yield increases and growing demand, the world will easily require all the idled European land, all the sustainably cultivable U.S. Conservation Reserve Program land, and all the "reserve" land identified by the FAO (assuming it is actually available). In the face of such great need, continuing losses of quality cropland are unacceptably large.[60]

LAND FOR THE NEXT GENERATION

Clearly, the global food production system will be seriously challenged in coming decades to feed a continually growing, increasingly affluent global population. Every hectare of sustainably croppable land that is degraded or lost means more pressure on yields to compensate for lost production. But if existing, sustainably farmed cropland is seen as a strategic resource, no less important to a nation's well-being than oil reserves or its armed forces, preservation can become a relatively straightforward matter.

Fortunately, models of successful soil conservation policies already exist in several areas. The United States, for example, has achieved encouraging results with the Conservation Reserve Program, which pays farmers to retire marginal lands under 10-year contracts. On the half of CRP land that is highly erodible, erosion fell from 8.6 tons per hectare per year to 0.6 tons between 1982 and 1992. In all, more than 60 percent of the soil savings on cropland in the United States since 1985 is credited to this program.[61]

U.S. farmers have also made great strides in adopting soil-conserving methods of production. Conservation tillage—a set of cultivation techniques that avoids wholesale overturning of the soil—was in use on more than a third of U.S. cropland by 1994. This and other conservation practices contributed to a 25-percent reduction in soil erosion in the United States between 1982 and 1992. A host of such techniques, including terracing, alternative cropping arrangements, use of shelterbelts, and other initiatives, can be promoted through extension services, agricultural research agencies, nongovernmental organizations, and other institutions with a presence in the field.[62]

In some areas, soils can be conserved by eliminating the conditions that force farmers to use them unsustainably. Poor farmers who till marginal hillsides or forestland are often cultivating the only area available to them. The damage done to their soils can in many cases be avoided by allowing them to farm land that is underused. In some parts of Latin America, more equitable land distribution would likely stimulate more intensive use of farmland by putting into cultivation

land that is now underused or idle.

The best soil conservation practices in the world, however, are of little use to cropland that is paved over. Measures to preserve farmland are needed to ensure that the cropland base shrinks as little as possible in coming decades. In many European and a few Asian countries, agricultural land is already given the high levels of protection that characterize a strategic asset. Permission is needed to develop agricultural land in the United Kingdom, for example. But because development of rural land is presumed to damage the quality of open countryside, development permits are typically not granted. In Norway, real estate transfers of all kinds require a concession from the King, which serves to control changes in land use. By giving planning agencies in other countries a mandate to protect farmland and the authority to do so, losses could be sharply curtailed.[63]

The best soil conservation practices in the world are of little use to cropland that is paved over.

Zoning authority is a tool used extensively in Europe to protect farmland. Adjacent to some cities in the United Kingdom, a "greenbelt" several kilometers wide is established on which development is virtually prohibited for long periods. In addition to saving farmland, the greenbelts separate neighboring cities, preserve rural landscapes, and avoid the suburban sprawl found in many parts of the United States. In contrast, zoning authority is far weaker in the United States: only some 400 local governments employ agricultural zoning, and only three states have state-wide zoning programs designed to protect farmland. Wider use of zoning could

State of the World 1997

become an important tool in farmland protection.[64]

Where land is more freely developed, as in the United States, a regulatory approach may not always be politically viable. In such cases, a stiff farmland conversion tax may be needed. This tool would give owners a strong disincentive to take their land out of farming. It would essentially protect the interests of future generations—those whose voice is not heard in today's market transactions on land.

Without strong regulation of farmland use, control of cropland losses is difficult.

Cropland losses could also be reduced by requiring greater density in urban and suburban building. In the agriculture-rich Central Valley of California, for instance, where population is expected to triple by 2040, cropland losses could be cut by an estimated 55 percent simply by building 15 residential units per hectare rather than the more typical 7 units. A denser urban environment also facilitates the use of sustainable transportation systems, saves money on infrastructure of many kinds, and can promote a greater sense of community.[65]

Without strong regulation of farmland use, control of cropland losses is more difficult. Voluntary arrangements that rely on financial incentives, such as the purchase of development rights from landowners, have shown only modest success in preserving land. Under these arrangements—also known as conservation easements—a farmer agrees not to develop cropland for nonfarm purposes in return for tax benefits or a cash payment. Where easements are perpetual, subsequent owners of the farm are also bound by the development restriction,

and the land remains in agricultural production permanently. In the United States, 169,000 hectares of farmland in 16 states have been preserved since 1976 through the purchase of development rights. But the gains are relatively small: more cropland is converted to other uses in the United States in one year than was saved in the 20 years of conservation easement arrangements.[66]

As regulatory measures and conversion taxes are adopted to preserve cropland, other measures will need to be brought into line. Some farmers near cities are forced to sell their land to pay the higher property taxes that result when land becomes attractive to developers. Taxing farmland at its agricultural value rather than its development value would let farmers pay lower property taxes, making it more profitable for them to remain on the land. Similarly, burdensome estate taxes often force inheritors to sell all or part of their new holdings to meet their tax obligations. Restructuring estate taxes to preserve farmland is especially necessary in industrial countries, where the farming population is aging and where large areas of farmland will change hands in the next two decades as current owners retire or die. More than half of Japanese farmers, for example, will be 65 or older by the end of this decade. As farming populations age and farming constituencies weaken, the pressure to convert farmland to nonfarm uses increases.[67]

Pressure on agricultural land can also be minimized by reducing demand. In the short run, the easiest way to reduce grain consumption is to lower the intake of meat and milk, grain-intensive foods. Roughly two of every five tons of grain produced in the world is fed to livestock, poultry, or fish; decreasing consumption of these products, especially of beef, could free up massive quantities of grain and reduce pressures on land. Indeed, the most prosperous nations have plenty of room to cut down their meat (and therefore grain) consumption. Average annual grain consumption is just over 300 kilograms per person globally, yet people in 18 nations consume well over 500 kilograms, and the average American consumes more than 800. If the greatest consumers of grain had eaten on average 400 kilograms of grain in 1995—the Italian level of consumption—13 percent more grain would have been available that year. This represents what can be grown on more than 70 million hectares of land.[68]

In the long run, reducing demand will require slowing the rate of population growth. In a land-tight world, the policies that have been effective in re- ducing population growth, such as quality education for girls, economic security for women, and access to family planning, have a direct impact on the extent and use of cropland. As governments think strategically about the agricultural land base, population policy cannot be ignored.

The need to protect the extent and quality of cropland is no less urgent today than it was for the ancient Sumerians. Once we recognize farmland as the base of our civilization as well as our food supply, measures to preserve land become easy to identify and implement. In an increasingly crowded world, there is little time to waste in protecting our agricultural heritage.

4

Preventing Chronic Disease in Developing Countries

Anne Platt McGinn

Developing countries are typically known for high levels of poverty and infant mortality, low life expectancies, and a preponderance of infectious disease. But that picture is changing. Because of economic growth, urbanization, and overall improvements in public health and diet, health patterns in developing countries are no longer so simple. As these nations continue to struggle with the health burdens of underdevelopment, they are discovering new ills to be addressed, such as heart disease, stroke, and cancer.

Improved standards of living lead to different health risks—and sometimes unhealthier life-styles. Some people in developing countries are eating higher on the food chain—more fatty foods, meat, and refined grains—as international trade and urbanization alter food supplies. At the same time, they are getting less exercise as they rely more on cars for transportation and on machines for work, which can lead to obesity, heart and lung maladies, and premature death. And disability from alcohol abuse is becoming a more common problem,

even in Islamic countries, where liquor is banned by religious practice.[1]

As these changes occur, governments face difficult challenges. One of these is to understand the underlying influences on human behavior and health. Economic development and rising incomes, for example, enable people to buy meat, alcohol, tobacco, and other items thought of as luxury goods, while television and global marketing try to build the appeal of an affluent life-style. Addressing these underlying contributors to disease is crucial; otherwise, any response will be just a temporary band-aid, not a solution with long-lasting effect.

Population growth and demographic changes are also playing a role. In developing countries, aging populations are contributing to some of the rise in chronic disease as people live longer and increase their chances of becoming ill.

The transition from a burden of predominantly infectious disease to a mix of chronic and infectious disease is occurring throughout the developing world. (See Table 4–1.) (Some infections are chronic conditions, but in this chapter "chronic" is used in lieu of noncommunicable diseases and "infectious" is used for communicable ones.) Although this transition is most advanced in Eastern and Central Europe, Latin America, and Southeast Asia, populations of sub-Saharan Africa and South Asia are also affected. And this is changing the picture of world health.

THE BURDEN OF CHRONIC DISEASE

In Shanghai County, China, heavy use of tobacco precipitated a vast shift in mortality patterns in less than 20 years. In the early sixties, infectious disease, respiratory illness, and accidents were the leading causes of death. By the end of the seventies, cancer, stroke, and heart disease had taken over as the leading killers in this rural and urban county near the city of Shanghai. Indeed, by 1989, cardiovascular diseases—heart disease and stroke combined—were the leading cause of death nationwide.[2]

The same pattern is emerging in many developing countries. In Latin America and the Caribbean, for example, nearly twice as many people die from chronic diseases as from infectious ones. A similar pattern exists in the Middle East and some Asian countries. By 2020, chronic diseases are expected to outnumber infections as the cause of death globally by four to one. In developing countries, they will account for 7 out of 10 deaths and nearly 60 percent of all illness and disability.[3]

These illnesses have long been recognized as killers in industrial countries. Yet 58 percent of the world's 6 million cancer deaths in 1993 occurred in de-

Table 4–1. Current and Projected Burden of Chronic and Infectious Diseases and Injuries in Selected Countries and Regions

Country or Region	1990	2020
	(percent of disability-adjusted life years[1])	
All developing countries		
Chronic diseases	36	57
Infectious diseases	48	22
Injuries	15	21
Latin America		
Chronic diseases	48	68
Infectious diseases	35	13
Injuries	16	19
China		
Chronic diseases	58	79
Infectious diseases	24	4
Injuries	18	16
India		
Chronic diseases	29	56
Infectious diseases	56	24
Injuries	15	19

[1]Disease burden is commonly measured in terms of disability-adjusted life year (DALY). To calculate disability, researchers add the loss of healthy years of life and premature loss of life, and weigh it against the risk of dying at a certain age combined with the burden of illness over a lifetime. Columns within categories may not add to 100 due to rounding.

SOURCES: Ad Hoc Committee on Health Research Relating to Future Intervention Options, *Investing in Health Research and Development* (Geneva: World Health Organization, 1996).

veloping countries because of inadequate preventive care and high pollution levels. By 2010, the number of new cancer cases will double in developing countries even if current rates of incidence remain the same, solely because of projected increases in the number of people over age 60. Yet the incidence rate will not stay the same: because of increasingly western life-styles and urbanization, it is expected to increase significantly—more than doubling the cancer burden in the Third World. The same is true for other life-style chronic diseases:

aging populations will increase the total numbers of disease, while greater exposure to risks will increase the rates of disease.[4]

The economic burden of chronic disease threatens to overwhelm health services that are already under financial strain. More than 60 percent of cancers that will develop in the next several decades are expected to occur in parts of the world that have the fewest economic and medical resources available to treat chronic disease. In the United States alone, diet-related diseases—including heart disease, cancer, and stroke—cost nearly $180 billion a year in medical expenses and lost productivity. Developing countries can ill afford such high costs in addition to a continuing burden of infectious diseases.[5]

There are also social and environmental costs associated with a western diet and life-style. While difficult to quantify, these range from lost income and domestic violence to displaced crop production and accelerated deforestation to cure tobacco.[6]

Fortunately, many of these illnesses and deaths can be prevented. In the United States, for example, 320,000 deaths from chronic diseases in 1995 could have been avoided by changes in diet and exercise. Recognizing the key risk factors—a poor diet, alcohol and tobacco use, and lack of exercise—and heeding early warning signs can help prevent chronic disease.[7]

Of course, human genetics and environmental exposure also play a role in the incidence of disease. But it is difficult for individuals to change their environmental risk and nearly impossible to alter their inherited risk. Life-style choices are one aspect of health that individuals can readily control. And societies can influence and encourage healthy life-styles, and can reinforce the message of prevention.[8]

In one sense, the fact that western life-styles have only recently been adopted in developing countries is a sign for optimism that unhealthy trends can be reversed. It provides enormous opportunities for individuals and local groups to improve education about risks and to encourage healthier living habits. Consumer groups and the media can work to counteract advertising for high-fat foods, tobacco, and alcohol, for instance. Schools, health clinics, and employers can teach people about the risks of smoking and excessive drinking. The possibilities for preventive education and health promotion are endless.

But that will not be enough. It takes more than just individual behavioral changes to reduce the burden of chronic disease. Tackling this enormous problem also requires careful planning and restructuring of health priorities as well as action to address the underlying causes.

DIETARY CONTRIBUTIONS TO HEALTH

Our primitive ancestors gathered fruits, vegetables, nuts, and seeds and caught fish and game, while people living in agricultural societies harvested a variety of grains and vegetables. Measured in terms of calories, between 60 and 75 percent of food energy in a traditional diet comes from starches and other complex carbohydrates, as opposed to sugars, which are simple carbohydrates and constitute 5 percent of food energy. Another one fifth of food energy comes from fat, usually from animal products. The remaining 5–15 percent of dietary energy consists of protein. (See Table 4–2.)

Healthy modern diets have evolved from this traditional combination of

Table 4–2. Dietary Components of Traditional, Mediterranean, and Western Diets Compared with WHO Recommendations

Dietary Components	Diet			WHO Recommendations
	Traditional	Mediterranean	Western	
	(percent)			
Total carbohydrates	65–80	>50	50	55–65
Complex (starch)	60–75	n.a.	28	45–55
Simple (sugar)	5	n.a.	22	10
Fats and oils	<20	30–37	38–43	20–30
Saturated	~10–15	<8	18–30	10–15
Protein	10	8–12	12	8–12
	(milligrams per day)			
Cholesterol	<100	~300–500	~500	<300
	(grams per day)			
Salt	5–15	n.a.	15	5
Fiber	60–120	7–11	7	>30

SOURCES: G. Spiller, ed. *The Mediterranean Diets in Health and Disease* (New York: Van Nostrand Reinhold, 1991); N. J.Temple and D. P. Burkitt, eds., *Western Diseases: Their Dietary Prevention and Reversibility* (Totowa, N.J.: Humana Press, 1994); World Health Organization (WHO), "Diet, Nutrition, and the Prevention of Chronic Diseases," WHO Technical Report Series No. 797, Geneva, 1990; W. Willett, "Diet and Health: What Should We Eat?" *Science,* 22 April 1994.

foods. People who eat a healthy diet to-day still consume most of their energy in the form of carbohydrates. The typical Mediterranean diet, for instance, includes a large amount of grains, fruits, and vegetables, with moderate amounts of wine. Nearly one third of dietary energy in this area is consumed in the form of fats and oils, although intake of unhealthy, saturated fats is limited in Mediterranean cuisine. A typical Asian diet consists of grains (especially rice), vegetables, fish, and small amounts of other meats, and is relatively low in fat and sugar but high in salt.

In contrast, the diet characteristic of many industrial societies today represents a break with dietary evolution. It not only contains more total calories, but it includes large amounts of fat, sugar, salt, and dietary cholesterol, with small portions of starches, fruits, and vegetables. Westerners tend to eat more animal products—such as red meat, eggs, milk, and cheese—which are higher in fat, cholesterol, and calories than plant-based sources of protein are. The western diet contains nearly twice the level of sugar and saturated fat recommended by the World Health Organization (WHO). As these increase at the expense of starches, complex carbohydrates are about one third below the level recommended by WHO.[9]

This high-fat, high-calorie diet combined with a lack of exercise can lead to obesity, a visible manifestation of the western diet and life-style. Overconsumption of fats, salt, and meat also contributes to less obvious health problems, including high blood cholesterol and hypertension (abnormally high blood pressure). When a person's diet is high in saturated fat and cholesterol, the concentration of cholesterol in the blood rises. Excess cholesterol gets deposited in the arteries, clogs the passageways, and can eventually cut off the blood supply to the heart. This process, called atherosclerosis, can trigger a heart attack. High blood pressure, caused by high salt intake and other factors, also increases the risk of a heart attack. It forces the heart to work harder and be less efficient at pumping blood, thereby straining the heart muscle.[10]

Obesity, high blood cholesterol, and hypertension are precursors to other diet-related chronic diseases such as heart disease, stroke, and cancer—which combined killed 1.2 million Americans in 1993. Recent studies by the American Cancer Society attribute one third of all cancers in the United States to a high-fat diet.[11]

These health risks translate into staggering economic costs. In 1993, heart disease, stroke, and cancer cost the United States more than $100 billion in medical expenses. Lost productivity and economic output from chronic disease accounted for an additional $79 billion, nearly doubling total costs.[12]

In developing countries, changes in eating habits are occurring mostly among the rich elite and urban populations, not among average citizens or the poor. Although this represents only a small percentage of people in developing countries, it is a significant group, as it indicates where other people may be heading. Also, the health of the elite indirectly affects the well-being of others: following the lead of industrial nations, developing countries are already dedicating a disproportionate share of resources to the medical needs of the few, at the expense of the ongoing needs of the poor.

Although doctors and research scientists know what constitutes a healthy diet and what diets minimize chronic disease, people are not moving toward that standard. In fact, more people are following the western model. A look at the trends in consumption of oil, fat, and meat shows where developing countries, and consequently the world, are heading.

The amount of oil in the diets of people in developing countries remains far below levels in industrial countries,

although the gap is narrowing rapidly. Worldwide, dietary oil consumption per person increased almost fourfold over the past 30 years. The increase was much greater in newly industrializing countries. Between 1965 and 1995, people in Taiwan, South Korea, Singapore, and Hong Kong increased the amount of oil in their diet elevenfold, from 1.5 to 17.1 kilograms per person a year. (See Figure 4–1.) (By comparison, in 1995 North Americans had 28.4 kilograms of oil in their diets.) In the Middle East, Latin America, and Southeast Asia, the figure reached about half the level of the western diet during the past 30 years. Most of the growth was gradual, except in Southeast Asia, where the increase came just in the last decade. These changes, however, are by no means universal: in South Asia and sub-Saharan Africa, the problem is undernutrition; dietary oil consumption there remains the lowest in the world, at 6.8 and 4.8 kilograms per person respectively.[13]

Not only do people have more oil in their diet than they used to, but the type of oil has shifted toward the unhealthy variety. Saturated, unhealthy oil now represents a larger proportion of the total

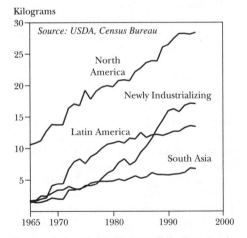

Figure 4–1. Total Dietary Oils Per Capita in Selected Regions, 1965–95

consumed. Worldwide, the ratio of "good" to "bad" oils declined from 4.5:1 in 1975 to 2.4:1 in 1995, with unhealthy palm oil making up a larger share of total consumption.[14]

These different types of dietary oil are associated with different health effects. Although people who follow a Mediterranean diet or a western one all eat more fat than WHO recommends, the type of fat they eat differs significantly. In the Mediterranean diet, most fat is relatively healthy, unsaturated oil that tends to decrease blood-cholesterol levels. In a western diet, people consume not only more total fat, but also a larger share of unhealthy, saturated fat that clogs blood vessels and accelerates atherosclerosis. In a western diet, 18–30 percent of dietary food energy comes from saturated fat. This is one reason why rates of coronary heart disease are more than five times higher among American men than Greek men, and about four times higher for American women than Greek women.[15]A large amount of fat is hidden in the diet. While dietary oil is important, it is also an incomplete measure of fat consumption. More than two thirds of saturated fat, for example, comes from meat, milk, and eggs. When people eat more meat, therefore, they consume more fat.[16]

Generally, people in developing countries eat less than half as much meat as people in industrial countries do. As with fats and oils, per capita consumption has increased dramatically in newly industrializing countries, where it reached 34.8 kilograms in 1995, up from 6.9 kilograms in 1965—a boost of nearly 400 percent. In other developing countries, however, per capita meat consumption has not increased significantly since 1965 due to rapid population growth, constrained agricultural resources, and the price of meat. Quite simply, many people in developing countries cannot afford to eat meat on a regular basis. In Latin America, for example, annual meat consumption stands at 25.9 kilograms per person—about where it did in the newly industrializing countries 10 years ago.[17]

Men and women in urban areas of Ghana are four times as likely to have hypertension as people in rural areas.

Current meat consumption trends in China, however, are especially troubling, as they point to the direction that other developing countries may be heading in. Demand for all red meat in China quadrupled between 1975 and 1995, and is expected to keep rising in the near future. If it does, the most populous country in the world can expect to see a growing incidence of heart disease, stroke, and cancer.[18]

Because the western diet is still new in developing countries, diet-related chronic diseases are just beginning to emerge and the full effects may not be seen for 20–30 years. Disease patterns in parts of Asia, Latin America, and Eastern Europe have shifted toward western trends, while in South Asia and sub-Saharan Africa, the picture of health is still dominated by infectious disease and malnutrition.

The burden of chronic disease is most evident among the elite and urban populations, who have been eating western foods the longest. Men and women in urban areas of Ghana, for instance, are four times as likely to have hypertension as people in rural areas. In cities like Nairobi, Johannesburg, and Mumbai (formerly Bombay), hypertension and heart disease are major health concerns among the elite.[19]

In Latin America and elsewhere, obesity has become a common affliction among women and children. In Costa

Rica and Nicaragua, an estimated 15 percent of women in their forties are obese, compared with just 4.4 percent of men. And in Trinidad, nearly one third of women age 40 or older are obese, according to the WHO Nutrition Program. (By comparison, 15 percent of women and 12 percent of men in the United States are obese.) Perhaps more troubling is that in Jamaica and Chile, an estimated 10 percent of pre-school-aged children are severely overweight, while in the city of Bangkok, more than 15 percent of schoolchildren are obsese. If this condition persists through adulthood, they may suffer from heart disease or stroke in the next 20–30 years.[20]

In China, as noted earlier, urbanized areas such as Shanghai County have already experienced a shift from infectious to chronic disease. As diets have changed, the trends have advanced beyond precursor conditions like hypertension and obesity to more complicated illnesses, such as stroke and cancer.

Stroke is the leading cardiovascular disease in China. It kills an estimated 1 million Chinese every year and disables another 2 million people. In 1990, the latest year for which data are available, deaths from stroke outnumbered those from coronary heart disease almost three to one. Coronary heart disease accounted for 20 percent of deaths from cardiovascular disease among urban Chinese and 10 percent of those in rural areas, according to the Chinese Ministry of Public Health. But with increasing consumption of fat and red meat and with more smoking, China's disease pattern may soon shift to one more closely resembling that in industrial countries—more heart disease than stroke.[21]

A 1990 World Bank study on the health transition in Brazil found that deaths from heart disease, stroke, cancer, and injuries rose from 38 percent of total mortality in 1960 to 54 percent

in 1986. This increase occurred at the same time that deaths from infectious disease declined 70 percent. By 2010, chronic illnesses are expected to account for nearly three fourths of all deaths in Brazil—far outnumbering infectious diseases.[22]

While Brazil and China are further along in the health transition, others are quickly catching up. Cardiovascular diseases are expected to soon be responsible for one out of four deaths in developing countries. By 2020, heart disease and stroke are expected to kill 13.8 million people in developing countries alone. In areas where mortality from stroke is already increasing, such as Cuba, Venezuela, Israel, and Sri Lanka, the trends will become more pronounced, especially among the urban and professional classes. In parts of China, Egypt, and Poland, the prevalence of hypertension is already approaching levels seen in Finland, which has one of the highest mortality rates from stroke among middle-aged men in the world.[23]

The key to halting the movement toward more chronic diseases is to treat the underlying causes along with the precursor conditions. Because stroke and heart disease have different risk factors, they require different prescriptions. (See Table 4–3.) Stroke is linked to hypertension, obesity, and high salt and alcohol intake, whereas heart disease is connected with a diet high in saturated fat, hypertension, diabetes, and smoking. Clarifying the risks factors helps policymakers recognize those that are unique to each disease, such as salt or saturated fat, and address the overlapping risks, such as hypertension. It also helps to target treatment and to understand the dangerous synergies among diet, drinking, and smoking.[24]

While no diet is risk-free, there are literally thousands of different combinations of food that humans can eat to stay healthy and minimize the overall risk

Table 4–3. Mortality from Chronic Diseases Worldwide, 1993, and Dietary and Life-style Preventive Measures

Disease	Deaths	Dietary and Life-style Preventive Measures
Heart disease	5.4 million[1]	Avoid obesity; exercise regularly; reduce fat intake, especially saturated and animal fat; reduce animal protein; maintain low cholesterol level; increase fruit and vegetable consumption; moderate alcohol intake eliminate smoking; treat hypertension and diabetes.
Stroke	3.9 million	Reduce salt intake; reduce body weight; eliminate smoking; treat hypertension and diabetes.
Diabetes mellitus	170,000	Reduce body weight; improve nutrition.
Cancers		
Lung	1.04 million	Eliminate smoking.
Stomach	734,000	Increase fruit and vegetable consumption; reduce salt intake.
Colon and rectum	468,000	Reduce fat and protein consumption; increase vegetable consumption.
Larynx, lip, and mouth	458,000	Eliminate smoking; reduce alcohol consumption.
Liver	367,000	Reduce alcohol consumption; vaccinate against Hepatitis B.
Breast	358,000	Reduce fat and animal protein consumption; avoid obesity.
Esophagus	328,000	Eliminate smoking; reduce alcohol consumption.
Pancreas	214,000	Eliminate smoking.
Bladder	135,000	Eliminate smoking.

[1]Includes all forms of heart disease.

SOURCES: Deaths from Report of the Director-General, *State of World Health* (Geneva: World Health Organization (WHO), 1995); National Research Council, *Diet and Health: Implications for Reducing Chronic Disease Risk* (Washington, D.C.: National Academy Press, 1989); United Nations Environment Programme, *Environmental Data Report, 1991–92* (New York: Oxford University Press, 1992); WHO, "Diet, Nutrition and the Prevention of Chronic Diseases," WHO Technical Report Series No. 797, Geneva, 1990.

of chronic disease. An optimal diet—rich in carbohydrates, vegetables, and fruits, and low in fats, sugars, and salt—goes a long way toward preventing chronic disease. A healthy diet helps to reduce obesity, hypertension, and high blood-cholesterol levels. Combined with exercise, a well-balanced diet will help prevent cardiovascular diseases and cancers.

Although diet changes alone will not prevent chronic disease from occurring, they certainly can help reduce the existing burden and prevent future illness. Eating less meat and more plant-based protein, such as legumes and soy, may hold the key to prevention. Researchers from Cornell University collected data in the early eighties and found rural Chinese who ate a plant-based diet had a low incidence of coronary heart disease, breast cancer, and large bowel cancer. They attributed the good health they found in China to plant-based protein sources that reduce the risk of chronic disease.[25]

Rather than aspiring to a western diet, people in developing countries would be better off eating like people in Mediterranean areas. In this case, as noted earlier, carbohydrates and vegetables make up the bulk of energy, while fats are limited to healthy oils, and protein is from low-fat meat and plants. The health benefits of this particular diet are clear: a study by researchers at the Harvard School of Public Health found that people in rural Greece who still consume a traditional diet live longer and have lower rates of premature mortality than Greeks whose diets have become westernized.[26]

The bottom line is that the western diet is neither inevitable nor desirable. There is a lot of diversity and variability in diet patterns, even among westerners. One key to reducing the dietary contribution to chronic disease is education about the health risks and benefits of food choices. As consumers in developing countries face an onslaught of western fast-food chains, food exports, and advertisements, they would do well not to succumb to the unhealthy habits of westerners. With the right kind of information, people can maintain the healthy aspects of their own traditional diet, and supplement it with fresh fruits and vegetables.[27]

ALCOHOL'S HIDDEN TOLL

Alcoholic drinks—such as *ulanzi*, a bamboo-based alcoholic drink in Tanzania; palm wine in The Gambia; and other traditional drinks—have been part of rituals for generations in developing countries. But the cultural practices and religious beliefs that used to stem the tide of excessive drinking are being eroded by advertising and government promotion. Alcohol is no longer reserved for special occasions. It has been removed from the structure of worship and celebration, and as a result communities now face the effects of alcohol abuse: more binge drinkers and an increasing toll of injury and trauma. Even in the Islamic world, where alcohol is prohibited by religious belief,

active alcoholics have been found in Saudi Arabia and Bahrain.[28]

Ethyl alcohol acts as a stimulant in small amounts, which can be appealing. When used in moderation, alcohol can be harmless. But in large amounts, ethanol acts as a depressant. The threshold of harm varies from person to person and is therefore difficult to pinpoint. Unlike food—which is necessary for survival—alcohol can harm an individual through physical and psychological dependency.[29]

But a person does not have to be addicted to alcohol to lose healthy years of life. Regular alcohol consumption is linked to high blood pressure and increased risk of stroke, heart disease, obesity, liver disease, and cancer. Consistent drinking, even in moderate amounts, causes more liver disease than occasional binges do. Excessive alcohol use over a long period of time is toxic to the liver and causes severe inflammation, or liver cirrhosis, which may lead to liver cancer.[30]

Nutritionally, alcohol offers only empty calories that replace better sources of energy in a person's diet. At high levels of consumption, alcohol actually causes the body to excrete nutrients. People who get more than 30 percent of their dietary energy from alcohol lose vitamins A and C, thiamin, calcium, iron, fiber, and protein. Although there is evidence that moderate amounts of wine may help prevent heart attacks, the net health and social risks outweigh these benefits in areas where heart disease is not a major threat.[31]

Worldwide, alcohol abuse killed an estimated 1.2 million people in 1993, the latest year for which global data are available. Nearly four out of five of these deaths reflect years of drinking. Most of these people were killed by damage to their liver. An estimated 390,000 people were killed by cirrhosis of the liver, and 300,000 people died from cancer of the esophagus or liver that was precipitated by drinking.[32]

Alcohol also kills in less direct ways. For instance, 5 percent of people who died from alcohol-related causes in 1993 had alcohol dependence syndrome, and 37 percent were killed in drunk driving accidents worldwide. These are caused not just by drunk drivers but by pedestrians, cyclists, rickshaw drivers, and passengers who are drunk. In Papua New Guinea, 85 percent of fatal road accidents during the eighties involved either drunk drivers or drunk pedestrians. Recent studies in South Africa estimated that half the deaths due to traumas for adults aged 14 to 60 can be attributed to alcohol. As a risk factor for injury, alcohol is estimated to cost South Africa $1.2 billion a year.[33]

Alcohol kills people who do not even drink. Intentional injuries such as homicide and domestic violence are more likely to be committed by a drinker than a nondrinker. Among Russians, the world's leading drinkers, almost 70 percent of crimes each year are committed while under the influence of alcohol. An estimated 100,000 Russians die every year from alcohol-related illnesses and accidents. And a survey in Mexico found that nearly half the people convicted of homicide admitted to being intoxicated at the time of the murder.[34]

Worldwide, alcohol consumption represents a global health and safety issue. Alcohol causes nearly three times the disability and illness that tobacco does, according to a 1996 report by WHO, the World Bank, and the Harvard School of Public Health. Alcohol abuse and various forms of psychiatric illnesses such as depression, schizophrenia, and bipolar disorder together account for 28 percent—nearly one third—of the global burden of disability. Alcohol is the fourth leading cause of disability, after unipolar depression, anemia, and falls.[35]

Nonfatal disability from alcohol takes many forms and is devastating for individuals and societies. Regular drinkers lose their memory, their jobs, and their earning potential. The latter loss is high in developing countries, where earning capacity is more likely based on physical labor and thus affected by drinking and alcohol-related disability and injury. Employers, communities, and governments also pay when people drink, as they lose income and productivity. In the United States, for instance, alcohol's toll topped $98 billion in 1990 in combined medical costs, lost productivity, and premature mortality—a 40–percent increase since 1985.[36]

Families suffer too: money that could be spent on food is often used to satisfy someone's drinking habit. A study from the Dissin region of Burkina Faso, for example, found that men spent $84 each year—44 percent of the per capita income in that country—on beer. Data from the National Trauma Research Center in South Africa show that more than 65 percent of domestic violence in the Cape Metropolitan Area and 75 percent in rural areas of the southwestern Cape are estimated to be alcohol-related.[37]

Although consumption and production data exist for only a few developing countries, data from the World Bank show that between 1970 and 1989, alcohol consumption increased in Central and Eastern Europe and in Latin America, especially Colombia, Brazil, and Mexico. For the first time ever, in 1994 the Chinese drank more beer than Germans did. Total world production of beer nearly doubled between 1970 and 1989, with most of the increase occurring in developing countries. Beer production in China is expected to nearly double between 1994 and 1998, to more than 22 billion liters a year, making that country the leading alcohol producer in Asia.[38]

Global consumption is underestimated—often by up to one third—because many people brew their own alcohol. Some of these mixtures are more potent, and more dangerous, than commercially available alcohol. In some African villages, women turn to making alcohol at home as a last resort to earn income for their families. Ironically, they sell the home brew to their husbands and get money that the men would otherwise spend on alcohol outside the home. This dangerous cycle encourages men to continue drinking, although it can help families make enough money to buy food, clothes, and other goods. If other, more productive job opportunities were available, women and men might be able to break the vicious circle of drinking and brewing at home.[39]

Countries that rely on alcohol for economic develpment are in denial about the risks and costs of dependency on this product.

Some governments, such as those in China, the Czech Republic and Mexico, believe that alcohol production is economically beneficial, and they are actively promoting production and consumption. But like alcoholics who refuse to believe they have a problem with drinking, countries that rely on alcohol for economic development are in denial about the risks and costs of societal dependency on this product. From a social standpoint, there is no doubt that actively promoting alcohol consumption "invites a future of alcohol-related illnesses, social disruption, and physical dependency," as researcher Lori Heise notes.[40]

As drinking-age laws are enforced and healthier life-styles are promoted in industrial countries, aggressive marketing of alcohol is likely to shift to developing countries. Without effective regulation and consumer education, alcohol-related problems will increase. For some people,

the threshold between experimentation and potential lifelong dependency is all too easy to reach. Adolescents are especially vulnerable to the lure of alcohol because they form psychological and physical dependencies much faster than adults do.[41]

In Africa, for example, beer drinking only recently became popular due to advertising campaigns and expanding markets. As a result, many people who never drank before, such as young adults and even children, have begun drinking without any experience or knowledge of the dangers of overconsumption. Beer drinking in South Africa grew from 12.1 liters per person in 1970 to 39.4 liters in 1985—a threefold increase in just 15 years. By 1989, South Africans were already drinking an additional 50 percent. A survey among high school teenagers in Lesotho found that half the students believed moderate drinking was impossible and that the point of drinking was to get drunk. Advertising directed at teenagers, especially at sporting and music events, has most likely contributed to this mindset.[42]

Concerned citizens and government officials can work together to make alcohol abuse socially unacceptable and to eliminate high-risk behavior. In July 1996, the government of Haryana, India, near New Delhi, enacted a statewide prohibition on alcohol consumption, production, and sale. Women activists pressured government officials for this because severe drunkenness had kept communities in the grips of poverty for years. With the ban in place, one woman declared, "For the first time in years, we [women] can go out without fear of being harassed." It remains to be seen how successful the prohibition is. Backyard producers of *arrack,* a liquor distilled from palm soap, molasses, rice, or grain, were operating in Haryana soon after the ban went into effect.[43]

If developing countries are intent on reducing the toll of alcohol-related chronic disease, one step they can take is to reduce the availability and desirability of alcohol, both government-sanctioned supplies and home brew. A tax on alcohol sales can provide needed revenue to treat alcohol-related illness, while enforcement of drunk driving laws and restrictions on advertising may help deter people from drinking. A 1988 study in the *Journal of Health Economics* concluded that taxing beer by 20 percent could reduce traffic fatalities by one third in the United States.[44]

HEALTH UP IN SMOKE

Within 25 years, tobacco-induced illness is expected to overtake infectious disease as the leading threat to human health worldwide. Developing countries are especially at risk because more people are smoking and, on average, each person is smoking more manufactured cigarettes—a potent and concentrated form of tobacco—than 20 years ago.[45]

Developing countries are also vulnerable because tobacco growing and manufacturing account for an increasing share of their revenues through direct sales and taxes. For each 1,000 tons of tobacco produced, however, nearly 1,000 people will eventually die from tobacco-related illnesses. As foreign investors and western tobacco conglomerates encourage developing countries to expand their markets, governments find themselves unable to pay for its legacy. Tobacco is therefore a threat not only to human health, but also to sustainable development.[46]

According to WHO, nearly one out of every five people on the planet smokes cigarettes. An estimated 800 mil-

lion smokers live in developing nations, while 300 million live in industrial countries. Of these 1.1 billion people, the odds are that one in three of them will die prematurely from smoking, losing about 22 years of life compared with average life expectancy.[47]

Worldwide, tobacco-related illnesses are estimated to cost nearly $200 billion a year in direct health care expenses and lost productivity. One third of this cost—$66 billion—is already borne by developing countries, a total that is expected to skyrocket as tobacco use spreads even further.[48]

Between 1971 and 1991, per capita consumption of cigarettes in developing countries increased by an average of 2.5 percent a year—with consumption growing the most in the Western Pacific region. (See Table 4–4.) In contrast, smoking in industrial countries either declined or stayed the same during this period.[49]

Given this growth in developing countries, tobacco use will soon become the world's leading cause of death. Richard Peto, an epidemiologist with the Imperial Cancer Research Fund's Cancer Studies Unit at Oxford University, calculated that in 1995, tobacco use killed 3 million people, 1 million of whom lived in developing countries. By 2025, he estimates, tobacco use will kill at least 10 million people a year. More than 7 million of these smokers will die in developing countries—a 700-percent increase in just one generation.[50]

"Unless smoking behavior changes, three decades from now premature deaths caused by tobacco in the developing world will exceed the expected deaths from AIDS, tuberculosis, and complications of childbirth *combined*," according to the World Bank's *1993 World Development Report*. In a follow-up report on the global burden of disease, researchers from Harvard University,

Table 4–4. Cigarette Consumption Per Adult, by Region, 1971, 1981, and 1991[1]

WHO Region	1971	1981	1991	Annual Change, 1971 to 1991
	(number)			(percent)
Europe	2,360	2,500	2,340	0.0
Western Pacific	1,100	1,610	2,010	3.0
North and South America	2,580	2,510	1,900	–1.5
South-East Asia	850	1,140	1,230	1.8
Eastern Mediterranean	700	940	930	1.4
Africa	460	570	590	1.2

[1]Data represent the average for 1970-72, 1980-82, and 1990-92.
SOURCE: World Health Organization, Tobacco or Health Program, "The Tobacco Epidemic: A Global Public Health Emergency," *Tobacco Alert: Special Issue*, World No-Tobacco Day, 1996.

WHO, and the World Bank argued that "this [tobacco] is a global health emergency that many governments have yet to confront."[51]

When people smoke, they inhale a dangerous and often lethal mix of carbon monoxide, nicotine, and almost 4,000 other chemical compounds, including a potent carcinogen. Carbon monoxide displaces oxygen in the body's blood. As a result, a smoker's lungs must work harder to oxygenate blood, which leads to difficulty breathing, constant spitting and coughing, and higher rates of respiratory infections. This also causes bronchitis and emphysema, which begin to affect smokers soon after they take up the habit. Because of the long-term disability associated with bronchitis, this condition is the most expensive health problem related to tobacco use. Smoking is a threat to others, too, in the form of secondhand smoke. Children who breathe a parent's smoke, for example, have higher rates of bronchitis and pneumonia.[52]

Another danger from smoking is caused by nicotine, an addictive substance that increases the heart rate by 10–25 beats per minute, or 36,000 beats per day. Smokers have a greater risk of irregular heart beats, which can cause a heart attack. Smoking also constricts blood vessels, triggering increases in blood pressure of 10–15 percent—an important risk factor for both heart attacks and stroke. Over time, people build up a tolerance to nicotine that makes it difficult to quit smoking and to reduce these health risks.[53]

Young adults are especially vulnerable to tobacco's health risks: the younger a person is when he or she starts to smoke, the more likely that person is to be a regular smoker as an adult. And the risk of lung cancer is much greater among smokers who begin before age 20 than among those who start later in life.[54]

Although cancer is the first illness to come to mind when smoking is mentioned, tobacco use kills more people from a combination of 25 different diseases, including heart disease and stroke, than from lung cancer. In the United States, for example, 434,000 people died in 1993 from tobacco-related illnesses: one fourth were killed by lung cancer, but nearly half died from heart disease and stroke.[55]

In 1993, tobacco use was responsible for 1.1 million cancer deaths worldwide—one out of every seven. Although lung cancer is the leading type of tobacco-related cancer, smoking also increases the risks of cancer in the mouth, larynx, pharynx, esophagus, pancreas, kidney, and bladder. Given the delay of 20–25 years from when people first start smoking to the appearance of a tumor, lung cancer alone is expected to more than double by 2020—from 945,000 deaths in 1990 to 2.4 million—almost entirely because of tobacco use.[56]

In developing countries, on average 48 percent of men smoke, compared with just 8 percent of women. Consequently, more men suffer and die from tobacco-related illnesses. But this may soon change as cigarette manufacturers and tobacco marketing executives try to expand their market by targeting women and young adults.[57]

Their marketing strategy seems to be working. More teenage girls smoke than boys in Latin America, so women smokers are likely to outnumber men within 20 years if today's patterns continue. In Chile, women in the health profession are astonishingly among the heaviest smokers in the country, with close to 50 percent lighting up regularly. Realizing the dangers of this trend, a women's anti-smoking network was established in 1991.[58]

Teenagers and young adults worldwide are lighting up like never before. In newly industrializing countries like South Korea, 61 percent of teenage boys smoke, compared with 29 percent in the United States. Some children even start smoking earlier than their teenage years. A 1988 survey of elementary school children ages 10 through 12 in Beijing found that 28 percent of boys and 3 percent of girls had smoked during the past month. Nearly half them had tried smoking between ages 5 and 9.[59]

Peer pressure, having parents who smoke, and not believing that smoking is harmful are some of the reasons why children smoke. If current trends are not reversed, an estimated 200 million children will become smokers in China by 2025; at least one out of four them will be killed by the habit. As one business magazine so aptly put it, the tobacco industry is a business that "slowly kills its best customers."[60]

The desire to smoke comes at a stiff price for individuals and families. In both industrial and developing countries, buying cigarettes typically takes 1–5 percent of a family's income each year, according to World Bank estimates. Even for countries that harvest tobacco and produce cigarettes, the cost of smoking can be devastating. Out of 22 tobacco-producing nations in sub-Saharan Africa, only Malawi and Zimbabwe have a trade surplus from tobacco. The U.N. Food and Agriculture Organization estimates that by 2000, nearly three fourths of the world's tobacco leaf will be produced in developing countries, particularly in Asia, Africa, and Latin America.[61]

It simply does not make economic sense for a government to promote smoking while at the same time bearing the brunt of health care costs caused by tobacco use. China exemplifies this irrational policy. The tobacco industry is China's largest source of revenue. Profits and taxes to the Chinese government totalled $8.6 billion in 1995. Yet just two years earlier, the annual direct health costs and indirect productivity losses from smoking were estimated at $11.3 billion by China's Academy of Preventive Medicine.[62]

Fortunately, it is never too late to quit smoking. Regardless of how heavy a smoker someone is, when that person quits, the health risks start to decline to those of nonsmokers. Within one year, the risk of heart disease is cut in half; within 15 years, the risk of lung cancer declines to that of a nonsmoker.[63]

Recently, some governments have tried to discourage the use of tobacco by controlling advertising. In Russia, for example, President Yeltsin banned advertising for tobacco and alcohol products in February 1995. While similar bans have been enacted in the past and enforcement has been questionable, the Health Ministry has vowed to take any money that television stations make running banned ads. In 1992, China restricted tobacco advertising, although this has had little apparent effect on consumption.[64]

Restrictions on advertising, bans on tobacco-industry sponsorship of sports and art events, and prohibition of tobacco logos on free giveaways have been enacted in various forms throughout Latin America, sub-Saharan Africa, and Asia. In France, a comprehensive tobacco law includes a ban on all forms of advertising, labelling requirements, and strict monitoring of compliance. After the tobacco control law went into effect, in 1991, tobacco consumption declined by 7.3 percent by 1995.[65]

Although these tools may prove effective in minimizing the spread of tobacco companies' deadly message, without education and disincentives, personal behavior is unlikely to change. As western tobacco companies increase their marketing efforts, public officials would do well to monitor and prevent teenagers from starting to smoke.

Prevention in combination with aggressive stop smoking programs and eco-

nomic incentives offer significant hope. In several industrial countries, cigarette taxes have been implemented to pay for some of the health costs of smoking. In Finland, for example, 0.45 percent of tax revenue is dedicated to tobacco control activities, while in Nepal, Portugal, and Romania, a portion of tobacco tax revenue is used to finance specific health programs.[66]

Taxes also serve as a deterrent to start or continue smoking. On average, a 10-percent increase in the price of a pack of cigarettes corresponds with a 4-percent decline in the number of smokers. (See Table 4–5.) Because teenagers and young adults are especially sensitive to prices, a 10-percent rise in price corresponds with a 10-percent decline in smokers in this group, thereby helping to limit the number of new smokers.[67]

LEADING HEALTHIER LIVES

As developing countries come to grips with the growing burden of chronic dis-

Table 4–5. Cigarette Taxes and Effects on Tobacco Consumption, Selected Countries

Country	Change in Tax	Effect on Consumption
New Zealand	$1.97 increase, 1980–91	Sales declined 37 percent.
Canada	Federal tax increase of 555 percent, 1980–91	Consumption declined 32 percent.
India	Excise tax doubled, 1986	Sales declined 15 percent.
Papua New Guinea	10-percent increase, 1973–86	Consumption declined 7 percent.
United States, Michigan	50¢ tax increase in 1994	Sales declined 30 percent.
United Kingdom	15-percent tax cut, 1987–90	Smoking increased more than 2 percent overall, and 25 percent among people under 18.

SOURCES: New Zealand and United Kingdom from Hal Kane, "Putting Out Cigarettes," *World Watch,* September/October 1992; Luc Martial, Canadian Council on Smoking and Health, Ottawa, Ont., Canada, private communication, 28 October 1996; India from World Bank, *World Development Report 1993* (New York: Oxford University Press, 1993); Papua New Guinea from Dr. Derek Yach, Division of Development of Policy, Programme, and Evaluation, World Health Organization, Geneva, private communication, 27 October 1996; Michigan from Hal Kane, "Cigarette Taxes Show Ups and Downs," in Lester R. Brown, Nicholas Lenssen, and Hal Kane, *Vital Signs 1995* (New York: W.W. Norton & Company, 1995).

ease, an important lesson can be applied from experience with infectious disease. As Richard Feachem, director of health policy at the World Bank, points out, "The best time to spend a dollar on HIV/AIDS control is when you've got no HIV in your country. The cost-effectiveness of control declines markedly as prevalence rises." The same holds for diet, alcohol, and tobacco: the best time to invest in prevention is before there is a problem.[68]

Preventive health, not expensive, curative medicine, is the key to reducing the toll of chronic disease. While the message of prevention applies everywhere, developing countries are in a unique but potentially tragic situation. Because changes in eating, drinking, and smoking are occurring more rapidly there than they did in industrial countries three generations ago, and because they affect more people, the costs of chronic disease in money and lives threatens to be much higher. If action is taken now to stop this ongoing and future threat, these nations will be able to avoid needless suffering and death, as well as the burden of chronic disease that industrial countries currently struggle with.

Diseases that stem from common causes, such as unhealthy diets, drinking, and smoking, can be tackled by encouraging healthy living habits and providing preventive health services. By addressing the connections between what people eat, drink, and smoke and their long-term health, individuals and community groups in industrial countries have been able to reverse some chronic disease trends. Mothers Against Drunk Driving (MADD) is a well known example of a group of concerned individuals who worked to publicize a problem, raise awareness, support victims of drunken driving, and coordinate safe alternatives such as designated drivers. A preventive health approach such as this is not only more cost-effective than frag-

menting by disease or risk factors, it also promotes broader aspects of health, including people's emotional well-being. Ongoing education about health and safety risks is important to counter misleading and seductive advertisements, especially for young adults.[69]

Some developing-country officials are beginning to realize that prevention is needed now. In August 1995, cancer researchers from all over the developing world met in Djerba, Tunisia, to discuss the growing burden of cancer. The three main conclusions of the meeting addressed the need to increase awareness; begin detection, prevention, and treatment early; and establish partnerships with nongovernmental organizations (NGOs) and community groups.[70]

But it takes more than government declarations to prevent disease. It takes physicians and parents teaching children about the dangers of smoking, and private corporations that choose not to exploit vulnerable populations in search of profits. NGOs are needed to mobilize public support for legislation protecting consumers, while effective media coverage could expose the impact of the globalization of trade on health and social development.

Community groups worldwide are responding to changing risks and threats to human health. In the Czech Republic, for example, anti-smoking programs based in health clinics have had considerable success at helping people stop. Patients treated for reconstructive heart surgery and heart attacks at two hospitals in Dubec, near Prague, measured declines in smoking of 40 percent and 72 percent respectively. This high rate of success was achieved through stop smoking programs and life-style changes to reduce blood cholesterol and blood pressure levels.[71]

In many developing regions, primary health care facilities focus on childhood and maternal health. By building on the proven success of these programs, clinics can adapt to the changing picture of health. Health messages can be tailored to aging populations while also emphasizing the vulnerability of young adults. Health workers can provide technical support for community-based programs on how to lose weight and stop drinking too much and smoking. This balance is admittedly difficult to achieve, but by blending education, health, employment, and even environment ministry mandates, developing countries can achieve considerable progress at little cost.Prevention does not require a colossal investment of money or resources. The World Bank study on Brazil's health transition, for example, concluded that "an initial 'core' preventive program (which might include campaigns to prevent smoking, alcohol and drug abuse, traffic accidents, and AIDS, and to promote exercise, and a national cervical cancer screening program) would require only about 3% of total public resources spent on health."[72]

Despite the common sense of this approach, expensive treatments rather than cost-effective prevention are being adopted in some areas. Most developing countries cannot afford the level of treatment available in industrial countries while also dealing with infectious diseases. Hypertensive medication, for example, is an expensive option for treating high blood pressure. Instead, nonpharmacological therapy—such as avoiding obesity, reducing salt and alcohol intake, and increasing exercise—is a more sensible option. In addition, more research is needed to develop cost-effective treatments for chronic disease.[73]

Food policies that discourage overconsumption of fat and meat are best for human health. In some areas, such as China and other Asian countries, promoting nutritional health means preserving traditional diets, cooking methods, and

cultural preferences rather than succumbing to western influences. In other areas, such as sub-Saharan Africa and Latin America, local diets can be supplemented with a variety of healthy foods that provide adequate nutrients and moderate amounts of fat, cholesterol, and additives. Food pricing schemes can be established based on health benefits from grains, meats, fruits, and vegetables.

Health workers can provide technical support for community-based programs on how to stop smoking and drinking too much.

When people know the facts, they often change their eating habits. Since 1970, life-style changes have resulted in a drop in coronary heart disease in the United States and Australia. Between 1970 and 1980, mortality from coronary heart disease declined 36 percent in the United States (although it still accounts for 20 percent of all deaths there). Consumption of low-fat milk and leaner meats increased at the expense of whole milk and red meat; as a result, saturated fat consumption declined. Average fat consumption dropped from 42 percent of dietary energy in 1965 to 37 percent in 1990, while complex carbohydrates increased from 22 to 29 percent. Improved medical care has also contributed to the decline in deaths from coronary heart disease.[74]

With tobacco, however, moderation is unacceptable. Reduction and eventually complete elimination of tobacco use is the goal. To do this, a tax on tobacco helps, as noted earlier. In India, cigarette sales declined by 15 percent after the excise tax on most of the popular brands more than doubled in 1986. In Papua New Guinea, a 10-percent increase in the tobacco tax reduced consumption by 7 percent. Experience from industrial countries shows that sometimes getting the political support for a tax is almost as difficult as trying to quit smoking, so gathering public support is crucial for the success of any progressive tax.[75]

For anti-smoking efforts to be effective, one underlying cause of the problem—the lack of alternatives to making a living—must also be addressed. Rather than subsidizing tobacco production, for example, governments can gradually dismantle incentives to grow tobacco and encourage farmers to plant other crops. In Zimbabwe, researchers found 53 other crops that could be grown in areas where tobacco is currently harvested. And some of them would make more money for farmers. Maize, for instance, was estimated to make 36 percent more profit per hectare than tobacco.[76]

Another underlying cause of chronic disease is the promotion of alcohol and tobacco by governments who subsidize and profit from sales of these goods. Clearly, these development choices will come back to haunt society in the form of lost productivity, premature deaths, illness, needless suffering, and health care costs.

If current trends in western diet and in alcohol and tobacco use continue, developing countries will face an enormous social and economic burden of chronic disease on top of the continued burden of infectious disease. On the other hand, if governments seize the opportunity to learn from the mistakes of industrial countries, developing countries will avoid increases in chronic disease and reduce the incidence where it already exists.

The interactions between diet, alcohol, and tobacco are too complex to wait until chronic disease is a full-blown problem. Given the added variables of rising incomes, urbanization, and aging populations, the stage for a dramatic shift in the picture of health has already been set in developing countries. It is up to governments, individual citizens, and private companies to determine the outcome of this transition—and the health of people worldwide.

5

Tracking the Ecology of Climate Change

Chris Bright

The early eighties were a global ordeal by fire and water. South Africa's Klaserie game reserve was parched and 33,000 game animals died of thirst; across the border in Botswana, the immense wetland of the Okavango River delta shrank by a third. In Borneo, tracts of lowland rain forest went up in flames, probably for the first time ever, and brush fires scorched 350,000 hectares of eastern Australia. In the central Pacific, torrential downpours on Christmas Island washed out a colony of 17 million seabirds, while farther east, plankton populations crashed, forcing a collapse in the fish populations that prey on them, and coral reefs died.[1]

In a world with less and less room for the wild, the effect of such natural disasters on nature itself is becoming a social issue. The earth's remaining natural areas are home to the planet's greatest stores of evolutionary wealth. Quite apart from their intrinsic value, it is becoming increasingly clear that such areas create wealth in a very literal sense. They do it not just by furnishing us with lumber or fish or new drugs, but by main-

taining the natural functions that underlie all economic activity. (See Chapter 6.) The social value of such natural services as pollination, which makes agriculture possible, and water purification, which makes cities possible, is so great as to be nearly incalculable. We literally cannot live without them.

There is another, more ominous social dimension to the ordeal of the early eighties: it may not have been an entirely natural disaster. Many of the disruptions have been related to a weather pattern known as El Niño, Spanish for "the little boy." The name commemorates the Christ Child because El Niños begin in the Christmas season, as an influx of a warm current into the normally cold waters off the coast of Ecuador and Peru. That event is associated with unusual weather over the western Pacific, and as this churning of air masses and currents works outward, El Niño can eventually rearrange a good deal of the global climate. In January 1996, a statistical computer model examining this phenomenon concluded that even though El Niños are a natural part of the earth's climate, nature alone probably cannot explain the recent increases in their severity and length.[2]

The recent El Niños are probably linked to another climate variable that seems to be acting in an "unnatural" way: temperature variation. There has been a general upward trend in average annual global temperature, from about 14.5 degrees Celsius in 1866, when reliable records begin, to around 15.4 degrees in 1995—the warmest year on record. (See Figure 5–1.) That trend correlates closely with an increase in atmospheric levels of heat-trapping greenhouse gases, principally carbon dioxide (CO_2), which is released in enormous quantities by the burning of coal and oil. Carbon dioxide is naturally present in the atmosphere, but current concentrations now stand at around 360 parts per million, some 25–30 percent higher than they have been at any time within the last 160,000 years.[3]

There is no proof positive that the warming trend is anything other than nature at work. But sophisticated computer modeling and actual measurements of the atmosphere are now converging with uncanny accuracy: in cyberspace, scientists can link up the atmosphere, oceans, and other major pieces of the world's climate machine, and ask what the extra CO_2 might do. Increasingly, the computer answers are corroborated by direct observation.[4]

By 1995, the fit looked too close to be pure coincidence; the Intergovernmental Panel on Climate Change (IPCC), a network of more than 2,000 scientists and policy experts assembled by the United Nations to advise governments on climate policy, concluded that human activity is warming the earth. Future warming, according to the IPCC, will probably be in the range of 1–3.5 degrees Celsius by the year 2100, depending on air pollution trends. That may not sound like much, but the last time temperatures substantially exceeded current levels, 125,000–115,000 years ago, hippopotamuses were living in what is now Britain.[5]

The possibility of rapid climate change is not just the stuff of academic hypothesis. There is a growing body of hard evidence for very rapid climate shifts in the earth's past—even in geologically "recent" eras. Some 11,600 years ago, at the end of a very cold era, average global temperatures shot up an estimated 7 degrees Celsius in only 20–50 years. Ocean currents changed abruptly, African lakes appear to have dried up, and atmospheric methane rose—a strong signal of widespread shifts in vegetation, since the gas is released by rotting plants. A major climate shift appears to have occurred in just the span of one human generation.[6]

Climate computer models only work on a very broad scale, so it is hard to say specifically what the current trends portend. But in general, scientists expect higher latitudes to warm much more than the tropics. Sea levels will rise, largely because warm water expands, but also in response to melting polar ice. Hurricanes may grow stronger and more frequent, in response to the increased energy of the

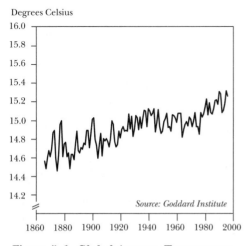

Figure 5–1. Global Average Temperature, 1866–1995

warming seas and air. And worldwide, the climate may become more extreme—droughts, floods, and heat waves are likely to occur more frequently.[7]

Investigating the possible effects of such changes on the planet's ecosystems has become a major scientific enterprise. Some studies already detect climate change at work, although with varying degrees of certainty. Others are exploring future ecological effects, or possible mechanisms of change. In general, ecologists are concerned about two aspects of the present warming that distinguish it from past climate fluctuations. First, the physical disruption of many natural landscapes will greatly constrain ecosystem responses. (Imagine trying to play chess with half the squares off limits to your pieces.) Second, the overlap with various other forms of ecological degradation will greatly increase the odds of abrupt and dangerous results. (Imagine that your opponent has several queens.) Even without these two liabilities, the prospects of rapid climate change would be well worth avoiding; with them, the risks increase enormously. Exploring the ecology of climate change is a matter of trying to understand those risks.

INSIDE THE GREENHOUSE

Despite the considerable temperature swings that can occur without apparent harm in the course of a day, a season, or a year, an overall upward nudge in the temperature pattern can have profound ecological effects. In many parts of the world, a slight rise in average annual air temperature could greatly increase the risk of insect outbreaks—to the detriment of both natural landscapes and crops. Warmer water temperatures could mean widespread disruption of aquatic ecosystems and an unpredictable addi-tional burden on the world's major fisheries, which are already being pressed beyond their long-term capacity. Temperature-driven changes in rainfall patterns are probably now contributing to spreading drought in Africa, Europe, and elsewhere. And rising sea levels are invading coastal wetlands—among the world's most threatened natural areas.

Many of these changes begin with simple physiological effects, such as in plant metabolism. Within the limits of its temperature tolerance and assuming its other needs are met, a plant will tend to grow faster in warmer weather. This fact is often seized on to argue that climate change will be "good"—or at least that it will not necessarily be bad. But mechanical extrapolation like this does not really tell us much about ecological effects.[8]

Outside the lab, a plant's success may be limited by many factors, one of the most important being insect attack. The relationship between plants and insects is a basic force shaping terrestrial ecosystems. Of the 1.82 million species of living things thus far identified, 1.04 million are insects. Some 325,000 species of "green" (photosynthetic) plants and fungi have been named, but the entire vertebrate line—fish, reptiles, amphibians, birds, and mammals—accounts for only about 41,000 species. Relatively few vertebrates probably remain to be discovered, but it is likely that tens of millions of insect species are still unknown. (And an even larger number of microorganisms may await discovery.)[9]

As with plants, warm weather speeds up insect metabolism: in warm years, insects often grow quicker, breed more frequently, and migrate sooner. The European corn borer, for example, is a major crop pest in both Europe and North America. Over the past few decades it has extended its range northward on both continents, and enlarged the areas where it manages to produce more than a single generation in the course of a year. At present, scientists credit changes in agriculture as the main cause, but climate projections for Europe suggest that by 2020, the borer will launch its migratory flights up to 25 days earlier than at present, and that it may be able to colonize areas of northern Europe that it now rarely visits.[10]

In the forests of western Canada and Alaska, where warm years are frequently associated with pest outbreaks, a warming trend may be driving an invasion of the spruce budworm, which has been moving across the continent from the east. The budworm, which attacks new growth on conifers, now causes more forest losses in Canada than any other insect. It also illustrates what climate change can do for an insect. A single outbreak can produce 7,200 trillion individual budworms; assuming standard insect mutation rates, that virtually guarantees the presence of billions of rare genetic combinations. In the boreal forests (those in the northern parts of the world), some areas could well become too warm or dry for spruce or fir. But for any likely Canadian climate scenario, there will almost certainly be a budworm genotype that will fit. Because of their huge genetic arsenal, insects like the budworm are in effect "preadapted" to climate change.[11]

Many aquatic organisms are highly sensitive to temperature as well. In the streams of the U.S. Pacific Northwest, for example, water temperatures above 19 degrees Celsius allow redside shiners to outcompete juvenile steelhead trout—an important commercial species. By altering such competitive balances, warming water could endanger a species even if the temperature remains well within the range of its physiological tolerance. Other dramatic ecological consequences could follow as well. In 1987, for instance, one of the toxic plankton species implicated in red tides (episodes of massive plankton reproduction that can poison large areas) followed an unusually warm current out of its native range, the Gulf of Mexico, and up the U.S. East Coast. This caused substantial fish kills—along with human nerve poisoning through contaminated shellfish.[12]

As the oceans warm, these kinds of shifts are liable to show up elsewhere. Some recent research indicates that the waters off western Canada may warm by 2 degrees Celsius by 2070, which would reduce the summer range of Pacific salmon species by 50 percent and eliminate the winter range entirely. In effect, the salmon would be forced to bend their migration route north into the Bering Sea—a prospect whose success and consequences would be very difficult to predict. By altering the distributional overlap of species, shifts in water temperature may break important knots in the food web.[13]

In warm years, insects often grow quicker, breed more frequently, and migrate sooner.

In certain animals, temperature fluctuation plays an even more basic role in population dynamics. In some fish, crustaceans, and reptiles, ambient temperature at a critical period in embryonic development helps determine gender. In certain turtles, for instance, warmer temperatures mean more females—and proportionately fewer males. The warming may already be skewing the sex ratios of certain turtle populations badly enough to threaten their existence. Among the species affected is the loggerhead sea turtle, an endangered species.[14]

A warming world is likely also to grow rainier, yet paradoxically, it will probably be a world of spreading drought as well.

The hydrological cycle, as scientists call it, will tend to feed a higher volume of water into the world's precipitation, but the additional rainfall will not be evenly distributed. Although the climate models are not precise enough to map out precipitation in much detail, they generally agree that many continental regions are likely to get drier—especially those already subject to drought. Many wet regions may get even wetter. The temporal distribution of precipitation is likely to be uneven as well—rainfall may become more "concentrated" into heavy rains than it currently is.[15]

Perhaps the biggest threat from changes in the hydrological cycle is drought, and studies of the problem in various parts of the world have begun to invoke climate change as a factor. An IPCC study concluded last June, for example, that climate change will eliminate 85 percent of the wetlands remaining in Spain and Greece. Mediterranean wetlands are already under intense pressure from drought and from the demands of farms and cities. Spain has lost two thirds of its inland wetlands since 1965.[16]

Average global sea level has probably risen about 18 centimeters over the past century.

Even relatively mild droughts may stunt plant growth, boost insect attacks, or spread disease. In balsam fir, an important conifer in North American boreal forests, lack of moisture can cause a near tripling of sugar concentrations in new growth. That stimulates feeding in the spruce budworm, which often thrives in dry years. In some trees, moisture stress can throw off the balance between the tree and a normally harmless fungus living within it; in effect, the fungus may become a new disease.[17]

At its worst, drought becomes desertification—vegetation dwindles, leaving the soil exposed to erosion by wind and what little rain there is. The remaining soil absorbs less and less water, which exacerbates erosion from runoff. Dryland scrub becomes sparse grassland and then barren hardpan. Under extreme conditions, such desertification is, for all practical purposes, irreversible. Nearly 20 million square kilometers, or 15 percent of the planet's land surface, may already be affected to some degree by desertification—principally in northwest China, central Asia, and the African Sahel. (The area includes some of the less extreme natural deserts; deserts themselves cover about 30 percent of the world's land surface.) The first stages of desertification may be emerging in Europe as well—in Spain, Portugal, Greece, and Italy. Overgrazing, fuelwood cutting, overcultivation, and water diversion are often cited as the main causes for much of the problem. But in Africa and now in southern Europe, extended drought has become an important part of the equation.[18]

Even where there might still seem to be plenty of water, changes in the hydrological cycle could be ecologically disruptive. Aquatic communities in rivers and streams, for instance, are often built up around a particular rate and rhythm of water flow—changes in hydrology can alter the assemblage of species in a river.[19]

Similar changes could also threaten tropical rain forests, even though the climate models are not predicting that these forests will dry up. Research in Central American rain forests has shown that tree fruit production can be finely tuned to the rhythm of rainfall; a shorter rainy season may prevent flowering even when plenty of moisture is still available for growth. Many rain forest trees flower only every few years; those that bear fruit annually are therefore crucial to the community. If changes in rainfall cause some species to shift their flowering to a slower cycle, the consequences could be disastrous for the insects that pollinate the flowers, and the birds and mammals that depend on the fruit. Changing rainfall patterns during the 1986–87 El Niño may have caused the extinction of the golden toad, which lived in Costa Rica's high-altitude cloud forest and required spring rainwater pools in order to breed. Such changes could injure many highly specialized rain forest creatures.[20]

Warmer temperatures will also mean rising sea levels. Most of the rise will be caused by thermal expansion of the water itself, but the melting of some glacial and Antarctic ice will contribute to the effect. The process is already well under way: during the past 50 years or so, an area of ice the size of the state of Delaware in the United States (about 8,000 square kilometers) has disappeared from the Antarctic peninsula. Average global sea level has probably risen about 18 centimeters over the past century, and is currently rising at 0.1– 0.3 centimeters per year.[21]

The effect of this process on particular coasts varies considerably, due to deposition of river sediment, coastal subsidence, and other factors. But it is clear that the rising seas pose an immediate threat to coastal wetlands—ecologically critical areas that development may already be destroying at a rate of 0.5–1.5 percent a year worldwide. Sea level rise of the order anticipated could flood 50 percent of the world's remaining coastal wetlands in the course of the next century. Recent studies have already documented wetlands lost to the sea along the Gulf of Mexico and the U.S. Atlantic seaboard.[22]

In the tropics and subtropics, rising seas will threaten mangrove forests—the stilt-rooted thickets that occupy the tidal zone of some 25 percent of tropical shoreline. Mangroves stabilize shorelines and provide habitat for an extremely diverse community of both marine and terrestrial species. One of the reasons for the drastic projected losses of coastal wetland is the impossibility of retreat: coastal areas in many parts of the world are among the most intensively developed. Even where the topography might permit a wetland community to "migrate" inshore, development has often blocked the path.[23]

An increase in the number or strength of tropical oceanic storms may intensify pressure on the coasts. It is not clear whether the spate of unprecedented storm disasters since 1990 represents a trend in this direction, but some scientists argue that the warming oceans and atmosphere may be increasing the amount of energy available to storm systems. According to one estimate, a 3–4 degree Celsius rise in sea surface temperatures could produce hurricanes with 50 percent more destructive power than current ones, and with sustained winds as high as 350 kilometers per hour. Perhaps because these storms are "natural" events, their ecological effects have received relatively little attention. But even at their current level, their toll is probably substantial in ecosystems under intense pressure. According to one study, a 50-percent increase in destructive storm potential would spell the end of many island and coastal tropical forests.[24]

BROKEN LANDSCAPES

Inside a North Carolina pine forest, 16 tall metal towers stand in a circle 31 meters in diameter. Although the trees inside the circle look no different from the ones outside, the tubes are conjuring up the forests of the future. They are pumping out extra carbon dioxide— enough to raise the CO_2 content of the air within the circle to 550 parts per million, about double the level that existed at the turn of the century. This is the scenario that many researchers predict for the middle of the next century. Studies like these are attempting to define how plants might respond to a relatively sudden doubling of atmospheric CO_2. The results, combined with field research into the effects of warming itself, are revealing a complex of pressures that could eventually reshape much of the world's forest and rangeland.[25]

At points along the northern rim of boreal forests, researchers have documented increased tree growth over the last couple of decades.

The pines in the circle will be monitored over the long term, but scientists reported some preliminary observations in 1995, including a 65-percent increase in photosynthesis. Since CO_2 is one of the raw materials of photosynthesis, researchers anticipate some degree of "CO_2 fertilization" as the gas continues to accumulate in the atmosphere. The finding in North Carolina was an important confirmation of much simpler laboratory experiments, which frequently show increased growth under higher CO_2 levels. But variations in metabolism cause various species to react differently; in some plants, extra CO_2 can even slow growth because it boosts the rate at which plants "exhale" carbon. The total range of documented growth responses runs from a negative 43 percent to a positive 375 percent.[26]

This range suggests that in any particular community, some plants will do well under increased CO_2 while others do poorly. In the forests of eastern North America, for example, sugar maple often competes with white pine in mixed stands. Since the maple may do substantially better in an enriched CO_2 atmosphere, the ecological balance may tip in its favor. Some studies suggest that entire categories of plants might gain a similar competitive advantage: annuals might do better than perennials, and deciduous trees better than evergreens. By favoring some species over others, CO_2 fertilization could join pollution, habitat loss, and a host of other pressures that are corroding the world's vegetational mosaics.[27]

The potential strength of CO_2 fertilization is difficult to gauge. It is possible that plants showing a strong initial response to extra CO_2 will eventually acclimate—their metabolisms may return to their earlier rates. In the mountains of central Italy, there are fissures that naturally emit high levels of carbon dioxide, and the plants growing nearby seem to be completely acclimated. Scientists studying wood cores taken from mature trees have not yet been able to find clear effects of the CO_2 increase that has already occurred (although there is some evidence of this in very cold areas).[28]

But within the larger ecological context, there are good reasons for viewing CO_2 fertilization as another significant dimension of risk. One commonly noted effect of the process is a drop in plant tissue nitrogen concentrations, since a plant's nitrogen uptake may not keep pace with its increased carbon uptake. That makes plant tissues less nutritious— and that in turn can affect the behavior of many other organisms. Recently in Canada, for instance, an aspen stand growing in a CO_2-enriched atmosphere was found to harbor soil fungi that were releasing spores at two to four times the normal rate. Since the fungi feed on dead plant debris, a tentative explanation is that they are putting more energy into reproduction as a stress reaction to less nutritious food. (Such a reaction could be a kind of evolutionary insurance policy, because it would help the fungi spread elsewhere if local conditions become unfavorable.) These fungi play a key ecological role, as their digestion liberates nutrients locked up in the plant debris; weaker fungi could mean a weaker ecosystem.[29]

Less nutritious plants could affect plant-eating insects as well. Experiments have shown that insect growth is generally stunted on a diet of CO_2-fertilized plants, but as the bugs struggle to get the nitrogen they need, their feeding actually tends to increase—an average of 44 percent in 19 different studies. This compensatory feeding varies greatly, however, and current research is nowhere near providing a realistic projection of the process in nature. Nearly all the work done thus far has focused on leaf-chewing insects; virtually nothing is known about the possible reactions of other kinds of plant eaters. Nor can scientists predict changes in the performance of allelochemicals—substances that plants manufacture to discourage insect feeding and competition from other plants. But it is known that the effects of these chemicals vary greatly at different temperatures.[30]

Perhaps most plant species will simply acclimate to higher levels of carbon dioxide. Or perhaps the effect of nitrogen-poor foliage will be largely "lost" amidst all the other pressures acting on plant-eating insects. Yet despite all the uncertainties in the current research, the potential for disruption is clear. Suppose one or two tree species in a community begin to grow more quickly and do not acclimate. Suppose their insect attackers begin to shift their feeding preferences to other species that have acclimated and are therefore already at a competitive disadvantage, because the extra CO_2 is no longer boosting their growth rate. Thus, by subtle increments, could a slight change in the chemistry of the air reduce the richness of a forest.[31]

Such pressures could intensify the changes already under way as a consequence of warming. At points along the northern rim of the world's boreal forests—in Finland, northern Canada, and Alaska—researchers have documented increased tree growth over the last couple of decades, along with forest advances beyond the former tree line, out onto the tundra. The forests seem to be reacting to an upward trend in annual minimum temperatures—northern winters, that is, are a little less cold than they used to be.[32]

"Tree migration" is one of the ways forests have responded to previous changes in the world's climate. But the forests do not move collectively, because tree species vary greatly in their abilities to occupy new habitat. After the retreat of the ice sheets that covered much of the northern hemisphere during the last glaciation, for example, the cold-tolerant, wind-pollinated, light-seeded white spruce may have blown into new territory at a lightning speed of up to 2 kilometers a year on average, while the temperate, heavy-seeded American chestnut labored along at just 100 meters a year.[33]

Ecologists expect to see migration on both edges of the boreal realm; the forests will probably advance out onto the tundra in places, and retreat along their southern edges. So could the boreal forests adjust to climate change just by moving north? Unfortunately, the answer is no, for several reasons. At the forecast rates of warming, an entire forest assemblage would have to "move" poleward at 1.5–5.5 kilometers a year to maintain its current temperature regime—an ecological impossibility. (The white spruce migration may have been aided by glacial winds that do not exist today.) Even if such movement were possible, soil conditions on the tundra greatly limit opportunities for colonization, while the warming and drying in the southern parts of the boreal zone are likely to provoke far larger and faster die-offs—dead forests that might one day be reoccupied by temperate-zone species. The vast boreal forests, which ring the Arctic and presently cover about 17 percent of the planet's land area, might eventually be reduced to 10–50 percent of their current extent.[34]

Cold weather is as essential for northern communities as heavy rain and warmth are for a tropical rain forest. It is true that much of the northern flora has survived abrupt shifts of climate in the past—events that would have selected for a fairly robust genetic diversity within many species. But field evidence is already turning up some signs of strain. A long-term study of Alaskan tundra found a decline in species diversity during the eighties, the warmest decade on record in the region. In Scandinavia, unusually long growing seasons in recent years seem to be preventing some alpine plants from entering winter dormancy, thereby leaving flower buds and growing tissue exposed to frost. Even plants that do better will not necessarily benefit ecosystems as a whole: in Scandinavian alpine areas, the movement of shrubs farther upslope is likely to reduce the amount of ground lichen—the basic winter food for caribou.[35]

One of the most important manifestations of climate change in the world's plant communities is likely to be the invasion of nonnative "exotic" plants—species that, for one reason or another, can profit from new climatic conditions. Exotics can be dangerous because they often arrive in a new range without the diseases and other pressures that keep their populations in check in their native ecosystem, and because their new neighbors may not have evolutionary adaptations that work well in fending

them off. So while exotic invasions may seem at first sight to be a "good" thing for biodiversity, because they add species to an ecosystem, the long-term effect is generally the opposite. Exotics often suppress natives, and sometimes drive them into extinction. The spread of exotics has reached levels many times beyond the natural rates of invasion, and climate change is likely to accelerate this process.[36]

Climatic factors are already an important part of many plant invasions. In northeastern Australia, for instance, unusually wet weather in the seventies and eighties promoted the spread of parkinsonia and mesquite; vast thickets of these exotic shrubs now cover what was once grassland. To the south, a drought during the early nineties caused a substantial dieback of native forest, and the extra sunlight penetrating the broken canopy helped spread an infestation of various exotic vines and shrubs, which are likely to interfere with the regeneration of the forest. Farther west, along the coast of the Northern Territories, extensive flooding in the Adelaide river region during the seventies is thought to have been a factor in unleashing an invasion of a shrubby neotropical tree, *Mimosa pigra*. Some 45,000 hectares of what was once rich, biologically diverse wetland are now dense, monotonous stands of mimosa—proof that extreme weather events can work long-term ecological change.[37]

Further warming will almost certainly provide additional opportunities for aggressive exotics. In the western United States, the mild, wet winters and dry summers forecast for much of the region are likely to favor cheat grass and Russian thistle, two disruptive invaders from Eurasia that are already very widespread. Cheat grass alone now dominates 40 million hectares of western North America. In Australia, Africa, and elsewhere, native grassland is retreating before invasions of woody shrubs; preliminary research suggests that because they use a slightly different type of photosynthesis, the shrubs may already be benefiting from the elevated levels of carbon dioxide.[38]

Although no particular type of flora is likely to lose out everywhere, the world's forests may suffer disproportionately from the changing climate and the invasions that follow. Tree species particularly adapted to present local conditions may disappear and a great deal of forest may be converted to grassland. According to one estimate, a full third of the world's forest area is at risk from climate change.[39]

PESTS, PATHOGENS, AND WILDLIFE

The effects of warming will not be limited to vegetation: animals and microbes will respond as well. That complicates the picture immensely—and further reduces the odds of ecological stability. Insects, with their fine-tuned responses to temperature, can be expected to shift their ranges rapidly in response to changing weather. One recent study has documented the northward movement of the Edith's checkerspot butterfly in western North America. A warming of 0.6 degrees Celsius appears to have "shifted" the butterfly northward about 150 kilometers over the past century. In Costa Rica, a more recent warming trend seems to have allowed the yellow fever mosquito to vault the country's central mountain range—formerly too cool for it—and occupy the western half of the country.[40]

The world's landscapes are full of such possibilities. In the western United States, for example, a 2.5-degree-Celsius increase in annual mean temperatures would allow the balsam woolly adelgid, an insect invader from Europe, to overwinter in alpine fir forest. The adelgid has a voracious appetite for certain types of conifer needles; its colonization of the western forests could mean a repetition of the disaster in the eastern part of the continent, where it has killed entire stands of fir in the Appalachian mountains. Farther north, late frosts are the mechanism that usually ends spruce budworm outbreaks, because the frosts destroy the new growth that the budworm feeds on. Fewer frosts could mean longer outbreaks; already in one area in northern Canada, 18 years passed before a June frost was hard enough to halt an outbreak.[41]

Many of the world's most dangerous insects almost by definition are poised to follow the retreat of temperature barriers.

Practically any region on earth will harbor some insect species—native or exotic—that are functioning near the limits of their temperature or moisture tolerance. Many of the world's most dangerous insects—for agriculture, forestry, and public health—are tropical or subtropical in origin; almost by definition they are poised to follow the retreat of temperature barriers. And given their ability to spread quickly, many insect species can be expected to move into new habitat practically as soon as it becomes available. In Europe, for instance, the rate at which invading insects are colonizing new terrain seems generally to be faster than 2 kilometers a year and is sometimes as fast as 100 kilometers a year. In insects, mobility may prove to be another form of "preadaptation" to a changing climate.[42]

Of course, bigger animals may move as well, as their present habitats begin to shrink or as new opportunities open up elsewhere. One serious vertebrate pest that is likely to profit from climate change is the cane toad, a large amphibian from South America that was introduced widely in the tropics and warm temperate regions in an ill-conceived effort to control insects in sugarcane plantations. The toad is an aggressive and indiscriminate predator; its own would-be predators are usually discouraged by its skin toxins. In Australia, where the toad is already enjoying a huge success, climate modeling forecasts a substantial range extension in areas likely to grow warmer and wetter.[43]

Warming water temperatures are also likely to favor the spread of aquatic exotics. Aquatic ecosystems all over the planet are primed with dangerous exotics that stand to benefit from climate change. For example, the Mozambique tilapia, a popular aquaculture fish, has been released into the lakes and rivers of virtually every tropical and subtropical country. The tilapia is displacing native fish in many of these countries, and warmer temperatures may allow it to expand into temperate waters. Off the coast of California, a northward invasion of certain mollusk species has already been attributed to warmer water.[44]

A more subtle danger is the climate-driven movement of pathogens and parasites. These organisms play a largely hidden but crucial role in shaping an ecosystem; they help control the populations of their hosts, thereby maintaining competitor balances and healthy predator-prey ratios. But climate change could upset these balances by boosting infection rates or favoring the spread of new diseases. In Tasmania, for example, increasing rainfall and temperature would probably promote the spread of *Phytophthora cinnamomi,* an exotic fungal

plant disease that is already threatening the island's native flora.[45]

Many pathogens are transmitted by insects and may therefore profit from insect sensitivity to climate. In northern regions, mild winters are sometimes a prelude to large and early migrations of aphids—tiny insects that live off plant juices, destroying new growth and spreading plant viruses. In Europe, at least one important group of aphid-transmitted cereal pathogens, the barley yellow dwarf viruses, is expected to gain from warmer temperatures not just by spreading, but by infecting earlier in the growing season, which could greatly increase the viruses' burden on cropland.[46]

Insects may not need to migrate in order to spread disease. Warming can increase an established insect population, to the benefit of any pathogens it hosts. Warming can also boost the pathogen's rate of development—a factor of considerable potential in some human diseases, such as malaria, in which the average life expectancy of the insect vector can be so short that the pathogen does not always have time to mature before the vector dies. Other factors are sometimes at work as well. The mosquito that transmits another human disease, dengue fever, is stunted by warmer temperatures; that means it has to feed more frequently, which increases opportunities for infection. For humans and nonhumans alike, a warmer world is likely to be a more disease-prone world.[47]

BROKEN TIME

Rapid warming is likely to break up the temporal as well as the spatial relationships in a community. Climate change may already be affecting seasonal cycles, according to a recent statistical analysis of some 300 years of temperature records, culled from various historical sources. The study looked beneath the obvious temperature patterns and concluded that the timing of the seasons in the northern hemisphere began to change quickly around the twenties, in erratic, local ways. Spring comes earlier in some places and later in others; winter advances or retreats as well.[48]

Ecologists may already be seeing the results of this slippage in seasonal timing. A study of migratory songbird arrivals in New York State, for example, found that 39 of 76 species are now arriving significantly earlier than they did around 1900. Six species of local plants are blooming earlier as well. In Canada, snowgoose broods along the northwestern shore of Hudson Bay are hatching out, on average, 30 days earlier than they did in 1950.[49]

But from an ecological point of view, a season is more than a particular temperature. Warming cannot "move" seasons around in the calendar, any more than it can move ecosystems from place to place; instead, it is likely to disrupt many seasonal rhythms. Some of the most vulnerable mechanisms involve photoperiod responses—metabolic clocks that are set by seasonal changes in the length of day and night. In many temperate zone plants, for instance, a springtime light pattern helps stimulate flowering or leaf production. The timing of this response is often very precise; even within a single species, a southern population might have a photoperiod response that differs from a northern one. That precision allows plants to fine-tune leaf production so that it coincides with spring rains, or to get a jump on plant-eating insects, or to flower when pollinators arrive. But this strategy only works when it is calibrated to actual climate conditions; a change in the timing of the rains or a warmer spring that

speeds the emergence of insects could throw the response off—perhaps enough to affect the fate of a population.[50]

For humans and nonhumans alike, a warmer world is likely to be a more disease-prone world.

Some animals—especially migratory species—have a photoperiod response as well, which may make them susceptible to the same kind of miscuing. The broad-tailed hummingbird, for instance, uses day length to tell it when to begin its spring migration into the Sierra Nevada mountains of the U.S. Southwest. The bird arrives just as certain subalpine plants are coming into bloom—a feat of timing that allows the bird to feed and the plants to be pollinated. But these plants do not time their flowering by photoperiod—they bloom in response to runoff from melting snow. Under doubled-CO_2 conditions, spring melt in the Sierra Nevada could come two months earlier than it does now—with disastrous results for both the plants and their pollinator.[51]

A similar sort of miscuing may occur in aquatic ecosystems. In the Pacific sockeye salmon, photoperiod may help trigger the migration up the Columbia River of the U.S. Northwest. Under stable conditions, that response could be a valuable indicator of the temperature in the far upriver reaches where the salmon breed, but over the past half-century or so the river has warmed (due largely to dam building, drainage, and other forms of interference with the natural rates of flow). A recent study suggests that the rigid photoperiod response may prevent the salmon from migrating upriver early enough to compensate for the warming.[52]

Other migration mechanisms could be thrown off as well. Delaware Bay, for example, is the most important stopover site on the U.S. East Coast "flyway." More than 1 million shorebirds arrive there in May on their way from the tropics to the Arctic. That is when the waters are warm enough to trigger mating and egg-laying in the horseshoe crab; the crabs and their eggs are what fuel the subsequent leg of the birds' journey. The birds' arrival in the Arctic, in early June, is timed so that hatching will occur just before the emergence of certain insect populations, another important food source. Ecologists are concerned that warming in the Arctic could cause the insect populations to peak earlier than they do now. But the birds, with their itinerary tied to the horseshoe crab mating season, probably would not be able to adjust their arrival time.[53]

Such predicaments reveal an important ecological double standard when it comes to migration. Migratory vertebrates—whether Arctic breeding birds or Pacific salmon—are generally "locked in" to their itinerary. They must migrate, and their success generally requires accurate timing. That makes them very vulnerable to climate change. But the vast hordes of migratory insects—aphids, planthoppers, locusts, and others—are liable to adapt readily to migratory disruption. For most of these species, migration is optional—if conditions are suitable at home, they may stay put. And migration in insects seems generally to be an adaptation to unreliable, changing conditions.[54]

The temporal and spatial convulsions of a warming world are not likely to create stable new communities, because the kinds of checks and balances that develop over long spans of time will be absent. New plant assemblages, for instance, may lack pollinators or seed dispersal agents. Outbreaks of exotic insects, uncontrolled by predators or disease, may impoverish forests and range-land. Local diversity—the variety of life that makes one place different from another—will tend to slip away as more and more of life's resources are absorbed by tough, opportunistic organisms that thrive on instability.

TROUBLE COMPOUNDED

We usually think of environmental threats acting in isolation, but of course they do not. Climate change is likely to overlap with various other pressures to cause problems far greater than would have been anticipated by the study of climate alone. Norman Myers, an ecologist who is studying such overlaps, explains that some of our biggest problems may be the most difficult to see. "Even our most advanced climate models," he writes, "tend to discount, by virtue of their very structure, the possibility of certain kinds of synergistic interactions in the real world, leading to threshold-type repercussions. Far from knowing how to incorporate such complex interactions into our models, we scarcely know how to identify and define them as yet."[55]

In some eastern Canadian lakes, one synergism manifests itself periodically by festooning the shoreline with brilliant purple algae. This is a fairly new phenomenon, but it is not an invasion: it is evolution. The brilliant pigment reflects ultraviolet (UV) light, thereby lowering the dose of dangerous UV radiation the algae absorb. UV radiation is a component of sunlight, but much of it is filtered out by the ozone layer high in the atmosphere—the layer now famous for the "ozone hole" caused by the release of chlorofluorocarbons and other ozone-depleting substances (see Chapter 9). The algae are adapting to higher UV levels, but the extra dose is not caused primarily by the weakening ozone layer. It is an effect of drought.[56]

David Schindler, an ecologist at the University of Alberta, has been studying that drought in the Experimental Lakes Area (ELA), a group of lakes in northern Ontario set aside specifically for scientific research. Over the past two decades, the ELA has warmed by about 1.6 degrees Celsius and precipitation has dropped by 25 percent—the sort of change broadly consistent with what a doubled-CO_2 scenario likely has in store for the interior of North America.[57]

Streams in the area are drying up, so less plant debris and other organic matter is flowing into the lakes. Schindler found that the debris has an important function in the lakes: some of it dissolves, and dissolved organic carbon (DOC) absorbs UV light, preventing it from penetrating more than a short distance into the water. In the process, the DOC breaks down, so a constant resupply is necessary for maintaining the UV shield. With less DOC coming in, the lakes are growing increasingly transparent to ultraviolet light. In boreal lakes, UV-B (the most dangerous UV wavelength to penetrate the atmosphere) is usually absorbed within 20–30 centimeters of the surface; in these lakes, it penetrates to nearly 1.5 meters.[58]

Some of the ELA lakes were experimentally acidified to simulate the effects of acid rain. (Acid rain, a product of air pollution from coal burning, the smelting of metal, and various other industrial processes, is a major problem in boreal lakes.) The acidity broke the DOC down or caused it to clump together and settle out of the water column entirely. The result was an even greater UV transparency. In one lake, UV-B penetrated to nearly 3 meters—and real acid rain sometimes pushes DOC levels even lower than those at the ELA. Of the nearly 700,000 lakes in eastern Canada, Schindler estimates that some 140,000 are already suffering from deeper UV penetration.[59]

In a destructive synergism such as this, several forces combine to produce a result greater than the sum of their individual effects. The potential for such overlaps is pervasive. UV exposure is increasing the most at higher latitudes—precisely where the greatest temperature changes are forecast. And air pollution is acidifying Eurasian boreal lakes as well as Canadian ones. Warmer temperatures are likely to increase acidification by speeding up the rate of soil decomposition, which will boost the concentration of acidic nitrogen compounds in rainwater runoff.[60]

But the problem will not be limited to these factors, or to northern regions. In the U.S. Southeast during the mid-eighties, ozone air pollution combined with hot, dry weather to cause declines in loblolly pine, a mainstay of the region's $4.5-billion forestry sector. (Even though ozone is a natural component of the upper atmosphere, it is a serious air pollutant at ground level, where it is produced mainly in a reaction based on car exhaust.) Similar ozone-drought synergisms may be affecting trees in Britain.[61]

As with drought, air pollution also seems to trigger disease and pest outbreaks, although the precise mechanisms are not well understood. Another form of pollution, trace metal contamination, has been shown to increase the toxicity of acid rain in the soil, and to lower plant resistance to insect attack. Fed on toxic soils, acidified water, and dirty air, the world's terrestrial ecosystems are liable to grow steadily less resistant to the quiet menace of climate change.[62]

Synergisms are a threat in the oceans too, as is apparent from the state of a crucial marine ecosystem: coral reefs. In terms of species diversity, coral reefs are the richest ecosystem in the oceans and the second richest on earth, after tropical forests. It has been estimated that at least 65 percent of marine fish species depend on reefs at some time during their life cycles. But coral is extremely vulnerable to heat stress; the El Niño of the early eighties caused extensive coral dieback in reefs throughout the Pacific, and may even have driven several coral species into extinction. Tropical sea surface temperatures could warm 1–2 degrees Celsius by 2050 or 2100. One IPCC report explained the implications for coral: "The magnitude of such an increase, in addition to the rapid rate of change, leaves virtually no margin for corrective action."[63]

If such a warming occurs, however, the effects may be magnified drastically by a host of other pressures. In the wake of the last El Niño, outbreaks of starfish and sea urchins are destroying many weakened coral reefs throughout much of the Pacific and Indian oceans. In the central Atlantic and Caribbean, high water temperatures have brought on spreading infections of an extremely virulent coral disease. In some Caribbean reefs, overfishing has reduced populations of plant-eating fish so greatly that seaweeds are now smothering corals that had only begun to rebuild after the destruction of Hurricane Allen in 1980.[64]

And as atmospheric CO_2 levels rise, more of the gas will be absorbed into the oceans; that will tend to reduce seawater concentrations of calcium carbonate, the material corals need to build their skeletons. Extra CO_2 may also fertilize algae and seagrasses, which are already displacing coral in many areas as a result of nitrate pollution. In the oceans, just as on land, destructive synergisms may eventually emerge as the principal threat of climate change.[65]

NATURAL AREAS CONSERVATION AND ENERGY REFORM

Preserving the planet's remaining natural areas is one of our most urgent responsibilities. Such places are fundamental to every economy in the world, no matter how divorced from "nature" it might appear to be, and no conceivable development will lessen that dependence. There is no substitute for a stable hydrological cycle, healthy pollinator populations, or the general ecological stability that only natural areas can confer. We need these places in ways that are direct enough to satisfy even the most hard-nosed economist, but we also need them for reasons that are harder to quantify.

It may be difficult to prove, but it is hard to avoid concluding that ecological and cultural health are related. Environmental and cultural degradation are inextricably entangled in so many places: the destruction of the forests and indigenous forest cultures in Indonesia, Canada, or Brazil; the ecological and social collapse of the Aral Sea basin; the flattening of North American life and landscapes into homogenous shopping malls. The struggle to save wild places is thus also an act of economic and cultural self-preservation.

To future generations, however, that struggle will seem a grotesque exercise in futility if we continue to pump carbon into the atmosphere at anything even remotely approaching the current rate. Wildlands and our carbon culture will not continue to fit on the same planet: they are fundamentally incompatible. The contradiction, unfortunately, has yet to sink in fully. The United States, for instance, spends roughly $2 billion a year on natural areas management, but remains the world's largest carbon emitter by far. And the U.S. government is slashing federal funding for research into renewable energy technologies—the sector that must ultimately provide the solution to climate change.[66]

Yet wealthy societies routinely spend heavily to anticipate dangers far more remote than the risks that climate change poses. That kind of reckoning, for instance, is typical of defense budgets. Individual people do much the same thing by buying property and health insurance. By the same token, we can buy ourselves some degree of insurance against climate change. In part, this will involve more sophisticated ways of drawing the boundaries of natural areas. Wildlife corridors, for example, can be created to allow movement from one natural area to another. Where possible, coastal wetland preserves could be extended farther inland, to allow for sea level rise. Such adjustments may be achieved by the outright purchase of land, or by the use of conservation easements, an arrangement in which landowners "sell" their rights to develop property, while retaining ownership of the land itself. (See Chapter 3.)[67]

Within natural areas, a much more "hands-on" management approach will probably be required. Land management agencies will probably need to invest more heavily in exotic-species control programs, for example, and more intervention on behalf of endangered species may also be required. Such efforts are likely to claim a growing share of conservation budgets, as land managers face a host of labor-intensive tasks—everything from chopping out thickets of invasive exotic trees to hand-pollinating native plants that have lost their natural pollinators, as is already done in some Hawaiian natural areas.[68]

In the business world, insurance against climate change could take the form of government-industry partnerships, perhaps on the model of the U.S.

Initiative on Joint Implementation. This pilot program is designed to reduce greenhouse gas emissions through partnerships between government agencies, utilities, or private corporations in the United States and their counterparts in the developing world. The programs typically involve the use of alternative energy or reforestation to compensate for emissions elsewhere.[69]

The struggle to save wild places is also an act of economic and cultural self-preservation.

Mitigation efforts on all these fronts will be essential. But they do not constitute a cure for climate change, because they do not attack the basic mechanisms that have turned modern economies into carbon emission machines. Coming to grips with our fossil fuel addiction will require enormous changes in both public and private life, especially in industrial countries. Although the way to achieve these reforms must vary to fit local needs and politics, many of the broad objectives are already clear. Among the techniques are tax codes that favor renewable energy and natural gas (the cleanest of the fossil fuels) over oil and coal, energy efficiency programs, renewable energy R&D, drastic reductions in the use of private cars, and removal of systemic economic biases that promote the use of coal and oil (see Chapter 8).

The task might seem next to impossible, but there are some reasons for hope. A critical point of leverage is provided by the Framework Convention on Climate Change signed in Rio de Janeiro in 1992. Under the convention, industrial countries are supposed to cut their greenhouse gas emissions to their 1990 levels by 2000. That step is intended as a preliminary to much deeper cuts later on, when better technologies and procedures are developed. Thus far, the convention has achieved rather limited success on the ground. (See Chapter 1.) Even so, it may be the single most effective tool available for working fundamental reform. Yet the convention's supporters have not fully engaged one of its largest potential constituencies—people and groups concerned about the preservation of natural areas.[70]

Among the general public, broad support for conservation could be translated into direct pressure on governments to live up to their climate commitments. Educational programs like the Climate Change Campaign of the World Wide Fund for Nature could be a mechanism for building that pressure. Another part of the constituency consists of private industries likely to suffer directly from climate change. Already, the nearly $1.5-trillion-a-year insurance industry—aware that climate-related disasters could bankrupt it—is joining the debate on climate change.[71]

Food products companies are also prime candidates for a climate coalition: growing demand for their products will not guarantee their continued prosperity, since climate change could injure the fisheries and fields they depend on, or force them to spend much more on managing that production. Forest products companies are in a similar position—climate change is likely to take its toll not just on natural forests, but on tree plantations. An industrial alliance of "natural areas users" could be a potent ally for the renewable energy industries, which are already represented at climate talks by umbrella groups such as the Business Council for Sustainable Energy.[72]

But the climate convention is only a beginning. Facing up to climate change will require a profound revision of the consumer ethic basic to industrial societies: somehow, both individually and collectively, we will have to rediscover the value of material restraint. Yet it would be incorrect to see such climate realism as a narrowing of possibilities. Huge economic opportunities lie ahead: renewable energy technologies are now developing so rapidly that few people except the experts even know what the state of the art is. For certain applications, solar and wind power have already come of age; other technologies, such as hydrogen-powered fuel cells, electric cars, and high performance flywheels, are now approaching maturity.[73]

The biggest opportunities may be cultural. In the changing climate, we can see that nature is no longer a force distinct from people; we influence it profoundly, and on a global scale. The world's dominant societies, however, have yet to grasp the consequences of their own enormous economic strength. The consumer culture is still fundamentally a device for clearing the natural world away, for simplifying it and extracting products from it.

But reversing the processes of environmental degradation will require more than just an awareness of the dangers we face. We will need a positive vision as well—a kind of "ecological literacy" that will allow us to appreciate a healthy ecosystem as something far greater than a set of potential commodities. Ultimately, facing up to the threat of climate change is a way of rebuilding the myriad necessary connections between humanity and the natural world.

6

Valuing Nature's Services

Janet N. Abramovitz

Nature's "free" services form the invisible foundation that supports our societies and economies. We rely on the oceans to provide abundant fish, on forests for wood and new medicines, on insects to pollinate our crops, on birds and frogs to keep pests in check, and on rivers to supply clean water. We expect that when we need timber we can harvest it, that when we need new crops we can find them in nature, that when we drill a well we will find water, that the wastes we generate will disappear, that clean air will blow in to refresh our cities, and that the climate will be stable and predictable. Nature's services have always been there free for the taking, and our expectations—and economies—are based on the premise that they always will be.

Yet economies unwittingly provide incentives to misuse and destroy nature by underappreciating and undervaluing its services. Nature in turn is increasingly less able to supply the services that the earth's expanding population and economy demand. It is not an exaggeration to state

that the continued loss of nature's services threatens not only today's human enterprise, but ultimately the prospects for our continued existence.

How did this unhealthy dynamic come into being? Nature is viewed as a boundless and inexhaustible resource and sink. Human impact is seen as insignificant or beneficial. The very tools used to gauge the economic health and progress of a nation can reinforce and encourage these attitudes. The gross domestic product (GDP), for example, supposedly measures the value of the goods and services produced in a nation. But the most valuable goods and services—the ones provided by nature, on which all else rests—are measured poorly or not at all. The unhealthy dynamic is compounded by the fact that activities that pollute or deplete natural capital are counted as contributions to economic well-being.

In the human economy, it is easy to distinguish between goods and services. In nature's economy, such a distinction is less useful as goods and services are highly integrated in subtle and complex ways. Indeed, treating nature as a box filled with unrelated objects that we can remove or replace at will, with little or no effect, is ultimately counterproductive.

Nature's ecosystem services include producing raw materials, purifying and regulating water, absorbing and decomposing wastes, cycling nutrients, creating and maintaining soils, providing pollination and pest control, and regulating local and global climates. (See Table 6–1.) Forests, for example, do much more than supply timber. They provide habitat for birds and insects that pollinate crops and control disease-carrying and agricultural pests. Their canopies break the force of the winds and reduce rainfall's impact on the ground, which lessens soil erosion. Their roots hold soil in place, further reducing erosion. A forest's watershed protection values alone can exceed the value of its timber. Forests also act as effective water pumping and recycling machinery, helping to stabilize the local climate. And

Table 6–1. Nature's Services

Raw Materials Production
   (food, fisheries, timber and building
   materials, non-timber forest products,
   fodder, genetic resources, medicines,
   dyes)
Pollination
Biological Control of Pests and Diseases
Habitat and Refuge
Water Supply and Regulation
Waste Recycling and Pollution Control
Nutrient Cycling
Soil Building and Maintenance
Disturbance Regulation
Climate Regulation
Atmospheric Regulation
Recreation
Cultural
Educational/Scientific

SOURCE: Worldwatch Institute.

through photosynthesis, plants generate life-giving oxygen and hold vast amounts of carbon in storage, which stabilizes the global climate.[1]

Around the world, the conversion, degradation, fragmentation, and simplification of ecosystems has been extensive. (See Table 6–2.) In many countries, including some of the largest, more than half the territory has been converted from natural habitat to other uses, much of it unsustainably and irreversibly. In countries that stayed relatively undisturbed until the eighties, significant portions of remaining ecosystems have been lost in the last decade. These trends have been accelerating everywhere. Lost with these natural ecosystems are the valuable services they provide.

Nature's living library—the genes, species, populations, communities, and ecosystems in existence today—represent a wealth of options for future generations and for change in the biosphere. Unfortunately, we are running a "biodiversity deficit," destroying species and ecosystems faster than nature can create new ones. Species alone are now vanishing 100 to 1,000 times faster than natural extinction rates as a result of human actions.[2]

By reducing the number of species and the size and integrity of ecosystems, we are also reducing nature's capacity to evolve and create new life. In just a few centuries we have gone from living off nature's interest to spending down the capital that has accumulated over millions of years of evolution, as well as diminishing the capacity of nature to create new capital. Humans are only one part of the evolutionary product. Yet we have taken on a major role in shaping its future production course and potential. We are pulling out the threads of nature's safety net even as we need it to support the world's expanding human population and economy.

DEVELOPING AND PRODUCING RAW MATERIALS

One of nature's most obvious services to humanity is the development and production of commodities vital to our well-being. Nature synthesizes and produces food, fiber, fuel, fertilizers, building materials, medicines, and objects of aesthetic value. Providing this service requires healthy ecosystems, which are in increasingly short supply.

The enormous variety and value of goods produced and collected in wild areas, and their importance to local livelihoods and national economies, is truly a global phenomenon. Rattan, for instance—a vine that grows naturally in tropical forests—is woven into furniture and other products. The global trade in rattan, worth $2.7 billion in exports each year, employs a half-million people in Asia alone. Coastal and inland wetlands around the world—some of the most threatened habitats—support extremely valuable commercial and artisanal fisheries. Seventy percent of U.S. commercial fish species use coastal wetlands and estuaries during part of their life cycle; in the Gulf of Mexico, more than 95 percent do. In 1991, in just the United States, fish valued at $3.3 billion were hauled up at the docks; the fish processing and sales industry generates 10 times that amount each year.[3]

All modern crop varieties were originally produced using landraces developed by farmers around the world from wild plants over hundreds and thousands of years. One reliable estimate places the contribution to the global economy of these landraces and wild relatives at $66 billion. Wild wheat from Turkey, for example, provides disease resistance for many cultivated varieties, a contribution valued at approximately $50 million a year. As plant breeders continue seeking genes to improve crop characteristics such as vigor, yield, salt tolerance, and resistance to pests and diseases, the old varieties and wild relatives have enormous value. The origins of today's globally important crops are found in every region of the world, from coffee in Ethiopia to tomatoes and potatoes in South America, apples in Russia, cotton in Africa, sunflowers in the United States, and grains in the Near and Middle East. New crops and commodities are still being discovered.[4]

The world's largest biochemical R&D industry is the one that nature has operated for millions of years. For more than 80 percent of the people in developing countries, traditional medicine is still their primary form of health care. Even in the United States, 25 percent of all prescriptions dispensed between 1986 and 1990 and 60 percent of nonprescription medicines contain active compounds extracted from natural products, primarily plants. The heart medicine digitalis, antimalarial quinine, antibiotics, and aspirin are among the drugs that originated in nature. All told, medicines from natural products are worth about $40 billion a year worldwide.[5]

New medicines are continually being developed from a huge variety of life forms: Microorganisms have been the source of more than 3,000 antibiotics. Taxol, derived from the pacific yew tree of North America, is a promising treatment for ovarian and breast cancer, and a common temperate weed brings relief from migraine headaches. Venomous snakes are the source of anticoagulant drugs, and amphibians produce neurotoxins used in medical research.[6]

Many scientists view microorganisms and marine ecosystems as the largest untapped sources of valuable new compounds and medical models. These range from antiviral compounds in corals to antitumor agents in sponges. The

**Table 6-2. Historic Extent of Ecosystem Conversion and Recent Rate
of Forest Conversion in Selected Countries**

Country	Converted Area[1]	Share of Area Converted	Share of Forests Converted, 1980–90
	(thousand hectares)	(percent)	(percent)
Africa			
Sudan	123,178	52	10
South Africa	95,522	78	8
Nigeria	72,536	80	7
Chad	48,260	38	7
Mozambique	47,208	60	7
Tanzania	38,654	44	12
Zambia	35,321	48	10
Angola	32,620	26	7
Mali	32,517	27	8
Madagascar	27,322	47	8
Botswana	26,021	46	5
Zaire	22,942	10	6
Côte d'Ivoire	16,773	53	10
The Americas			
United States	426,948	45	n.a.
Brazil	238,855	28	6
Argentina	169,747	62	6
Mexico	99,338	52	12
Colombia	46,186	44	6
Peru	30,734	24	4
Bolivia	28,908	27	11
Paraguay	23,979	60	24
Venezuela	21,968	25	12
Nicaragua	6,784	57	17
Ecuador	5,155	19	17
Honduras	3,551	32	19

ability of sharks and amphibians to avoid infections has led to the discovery of new antimicrobial compounds that are being tested as contraceptives and for treating sexually transmitted diseases. Sea snails are the source of highly refined pain-killing chemicals now being tested for human use. One scientist describes these as "little chemical factories that are in essence doing what drug companies are trying to do. They've created thousands of chemical compounds and refined them to be exquisitely sensitive and potent."[7]

Even when useful chemical compounds from nature can be reproduced in the laboratory, scientists still rely on millions of years of nature's chemical synthesis and testing to provide them with the compounds to copy. Yet less than 1 percent of flowering plant species and an even smaller share of less-studied groups such as microorganisms and aquatic species have been examined for their medical and biochemical value. Some economists have estimated the lost pharmaceutical value from plant species extinctions in the United States alone at almost $12 billion.[8]

All too often, people simply assume that the greatest value that can be de-

Table 6–2. (*Continued*)

Country	Converted Area[1] (thousand hectares)	Share of Area Converted (percent)	Share of Forests Converted, 1980–90 (percent)
Asia/Oceania			
Australia	460,286	60	n.a.
India	194,280	65	6
Indonesia	48,912	27	10
Thailand	22,129	43	29
Myanmar	10,681	16	12
Philippines	10,673	36	29
Bangladesh	10,538	81	33
Viet Nam	8,500	26	14
Malaysia	4,988	15	18
Cambodia	4,407	25	10
Lao People's Democratic Republic	1,609	7	9
Europe			
Russian Federation	211,126	12	n.a.
Ukraine	41,890	72	n.a.
France	30,203	55	n.a.
Spain	29,956	60	n.a.

[1]Converted land represents forest plantations, croplands, and permanent pastures except for Australia, France, the Russian Federation, Ukraine, the United States, and Spain, which exclude forest plantations.
SOURCE: U.N Food and Agriculture Organization (FAO), "FAOSTAT-PC" (electronic database), Rome, 1995; FAO, *Forest Resources Assessment, 1990: Global Synthesis,* FAO Forestry Paper 124 (Rome: 1995); World Resources Institute, U.N. Environment Programme, U.N. Development Programme, and World Bank, *World Resources 1996–97* (New York: Oxford University Press, 1996).

rived from an ecosystem is maximizing its production of a single commodity, such as timber from a forest. In fact, that is usually the least profitable and least sustainable use of a forest. From non-timber forest products (NTFPs) to watershed protection to climate regulation, other values can be enormous. Not only are other uses more valuable in the short run, they can also be sustained over the long term and benefit more people. To consider these various options, alternative management strategies for the mangrove forests of Bintuni Bay in Indonesia were compared. When non-timber uses such as fish, locally used products, and erosion control were included in the calculations, the most economically profitable strategy was to keep the forest standing, yielding $4,800 per hectare. The timber cutting value was only $3,600 per hectare. Not cutting the forest would ensure continued local uses of the area worth $10 million a year (providing 70 percent of local income) and protect fisheries worth $25 million a year.[9]

In India, these "minor" forest products account for three fourths of the net export earnings from forest produce. Non-timber forest products also provide more than half of the formal employment in the forestry sector. In Thailand, the value of rattan exports is equal to 80 percent of the legal timber exports. And in Indonesia, hundreds of thousands of people make their livelihoods collecting and processing NTFPs for export, a trade worth at least $25 million a year.[10]

Perhaps even more valuable is the role of harvested wild goods in local economies and households. They are part of flexible and sustainable livelihood systems that provide food and income security. Wild products collected for personal consumption as well as traded in markets include vegetables, fruits, game meat, fish, medicines, dyes, and materials for thatching, cording, and weaving. In rural Laos, at least 141 forest products are collected, mainly by women, for sale or home use. In Ghana, most people depend on wildlife for most of their protein. Access to wild resources can literally be life-saving during times of famine and in the gap before the next agricultural harvest.[11]

Mangrove and coastal wetlands buffer coasts from storms and erosion, cycle nutrients, serve as nurseries, and supply critical resources.

Earnings from collecting and processing wild products are substantial. In Belize, for example, gathering medicinal plants yields 2–10 times the annual income of farmers on formerly forested lands. In Nigeria, collecting the wild duba palm from the Hadejia-Jama'are floodplain for thatching and weaving earns two to three times as much as agricultural wages. Even in more developed countries, collected wild products have economic importance. In the temperate rain forests of the Pacific Northwest coast of North America, unemployed timber workers can earn hundreds of dollars a day collecting wild mushrooms for sale in the region's cities.[12]

Access to and income from wild products is especially important to people who are usually excluded from more formal employment. Most workers in the world's formal and informal NTFP economy are women. Even among the renowned Amazonian rubber tappers, women are responsible for the processing that adds significant value to the products. Since a much larger share of women's income goes to support their families' health and welfare, this undercounted economy makes a substantial contribution. In India, NTFPs meet the household needs of tribal and forest communities and the landless, and the collection, processing, and sale of these products are their most important source of income. In fact, Indian biologist Madhav Gadgil notes that "a third or more of Indian people behave as 'ecosystem people'—households whose quality of life is intimately linked to the productivity and diversity of living organisms in their own [areas]." Unfortunately, the well-being of many of the world's ecosystem people—and of ecosystems—is in jeopardy due to economic and policy forces beyond their control.[13]

When areas are converted or managed for a single commodity, other benefits and services are lost. One recent and vivid example of this phenomenon is the widespread conversion of coastal mangrove systems to industrial aquaculture operations. Mangrove and coastal wetlands play critical roles linking the land and the sea. They buffer coasts from storms and erosion, cycle nutrients, serve as nurseries for coastal and marine fisheries, and supply critical resources to local communities. A major driving force in the accelerated loss of these critical ecosystems in the last two decades has been the explosive growth of intensive commercial aquaculture, especially for shrimp export.

This booming industry might at first glance appear to be a positive development path for developing countries. Shrimp aquaculture production more than quadrupled between 1985 and 1994, with a global market value of over $8 billion a year. But a closer look reveals quite a different picture. In the growing list of countries where this has become an important industry, up to half of mangrove areas have been converted to intensive aquaculture. The Philippines has lost 78 percent of its coastal wetlands and mangroves, Ecuador has lost 70 percent, and Thailand and Indonesia, about one third. Worldwide, shrimp ponds have consumed about 2.7 million hectares of rich coastal ecosystems. The "footprint," or impact, of the loss extends far beyond the immediate area.[14]

Wetlands that have been converted to intensive aquaculture can bring in as much as $11,600 per hectare a year. But using natural mangroves for fish, game, fuel, wood, food, fodder, medicines, and other uses can yield $1,000 to $10,000 per hectare a year. More to the point, these other uses can be sustained indefinitely, whereas aquaculture operations are viable for only 5–10 years. After that, they are the aquatic equivalent of a strip mine: they can no longer support life and are prohibitively expensive to rehabilitate.[15]

Beyond their unsound economics, aquaculture farms cannot perform the valuable services of natural ecosystems mentioned earlier. In India and Bangladesh, for instance, after only one year of aquafarm operation, nearby fishers reported that their wild shrimp catch had dropped by 80–90 percent. Not only do local people permanently lose access to critical resources, but strip-mine aquaculture produces a net loss of employment as well. Furthermore, much of the conversion has been heavily subsidized and benefits a relatively wealthy minority. Most of these new operations are owned not by local people but by outside investors looking to maximize short-term profit.[16]

APPRECIATING SERVICE PROVIDERS

Nature nurtures innumerable species that are not harvested directly but that provide important "free" services. These creatures pollinate crops, keep potentially harmful organisms in check, build and maintain soils, and decompose dead matter so it can used to build new life. Nature's "service providers"—the birds and bees, insects, worms, and microorganisms—show how small and seemingly insignificant things can have disproportionate value. Unfortunately, their services are in increasingly short supply because chemicals, disease, hunting, and habitat fragmentation and destruction have drastically reduced their numbers and ability to function. In the words of Stephen Buchmann and Gary Paul Nabhan, coauthors of a recent book on pollinators, "nature's most productive workers [are] slowly being put out of business."[17]

Pollinators, for example, are of enormous value to agriculture and the functioning of natural ecosystems. Without them, plants cannot produce the seeds that ensure their survival—and ours. Unlike animals, plants cannot roam around looking for mates. To accomplish sexual reproduction and ensure genetic mixing, plants have evolved strategies for moving genetic material from one plant to the next, sometimes over great distances. Some rely on wind or water to carry pollen to a receptive female, and some can self-pollinate. The most highly evolved are those that use flowers, scents, and nectars to attract and reward animals to do the job. In fact, more than 90 percent of the world's quarter-million flowering plant species are animal-pollinated.[18]

Developing a mutually beneficial relationship with a pollinator is a highly effective way of ensuring reproductive success, especially when individuals are isolated from each other. Performing this matchmaking service are between 120,000 and 200,000 animal species, including bees, beetles, butterflies, moths, ants, and flies, along with more than 1,000 species of vertebrates such as birds, bats, possums, lemurs, and even geckos. New evidence shows that many more of these species than previously believed are threatened with extinction.[19]

Eighty percent of the world's 1,330 cultivated crop species (including fruits, vegetables, beans and legumes, coffee and tea, cocoa, and spices) are pollinated by wild and semiwild pollinators. Without these services, crops yield less and wild plants produce few seeds—with large economic and ecological consequences. One third of U.S. agricultural output is from insect-pollinated plants (the remainder is from wind-pollinated grain plants such as wheat, rice, and corn). Honeybee pollination services are 60–100 times more valuable than the honey they produce. The value of wild blueberry bees is so great, with each one pollinating 15–19 liters of blueberries in its life, that they are viewed by farmers as "flying $50 bills."[20]

In the United States, more than half the honeybee colonies have been lost in the last 50 years, with 25 percent lost within the last 5 years alone. Widespread threats to pollinators include habitat fragmentation and disturbance, loss of nesting and overwintering sites, intense exposure of pollinators to pesticides and of nectar plants to herbicides, breakdown of "nectar corridors" that provide food sources to pollinators during migration, new diseases, competition from exotic species, and excessive hunting. A "forgotten pollinators" campaign was recently launched to raise awareness of the importance and plight of these service providers.[21]

Ironically, many modern agricultural practices actually limit the productivity of crops by reducing pollination. The high levels of pesticides used on cotton are estimated to reduce annual yields by 20 percent (worth $400 million) in the United States alone by killing bees and other insect pollinators. One fifth of all honeybee losses involve pesticide exposure; honeybee poisonings may cost agriculture hundreds of millions of dollars each year. Wild pollinators are most vulnerable to chemical poisoning because their colonies cannot be picked up and moved in advance of spraying the way domesticated hives can. Herbicides can kill the plants that pollinators need to sustain themselves during the "off-season" when they are not at work pollinating crops. Plowing to the edge of fields to maximize planting area can reduce yields by disturbing pollinator nesting sites. Just one hectare of unplowed land, for example, provides nesting habitat for enough wild alkali bees to pollinate 100 hectares of alfalfa.[22]

Domesticated honeybees alone cannot be expected to fill the gap left when wild pollinators are lost. Only 15 percent of the world's major crops are pollinated by domesticated and feral honeybees, while at least 80 percent are serviced by wild pollinators. In addition, because honeybees visit so many different plant species, they are not very "efficient"— that is, there is no guarantee that the pollen will be carried to a potential mate of the same species and not deposited on a different species.[23]

In peninsular Malaysia, the bat *Eonycteris spelea* is thought to be the exclusive pollinator of durians, one of the most highly valued fruits in Southeast Asia. The bats' primary food supply is a coastal mangrove that flowers continuously throughout the year. The bats routinely fly tens of kilometers from their roost sites to the mangrove stands, pollinating durian trees along the way "almost as a dietary afterthought." Unfortunately, mangrove stands in Malaysia and elsewhere are under siege from coastal development. Without this year-round mangrove resource, the bats are unlikely to survive.[24]

Pollinators that migrate long distances, such as bats, monarch butterflies, hummingbirds, and other birds, need to follow routes that offer a reliable supply of nectar-providing plants for the full journey. Today, however, such nectar corridors are being stretched increasingly thin and are breaking. When the travellers cannot rest and "refuel" every day, they may not survive the journey.

The migratory route followed by long-nosed bats from their summer breeding colonies in the desert regions of the U.S. Southwest to winter roosts in central Mexico illustrates the problems faced by many service providers. To fuel trips of up to 150 kilometers a night, they rely on the sequential flowering of at least 16 plant species—particularly century plants and columnar cacti. Along much of the migratory route, the nectar corridor is being fragmented.[25]

On U.S. and Mexican rangelands, ranchers are converting native vegetation into exotic pasture grasses for grazing cattle. In the Mexican state of Sonora, an estimated 376,000 hectares have been stripped of nectar source plants. In parts of the Sierra Madre in Mexico, an additional threat is overharvesting of century plants to make a bootleg alcoholic drink called mescal. And the latest threat may come from dynamiting and burning of bat roosts by Mexican ranchers attempting to eliminate vampire bats that feed on cattle and spread livestock diseases. According to Bat Conservation International, the long-nosed bats are one of several bat species suffering dramatic declines as a result of being caught in the vampire crossfire. The World Conservation Union–IUCN estimates that worldwide, 26 percent of bat species are threatened with extinction.[26]

Many of the disturbances that have harmed pollinators are also hurting creatures that provide other beneficial services, such as biological control of pests and disease. Much of the wild and semiwild habitat inhabited by beneficial predators like birds has been eliminated. Chemicals have killed beneficial insects along with the pests. The "pest control services" that nature provides are significant. Bat colonies in Texas can eat 250 tons of insects each night. Without birds, leaf-eating insects are more abundant and can slow the growth of trees or damage crops.[27]

One third of U.S. agricultural output is from insect-pollinated plants.

The loss of nature's pest control services has also contributed to the rise of vector-borne diseases and to increased reliance on harmful chemicals to try to control ever-more-abundant pests. In one illustrative case, Bangladesh's export of frogs' legs in the seventies and eighties led to a steep decline in frog populations—and to increased outbreaks of agricultural pests and waterborne diseases. Loss of the frogs' pest control and fertilizing services also led to a 25-percent increase in pesticide imports. By 1989, Bangladesh was spending three times as much each year on pesticides—$30 million—as it was earning from exporting frogs' legs. Within a year of banning these exports, frog populations began to rebound and pesticide imports dropped by 30–40 percent. The precise reason for the recent decline of the world's 5,000 or so species of frogs and other amphibians is not as clear, but the loss of their services has serious consequences, as Bangladesh discovered.[28]

Soil is more than just a place where plants can put down their roots. It is also home to an incredible array of valuable microorganisms who are the workers in nature's "underground economy." Insects, worms, and microorganisms in the soil provide the priceless services of decomposing organic material, making nutrients available to plants, controlling diseases, and improving the texture and water-holding capacity of soil. The tiny tunnels they dig provide space for air, water, and roots to move through the soil. The sheer volume and variety of these creatures is amazing. A hectare of healthy soil contains thousands of kilograms of earthworms, insects, spiders, fungi, bacteria, algae, and protozoa. Scientists have recently discovered that microbes deep in the planet's crust (some several kilometers below the surface) are even responsible for generating oil and mineral deposits such as gold.[29]

Changes in land use have reduced the abundance and diversity of these soil service providers. Stripping the land of vegetation removes the organic matter and nutrients that microfauna break down and return to the soil. Exposing soil also makes it more vulnerable to erosion, as well as hotter and drier and therefore less hospitable to these creatures. The use of chemicals kills the beneficial organisms as well as the harmful.

How can we encourage nature's service providers? By protecting them, their habitat, and the relationships among them. No-till farming methods can reduce soil erosion and allow nature's underground economy to flourish. Substantial reductions in the use of agricultural chemicals that harm service providers (and people) can help. Across the whole landscape, migratory routes and nectar corridors need protection to ensure the survival of nature's pollinators and pest control agents.[30]

Buffer areas of trees and native vegetation can have a number of beneficial effects. They can serve as havens for resident and migratory insects and animals that can pollinate crops and control pests. Buffer areas also help reduce wind

erosion and control pollution that escapes from agricultural fields. Such zones have been eliminated from many agricultural areas that have been "modernized" to accommodate new equipment or larger field sizes. The "sacred groves" in South Asian and African villages still provide such havens, and buffer areas can be reestablished in so-called modernized areas.[31]

CYCLING AND RECYCLING

Many of nature's services arise from its ability to regulate and recycle water, nutrients, and waste. But human disruptions have impaired this ability to filter and regulate water, to recharge groundwater supplies, and to move nutrients and sediments—indeed, to support life.

One of the most basic aspects of the cycling and recycling service is that water falls as precipitation, running across the landscape to streams and rivers and ultimately to the sea. Human actions have even changed that fundamental force of nature by removing natural plant cover, plowing fields, draining wetlands, separating rivers from their floodplains, and paving over land. In many places, water now races across the landscape much too quickly, causing flooding and droughts. In the Mississippi basin, for example, conversion of forests, prairies, wetlands, and floodplains to agriculture over the past 150 years has dramatically accelerated soil erosion, flood damage, and loss of native species. These changes have also reduced the water-holding capacity of the soils by as much as 70 percent.[32]

The slow natural movement of water across the landscape is also vital for refilling nature's underground water storage tanks—aquifers—that supply much of our water. One 223,000-hectare swamp in Florida has been calculated as worth $25 million a year just for its services of storing water and recharging the aquifer. Around the globe, vast expanses of wetlands have been drained and can no longer perform these valuable services.[33]

In other places, people take so much water that rivers run dry before they reach the sea and cannot deliver the fresh water, sediments, and nutrients needed by coastal and marine systems. Excess diversions also allow salt water to "intrude" into surface and groundwater supplies. On Europe's heavily populated Mediterranean, Black, and Baltic coasts, groundwater reservoirs have already been harmed by saltwater intrusion. Overdrawing groundwater depletes this renewable resource at a nonrenewable rate and can even reduce the capacity of an aquifer to store water in the future.[34]

One way to picture the value of nature's free services is to estimate what it costs society to replace them. The huge expenditures for building and maintaining infrastructure such as water treatment, irrigation, levees, and flood control illustrate a few of the economic costs. The value of mangroves for flood control alone, for instance, has been calculated at $300,000 per kilometer in Malaysia—the cost of the rock walls that would be needed to replace them. New York City has always relied on the natural filtering capacity of its rural watersheds to cleanse the water that serves 10 million people each day. Rather than spend $7 billion to build water treatment facilities, the city will pay one tenth that amount helping upstream counties protect the watersheds around its drinking-water reservoirs.[35]

The great values placed on watersheds comes from their ability to absorb and cleanse water, recycle excess nutrients, hold soil in place, and prevent flooding. When plant cover is removed or disturbed, water and wind can race across the land carrying valuable topsoil with them. Exposed soil is eroded at several thousand times the natural rate. Under normal conditions, each hectare of land loses somewhere between 0.004 and 0.05 tons of soil to erosion each year—far less than what is replaced by natural soil building processes. On lands that have been logged or converted to crops and grazing, however, erosion rates are many thousands of times higher than that. The eroded soil carries nutrients, sediments, and chemicals valuable to the system it leaves, but often harmful to the ultimate destination.[36]

The cost of this unsustainable behavior is quite large. In the United States, for example, which has relatively low erosion rates compared with the rest of the world, replacing lost nutrients, water, and so on from eroded land costs about $196 per hectare. The total cost of on-site and off-site damages (such as health costs, dredging waterways, and water treatment, but not including damage to aquatic life) from U.S. agricultural erosion is about $44 billion per year. Worldwide, costs are roughly $400 billion per year.[37]

Disruption of nature's nutrient cycling is apparent in the vast areas rendered infertile and the aquatic ecosystems dying from eutrophication—that is, from too many nutrients. The North, Baltic, Arabian, and Black Seas, the Chesapeake Bay, the Bay of Bengal, and the Pacific coasts of North and South America all suffer from periodic fish kills or the complete collapse of fisheries caused by nutrient overload. The "dead zones" in the Gulf of Mexico—thousands of square kilometers of water that have been robbed of oxygen by the excessive growth and death of algae—are caused by nutrients in the fertilizers and wastes that run off from farms and homes throughout the Mississippi River system. Around the Albermarle-Pamlico estuary of North Carolina, an important nursery for Atlantic fisheries, locals now call July through October "fish kill season."[38]

Once swamps and wetlands were viewed as wasted land, productive only if drained or filled. Today, their roles in cleansing water, recycling nutrients, recharging aquifers, controlling floods, and supporting productive resources such as fish, wildlife, and wild produce are being recognized. Their function as a line of defense in protecting coastal and ocean ecosystems from land-based pollution is clear. So is their ability to protect coasts from storms. Some of the highest measured values from wetlands (up to $40,000 per hectare) are near cities, where they provide critical water supply, nutrient abatement, and flood control services. Despite these demonstrated values, wetlands and watersheds are still converted to other uses, primarily agriculture, on a wide scale. Conservative estimates are that the United States and Europe have lost more than half of their wetlands, and Asia, 27 percent. The losses have been far higher in many nations and for many types of wetlands.[39]

Properly restored or constructed ecosystems can provide many of the services people require. For example, many countries are now using the assimilative capacity of natural or created wetlands as a cost-effective way to control and filter storm water and industrial and agricultural runoff, to decompose human waste, and to cleanse water. On agricultural lands, buffer strips of trees together with restored or constructed wetlands can reduce runoff of major pollutants such as sediments, phosphorus, and nitrogen by 80–100 percent. In both industrial and developing countries, wetland services are a low-cost, low-technology alternative to sewage treatment plants.[40]

Restored ecosystems can also bring back some of the flood control services that nature once provided—at lower cost

and greater effectiveness than structural alternatives such as dams and levees. Studies have found that for each 1-percent increase in wetlands, flooding downstream is decreased by 2–4 percent. And watersheds that are 5–10 percent wetlands can reduce the peak flood period by 50 percent compared with watersheds that have no wetlands. If just half of the Mississippi Basin's lost wetlands were restored in strategic locations, for example, they could control a flood of the magnitude of the one in 1993. This would affect only 3 percent of the land, but might prevent a repeat of the $12–16 billion catastrophe of that year.[41]

Even more effective than mitigating the impacts of activities or rejuvenating degraded ecosystems is maintaining healthy ecosystems. A few studies have measured the aggregate values of ecosystems and the unanticipated losses of economic, social, and ecological benefits that can ensue when the systems are degraded. One well-studied region is the floodplain between the Hadejia and Jama'are Rivers in northern Nigeria. It is an extraordinarily rich area that has a long history of supporting a large population (about 1 million today) at high income and nutritional status.[42]

In this region of Africa, people have developed sophisticated ways of using the flood pulse and dry areas to maximum effect without exceeding the floodplain's carrying capacity. The naturally functioning wetland supports traditional flood- and drought-adapted agriculture, fishing, dry-season grazing, and collection of a wide variety of useful products such as fuelwood, thatching, wild foods, and fertilizers. The region beyond the floodplain also benefits from the agricultural surpluses, the dry-season grazing available to seminomad pastoralists, and the recharge of groundwater supplies in this arid region. The wetland, which once covered 2,000–3,000 square kilometers, is now less than 900 square kilometers, following the droughts of the eighties and the construction of upstream dams.[43]

Despite the productivity, sustainability, and relative prosperity of the region, the floodplain is eyed as a source of water for modern agricultural development schemes. An extensive economic assessment measured the costs and benefits of such development compared with existing uses. (See Table 6–3.) The net economic benefits of the project (after subtracting project costs) total $29 per hectare, while those of existing uses are $167 per hectare. The economic benefit of the water itself when diverted for irrigated agriculture is 4¢ per 1,000 cubic meters versus at least $48 per 1,000 cubic meters when left in the floodplain to support traditional uses.

When the values of other ecosystem services (such as waterfowl habitat, grazing benefits, and aquifer recharge) and the extensive social benefits are added

in, the value of this naturally functioning floodplain in northern Nigeria is even higher. Thus, diverting water makes no economic sense. From an economic "efficiency" perspective alone this would be a bad deal, even without considering sustainability and equity. In developing and industrial countries alike, the benefits of healthy, functioning ecosystems nearly always outweigh the alleged benefits of degradation and conversion.

NATURE'S STABILITY AND RESILIENCE

A fundamental service provided by nature is ensuring that ecosystems and the entire biosphere are relatively stable and resilient. The ability to withstand disturbances and bounce back from regular "shocks" is essential to keeping the life-support system operating. Maintaining the integrity of the web of species, functions,

Table 6–3. Comparison of Benefits from Alternative Uses of Hadejia-Jama'are Floodplain, Nigeria

Costs and Benefits	Per Thousand Cubic Meters of Water		Per Hectare	
	Without Irrigation	With Irrigation	Without Irrigation	With Irrigation
	(dollars)			
Economic Benefits				
Agriculture	32.40	1.60	113.07	1299
Fishing	10.53	—	36.80	—
Fuelwood	4.93	—	16.93	—
Project Cost	0.00	1.56	0.00	1270
Net Economic Benefits	47.86	0.04	166.80	29

SOURCE: E.B. Barbier, W.M. Adams, and K. Kimmage, "An Economic Valuation of Wetland Benefits," in G.E. Hollis, W.M. Adams, and M. Aminu-Kano, eds., *The Hadejia-Nguru Wetlands: Environment, Economy, and Sustainable Development of a Sahelian Floodplain Wetland* (Gland, Switzerland: World Conservation Union–IUCN, 1993).

and processes within a system and the webs that connect different systems is critical for ensuring stability and resilience. As systems are simplified and their webs become disconnected, they become more brittle and vulnerable to catastrophic, irreversible decline. From global climate change and the breakdown of the ozone layer to the biodiversity deficit, the collapse of fisheries, frequent outbreaks of red tides, and increasingly severe floods and droughts, there is now ample evidence that the biosphere is becoming less resilient.[44]

Unfortunately, much of the economy is based on practices that convert natural systems into something simpler for ease of management or to maximize the production of a desired commodity (trees or wheat or minerals, for example). But simplified systems lack the resilience that allows them to survive short-term adversities (like disease or pest outbreaks, forest fires, or pollution) or long-term alterations such as climate change. A tree plantation or fish farm may provide some of the things we need, but it cannot supply the array of goods and services over a range of conditions that natural diverse systems do.[45]

Simplified systems lack the resilience that allows them to survive short-term adversities or long-term alterations such as climate change.

The results of decisions to maximize agricultural productivity while eliminating diversity show the consequences of making systems uniform and brittle. Today, fewer than 100 species provide most of the world's food supply, and within these species, genetic diversity has been drastically reduced. In eight major crops in the United States, for instance, fewer than nine varieties accounted for 50–75 percent of the total.[46]

It is increasingly common for one genetically uniform variety to cover nearly all of a region's cropland. In Indonesia, 74 percent of rice varieties come from a single maternal plant, and across Asia a single rice variety covers nearly 4.5 million hectares. Diseases and pests can quickly destroy genetically uniform stands of crops, trees, and even fish. In 1972, 15 million hectares of winter wheat fields in the Soviet Union were sown to a single variety, which proved particularly susceptible to a colder-than-normal winter. Virtually the entire crop was lost.[47]

Similarly, all major commercial banana varieties have been bred from the Cavendish banana, and have no genetic resistance to black sigatoka, a fungal disease. The disease can only be controlled with regular doses of fungicides, which Central American, Colombian, and Mexican banana producers spent at least $350 million on in just eight years. The price of chemical control is beyond the reach of many small-scale farmers, and banana yield reductions as high as 47 percent have been reported in the region.[48]

Despite the proven benefits of genetic diversity, landraces and the wild relatives of crops have been lost to an alarming extent. Between 1949 and the seventies, China lost 90 percent of its 10,000 wheat varieties, a downward trend that continues. In Indonesia, more than 1,500 local rice varieties have become extinct in the past 20 years. And up to 96 percent of the commercial vegetable varieties grown in the United States around 1900 are now extinct. The Convention on Biological Diversity and a new global plan of action on plant genetic resources seek to galvanize efforts to conserve these essential resources and ensure that they are used sustainably.[49]

Another sign that nature is becoming less resilient is the doubling of outbreaks of red tides in coastal ecosystems during the last two decades. These poisonous algal blooms can cause open sores on fish, accumulate toxins in shellfish, and be deadly to humans. Some of these little-known organisms have toxins 1,000 times stronger than cyanide. Outbreaks have been tied to high nutrient levels in coastal waters due to run-off from fertilizers and from human and animal wastes. Red tides and coastal stress are now truly global phenomena. A recent analysis by the World Resources Institute found that at least 51 percent of the world's coastlines are under moderate or high threat due to population density, urbanization, industrial development, and so forth.[50]

Coastal wetlands reduce vulnerability to floods, erosion, and storms. This "flood insurance" is important to subsistence and commercial fishers, coastal resorts, and indigenous communities, and will become even more valuable under future climate change and sea level rise. It is far less expensive and less disruptive than suffering the alternatives. That we are harming nature's ability to provide this service is apparent in the growing amounts that insurance companies pay out each year for "natural" disasters and the rise in uninsured losses.[51]

Changes in land use also affect the capacity of ecosystems to regulate local climates. After forest cover is removed, an area can become hotter and drier because water is no longer cycled and recycled by plants. It has been estimated that a rain forest tree pumps 2.5 million gallons of water into the atmosphere during its lifetime. Ancient Greece, for example, was a moister, wooded region before extensive deforestation, cultivation, and the soil erosion that followed transformed it into the hot, rocky country of modern times. The global extent and spread of desertification provide ample evidence of the toll of lost ecosystem services.[52]

The cumulative effects of local land use changes have global implications as well. One of the planet's first ecosystem services was the production of oxygen over billions of years of photosynthetic activity, which allowed oxygen-breathing organisms such as ourselves to exist. Our future existence will continue to depend on ecosystems maintaining the proper balance of atmospheric gases like oxygen and carbon dioxide. There is no technological substitute for this vital service.

Humans have begun to impair this basic service by generating too much carbon dioxide and other greenhouse gases, and reducing the ability of ecosystems to absorb carbon dioxide. The benefits of intact forests for global carbon sequestration alone have been estimated at several hundred to several thousand dollars per hectare. The consequences of this service disruption are beginning to be evident in the form of global climate change. Maintaining nature's ability to regulate local and global climates will be even more valuable under the predicted climate change scenario. (See also Chapter 5.)[53]

There are, however, ways for people to use ecosystems that capitalize on nature while maintaining its stability and resilience—and its productivity. By maintaining a nearby forest and estuary, a diversity of crops, and variety within each crop, for instance, farmers are assured a sufficient harvest regardless of weather and pests. This may not yield the maximum under "ideal" conditions (which rarely exist), but it is smart "crop insurance." Many human societies have evolved strategies for not only coping with nature's inevitable rhythms and changes, but using those changes and "disturbances" to their benefit, such as flood-dependant agriculture and flood-plain fisheries. The bottom line is that for humans to be healthy and resilient, nature must be too.

LETTING NATURE DO ITS WORK

What can be done to stop the unraveling of nature's life-support system and ensure that it can continue to supply the services on which we depend? First, our understanding of the true extent and value of nature's services, and the tools and processes we use to make decisions, need to be redirected toward ensuring the sustainability of the planet's life-support system. Understanding and valuing nature's services, and ensuring that they are used equitably and within nature's limits, are essential to that sustainable path.

We need to understand the interconnected web of life that we are part of and that supports us. Public and policy education as well as more fundamental ecological research about nature's services and cycles, and the true extent of our reliance on them, are needed. Realizing the cumulative impact of our activities and learning how we can conduct the human enterprise within nature's regenerative capacity are essential.

Economies and societies often use faulty signals that encourage people to make decisions that run counter to their own long-range interests—and those of society and future generations. Economic calculations grossly underestimate the current and future value of nature. While a fraction of nature's goods are counted when they enter the marketplace, many of the goods are not measured. And nature's services—the life-support systems—are not counted at all.[54]

When nature's goods are considered free and therefore valued at zero, the market signals that they are only economically valuable when converted into something else. For example, the profit from deforesting land is counted as a plus on a nation's ledger sheet, but the depletions of the timber stock, watershed, and fisheries are not subtracted. Clearly the costs of environmental degradation and lost ecosystem services are external to economic calculations: the damage from a massive oil spill is not subtracted from a nation's GDP, but the amounts spent on cleanup and health impacts are counted as additions to the national economy.[55]

The market system is geared to maximizing current profits and discounting future benefits, which also sends the wrong message. Just as a piece of factory machinery is assumed to wear out in 10–15 years, natural resources are considered by economists to be less valuable over time. By this reckoning, it is more profitable to consume a resource today than to save it for tomorrow. There are a number of fallacies in this assumption. First, nature does not wear out like an old automobile. In fact, just the opposite—it becomes increasingly valuable with time. When used sustainably, nature's goods and services can be renewed and available indefinitely. Second, discounting disregards the rights of future generations to the planet's life-support system.

Another faulty economic signal is that financial benefits from resource use are realized by private individuals or entities, but the costs of any loss are distributed across society. Economists call this "socializing costs." Stated simply, private costs and benefits are counted, but social and environmental costs to current and especially future generations are "external" to the calculations. The people who get the benefits are different from the ones who pay the costs. Thus, there is little economic incentive for those exploiting a resource to use it judiciously or in a manner that maximizes public good.

In Thailand, for example, agricultural users who consume 90 percent of the water pay nothing for it, so there is no incentive to conserve. Meanwhile, Thailand is looking beyond its borders for more water and energy. The costs of building dams and diversions along the Mekong River—construction and debt costs, lost fisheries, agriculture, water, livelihoods, and so on—will be paid by the 52 million people in the downstream countries of Laos, Cambodia, and Vietnam. Worldwide, too often the costs and benefits of exploitation are unevenly and inequitably distributed, with most of the profits flowing to an increasingly wealthy and narrow minority.[56]

Fixing a more accurate price for nature by better "internalizing" the economic "externalities" is an important step, but it is also necessary to acknowledge that everything does not have a price. Much of nature's value is quite literally beyond measure. Evolution and resilience, for instance, are priceless. Assessing the total value, economic and otherwise, of an ecosystem requires looking at more than the amount of money that can be made from a piece of land. The nonmonetary benefits of nature's services and the costs of its absence must also be recognized. Beyond looking at the economic value of exploiting nature for a particular commodity, for example, it is also important to examine how many people—and which people—use the resources, and what portion of their livelihoods and larders nature provides. Community stability, self-sufficiency, and livelihood flexibility and security are extremely valuable, even though a monetary value cannot be assigned to them.

There are spiritual, cultural, religious, and aesthetic values of nature that are immeasurable yet powerful incentives for good stewardship. The desire to pass on a healthy environment to future generations is a part of most cultures. Many traditional resource management strategies and religious rituals and taboos may have been developed in response to the need to use biological resources sustainably. For example, the sacred

groves of India and Ghana as well as Indonesia's water temples are rooted in religious tradition, but they are now recognized as highly evolved forms of wise resource management as well.[57]

Clearly, it is not just market failures that are responsible for misvaluing and misusing nature's services. People devise the markets and the economic indicators, and they decide how they will be used. Too often, illogical and inequitable resource use continues in the face of evidence that it is ecologically, economically, and socially unsustainable because powerful interests are able to shape government policy by legal or illegal means, through corruption, favoritism, or discrimination.

Assessing the total value, economic and otherwise, of an ecosystem requires looking at more than the money that can be made from a piece of land.

A major step along a more sustainable path is recognizing that not everyone assigns the same value to goods and services, nor do they experience the same costs and consequences from their loss. Nature has different values at different times to different people, and not everything has a monetary value. For example, a forest may be most valued for its timber by some people and for its role in watershed protection, water regulation, and sustainable products harvest by others. Carbon sequestration may be an important global service but have no local value. Who decides what to measure, and the values that are assigned, profoundly influences how nature is used and ultimately its ability to continue providing services.

Although it may be unlikely that the full value of ecosystem services will ever be captured in economic terms, markets and policies can do a better job of reflecting the values of nature and all those to whom it is of value, and thus better maintain ecosystem services and processes. Charting a more sustainable path will require using better economic tools to measure and value nature's services, economic performance, and human well-being. Standard indicators have not been good at measuring environmental or human well-being.

As the authors of a new Genuine Progress Indicator (GPI) put it, "The GDP makes no distinction between economic transactions that add to well-being and those which diminish it....As a result, the GDP masks the breakdown of social structure and natural habitat; and worse, it portrays this breakdown as economic gain." While global GDP has been rising in recent decades, for example, the world's population living in poverty has been increasing, the distribution of income has become less equitable, the biodiversity deficit is growing, and the loss of nature's services has worsened. The values of nature's unmarketed goods and ecosystem services as well as the unpaid labor in households and communities must be incorporated into economic calculations and performance indicators.[58]

New performance indicators are being developed to give more accurate assessments of well-being and development. The GPI, for example, has been proposed by a group called Redefining Progress. It expands on the landmark methodology developed for the Index of Sustainable Economic Welfare by Herman Daly and John Cobb in 1989. The GPI counts the positive contributions of household and community work and subtracts for depletion of natural habitat, pollution costs, income distribution, and crime. (It does not, however, reflect the value of nature's services except when they are lost.) In contrast to rising GDP, the GPI in the

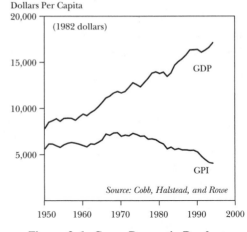

Figure 6–1. Gross Domestic Product Versus Genuine Progress Indicator, United States, 1950–94

United States has been declining since the seventies. (See Figure 6–1.)[59]

The new discipline of ecological economics is providing much-needed guidance on charting a more sustainable path. Revision of the GDP-based system of national accounts is now being taken seriously. And indicators will continue being refined to include estimates of the values of natural capital and ecosystem services. But it is not necessary to wait for a global consensus on these changes to begin taking action. Governments, lenders, businesses, and others can begin today by using the newer indicators and fuller valuation techniques that are already available. They can also end destructive subsidies, apply appropriate economic incentives, and link receipt of benefits to payment of costs. They can start by incorporating social and environmental indicators and nonmonetary criteria as fundamental parts of their decision-making processes.[60]

Governments can use positive economic and policy incentives to encourage things society wants more of, such as healthy ecosystems and employment;

can use disincentives to discourage things society wants less of, such as pollution; and can eliminate the perverse incentives in the form of subsidies and so on that are encouraging things that society does not want, such as environmental degradation, growing unemployment, and poverty. (See also Chapter 8.) For example, ending the subsidized use of water and using more efficient irrigation (often through lower-cost technologies) could significantly reduce the amount of water removed from freshwater systems and thus increase the amount that remains to provide fundamental ecosystem services.[61]

In project and local planning, most current cost-benefit analyses and environmental impact assessments are not up to measuring the true costs of depleting nature's capital and the real ecological and socioeconomic benefits of nature's services. Thus decisions made based on these measures (as with the GDP) will be flawed. Local entities, banks, private lenders, and businesses can use an expanded set of social and environmental indicators to judge the relative merits of development alternatives.[62]

When measuring the potential environmental impacts of planned developments (from dams and highways to irrigation and land use), investors and developers need to consider lost environmental benefits as well as social, economic, and ecological costs. For example, displacing communities in the name of progress tears the social fabric and the social safety net, frequently leading people to become environmental refugees and aggravating poverty and environmental destruction. As described earlier, the government of Indonesia used such a full assessment of development options for Bintuni Bay; the study showed that maintaining the mangrove ecosystem provided more economic benefits, more employment, more social stability, and a wider array of goods and

services than timber cutting would. And it could be sustained indefinitely.[63]

Laws and policies should be designed to protect nature's systems and services, not just individual elements in those systems. Management decisions should cover larger geographic areas and longer time horizons, and should shift from managing for individual elements (such as one species or use) to managing for ecosystem health and processes. The connection between pollinators, habitats, and pesticides illustrates the importance of maintaining healthy ecological relationships and processes. In Costa Rica, for instance, a new law has the explicit goal of maintaining important ecological services, in part by providing compensation to landowners for keeping their land in natural cover.[64]

In Costa Rica, a new law has the explicit goal of maintaining important ecological services.

At the international level (see Chapter 1), the Convention on Biological Diversity, now ratified by 162 countries, emphasizes the importance of maintaining healthy ecosystems and the sustainable and equitable use of nature's goods and services. And the climate change convention has made progress on halting the further loss of nature's climate control services. The oldest international conservation treaty, the Convention on Wetlands of International Importance especially as Waterfowl Habitat (also known as the Ramsar Convention) has shifted its emphasis from preservation of these areas for bird habitat to maintenance of ecosystem services.[65]

We can reduce and reverse the destructive impact of our activities by consuming less and by placing fewer demands on nature's services—for example, by increasing water and energy use efficiency. It is not necessary to undermine ecosystems services in order to produce the food and materials that people require. Food can still be produced using no-till farming methods that dramatically reduce soil erosion, fertilizer and chemical runoff into waters, and air pollution. This approach can also improve the organic matter content of soil and make it more hospitable to valuable microorganisms.

The continued conversion, simplification, and degradation of ecosystems needs to be reversed. And degraded habitat should be restored so it can perform critical services. Examples of steps needed in this direction include using artificial wetlands for flood control and nitrogen abatement, and promoting reforestation for watershed protection and carbon sequestration. Policies such as "no net loss of wetlands" can fail to protect the myriad values and services of wetlands. The goal should be no more loss of natural wetlands and restoration of degraded wetlands.

Finally, we can no longer assume that nature's services will always be there free for the taking. We must become more cautious and forward-thinking before taking any actions that disrupt natural systems and services and limit the options of future generations. We have already seen that the loss of ecosystem services can have severe economic, social, and ecological costs, even though we can only measure a fraction of them. We can rarely determine the full impact of our actions. The consequences for nature are often unforeseen and unpredictable. The loss of individual species and habitat, and the degradation and simplification of ecosystems, can impair nature's ability to provide the services we need. Many of these losses are irreversible, and much of what is lost is simply irreplaceable.

Maintaining nature's services requires looking beyond the needs of this generation, with the goal of ensuring sustainability for many generations to come. We must act under the assumption that future generations will need at least the same level of nature's services as we have today—the safe minimum standard. Thus reason and equity dictate that we operate under the precautionary principle. We can neither practically nor ethically decide what future generations will need and what they can survive without.

7

Transforming Security

Michael Renner

On April 6, 1994, the President of Rwanda, Juvénal Habyarimana, died in a mysterious plane crash. Within hours, members of the presidential guard, the armed forces, and militias made up of militant Hutus started a systematic slaughter directed primarily at the country's Tutsi population. The genocide, in which anywhere from 500,000 to 1 million people perished, ended only when rebel forces of the predominantly Tutsi Rwandan Patriotic Front (RPF) defeated the government's forces some three months later.[1]

The sheer magnitude and ferocity of the killings seemed motivated by a near-satanic level of hatred. Many observers saw the events as a prime example of how ethnic tensions can lead to violence. And indeed, the key perpetrators of the violence proved very adept at manipulating the meaning of ethnic identities; in an effort to conceal what amounted to premeditated mass murder, they stressed the ostensibly tribal nature of the killings.[2]

This chapter is adapted from *Fighting for Survival: Environmental Decline, Social Conflict, and the New Age of Insecurity* (New York: W.W. Norton & Company, 1996).

What has become a routine reference to "ancient hatreds" in the post–cold war era turns out to be a poor explanation of the circumstances that brought about this genocide. Rwandan society had been unraveling for several years. Rather than being a simple case of tribal bloodletting, the Rwandan apocalypse was rooted in a complex web of explosive population growth, severe land shortages, land degradation and rapidly falling food production, lack of nonagricultural employment, dwindling export earnings, and the pain of structural economic adjustment.[3]

These pressures, combined with long-standing discrimination against the Tutsi population and regional favoritism in dispensing government money, generated growing discontent and political opposition, triggered an invasion by the RPF, and led to increasingly savage competition among the country's elites. Rather than allow a transition to a multiethnic, nonauthoritarian system take place—a prospect that seemed likely in early 1994—extremist forces among the Hutu resorted to mass murder.

The events in Rwanda are powerful testimony for a long-ignored but increasingly obvious fact: violent conflict occurs much less frequently between sovereign nations now than it does within countries. Almost none of the major armed conflicts in the nineties have been unambiguously country-against-country. The nature of "security" has been transformed.

For too long, security has been defined primarily in military terms, an understanding that has led governments to create ever more powerful armies and develop ever more sophisticated weapons. But this preoccupation with "national security" has led decision makers to neglect other dimensions that may be much more relevant to their constituents' well-being, and hence to the social and political stability that is crucial if internal conflicts are to be avoided. Today, humanity is facing a triple security crisis: the effects of environmental decline, the repercussions of social inequities and stress, and the dangers arising out of an unchecked arms proliferation that is a direct legacy of the cold war period.

Conflicts typical of the contemporary world cannot be resolved at gunpoint. They require not a recalibration of military tools and strategies, but a commitment to far-reaching demilitarization. Indeed, the military now absorbs substantial resources that could help reduce the potential for violent conflict if invested in health care, housing, education, poverty eradication, and environmental sustainability.

This broader conception of security is often referred to as "human security" (as opposed to "national security"). It entails such seemingly disparate concerns as peace, environmental protection, human rights and democratization, and social integration. Concerns about human security are in a sense as old as human history, yet they are now magnified by the unprecedented scale of environmental degradation, by the presence of immense poverty in the midst of extraordinary wealth, and by the fact that social, economic, and environmental challenges are no longer limited to particular communities and nations.[4]

SECURITY IN THE POST–COLD WAR ERA

Far from the traditional image of war—clashing national armies—the "battlefield" in today's violent conflicts can be anywhere, and the distinction between combatants and noncombatants is blurred. The fighting is done as often by guerrilla groups, paramilitary forces, and vigilante squads as by regular, uniformed soldiers. Child soldiers are by no means an uncommon sight. Civilians are often not accidental victims but explicit targets of violence, intimidation, and expulsion. By some rough estimates, civilians accounted for half of all war-related deaths in the fifties, three quarters in the eighties, and almost 90 percent in 1990. Humanitarian relief supplies are frequently delayed and used as bargaining chips.[5]

As many countries may be bordering on war as are actually engaged in it, trapped in endemic political violence. From Haiti to the Philippines, highly inequitable social and economic conditions remain in place that trigger cycles of uprisings by the disadvantaged and oppression by the ruling elites. Some countries are facing generalized lawlessness and banditry—whether by marauding ex-soldiers (in several African nations), drug cartels (in Colombia), or various forms of organized crime (in Russia). Analysts are finding a growing privatization of security and violence—in the form of legions of private security guards, the proliferation of small arms among the general population, and the spread of vigilante and "self-defense" groups. A culture of violence—in which vicious responses to social problems are the norm—has taken root in many countries.[6]

The post–cold war era is increasingly witnessing a phenomenon of what some have called "failed states"—the implosion of countries like Rwanda, Somalia, Yugoslavia, and others. But they are only the most spectacular victims of the pressures and vulnerabilities of the current era—underlying forces that many other countries are subjected to as well but have managed, for the time being at least, to cope with more successfully.[7]

Several countries are among the ranks of what Professor James Rosenau of George Washington University calls "adrift nation-states"—where one or more of the following conditions is likely to be present: the economy is being depleted; the state is unable to provide anything like adequate services to its citizens; grievances are disregarded and political dissent is repressed; the social fabric is unraveling; and the political leadership is unable to cope with growing tensions among different ethnic groups, regions, and classes, or it plays different groups off against each other in an effort to prolong its rule.[8]

In short, an amalgam of forces is at work. But as was the case in Rwanda, the media and many other observers now almost habitually ascribe the outbreak of civil wars and the collapse of entire societies to just one factor: the resurfacing of "ancient ethnic hatreds" revolving around seemingly irreconcilable religious and cultural differences. Professor Samuel Huntington of Harvard University went so far as to postulate a coming "clash of civilizations"—ethnically motivated communal violence writ large.[9]

Of course, ethnic tensions do play some role. Roughly half of the world's countries have experienced some kind of interethnic strife in recent years. A 1993 study for the U.S. Institute of Peace found 233 minority groups at risk from political or economic discrimination. These groups encompassed 915 million people in 1990, about 17 percent of the world's population. Only 27 of the 233 groups "have left no record...of political organization, protest, rebellion or intercommunal conflict since 1945."[10]

A culture of violence has taken root in many countries.

Where ethnic tensions do exist, however, they did not arise in a vacuum. One of the continuing legacies of colonial and imperial rule is that boundaries are often arbitrary—drawn not to reflect local realities, but to serve the purposes of the imperial masters. As a result, people of the same culture, language, or ethnicity often found themselves separated by international borders and grouped with people of other backgrounds and origins, irrespective of whether they had previously coexisted peacefully, been at odds, or had no significant contact at all. To steady their rule, colonial administrations typically favored one local group, often a minority, over others—Tamils over Sinhalese in Sri Lanka, Tutsi over Hutu in Rwanda and Burundi, Christian Arabs over Sunni and Shia Moslems in Lebanon—which generated fatal resentments.[11]

Following independence, civic life in many of these states continued to be split along ethnic lines, with one group ruling at the direct expense of the other. Given severe economic underdevelopment and undemocratic, often repressive patterns of governance, the competition for power and resources among contending groups became intense. A 1990 study for the U.S. Institute of Peace found that more than half of 179 minority groups in the Third World feel disadvantaged; although some might be content with pressing for domestic changes in their favor, many have separatist leanings.[12]

On the surface, then, many conflicts do seem to revolve around ethnic, religious, cultural, or linguistic divisions. These divisions will likely dominate the perceptions of the protagonists themselves, because political leaders in virtually all these divided societies see playing the ethnic card as an essential way to capture and maintain power. Yet it is important to examine the underlying stress factors that produce or deepen rifts in societies, particularly since ethnic distinctions often lie dormant for long periods of time. As discussed in this chapter, disputes are often sharpened or triggered by glaring social and economic disparities—explosive conditions that are exacerbated by the growing pressures of population growth, resource depletion, and environmental degradation.

A major threat to the economic well-being of many countries is land degradation.

Together, these conditions can form a powerful blend of insecurities. Accompanied by weak, nonrepresentative political systems that are increasingly seen as illegitimate and incapable of attending to people's needs, these pressures can lead to the wholesale fragmentation of societies. As people turn to ethnic, religious, or other identity-based organizations for assistance and protection, "other" groups tend to be regarded as competing and threatening, and whatever bonds may have held societies together in the past grow more tenuous.

ENVIRONMENTAL PRESSURES

Aral'sk, once a harbor city situated at the northern-most tip of the Aral Sea, now lies 30 kilometers from the receding shoreline. The rivers feeding into the Aral were tapped heavily to supply water to huge Soviet cotton irrigation systems. Since 1960, the Aral Sea has lost 75 percent of its volume; the fish catch has dropped from 40–50,000 tons to zero, wiping out 60,000 jobs. Widespread salinization and waterlogging—due to grossly inefficient irrigation methods—have led to devastating crop yield losses.[13]

As the Aral has shrunk, winds pick up dust, salt, and toxic chemicals from the sea's exposed bottom and deposit them over a wide area. These airborne toxins are contaminating crops and endangering public health. A massive reduction in water diversion is needed to restore the Aral. But the Central Asian governments have been unable to agree on practical measures, and disputes over water allocation continue to erupt both among and within the countries of the region.

The Aral Sea story is one of the more egregious examples of how the depletion and deterioration of natural systems has become an important source of insecurity and stress in many societies. Desertification, soil erosion, deforestation, and water scarcity are worldwide phenomena that make themselves felt in the form of reduced food-growing potential, worsening health effects, or diminished habitability.

A major threat to the economic well-being of many countries is land degradation—principally through the plowing of highly erodible land, the salinization of irrigated land, the overgrazing of rangelands, and the loss of arable land, rangeland, and forests to expanding urban and industrial needs. Although the immediate reasons may be found in inappropriate practices or inefficient technologies, land degradation often is the result of social and economic inequities.

According to U.N. Environment Programme (UNEP) estimates at the beginning of the nineties, some 3.6 billion hectares—about 70 percent of potentially productive drylands—are affected by desertification. One third of all agricultural land is lightly degraded, half is moderately degraded, and 16 percent strongly or extremely degraded. Some 400 million poor people live in rural, ecologically fragile areas of the developing world characterized by land degradation, water scarcity, and reduced agricultural productivity.[14]

Currently 65 percent of the agricultural land in Africa, 45 percent in South America, 38 percent in Asia, and 25 percent in North America and Europe is affected by soil degradation. Among the soil erosion crisis areas are the Horn of Africa, eastern Iran, large patches of Iraq, the northwestern and northeastern corners of the Indian subcontinent, Central America, the Amazon basin, and several parts of China. In Mexico, for instance, at least 70 percent of agricultural land is affected by soil erosion.[15]

Because of population growth and unequal land distribution, large numbers of small peasants are cultivating highly fragile areas, such as steep hillsides and patches cleared out of rain forests, that are easily susceptible to erosion and the soils of which are quickly exhausted. Environmental consultant Norman Myers calls them "shifted cultivators"—a play on the traditional term shifting cultivators. In Rwanda, for example, half of all farming took place on hillsides by the mid-eighties, when overcultivation and soil erosion led to falling yields and a steep decline in total grain production. In Mexico, more than half of all farmers eke out a living on steep hill slopes that now account for one fifth of all Mexican cropland.[16]

Water, like cropland, is a fundamental resource for human well-being—for food production, health, and economic development. Yet in many countries it is an increasingly scarce resource, under threat of both depletion and pollution. Countries with annual supplies in the range of 1,000–2,000 cubic meters per person are generally regarded as water-stressed, and those with less than 1,000 cubic meters are considered water-scarce. By the beginning of the nineties, 26 countries—home to about 230 million people—were in the water-scarce category.[17]

Many rivers and aquifers—and not just in countries with acute water scarcity—are overexploited. Excessive withdrawal of river and groundwater leads to land subsidence, intrusion of salt water in coastal areas, desiccation of lakes, and eventual depletion of water sources. In the United States, more than 4 million hectares—about one fifth of the total irrigated area—are watered by pumping in excess of recharge. Aquifer depletion due to overpumping is occurring in crop-growing areas around the globe, including Mexico, China, India, Thailand, northern Africa, and the Middle East.[18]

Another problem is waterlogging and salinization brought about by poor water management. Salt buildup in the soil is thought to reduce crop yields by about 30 percent in Egypt, Pakistan, and the United States. Data are sketchy, but it is estimated that some 25 million hectares—about 10 percent of irrigated cropland worldwide—suffer from salt accumulation, and that an additional 1–1.5 million hectares are added to that figure each year.[19]

The already observable degradation of the earth's soil and water resources is likely to be compounded by climate change. Changing precipitation patterns, shifting vegetation zones, and rising sea levels caused by global warming threaten to disrupt crop harvests, inundate heavily populated low-lying coastal areas, upset human settlement patterns, imperil estuaries and coastal aquifers with intruding salt water, and undermine biological diversity (see Chapter 5).

Global warming could cause sea levels to rise anywhere from 15 to 94 centimeters during the next century (and more thereafter), with a current best estimate of about 50 centimeters. Some 118 million people living in coastal areas could be put at risk (population growth will increase this number). Bangladesh would be one of the most severely affected countries. The currently projected maximum sea level rise would inundate about 25,000 square kilometers of the country—17 percent of its territory. Virtually the entire country would be subject to repeated massive flooding.[20]

River deltas and coastal areas around the globe likely to be strongly affected by global warming include the Yangtze, Mekong, and Indus in Asia; the Tigris and Euphrates in the Middle East; the Zambezi, Niger, and Senegal in Africa; the Orinoco, Amazon, and La Plata in South America; the Mississippi in North America; and the Rhine and Rhone in Europe.[21]

The low-lying areas most at risk are precisely the places with some of the densest human settlements and the most intensive agriculture. All in all, UNEP anticipates that sea level rise, along with amplified tidal waves and storm surges, could eventually threaten some 5 million square kilometers of coastal areas worldwide. Though accounting for only 3 percent of the world's total land, this area encompasses one third of all croplands and is home to more than a billion people.[22]

Global warming's impact on agriculture—through rising seas, higher or more variable temperatures, more frequent droughts, and changes in precipitation patterns—is thus a major concern. Given already existing water shortages, agriculture in arid and semiarid areas is particularly vulnerable to climate change. Studies suggest that Egypt's corn yield may drop by one fifth and its wheat yield by one third, while Mexico's rain-fed maize crop may be reduced by as much as 40 percent.[23]

The human security implications of degraded or depleted lands, forests, and marine ecosystems, intensified by climate change, are many: heightened droughts and increasing food insecurity; reduced crop yields that force farmers to look for work in already crowded cities; environmental refugees from coastal areas seeking new homes and livelihoods elsewhere, possibly clashing with unwelcoming host communities; the disruption of local, regional, and possibly national economies; and the soaring costs of coping with the dislocations.

SOCIAL PRESSURES

Tens of thousands of Bolivian teachers, health care workers, miners, and oil industry workers went on strike in March 1996 in the nation's capital, La Paz. It was one of a series of desperate protests to push for an increase in wages. In Bolivia, as elsewhere in Latin America, many people are hard-pressed to find jobs or to make do with the often meager incomes that existing jobs give them. Strikes, unrest, and other forms of protest are becoming more frequent.[24]

The growth of GNP and other macroeconomic indicators in Latin America has been impressive in recent years. But with few exceptions, income distribution in the region remains highly skewed, providing the benefits of economic growth to relatively few. Even with continued growth, the region's poverty rate is not expected to drop below its 1990 level of 46 percent.[25]

As a group, Latin American countries have long displayed the most unequal income distribution in the world—disparities that grew even bigger during the eighties. In Argentina, Brazil, Costa Rica, Uruquay, and Venezuela, for example, the richest 5 percent gained during the eighties at the expense of the bottom 75 percent. Though the circumstances vary from region to region, Latin America is not alone in its experience of a highly uneven distribution of the benefits of economic growth (or the woes of economic contraction). The nations of East Asia are one of the few exceptions to a pattern of rising inequality, marginalization, and the resulting rifts and fractures found in many societies.[26]

The gap between rich and poor has grown to tremendous levels, both globally and within many individual countries. (See Table 7–1.) Worldwide, the richest fifth of the population now receives 60 times the income of the poorest fifth, up from 30 times in 1960. In the United Kingdom, the ratio between the top 20 and bottom 20 percent went from 4:1 in 1977 to 7:1 in 1991. In the United States, it went from 4:1 in 1970 to 13:1 in 1993.[27]

Those at the bottom of the economic heap have to contend with meager or unpredictable incomes despite long hours of backbreaking work, insufficient amounts of food and poor diets, lack of access to safe drinking water, susceptibility to preventable diseases, housing that provides few comforts and scant shelter, and the absence of social services that the better-off take for granted.

Rich-poor disparities are about much more than just the lack of access to modern conveniences or the inability to accumulate material wealth: they are often a matter of life and death. The life expectancy of the poorest Mexicans—53

Table 7–1. Ratio of Richest 20 Percent of Population to Poorest 20 Percent in Selected Countries, Eighties

Country	Ratio
South Africa	45
Brazil	32
Guatemala	30
Senegal	17
Mexico	14
United States	13[1]
Malaysia	12
Zambia	9
Algeria	7
China	7
South Korea	6
Germany	6
India	5
Japan	4

[1]Data for 1993.

SOURCES: U.N. Development Programme, *Human Development Report 1995* (New York: Oxford University Press, 1995); David Dembo and Ward Morehouse, *The Underbelly of the U.S. Economy* (New York: Apex Press, 1995); Reinhold Meyer, "Waiting for the Fruits of Change. South Africa's Difficult Road to Equality," *Development + Cooperation*, July/August 1996.

years—is 20 years less than that of the richest of their compatriots. In rural Punjab, a region straddling India and Pakistan, babies born to landless families have infant mortality rates one third higher than those born to landowning families.[28]

In most developing countries, where agriculture is a mainstay of the economy and key to people's livelihoods, land distribution is an indicator as important as the distribution of wealth. It, too, tells a story of immense imbalances. (See Table 7–2.)

Together with other trends, such as the marginalization of small-scale agriculture by cash-crop operations, the conversion of cropland to cattle ranching, and still-high rates of population growth, unequal and insecure land tenure forces large numbers of peasants to migrate to

Table 7–2. Land Distribution and Landlessness, Selected Countries or Regions

Country/Region	Observation
Brazil	Top 5 percent of landowners control at least 70 percent of the arable land; the bottom 80 percent have only 13 percent of the cultivable area.
Peru	Three quarters of the rural population are landless or near-landless.[1]
Central America	Guatemala: 2 percent of farmers control 80 percent of all arable land. Honduras: the top 5 percent occupy 60 percent. El Salvador: the top 2 percent own 60 percent, and almost two thirds of the farmers are landless or nearly landless. Costa Rica: top 3 percent have 54 percent of arable land.
India	40 percent of rural households are landless or near-landless; the 25 million landless households in 1980 are expected to reach 44 million by the end of the century.
Philippines	3 percent of landowners control one quarter of the land; 60 percent of rural families have no or too little land.

[1]Near-landlessness means that a rural family or household possesses too little land to sustain its members' livelihoods with farming alone.

SOURCES: Norman Myers, *Ultimate Security: The Environmental Basis of Political Stability* (New York: W.W. Norton & Company, 1993); U.N. Department of Public Information, "The Geography of Poverty," factsheet, March 1996; Myriam Vander Stichele, "Trade Liberalization—The Other Side of the Coin," *Development + Cooperation,* January/February 1996.

more marginal areas, such as hillsides and rain forests, where the limited fertility soon makes them move on. Others turn to seasonal or permanent wage labor on large agricultural estates, or end up seeking new livelihoods in already crowded cities.

On the whole, Latin American land tenure patterns are much more inequitable than those found in Asia and Africa. Brazil has one of the most lopsided patterns of land distribution: the top 1 percent of landowners control 45 percent of the arable land, while the bottom 80 percent have to make do with 13 percent. But there are exceptions. In South Africa, the apartheid legacy still lives on: some 67,000 white farmers own 87 percent of the arable land and account for 90 percent of agricultural production. In the Sudan, an estimated 90 percent of the marketable agricultural production is controlled by fewer than 1 percent of the farmers.[29]

Together with population growth, which forces peasants to subdivide plots

into smaller and smaller parcels from one generation to the next, unequal land tenure is causing increasing landlessness. In Rwanda, for instance, average farm size declined from 2 hectares per family to 0.7 hectares over the past three decades. In 1981, an estimated 167 million households worldwide (938 million people) were landless or near-landless; that number is expected to reach nearly 220 million by the end of the nineties.[30]

Sharp increases in what were already large social and economic discrepancies were to a great extent a consequence of structural adjustment programs imposed by the International Monetary Fund (IMF) and the World Bank since the early eighties. These loans came with strings attached—such as the reduction or elimination of subsidies, price controls, and social programs—that proved to be exceedingly bitter medicine not just for the poor but for significant parts of the middle class. In sub-Saharan Africa, structural adjustment initiated a vicious circle of retrenchment, leading to a decline in investments of 50 percent during the eighties.[31]

Most people in highly indebted African and Latin American countries suffered a severe drop in living standards during the eighties. In Mexico, for example, real wages declined by more than 40 percent in 1982–88. In 1983, a basket of basic goods for an average family of five cost 46 percent of the minimum wage; by 1992, it cost the equivalent of 161 percent. Deepening disparities have widened political rifts; one result was the uprising of impoverished peasants in the southern state of Chiapas in early 1994.[32]

Structural adjustment policies are part of a larger, neoliberal model of development that sees privatization, deregulation, trade liberalization, and world market integration as the road to economic salvation. In agriculture, this has meant giving priority to the larger cash crop producers (who are typically more oriented toward lucrative export markets and nonstaple and perhaps even nonfood crops) to the detriment of the numerically much larger subsistence or small-scale commercial farmers. In many countries, small farmers are losing access to credits, extension services, and other forms of support, such as guaranteed prices. In Chiapas in 1990, for example, 87 percent of agricultural producers had no access at all to government credit.[33]

Marginalized peasants may have little choice but to join the trek to urban areas. It would be one thing if those displaced could find jobs in cities and towns. But by and large a sufficient number of jobs, particularly jobs that pay a living wage, do not exist. Indeed, one reason for rising inequality and poverty—and a major threat to social cohesion and stability—is found in what various observers have termed the global jobs crisis. Out of the global labor force of about 2.8 billion people, at least

120 million people are unemployed, while 700 million are classified as "underemployed"—a misleading term because many in this category are actually working long hours but receiving too little in return to cover even the most basic of needs.[34]

Perhaps most unsettling is the reality of large-scale youth unemployment, which virtually everywhere is substantially higher than that for the labor force as a whole. High rates of population growth and the resulting disproportionately large share of young people in many developing countries translate into much greater pressure on job markets there. The world's labor force is projected to grow by almost 1 billion during the next two decades, mostly in developing countries hard-pressed to generate anywhere near adequate numbers of jobs. During the nineties, an additional 38 million people will seek employment each year in these countries. The uncertain and frequently negative prospects that many young adults face are likely to provoke a range of undesirable reactions: they may trigger self-doubt and apathy, cause criminal or deviant behavior, feed discontent that may burst open in street riots, or foment political extremism.[35]

Unemployment, underemployment, the threat of job loss, and the specter of eroding real wages are challenges for many workers across the globe, though the particular conditions and circumstances diverge widely in rich and poor countries. Failure to deal appropriately with sharpening social problems could have fatal political consequences. People whose hopes have worn thin, whose discontent is rising, and whose feelings of security have been stripped away are more likely to support extreme "solutions," and it is clear that some politicians stand ready to exploit the politics of fear.

In Rwanda, for instance, the Hutu leaders that planned and carried out the

---

genocide in 1994 relied strongly on heavily armed militias. Members of these militias were recruited primarily from among the uneducated, the unemployed, and young toughs. These were the people who had insufficient land to establish and support a family of their own and little prospect of finding a job outside agriculture. Their lack of hope for the future and low self-esteem were channeled by the extremists into an orgy of violence against those who supposedly were to blame for these misfortunes.[36]

Inequality, poverty, and lack of opportunity are, of course, nothing new. But today's polarization takes place when traditional support systems are weakening or falling by the wayside. In developing countries, there is an erosion of the bedrock of social stability—the webs and networks of support and reciprocal obligations found in extended family and community relationships (although these are admittedly often paternalistic and exploitative). In western industrial countries, the post–World War II welfare state that substituted or supplemented many family and community support functions has come under growing attack. The social fabric of many societies, whether affluent or destitute, is under greater strain as the paths of rich and poor diverge more sharply, and as the stakes of economic success or failure rise.

PEOPLE ON THE MOVE

The accelerating social, economic, and environmental pressures just described are at the root of large-scale population movements—both refugees and migrants—across the globe. The magnitude and speed with which these movements now take place in turn make people on the move an important factor in the amalgam of pressures and hence a potential contributor to conflict.

Anti-immigrant and anti-refugee feelings reflect the many pressures and insecurities that people everywhere are experiencing. Ours is an age in which global competition has vastly increased people's sense of economic vulnerability, in which social services and benefits are being pruned or slashed, and in which scarce land and water are increasingly being contested. Under such circumstances, the influx of large numbers of people is all too easily seen as menacing. Migrants or refugees are perceived as taking away jobs, imposing economic burdens, irredeemably altering the local culture and customs, or generally becoming unwelcome competitors for scarce resources and services. The experience of recent years shows how much political leaders in many countries have been tempted to use the issue of "outsiders" to seize or maintain political power.

The number of international refugees rose from slightly more than 1 million in the early sixties to about 3 million in the mid-seventies, and then soared to an estimated 27.4 million in 1995. But at least an equal number of people worldwide—and possibly many more—have been displaced within their own countries. These numbers do not even include people uprooted by environmental calamities or displaced by large-scale infrastructure projects. Over the past decade, for example, as many as 90 million people may have lost their homes to make way for dams, roads, and other development projects.[37]

Some 70 countries now have at least 10,000 refugees in their territories, but a relatively small number of countries account for the bulk of refugee populations. Adding together the ranks of the internationally and the internally displaced, the total number of the uprooted accounts for an astounding 63 percent of the population of Liberia, about

45 percent of Rwanda and Bosnia, and 20 percent of Afghanistan. With such enormous dislocations, there is little coherent society left to speak of.[38]

The other source of potential instability from people on the move is migration. The number of cross-border legal migrants is estimated to have reached about 100 million worldwide, while illegal migrants number anywhere from another 10 million to 30 million. More than 100 countries are now experiencing major migration outflows or inflows, according to the International Labour Organisation. A quarter of these nations are simultaneously a source and a recipient of migrants. Within countries, too, substantial flows of people can be seen, typically from rural to urban areas, and from poorer to more prosperous provinces. An estimated 20–30 million people migrate to cities within their own country each year.[39]

Over the past decade, as many as 90 million people may have lost their homes to dams, roads, and other development projects.

Traditionally, a sharp distinction has been made between migrants and refugees. Migrants are thought to leave largely of their own choosing, "pulled" by the prospect of a better job or higher earnings, whereas refugees are compelled to vacate their homes, "pushed" out by war, repression, or other factors beyond their control. But the categories are becoming blurred. People are increasingly leaving their homes for a mixture of reasons—both voluntary and involuntary. In some situations, migrants could be characterized as individuals who had the foresight to leave early, before local conditions deteriorated to the point where they were compelled to

move—that is, before human rights violations become massive, before economic conditions turned wretched, and before environmental deterioration made eking out an existence impossibly burdensome.[40]

A variety of forces are at work in uprooting people. They range from chronic violence and persecution to pervasive unemployment and disparities in wealth and income, land scarcities, unequal land distribution, and environmental degradation. Often, they operate not in isolation but in combination.

Among these factors, environment-related causes have to date received neither official recognition nor sufficient attention from the world's governments. For instance, desertification has uprooted one sixth of the populations of Mali and Burkina Faso. In Ethiopia, massive deforestation and soil erosion combined with population growth, inequitable land tenure systems, and inefficient agricultural practices to force large numbers of peasants out of the country's highland farming areas. Extremely unjust patterns of land distribution were behind the movement of Salvadoran peasants into neighboring Honduras that caused the two countries to go to war in 1969.[41]

Nobody knows how many people are being uprooted for environmental reasons—in part because there is not even an agreed-upon definition of the term, and in part because it is often hard to separate environmental from other causes. But it seems likely that the numbers of people affected will continue to rise, particularly as climate change proceeds.

Recent years have seen growing efforts, among both developing and industrial countries, to restrict the flow of migrants and refugees. But the movement of people is likely to increase sharply in coming years: The centrifugal forces of war, repression, and ethnic conflict remain strong in many countries and may lead to their violent disintegration. Degradation of critical ecosystems continues to undercut the livelihoods of tens, if not hundreds, of millions of people, while the full impact of climate change is yet to be felt. And the economies of many countries may be unable to provide anywhere near an adequate number of jobs for the rapidly growing ranks of young people. Restricting the flows of people—shutting people out—will not resolve the underlying problems humanity faces.

CONFLICTS BASED ON ENVIRONMENTAL AND SOCIAL STRESS

Unresolved environmental and social stresses have a detrimental effect on human security. But beyond generating hardships or uncertainty in the daily existence of many people, these stress factors also can lead to violent conflict.

On the whole, such conflict is more likely within than between individual countries. This is because the needs and interests of contending groups tied closely to land and environmental resources—peasants, pastoralists, ranchers, loggers, and other resource extractors— often remain unreconciled. These contending interests are typically bound up with issues of ethnicity, and people often clash over the kind of economic development to be pursued—small-scale versus large-scale, and subsistence versus commercial operations—and over the distribution of benefits derived. There is considerable scope for environmental scarcities and social inequities to feed on each other.

Large-scale resource extraction and infrastructure projects are often of questionable economic merit and have dev-

astating environmental impact. And they usually create two types of burdens: First, they lead to massive displacement of local populations because they disrupt traditional economic systems or render areas uninhabitable. Second, the environmental burden is disproportionately borne by these populations, even as they derive few, if any, economic benefits from these projects.

Typically, the affected populations are minority groups, indigenous peoples, and other vulnerable and impoverished communities such as subsistence peasants or nomadic tribes. Despite the ability of some celebrated cases to gain worldwide attention and support, the capacity of these groups to resist and defend their interests is very weak, and hence the consequence is more likely to be further marginalization than actual resistance and conflict.

One case that has received considerable attention, however, is on the island of Bougainville, where since 1988 guerrillas have been fighting a ferocious war of secession from Papua New Guinea. The conflict was triggered largely by the environmental devastation caused by copper mining. Mine tailings and pollutants covered vast areas of land, decimated harvests of cash and food crops including cocoa and bananas, and blocked and contaminated rivers, leading to depleted fish stocks. About one fifth of the island's total land area has been damaged during almost two decades of operations at the huge Panguna mine. The economic benefits went almost exclusively to the central government and foreign shareholders. Royalty payments to local landholders amounted to only 0.2 percent of the cash revenue of the mine, and compensation payments—for land leased and damage wrought—were seen as inadequate.[42]

Other struggles that have received notoriety include the battles of indigenous groups in Nigeria's delta region, who face a threat quite similar to that of Bougainvilleans. Among them, the Ogoni have waged a peaceful campaign demanding environmental cleanup and a fairer share of the economic benefits of oil production. Frequent oil spills, natural gas flaring, and leaks from toxic waste pits have exacted a heavy toll on soil, water, air, and human health. Much vegetation and wildlife has been destroyed; many Ogoni suffer from respiratory diseases and cancer, and birth defects are frequent. Despite huge oil revenues, the area remains impoverished. The military government responded to the Ogoni campaign with massive repression that destroyed several Ogoni villages, killed 2,000 people, and uprooted 80,000 more. The crackdown culminated in November 1995, when nine Ogoni activists were executed, despite international protests.[43]

The expected devastating impact of the gigantic Sardar-Sarovar dam project in India's Narmada river valley has also triggered intense opposition from affected communities. Close to 100,000 hectares of arable land would be flooded or lost to irrigation infrastructure. Aside from detrimental environmental and health consequences, the project is estimated to displace 240,000–320,000 people. The benefits would go to a small number of wealthy export farmers, while those displaced would come from among the Adivasi, an indigenous group. Marshalling broad international support for their cause, project opponents eventually compelled the World Bank to withdraw its crucial financial support. Some construction continues, but prospects for the project are uncertain.[44]

Throughout the Sahel, peasants and pastoralists are under pressure from large-scale commercial farming and ranching projects, bringing them into heightened conflict against each other and against outside encroachment. In the Sudan, the expansion of large-scale mechanized farming schemes displaced several million small producers. Some lost their land outright in expropriations; others were forced out indirectly by declining soil quality, the blockage of traditional herding routes, and the increasing scarcity of grazing areas. Because Sudan's fragile soils were rapidly exhausted, mechanized farming kept claiming fresh lands, a southward march seen increasingly as a hostile incursion by the local population. The dispute over mechanized farming was a key contributing factor to the renewed confrontation and civil war between north and south Sudan that broke out in 1983 and continues today.[45]

As noted earlier, unequal land distribution forces large numbers of landless or land-poor peasants to cultivate steep hillsides, rain forests, and other economically marginal and environmentally vulnerable areas. With land pressures high, competition among small peasants is intense, and confrontations with land barons, ranchers, and loggers lead to frequent land skirmishes.

In the Sudan, the dispute over mechanized farming was a key contributing factor to renewed confrontation and civil war.

In Brazil, peaceful efforts by the landless or near-landless to take over large, often idle estates have triggered bloody confrontations with landowners' private armies and with police forces controlled by local and state governments dominated by the big landowners. More than 1,000 persons have been killed in confrontations during the past 10 years. The pace of land occupations is accelerating; according to the key squatter organization Movimiento dos Trabalhadores Sem-Terra, some 85,000 landless families are currently involved.[46]

Takeovers by the landless have been met by wholesale repression in Central America, and they have caused endless skirmishes in a number of Mexican states. In Chiapas, a small number of farming and ranching elites control much of the best land. Among coffee producers, for instance, the top 0.15 percent (those with more than 100 hectares) own 12 percent of the coffee-growing land. Driving small peasants off their fields, cattle barons have made significant inroads since 1960; an estimated 45 percent of Chiapas's territory is now used as cattle pastureland.[47]

Most land struggles in Chiapas are taking place in the eastern half of the state. Virtually uninhabited until the mid-twentieth century, the region's Lacandón rain forest attracted waves of peasants fleeing land scarcity, dislocation from dam construction, and persecution where they competed not only with each other but also with loggers, ranchers, and oil prospectors.

Tree cover in the Lacandón declined from 90 percent in 1960 to 30 percent today, to the point that the border with neighboring Guatemala is clearly visible from space.[48]

With population growing rapidly and the distribution of arable land remaining highly inequitable, Chiapas has witnessed an intensifying conflict between desperate campesinos staging land takeovers and land barons unleashing private paramilitary bands and state police forces against the squatters. Land was a key issue behind the uprising of impoverished peasants, banding together in the Zapatista National Liberation Army, in January 1994.[49]

These struggles can be found in many regions around the world. But few efforts are on the horizon to address the many issues involved forthrightly. If anything, local and national governments are often ineffective or tend to side with those who already have power in these conflicts.

ELEMENTS OF A HUMAN SECURITY POLICY

Unlike traditional military security, human security is much less about procuring arms and deploying troops than it is about strengthening the social and environmental fabric of societies and improving their governance. To avoid the instability and breakdown now witnessed in countless areas around the globe, a human security policy must take into account a complex web of social, economic, environmental, and other factors.

There is much that national governments can do on their own to promote human security. But as important as these efforts are, human existence is paradoxically being shaped by both global and local trends. To be effective, national policies need to be complemented by improved international cooperation among countries and by a strengthening of civil society within countries. At the global level, a new bargain on social and environmental issues is crucial. At the local level, revitalizing communities and enhancing civil and human rights are essential. Achieving human security requires not only that global and local governance are improved, but that interaction between them be harmonized.

Global environmental governance is of increasing importance. During the past quarter-century, the number of international environmental treaties has skyrocketed—from about 50 in 1969 to 173 in 1994. Including less-binding types of accords and bilateral treaties, the number of international environmental instruments reaches almost 900. But many of these measures are weak on actual commitments. In fact, the gap between rhetoric and action is growing. Four years after the auspicious Earth Summit in Rio, international environmental diplomacy seems to have run out of steam due to a lack of political will. (See Chapter 1.) Breaking the logjam will take renewed commitment, innovations in environmental diplomacy (such as special incentives, differential obligations, and environmental alliances) to raise the global common denominator gradually, and increased financial support for developing countries.[50]

The 1995 World Social Summit in Copenhagen recognized—rhetorically, at any rate—that poverty, unemployment, and social disintegration are closely linked to issues of peace and security, and that there is an urgent need for a new global commitment, a global social compact, to reduce deep inequities that breed explosive social conditions, fuel ethnic antagonisms, and drive environmental decline.[51]

One key measure is more effective debt relief. Efforts by debtor nations to service their foreign loans have hemorrhaged their economies and increased the strain on an often already frayed social fabric—without even getting the countries off the debt treadmill. African governments now spend more than twice as much servicing foreign debts as they do on health and primary education for their people. Debt servicing has also led to environmentally disastrous resource extraction projects that put increased pressure on indigenous peoples and trigger evictions of small-scale farmers and pastoralists. So far, bilateral creditors have granted some rather modest debt relief, while multilateral creditors such as the World Bank and the IMF have been extremely slow to formulate a debt reduction plan of their own.[52]

Though hardly a new idea, another measure with multiple benefits is far-reaching redistribution of land. It would help counter the processes that fuel land wars and push the landless into ecologically fragile areas or into urban slums. In Brazil, for instance, so much land is left idle by absentee landlords that re-distributing it would virtually eliminate landlessness in that country. Redistributing land, guaranteeing secure land tenure, and improving the availability and quality of rural credit and extension services would help increase rural incomes, and thus transform what otherwise are unmet human needs into effective market demand. This in turn, as the experience of China and other East Asian countries has shown, helps stimulate industries that can provide much-needed employment outside agriculture. The resulting higher social and economic security is a crucial factor in restraining population growth.[53]

At the global level, a new bargain on social and environmental issues is crucial.

Equally important is the provision of credit to the urban and rural poor who are usually denied loans by commercial banks because of insufficient collateral. These micro-loans can help individuals and communities escape the poverty trap, and can generate jobs and income that will help communities gain a more secure footing so that they can again be anchors of society instead of sources of migrants and pools of festering resentment.[54]

Perhaps the best known example of micro-loans is the Grameen Bank in Bangladesh, which since 1983 has made loans to 2 million Bangladeshi families in 35,000 villages. This has inspired similar initiatives in countries around the world—from Guatemala to Ghana to Indonesia. The number of people served by micro-credit institutions—banks and cooperatives—has risen from 1 million in 1985 to about 10 million now. But this is still only a small percentage of those who are being denied credit by commercial banks.[55]

There are plans to convene a "micro-credit summit" in early 1997, in an effort to reach as many as 100 million of the world's poorest families by 2005. Even the World Bank, more known for its involvement in gargantuan projects, has now pledged some $200 million for micro-enterprises. Although the Bank's involvement is welcome, micro-credits probably work best if they continue to be administered and controlled at the grassroots level, rather than by a remote institution like the Bank.[56]

Safeguarding and enhancing the rights of citizens and communities—vis-à-vis both governments and corporations—is an integral component of a human security policy. Included here are traditional human rights and civil liberties such as freedom of expression and protection against government repression, as well as measures to ensure access to relevant information, to make corporate and bureaucratic decision making more transparent and accountable, and to improve community participation.[57]

At roughly $800 billion per year, military budgets worldwide are still bloated; they could easily shrink much further.

At a minimum, such rights will give communities tools to defend themselves against projects that imperil their well-being and existence, such as the Bougainville copper mine or the Sardar-Sarovar dam in India. But beyond purely defensive purposes lies a much greater realm: the active involvement of local communities in shaping development projects or other economic endeavors and in promoting good governance.

Although the struggle for human and civil rights, for transparency and accountability, is far from won, there is now an appreciable rise of civil society worldwide. The number of nongovernmental organizations (NGOs) is rising rapidly. NGOs are making inroads virtually everywhere, albeit often under threat of harassment, censorship, and violence in more repressive countries. And the phenomenon is not limited to individual nations: the independent Commission on Global Governance noted that the number of international NGOs (defined as those operating in at least three countries) grew from 176 in 1909 to 28,900 in 1993.[58]

NGOs have also played a crucial role in conflict prevention efforts. And a growing number of them are getting involved in a closely related area: promoting more democratic forms of governance and facilitating the emergence of more pluralistic, accountable societies. Actors as diverse as the Soros Foundation's Open Society Institute, the New York–based Committee to Protect Journalists, the German Friedrich Ebert Foundation, and the new Stockholm-based Institute for Democracy and Electoral Assistance are involved in a broad variety of activities ranging from political institution building and electoral support to legislative and judicial assistance and aiding the emergence of an active, viable civil society.[59]

Finance is the last key element in a human security policy. It is time to strike a new balance in our security investments—a balance that curtails the excessive reliance on traditional military means, promotes disarmament and the elimination of surplus arms, and corrects massive social and environmental investment deficits. Policies to prevent social breakdown, environmental degradation, and violent conflict require some substantial upfront investments, but they would cost much less than current reactive security policies. Moreover, they would help avoid the costly emergency measures that arise when societies splinter and disintegrate—measures that are already crowding out badly needed human security investments.

Building an alternative security system—based on far-reaching disarmament, demobilization of soldiers, conversion of arms factories, more effective peacekeeping, and nonviolent conflict resolution—might require some $40 billion annually. The global social and environmental investment needs—encompassing such areas as preventing soil erosion, providing safe drinking water, eliminating malnourishment, and providing adequate shelter—will take a larger amount, perhaps some $200 billion annually for several years.[60]

Where would the money come from to pay for these programs? We live in an era of anti-tax fervor and public belt-tightening, and hence the prospects for substantial additional resources are clouded at best. But large sums could be found by changing priorities within government budgets and by shifting resources. At roughly $800 billion per year, military budgets worldwide are still bloated; they could easily shrink much further than they have in the early post–cold war period and hence free up substantial revenues. For instance, a disarmament budget of $40 billion could be financed by cutting in half the amount that governments worldwide spend each year on military R&D alone.[61]

Development aid can play an important role in improving human security, yet it is often not targeted at the most appropriate areas. Calculations by the U.N. Development Programme indicate that even a modest reprioritization of

existing funds (under its proposal for a 20:20 Compact on Human Development) would increase the money going to human priority areas by about $40 billion a year.[62]

Debt relief could be another mechanism for mobilizing human security funds. If their foreign debts were cancelled (the full repayment is doubtful anyway), the 32 most severely indebted low-income countries worldwide would save some $10 billion a year in debt-servicing payments. It is time for lenders to cancel the bulk of the debts owed by these governments—some $200 billion—in exchange for a human security conditionality: commitments by the debtors to reduce their military expenditures and armed forces, and to invest resources that otherwise would have gone into debt servicing in areas of social and environmental need.[63]

Public flows of money are only part of the picture. At about $167 billion in 1995, private foreign direct investment was about three times as large as development aid. But public policy needs to set the parameters within which private flows of money can serve environmental and social needs far better than they do now—by setting appropriate standards and rules and providing incentives.[64]

Devoting greater resources to demilitarization, environmental sustainability, and social well-being may be regarded as incurring unwelcome expenses. Yet they constitute a set of highly beneficial, mutually reinforcing, and long overdue investments. Put simply, the choice before humanity is pay now or pay much more later. The cost of failing to advance human security is already escalating.

8

Reforming Subsidies

David Malin Roodman

In California's Central Valley, farmers can buy a thousand cubic meters of water from a federal project—enough to irrigate a few hundred square meters of vegetables—for $2.84, even though it costs the government $24.84 to deliver that water. Thanks to fertile soil and favorable climate, however, the water is actually worth at least $80–160 in the Valley, based on what nearby farmers pay for water from the state government. Cheap water was originally meant to give small farms in the United States a financial boost (though perhaps not one as big as this), but many large ones also benefit.[1]

In Indonesia, well-connected generals and business executives get rich buying logging concessions on a third of the country's territory at a third or less of actual value. Though the concessions are offered in the name of economic development, the resulting logging is attack-

ing the livelihoods of many rain forest residents and may slow overall growth even as conventionally measured—that is, before the loss of natural wealth is factored in. (See Chapter 6.)[2]

Both these stories are part of a larger pattern. Around the world, government policies shunt at least $500 billion a year toward activities that harm the environment, from overfishing to overgrazing. The full amount may be much greater: few countries have even tried to assess the magnitude of the subsidies they create, and none has completely succeeded. With the global tax burden standing at roughly $7.5 trillion a year, subsidies effectively elevate taxes—on wages, profits, and consumer spending—by at least 7 percent. Increased taxes on work, investment, and consumption are in turn discouraging these activities, placing a drag on the global economy. And this is an era of supposed worldwide fiscal austerity.[3]

An enumeration of the side effects of all these subsidies virtually catalogs today's environmental problems. (See Table 8–1.) Of course, governments

An expanded version of this chapter appeared as Worldwatch Paper 133, *Paying the Piper: Subsidies, Politics, and the Environment.*

Table 8–1. Selected Subsidies That Have Harmful Side Effects, by Activity

Activity	Examples of Subsidies	Side Effects
Mineral production	Low or zero royalties on oil and other minerals; aid for coal production in Germany, Russia, and other industrial countries.	Stimulating effects of low royalties are minimal, but those of subsidies to uncompetitive industries are significant, abetting climate change, acid rain, and landscape destruction.
Logging	Low timber royalties in developing countries; below-cost sales in North America and Australia.	Stimulating effects of low royalties are minimal, but below-cost sales accelerate deforestation and siltation of streams, and increase floods.
Fishing	Billions of dollars per year in subsidies for fuel, equipment, and general income support for fishers worldwide.	Promote overfishing, thus reducing catch, employment, and viability of marine ecosystems in the long run.
Agricultural Inputs	$13 billion a year lost on public irrigation projects in developing countries; billions more lost in industrial ones; subsidies for pesticides and fertilizers in some developing countries.	Encourage water waste, salinization; also higher rates of pesticide and fertilizer use, and thus pesticide poisonings among farm workers, soil degradation, and water pollution.
Crop and Livestock Production	$302 billion in annual support for farmers in western industrial countries; low fees for grazing on public lands in North America and Australia; tax breaks for land clearance in Brazil until 1988.	Encourage environmentally destructive farming and overgrazing.
Energy Use	$101 billion in fossil fuel and power subsidies in developing countries each year; comparable losses in former communist and western industrial nations.	Contribute to energy-related problems ranging from particulate emissions to climate change.

SOURCE: Worldwatch Institute, based on sources cited in text.

rarely set out to degrade the environment when they create these support systems. Rather, they offer most of them in the name of stimulating economic development, protecting rural communities dependent on resource-intensive industries, enhancing national security through energy or food independence, or helping the poor.

Unfortunately, it is hard to find a subsidy for environmentally destructive activities that does much good, and does so at reasonable cost. Some strive for obsolete or questionable goals. Others are largely ineffective. Still others have been undone by the very environmental destruction they encourage. Almost all others reach their intended beneficiaries to some extent, but only inefficiently: much of the money leaks into the hands of people who need it less.

In sum, most of these subsidies, as currently implemented, invite a four-pronged indictment: they fail on their own terms, they increase the cost of government, the higher taxes they engender discourage work and investment, and they hurt the environment. Clearly then, subsidy reform is an essential first step toward ensuring a just future for our children. It makes little sense for societies to begin making the polluter pay—as they ultimately must in order to achieve environmental sustainability—unless we first stop paying the polluter.

SUBSIDIES: HOW AND WHY

Few government policies are as unpopular in theory and as popular in practice as subsidies. The very word can cause economists to shudder, make taxpayers fume, deepen the cynicism of the poor, and enrage environmentalists. Yet to judge by the budgets and natural resource policies of governments around the world, subsidies are in permanent fashion.

A subsidy is defined here as a government policy that alters market risks, rewards, and costs in ways that favor certain activities or groups. The most visible subsidies are direct government payments that help hold down prices for consumers or prop them up for producers. Subsidies also take a dizzying variety of less obvious forms—ones that can be just as costly and are actually more popular with politicians because of their low visibility. Many subsidies, for example, accrue through special tax breaks. Whether subsidies elevate government spending or reduce government income, though, it is the general taxpayer—or more precisely, the unsubsidized taxpayer—who must ultimately bear their costs.

Subsidies also arise subtly when governments sell services and resources for less than it costs to provide them (as in the case of most public irrigation water) or for less than they are worth (low interest charges on loans for ranching in the rain forest). Or to take another nearly universal example, despite the accumulating reams of free trade treaties, most governments still aid domestic industries with tariffs and import quotas. The cost of protection mostly passes on to consumers through higher prices.

Another important but difficult-to-evaluate subsidy results when governments take on private risks. Early in the history of civilian nuclear power, for example, the U.S. government capped utilities' liability for damage from nuclear power plant accidents and assumed the rest of the risk itself, free of charge. Since the likelihood and costs of a nuclear accident are impossible to evaluate reliably, no private insurance company will take on the risk. Without this ongoing subsidy, the industry would never have developed and could not operate today. The subsidy is then, in a sense, invaluable to the industry.[4]

Similarly incalculable are the subsidies that occur when public authorities dedicate government-controlled land to commercial activities such as logging or mining at the expense of alternative uses of the same land—say, the various life-sustaining activities of indigenous peoples—that may be less commercially competitive but not necessarily less worthwhile. Indeed, the very idea of economic value begins to stretch thin when extended to such forced transfers of property rights. Economic value is based on the assumption of voluntary exchange: to say that something is worth a thousand dollars is to say that people would freely surrender it for that much money. But how do we calculate, for example, the costs in dollar terms to indigenous Dayak people in the Malaysian state of Sarawak of government sanctions for logging on their homelands?[5]

Some conservatives attack all subsidies as market manipulations destined to do more harm than good. Giving free play to Adam Smith's "invisible hand," they argue, is the best way to make an economy work for society. But there are good reasons to subsidize. Real economies never perform as perfectly as the unfettered ones in economic theories. One of the most widely acknowledged faults is the tendency toward oligopoly: the dominance of an industry by a few large companies, which tends to reduce competition and innovation over the long term. Even if such faults could be corrected, economists acknowledge that what they term efficient outcomes in textbooks—those that maximize material wealth—can end up working against collective visions of how society should be shaped, by allowing abject poverty to continue, for example. Both kinds of shortcomings of the market—its imperfections in practice and its inadequacies

even in theory—are cause for government intervention.[6]

Nevertheless, the impulse behind conservatives' skepticism is a healthy one. It is important to examine existing and potential subsidies carefully for effectiveness and worth. To the extent that subsidies reach unintended beneficiaries, create unintended incentives, or serve obsolete ends, they burden society with heavy environmental and financial costs.

To be most effective, subsidies need to be sharply targeted. They should reach only those meant to be helped. They should cease when they are no longer needed. Most fundamentally their benefits must justify their full direct financial and indirect environmental costs. Such principles are straightforward. Yet the reality is that few subsidies obey them. Many are ineffective or, because of poor targeting, inefficient, especially once the full direct and indirect costs are considered.

To be most effective, the benefits of subsidies must justify their full direct and indirect costs.

The remainder of this chapter considers subsidies with major environmental effects, which can be roughly broken into four categories, based on the policy goals best ascribed to them: stimulating overall economic development; protecting domestic industries for the sake of national security or workers; cutting costs for consumers, particularly the poor; and developing new technologies. Space constraints prevent discussion here of an important fifth category—the subsidies for car-dependent sprawl that arise when governments hide the cost of roads and road-related services. Almost all these subsidies are ripe for reform.

PERPETUATING THE COWBOY ECONOMY

In 1966, at a time when humanity was still recovering from the shock of seeing pictures of earth from space, economist Kenneth Boulding predicted that the insight of that moment would eventually penetrate the very workings of modern societies. The "cowboy" economies that increasingly characterized human civilization—economies that treated natural resources as limitless—were on a collision course with environmental limits. The day would come when they would need to transform into "spaceman" economies that, somewhat like astronauts do, would respect tight environmental limits, conserving resources and recycling waste. The longer societies delayed in embarking on this transition, Boulding noted, the more difficult it would be and the longer would economies tear at their own environmental supports.[7]

The oldest and perhaps most environmentally destructive subsidies now in place are the ones that effectively deny the inevitability of this transformation—those that artificially stimulate resource-intensive industries such as logging, mining, and livestock raising in the name of economic growth. The roots of modern subsidies for such activities lie in the histories of the nations settled by European emigrants, including Australia, Canada, and the United States. With their frontier days over, the special supports that these countries once gave such industries are ever harder to justify. Yet many live on.

The U.S. government alone has given away 400 million hectares over its history—half the country's continental expanse—and offers cheap access to millions more for some resource-based activities. Hardrock mining is still essentially free on a large fraction of public land in the United States and Canada.

In 1994, for instance, a Canadian concern bought 790 hectares of federal land in Goldstrike, Nevada, for $5,190; the tract contained gold worth $10 billion once mined—2 million times as much. All told, since 1873 U.S. taxpayers have forgone roughly $242 billion (in 1995 dollars) in potential mineral royalties on federal lands, equal to $900 per U.S. citizen and enough to pay off a twentieth of the accumulated federal debt. They have also accepted an estimated $33–72 billion in liability for environmental cleanup at abandoned mines.[8]

Not only do livestock and timber companies get access to government lands; they also get direct government assistance with their operations. Were the costs of this assistance passed back to the beneficiaries, logging and grazing on much public land would become unprofitable, and would cease. The U.S. and British Columbia governments, for example, lose millions of dollars managing public rangelands, only partly because they lease the lands at roughly a third of private rates.[9]

Government timber sales in parts of the United States and Australia, especially where young trees or steep terrain make logging expensive, bring in less than agencies spend administering the concessions, particularly building logging roads. Annual losses on forest administration hovered in the range of $300–400 million in the United States in the early nineties. In effect, the general taxpayer is paying timber companies to raze public forests. The biggest money-loser is the Tongass National Forest in Alaska, the world's largest remaining temperate rain forest. Providing roads and other services to private clearcutting operations there cost the government $389 million between 1982 and 1988, yet earned it only $32 million. In the Australian state of Victoria, the pattern is strikingly similar: there the government is losing some $170 million a year on net. Losses like these lead to the perverse conclusion that taxpayers would be better off banning such resource-intensive activities on many public lands and splitting the savings with industry—in other words, paying ranchers not to ranch and loggers not to log.[10]

There is little doubt that these generous resource giveaways have met their historical purpose of spurring European settlement of the parts of the New World. Indeed, they have contributed mightily to transformation of cultural and physical landscapes. Thousands of indigenous communities have been eliminated or squeezed onto small reservations. The ranges of many native species, such as the buffalo, have also shrunk to fragments. In the continental United States, 95 percent of the forests, including most public ones, have been logged at least once. In Australia and the arid American West, overgrazing of cattle has robbed land of much vegetative cover, freeing soils to erode and turning thousands of streams into muddy gullies.[11]

But since these subsidies were adopted, many of the economies of regions once dominated by resource-intensive industries have undergone dramatic transformations, making the subsidies increasingly archaic. Small-time miners and loggers have given way to mining and logging multinationals—established companies that, like other firms, should largely be expected to stand or fall on their own. Meanwhile, a new breed of settler is appearing. Service and manufacturing companies are moving in, attracted by the quality of the natural environment.

In the United States, western counties with open space are among the fastest growing in the country. In the resource-rich states of Idaho, Oregon, and Washington and the province of British Columbia, for example, 1 in 12 workers in 1969 made a living quarrying minerals, felling trees, or milling lumber; by 1993, 1 in 25 did. Public attitudes reflect this economic shift. A recent poll in the United States reported that 59 percent of adults opposed expanding mining and grazing on public lands; only 26 percent supported it.[12]

Though industrial countries have reached something of a dead end on the cowboy-style economic path, poorer countries have eagerly followed in their footsteps. As the colonial era finally came to a close at mid-century, the new governments in Latin America, Africa, and developing Asia adopted patterns of resource ownership and management from their colonial rulers. They claimed 80 percent of the world's tropical forests from traditional forest residents and owners, equally high shares of the minerals and water within their borders, and much of the land as well. Many began cashing in these natural resources, usually for much less than they were worth, hoping to jump-start economic development. Developing countries now mine four times as much unprocessed copper concentrate as they did in 1955, pump six times as much oil, and fell seven times as much timber for nonfuel use.[13]

Since 1873, U.S. taxpayers have forgone roughly $242 billion (in 1995 dollars) in potential mineral royalties on federal lands.

Although policymakers usually have argued that the transfer of resources into the hands of commercial industries stimulates economic growth, the results generally have been slower growth and more poverty. The more a developing country's economy depended on primary resource exports in 1971—that is, the more it seemingly played off of its inherited strengths—the less it had grown in per capita terms by 1989, according to a statistical analysis by Jeffrey Sachs and Andrew Warner, economists at Harvard University. On average, in fact, an increase of 17 percentage points in the share of primary resource exports in gross domestic product (GDP) in 1971 corresponded to a drop of 1 percentage point in average annual growth over the period. Meanwhile, resource-poor countries like South Korea and Taiwan experienced robust and lasting economic growth.[14]

One cause of this disappointment has been that unnecessarily low selling prices for public resources have meant much less potential funding for government investment in infrastructure, education, public health, and family planning—the very sort of funding that developing countries routinely seek from the World Bank and international donors.

The forgone revenues have often been glaring in the logging industry. Finding and cutting timber—which is not much harder than taking a walk in the woods—can be a quick, profitable business, making cheap logging concessions ideal for political patronage. For example, the government in Indonesia, a country pervaded by corruption, has sold timber concessions at a third or less of market value on a third of the country's territory since the late sixties. In 1990, it captured only 17 percent of the value of trees sold, earning $416 million. If the ratio of real to potential revenues had matched that for its oil concessions—85 percent—the government would have earned another $2.1 billion, equal to 40 percent of its foreign aid that year. Instead, the money mostly wound up in the bank accounts of a few dozen timber magnates with close ties to President Suharto and his family. Concession prices have been similarly low among other tropical timber exporters, including Côte d'Ivoire, Ghana, Malaysia, and the Philippines,

largely because of close ties between industry and policymakers.[15]

Indeed, since extractive industries are particularly hard on the environment, their longest-lasting local effects are often the destructive ones. Fencing of grazing lands for commercial cattle ranchers in Botswana has cut into the traditional range of native pastoralists. From Brazil to Côte d'Ivoire to the Solomon Islands, government sanctions for logging and incentives for forest clearance for ranches and farms have contributed substantially to deforestation, species loss, and the disintegration of indigenous cultures.[16]

Thus, as in industrial countries, natural resource subsidies in the developing world have done little to address contemporary economic priorities. Because they have rarely worked, and because they have often worsened the situation of the poorest of the poor, government resource giveaways need to be scaled back. The track record of most such subsidies in terms of slow growth, environmental damage, and impoverishment and violation of the human rights of local peoples is abysmal. Economy and society would be better off if local peoples were granted more control over their lands, and if resources were always sold at full value in order to better fund education, health care, and infrastructure—all vital ingredients in sustainable and equitable economic development.

DIKES AGAINST A RISING SEA

Though most resource extraction subsidies have been defended in the name of economic progress, some have served a more conservative impulse: to stem the economic tide when it turns against a resource-based industry. The most common rationales for protectionism are that it saves consumers from the apparent dangers of import dependence and it shields workers from job loss. However well intended, these subsidies—like most others—have usually been unnecessary, poorly implemented, or doomed by circumstances to failure.

In the case of subsidies meant to stave off the dangers of import dependence, too often the slogan of "national security" has substituted for careful thinking about when they are really necessary. Concentration of two thirds of the world's oil reserves in one volatile region is clearly a long-term threat to the economic stability of petroleum importers. But the sources of most other commodities, such as crops and coal, are scattered around the planet much better; here the dangers of import dependence are less clear-cut. Indeed, diversity of supply is often the key to security in the business world. More broadly, trade can increase the economic interdependence of nations, and perhaps reduce the likelihood of war or economic embargoes. In this light, it is ironic that the European Union, founded on the notion that trade begets security, dedicates most of its budget to what is probably the world's largest protectionist subsidy regime—the Common Agricultural Policy, at $97 billion a year.[17]

In the argument for protectionism on behalf of workers, the starting point has been that farmers, fishers, loggers, and miners have always led particularly insecure lives. Indeed, in recent decades, their jobs have proved more vulnerable than most to the steady march of automation. Worse, in many regions, the industries have literally run themselves into the ground by exhausting the resources on which they depend. The fact that resource-based industries such as logging and coal mining are overwhelmingly rural, giving rise to small, single-industry towns from the Oregon woods to the coal region of Vorkuta in the Russian Arctic, intensifies

the insecurity of individual workers. When the job bases shrivel, so, often, do the towns: many families must choose between unemployment and emigration. Thus industrial nations have often subsidized extractive activities in the belief that economic security for local communities is sometimes worth paying for.

Unfortunately, most of the subsidies granted in the name of either national security or job security have been far too costly to taxpayers, consumers, and the environment for the amount of good done. One problem—a partly avoidable one—has been clumsy targeting. For example, Germany, Japan, and some other industrial countries subsidize domestic coal production by the ton, not by the worker. Thus some of the subsidies end up in the pockets of investors, not laborers. As for subsidies in the name of national security, some have actually succeeded only too well, turning the dream of self-sufficiency into a nightmare of costly surpluses.[18]

The most spectacularly inappropriate targeting can be found in agriculture. One of the most universally echoed rationales for food production subsidies is that they are essential to the preservation of the family farm. Yet these rarely favor small farmers against large ones and farming corporations. In the United States, despite the intentions of the Depression-era program to shore up the family farm, most payments are based on how much food farmers grow, not how small their farms are. Not surprisingly, the number of U.S. farms fell by two thirds between 1930 and 1990, even as grain elevators bulged with millions of tons of surplus food. As a result of this concentration in ownership, 84 percent of the agricultural support payments—$8.5 billion—went to the top 30 percent of farms in 1991, ranked by gross income.[19]

It is true that production subsidies have enhanced the food self-sufficiency of most industrial countries, something particularly valued in the European Union, where memories still linger of wartime scarcities and international supply lines cut off by German U-boats. But the food subsidies have done far more than that. Today, chickens, sheep, pigs, and cattle eat 57 percent of the European Union's grain output, for example. Another 7 percent gets exported. Thus people in the European Union are producing three times as much grain as they eat. Clearly the subsidies have gone far beyond ensuring basic food security for the region in times of emergency.[20]

In Germany, it would be cheaper to shut down the mines and pay miners a handsome salary not to work.

In all western industrial countries, governments have historically attempted to limit food surpluses and found themselves drawn into a quicksand of market controls. They began by buying up surpluses and taking large losses by dumping them on international markets or even destroying them outright. The dumping depressed global prices, raising the cost of domestic price guarantees even further. To limit costs, countries began requiring farmers to take land out of production, sometimes actually paying farmers not to farm. (This did, however, give many tracts an ecologically valuable breather from intensive farming.) Constricting food supply lifted prices, costing consumers. In 1995, governments in western industrial countries spent $180 billion of taxpayers' money on agriculture, and effectively transferred another $122 billion from consumers to producers through high prices, for an average total of $22,000 per farmer—with richer farmers getting even more. Put otherwise, government policy inflated the food

budget of a family of four in these countries by an average $1,500.[21]

Subsidies for fishing have also been costly. The global fishing industry appears to have hemorrhaged red ink during most of the seventies and eighties, with losses reaching roughly $54 billion in 1989, or 44 percent of expenditures. Much of that gap, though no one knows exactly how much, was probably covered by government subsidies for purchases of boat fuel and fishing equipment, as well as general income support. But subsidies are one reason there are now enough boats, hooks, and nets to catch roughly twice the available fish supply—a gross imbalance that is generating powerful pressures for overfishing. Thirteen of the 15 major oceanic fisheries are in decline because fish are being hauled in faster than they reproduce. As a result, the global oceanic fish catch today stands at around 84 million tons a year, compared with an estimated potential of 100 million. In the increasingly vociferous battles over fishing rights, the livelihoods of the world's 14–20 million small fishers stand in the greatest peril.[22]

Incentives that miss workers and overstimulate output can be amended. But even if they are, many subsidies for resource-based industries will still face daunting odds, for some of the forces that threaten employment and production in domestic industries grow inexorably over the years. Like dikes built against a rising sea, offsetting subsidies have to rise just to stay even. It then becomes only a matter of time before they price themselves out of justifiability.

Some of these rising pressures threaten employment, but not output. Resource-intensive industries are inherently risky because of dependence on the weather, commodity price swings, and the uncertainties of minerals exploration. And riskiness favors large companies, which can survive lean years more easily than small ones can.[23]

The second strike against workers in such industries is automation, which makes it ever cheaper to substitute capital for labor, and which exploits economies of scale. For example, the average number of workers in the United States needed to fell and mill 9,400 cubic meters of lumber in a year declined from 20 to 16 during the eighties. And with the newest mills, the number is only 9. This is a major reason that the U.S. timber industry lost 10,000 jobs in the eighties even though the federal government sold enough timber from public forests—much of it below cost—to boost the national harvest to record levels.[24]

In industries based on nonrenewable resources, there is a third inexorable trend: the depletion of the resource itself. Multimillion-dollar tax breaks for domestic U.S. oil producers, for instance, did not keep their market share from slipping below 50 percent in the nineties as reserves gradually dwindled.[25]

The hard coal industry in Germany is experiencing some of these forces in combination. The country's sole deposit snakes from the Ruhr River to the Dutch border. As miners have delved ever deeper into this seam, the costs in time and equipment needed to raise a ton of coal have climbed, pushing up the price of protection. In addition, productivity—output per worker—has lagged behind the average for the entire economy, which is one reason that earnings in the industry have climbed much slower than wages. In 1982, the government granted the industry $30 in subsidies for each ton of coal it sold (in 1995 dollars); by 1995, the figure had nearly quadrupled to $119. Since total subsidies climbed only a little over half as much—from $2.9 billion to $6.9 billion—production had to fall 39 percent and employment 49 percent. Overall, the cost of protecting a mining job for a year with per-ton subsidies rose from $15,400 to an extraordinary $72,800. (See Figure 8–1.) It would

Figure 8–1. Western German Hard Coal Subsidies and Employment, 1982–95

be cheaper now to shut down the mines and pay miners a handsome salary not to work.[26]

The costs of these subsidized industries include more than just direct financial outlays. There are also indirect environmental costs. For example, agricultural runoff and seepage of fertilizers and pesticides are major sources of groundwater pollution in many countries. Studies in the United States and Europe have found clear associations between the level of subsidies in a region and the amount of farm chemicals used. As societies confront such environmental problems, subsidies for the industries that cause them will become increasingly hard to justify.[27]

The task for policymakers in reforming protectionist subsidies is threefold. First, they need to decide whether protection is needed and can deliver on its promises. In the case of oil production in oil-importing countries, for example, it essentially cannot, for they will only accelerate depletion of domestic reserves. Security arguments also generally seem weak for the current levels of support that many countries give to the production of coal, food, and other commodities. Many countries find themselves with surpluses of the commodities, with numerous potential suppliers scattered around the world, or both.

Second, they need to assess the potential gains from better targeting. In agriculture, just dropping the top-grossing farms from the subsidy rolls would cut budgetary costs dramatically, boost small farms, and reduce the artificial incentive for environmentally destructive farming. Basing the remaining subsidies on income rather than output—in effect, converting them to welfare payments—would improve effectiveness even more.

And finally, policymakers need to decide if, given such improvements, subsidies' benefits are worth the costs. There are no formulas for performing these cost-benefit comparisons or for determining exactly how fast transitional subsidies should be ended. Clearly though, it is generally best if subsidy phaseouts that seriously threaten single-industry communities or regions occur gradually. In some cases, the industries themselves can be shut down quickly while the subsidies continue for a few years, paying for worker retraining and providing incentives for new business start-ups. Losing a job is almost always hard on a family, and losing an employer in a small community is even worse. But the sooner societies make these course corrections, the more gently they can do it.

Shotgun Subsidies

In 1992, around the time world leaders were signing the first international treaty on climate change at the Earth Summit in Rio de Janeiro, two economists at the World Bank in Washington, D.C., decided to perform a simple mathematical exercise. Bjorn Larsen and Anwar

Shah gathered information on what people paid for energy in countries such as the United States, China, and the Soviet Union—those that burned most of the world's fossil fuels, which are the major source of the greenhouse gas carbon dioxide. They found that particularly in centrally planned countries, coal, oil, and natural gas cost much less than they did on world markets—a sure sign of subsidies. When they multiplied the price differences by the amount of fuel bought, they came up with a staggering figure. Collectively, the signatories to the climate treaty paid their own citizens more than $200 billion in 1991 alone to use fossil fuels and thus to emit carbon. To put that figure in perspective, only 15 nations earned that much in 1991.[28]

Though communist countries were the primary subsidizers of fossil fuels in the early nineties, almost all countries actually subsidize flows of energy and water in the name of holding down the cost of living for consumers, particularly poor ones. The poor typically spend proportionally more of their income than the rich on basic necessities such as fuel, drinking water, and irrigation-fed crops, and so can benefit proportionally more from subsidies for these commodities. In Indonesian cities, for example, the poorest one fifth of households spend 15 percent of their income on energy for lighting and cooking, while the top one fifth spend only 8 percent.[29]

But like subsidies meant to protect resource-based employment, most subsidies intended to help the poor suffer from clumsy targeting. They are, in effect, shotgun subsidies, implemented through across-the-board price controls that benefit the rich at least as much as the poor. Since there are other, more effective and efficient ways to aid the poor, ways that do not hurt the environment, these subsidies seem greatly overused. They may deserve a role in national budgets, but not one nearly so large.

As Larsen and Shah reported, governments in the former Eastern bloc spent lavishly to hold down the apparent price of energy. According to figures updated in 1995, these countries spent $135–180 billion in 1991—some 10 percent of GDP—to keep fuel costs to just a fraction of what they were in the West. Electricity subsidies totalled another $34–39 billion. Not surprisingly, signs of energy waste abounded, from grossly inefficient factories to overheated apartment buildings, where residents' only way of cooling off in winter was to open windows. Since then, however, market reforms and tight budgets have led these countries to phase many subsidies out. In Russia, energy prices for industry approached world levels in 1995, which partly explains why energy use and air pollution have dropped sharply. Because industry in formerly communist countries received such a large share of the energy subsidies measured by Larsen and Shah, it also seems likely that the global total has fallen substantially since 1991. However, backed by continuing subsidies, electricity prices for Russian consumers have held steady at 15 percent of world levels, while those for natural gas have actually fallen, from 11 percent of the world rate to an essentially nominal 1 percent.[30]

Developing countries also subsidize energy. They spent an estimated $65 billion in 1991 to fund price controls for fossil fuels, including kerosene, a major heating and lighting source for many low-income people, and diesel fuel, used in the public buses that are an important transport mode for the poor. Price controls also drove electricity prices down in developing countries from an average 7.6¢ per kilowatt-hour, where they had stood in the early eighties, to an average 5.2¢ by 1988 (in 1995 dollars)—about three fifths the true cost of additional supplies. Developing countries had to grant power companies some

$46 billion in handouts in 1991 to cover the losses from low prices.[31]

Western industrial countries also offer their energy industries financial support. In Italy, government appropriations and tax breaks effectively provide a fifth of the power industry's revenue. In addition to free nuclear accident insurance, the U.S. government offers utilities and fossil fuel producers a clutch of tax breaks worth some $5 billion a year. And it sells power from its own dams and nuclear plants so cheaply that it takes a loss of $4.4 billion each year.[32]

Globally, subsidies for water have been huge too. Indeed, it is almost unheard of for a public water project to come close to covering its costs. The U.S. government spent an estimated $45–93 billion more than it earned on public irrigation projects between 1902 and 1986 (in 1995 dollars). Costs in Australia and the former Soviet Union were similarly massive. In developing countries such as China, India, and Pakistan, public water projects lose an estimated $13 billion annually.[33]

It is almost unheard of for a public water project to come close to covering its costs.

Budgetary losses, however, understate the magnitude of many of these subsidies, since water and electricity from many projects are worth more than it costs to deliver them. It might seem fair for governments to charge just enough to cover their costs, and not make a profit even when they could. But selling something for less than it is worth encourages waste and bestows windfalls on resource recipients. Meanwhile, it forces governments to keep conventional taxes higher than they otherwise would need to be, which hurts an economy by discouraging work and investment. Farmers in California's Central Valley are already making a profit using water they buy from other sources at prices much higher than the federal government's, so selling water for what it is worth will affect food production much less than might be expected. Thus these irrigation subsidies emerge as little more than billion-dollar transfers from the pockets of taxpayers to those of a few lucky farmers.[34]

Low water and power charges have encouraged practices such as electric home heating and the cultivation of water-intensive crops like rice and alfalfa in arid regions—practices that often do not make economic sense once the full value of these resources is accounted for. Excessive power demand has contributed to the many side effects of energy use, from acid rain to global warming. And the illusion of cheap water has driven demand for ever more irrigation projects. Yet diverting large fractions of rivers has disrupted aquatic ecosystems by changing the amount and timing of water flows. Meanwhile, flushing huge amounts of water through agricultural lands has caused waterlogging and salinization. In the former Soviet Union, one third of irrigated land has been seriously damaged.[35]

Moreover, direct price controls on energy and water help the poor, if that is their intent, only inefficiently. Though higher-income people may spend less on energy, water, and food from irrigated lands relative to their means, they almost always spend more in absolute terms— and so receive more of the subsidies. In Argentina, Chile, Costa Rica, and Uruguay, for example, the richest fifth of the population each receives 30–50 percent more in water subsidies than the poorest fifth. The distribution of electricity subsidies tends to be even more skewed toward middle- and upper-income brackets, since these groups have better access to electricity and more appliances.[36]

Even among the poor, the benefits of cheap energy and water often accrue unevenly. Two billion people in developing countries have no electricity; a billion still lack access to clean water at any price. Moreover, particularly in rural areas, many people depend on traditional fuels such as wood and dung, thus missing out on kerosene subsidies meant for them. Similarly, limited access to clean water can result in tremendous disparities in welfare. One World Bank survey of 16 cities found that the residents forced to buy bottled water from street vendors paid 25 times as much on average as those with access to piped supplies. In rural areas, women and children in families without utility connections spend hours each day collecting fuel and water.[37]

Thus, almost all across-the-board supports for energy and water purchases seem badly misdirected. In countries where many people still lack access to power and clean water, governments would do better providing these to those without access instead of cutting prices for those who already have it. Where access is nearly universal, energy and water subsidies should perhaps be retained, but restricted to the poor. If societies want to help the poor buy food, then they should subsidize that directly and specifically. For without effective targeting, subsidies meant to redistribute wealth toward the poor defeat their own purpose.

FOSTERING TECHNOLOGIES FOR SUSTAINABILITY

One of the most fundamental flaws of today's economies is that they often insulate businesses and consumers from the environmental side effects of their actions. Even though one person's contribution to acid rain or smog harms other people's health and property, there is no practical way for the "victims" and "perpetrator" to meet in court or strike a compromise, especially since some of the victims are not even born yet. As a result, environmental destruction often seems cheap or free to its beneficiaries: in effect, they are cross-subsidized by the people whom they harm. Government intervention is indispensable to ending this self-destructive pattern.[38]

If traffic police handed out bonuses to people who stopped at red lights rather than ticketing those who did not, they would quickly drive local governments into insolvency. By the same token, any society that tries to subsidize itself all the way to sustainability, paying people not to pollute, will soon be bankrupt. Taxes and regulations on pollution and resource depletion are ultimately needed to level the economic playing field for environmentally sound ways of living and producing.

That said, targeted subsidies can sometimes play a useful role in protecting the environment—and will always be more popular. In late 1992, for example, a 1.5¢-per-kilowatt-hour tax credit for electricity from wind and biomass sailed through the U.S. Congress with little controversy. Only a few months later, President Clinton's energy tax proposal, which would have handicapped conventional sources by only 0.3¢ more, fell victim to vociferous industry and popular opposition. Subsidies for environmental protection, then, though a second-best policy solution, will likely be useful for decades to come.[39]

Funding specifically for research, development, and commercialization activities for new technologies can also grease the machinery of economic change. At their best, R&D subsidies work with the grain of culture, technology, and economics rather than against it, in order to leverage small amounts of money into

enough technological change that the subsidies themselves become obsolete. The strength of such subsidies lies not in the brute force of megabucks but in careful design and experimentation. They are more catalytic than coercive.

In practice, however, the track record of R&D subsidies has been poor. One important example of both the strengths and the dangers of targeted commercialization subsidies is provided by the Green Revolution—the combination of new grain varieties, pesticides, fertilizers, and irrigation that received active government support in developing countries starting in the sixties. Though not without serious social and environmental side effects, the Green Revolution did persuade millions of risk-averse farmers to grow food in new, high-yielding ways, which reduced hunger even among rapidly growing populations. The revolution is now largely complete. Yet many of the subsidies that helped spawn it persist, skewing farmers' decisions about when, for example, pesticides are worth the costs and health risks.[40]

One realm in which subsidies for environmentally important technologies have worked fairly well is energy efficiency. Three of the most successful technologies supported by the U.S. Department of Energy (DOE)—heat-reflecting windows, electronic ballasts for fluorescent lights, and variable-capacity supermarket refrigeration systems—are now saving enough energy to easily justify DOE's entire $425-million efficiency R&D budget.[41]

Though tiny, the $23.7-million public investment in these three technologies was pivotal to their development. In all three cases, it was small companies, which would have had difficulty embarking on such risky research on their own, that vied for the initial grants. Only when their efforts bore fruit did established firms take notice. Most likely, then, it would have taken much longer for the technologies to have developed without government help. The efficient windows, ballasts, and refrigerators already sold in the United States will save $8.9 billion in fuel costs over their lifetimes—375 times what DOE spent developing them.[42]

A key circumstance behind these impressive numbers is that with businesses and consumers spending so much on energy—$500 billion per year in the United States alone—one successful energy efficiency R&D grant can quickly save enough money to make up for dozens of failed ones. In contrast, public investments in new ways of producing energy have not paid off nearly as well. Western industrial countries alone spent $52 billion (in 1995 dollars) on energy R&D between 1990 and 1995. Forty-one percent of that was devoted to a single technology: traditional nuclear fission. Another 21 percent went for advanced fission and fusion technologies, which seem forever on the horizon. Only 17 percent went for renewable energy and energy efficiency technologies, which are growing rapidly in percentage terms and are less polluting and often more labor-intensive to produce and operate than conventional power plants. Thus the energy sources that are the least polluting, fastest-growing, and best job creators received the least support.[43]

People working at the grass roots, who have less money but a better sense of what is needed, have often had more success in catalyzing change. A U.S.-based nonprofit called Enersol, founded by a former nuclear and coal plant engineer, has parlayed modest grants from the World Bank, the Rockefeller Foundation, and other donors into the creation of a nearly self-sustaining solar industry in the Dominican Republic.[44]

Enersol's customers are rural peasants who want to bring electric light into their homes but have no access to the national electricity grid. The nonprofit does not pay for the imported solar panels, but instead has established a revolving loan fund that lets buyers spread payments over several years. The subsidy in this case is modest: some funding to train marketers and system installers and the willingness to risk losing part of the seed money should buyers default. But the leverage has been tremendous. By 1993, it had brought solar power to 4,000 families and created local employment. Other organizations are now copying the approach in China, Honduras, Indonesia, Sri Lanka, and Zimbabwe.[45]

These forays into technology commercialization and development hold several important lessons. The first is that including expiration dates in subsidies for specific technologies may be warranted to guard against their becoming entrenched despite failure or obsolescence. The second is that the bottom-up approach to technology commercialization typically works better than top-down because it tends to be more responsive to commercial imperatives such as making equipment reliable and meeting customers' needs. The last lesson is that, given governments' generally poor track record in picking winners, it may make more sense to favor broad-gauge subsidies, such as the U.S. tax credit for electricity generation from wind and biomass, over much R&D. By focusing more on results, governments can lessen the risk of subsidizing failures, and leave it to the market to pick winners.

Tellingly, the world's most successful wind power industries have arisen in countries where governments have spent little on R&D, instead favoring across-the-board production and investment incentives. Denmark, for example, instituted subsidies for both investment in and power generation from wind turbines in 1979, leaving the choice of technology to turbine buyers. It retired the investment credit in 1989 after advances had driven prices down and pushed installed capacity from next to nothing to nearly 300 megawatts. The industry continued to thrive.[46]

More recently, Denmark helped India spark a wind revolution of its own. Inspired by a demonstration wind farm built by the Danish foreign aid agency and spurred by tax breaks from the Indian government, local companies jumped into the wind business. At first they imported most of their components, but over time they cut costs and increased domestic value-added by drawing on the country's own manufacturing strength. By 1995 the Indian wind industry had created hundreds of new jobs and had catapulted to second in the world in annual capacity additions. The striking contrast with India's stagnant, problem-plagued domestic nuclear program suggests that wind technology is easily a better fit for the country's economy.[47]

SUBSIDY REFORM FOR SUSTAINABLE DEVELOPMENT

Worldwide, scattered subsidy reforms have occurred over the last decade. Fiscal more than environmental concerns have motivated most of them. Subsidy cutoffs following the collapse of communism in the former Eastern bloc are a prime example. Whatever has propelled them, the countries that have taken the first steps and, sometimes, missteps toward reform have offered the rest of the world valuable lessons on how best to proceed. That said, it is clear that many subsidies are as politically entrenched as ever. Clearly, comprehensive subsidy reform is no small task, but it is vital to making modern economies equitable and sustainable.

The conclusions that arise from applying the principles of good subsidy

policy described earlier to the subsidies in place today can be distilled down to a few fundamental recommendations: withdraw almost all subsidies that perpetuate the cowboy economy; phase out protectionist subsidies that are now or will soon become, like dikes against a rising sea, unnecessary, ineffective, or too costly; target with precision what are now shotgun subsidies or completely replace them with other methods of helping the poor; and use a combination of broad-gauged incentives and more bottom-up approaches to speed the development of environmentally beneficial technologies. (See Table 8–2.)

Reform would make subsidies more useful, eliminate almost all of the $500 billion or more in direct costs to taxpayers and consumers, and help the environment. Subsidy reform would lower taxes and consumer prices, reducing the penalties for work and investment that taxes create. At the same time, farmers, companies, and consumers would begin to reduce pollution and use resources such as water and energy more efficiently. Unsustainable and polluting industries, from coal mining to virgin papermaking, would lose some of their artificial market advantage over more sustainable competitors such as solar panel makers and paper recyclers. The sooner reform began, the more orderly it could be, and the less pain would result from the dislocation of workers in losing industries. To the extent that the poor would lose out from higher prices for water and energy, they would be compensated by new, more efficient subsidies aimed directly at them.

Recent movements in the direction of reform include Brazil's cancellation in 1988 of the generous investment tax credits it had once offered to ranchers and farmers who cleared land in the Amazon; officials there believe this change contributed to the temporary deforestation slowdown that began at that time. The U.S.

**Table 8–2. Critiques of and Remedies for Subsidies
with Harmful Environmental Side Effects**

Avowed Intent	Examples	Effects	How to Improve
Stimulating economic growth	Sales of timber, minerals, and land sometimes claimed by indigenous peoples, usually at below-market prices; tax breaks for forest clearance.	Usually slow economic traditional resource owners; cause massive environmental damage; reduce revenues.	Give traditional users more control over resources; sell resources at market rates; use savings to cut other taxes or fund public investment.
Protecting jobs in resource-based industries; protecting consumers from import dependence	Subsidies in most industrial countries for crop production, ranching, fishing, logging, or fossil fuel production.	Often fail to stem job losses or enhance national security; hurt workers in countries unable to offer subsidies; cost taxpayers and environment.	Convert subsidies for small opera-tors to welfare; phase out where ineffective or too costly.
Reducing the cost of living, especially for the poor	Subsidies for water, electricity, and fuels.	Waste money because they usually benefit the poor least; discourage efficiency and renewable energy use.	Offer "lifeline" rates or free fuel coupons to poor customers; expand access; fund alternatives such as solar panels.
Supporting technological change	Subsidies for irrigation pesticides, and fertilizers in developing countries as part of "Green Revolution"; nuclear R&D.	Often continue operating after transition has been achieved or has failed, imposing unnecessary fiscal and environmental costs.	Halt for mature or failed technolo-gies; subsidize the use of environmentally friendly ones; favor broad-gauged over selective subsi-dies.

SOURCE: Worldwatch Institute.

Congress has yet to reform the 1872 Mining Law, but it has placed a temporary moratorium on new mineral claims on public lands every year since 1994. Some developing countries, such as Indonesia, have cut agrichemical subsidies since the mid-eighties, partly in response to falling revenues from oil exports or the tightening vise of overseas debt, while encouraging the use of natural predators to control crop pests. And following the collapse of communism in the former Eastern bloc, the prices that businesses there pay for agrichemicals and fuel have shot up toward world levels. This has caused fertilizer and energy use to plummet, spurring the jolting economic contraction.[48]

When Belgium, France, Japan, Spain, and the United Kingdom eliminated or radically reduced coal subsidies, their combined output fell by half between 1986 and 1995. The imported coal that has replaced some of this output has in general contained less sulfur and ash, and has entailed less environmental damage in its mining. In the United Kingdom, moreover, coal consumption has also fallen, as natural gas from the North Sea has grabbed market share. As a result, U.K. carbon emissions have fallen during the nineties even as the economy has expanded—a rare phenomenon.[49]

Most of the coal subsidy cuts have been far from painless, unfortunately. In the United Kingdom—where the coal cutback of 27.5 million tons (48 percent) in three years was by far the largest and the most rapid—social ills such as high unemployment and drug abuse have struck many former coal towns. These tribulations dramatize both the seriousness of the trade-offs that policymakers sometimes face in deciding on subsidy reductions and the importance of trying to mitigate their effects.[50]

Though British Coal offered severance packages and some retraining, perhaps inevitably these have not been up to the formidable task of engineering a wholesale transformation of the job bases of dozens of local economies in just three years. Mine closing programs in Western Europe have often been slower, more generous, and more flexible. Miners in Baersweiller, Germany, for instance, will receive five years' notice if their pit is to close. In Belgian Flanders, the gradual mine closure program was once temporarily halted when local unemployment rose above the national average. Even in Europe, though,

serious unemployment has often resulted from mine closings, showing that there is usually no easy way out.[51]

The choices in coal policy are unusually tough because there is no getting around the fact that coal use is a major source of greenhouse gases and other pollutants; but in some resource-based industries it is easier to reduce environmental harm while protecting jobs. The European Union took advantage of the maneuvering room in agricultural policy in 1993 when it decreased guaranteed prices for major crops and instituted flat per-hectare payments. In 1996, the United States leapfrogged the European Union in this direction by completely abolishing price guarantees for most crops in favor of fixed payments based on farmers' past production levels. Both these reforms are intended to support farmers' incomes but end the market manipulations that burdened farmers with complex regulations and encouraged overproduction and environmentally destructive farming.[52]

New Zealand almost completely eliminated farming supports in the mid-eighties—partly at the prompting of farmers themselves.

Remarkably, New Zealand almost completely eliminated its farming supports in the mid-eighties—partly at the prompting of farmers themselves, through the agency of the national Federated Farmers group. The move was part of a broader government effort to cut subsidies that had crept into many sectors of the economy over several decades, leading to high taxes and inflation that hurt farmers at least as much as other workers. After some difficult years of adjustment, during which the government wrote off many bad loans to farmers, the agricultural sector became much more efficient, and rebounded. Interestingly, New Zealand is now one of the few industrial countries where the number of farmers is rising.[53]

As with subsidies for producers, many subsidies for consumers remain in place worldwide, though here too some countries offer good examples for others to follow. The U.S. government, for instance, targets heating bill assistance at poor households in order to hold down costs and minimize the subsidy-induced incentive for energy use and pollution. Such targeting is rarer in developing countries. In Indonesia, although across-the-board kerosene subsidies have reduced the cost of living for most families in the poorest one fifth of the population, 90 percent of the payments actually benefit better-off people. If the subsidy were restricted to the neediest recipients, it could give them 10 times the benefit for the same cost, or the same benefit for one tenth the cost.[54]

In countries like Indonesia, where governments are strapped for cash and most economic activity occurs off the books, identifying and targeting the neediest for subsidization can be a daunting task. Yet there are proven, cost-effective ways to sharpen, if not perfect, subsidy focus even in developing countries. These include targeting particularly poor neighborhoods and regions, and involving schoolteachers, who know local communities well, in determining which families are deserving. Sri Lanka used such approaches to distribute "kerosene stamps" among the poorer half of the population, in order to soften the blow of the 1979 oil shock. In the same spirit, Sri Lanka is also among at least a dozen developing countries that offer "lifeline" rates for electricity: discounts on the first 20 kilowatt-hours or so used each month, enough to power a couple of light bulbs every evening.[55]

One problem with resource consumption subsidies, no matter how carefully targeted or vital to the poor they are, is that they handicap cleaner alternatives. This is why the U.S. government also offers some funding to help poor people invest in efficiency upgrades for furnaces and home insulation. In doing so, it lowers the very heating bills it is helping to pay. By the same token, if Sri Lanka and other countries continue to pursue a policy of using cheap energy to mitigate poverty, they will succeed better by subsidizing all the forms of energy used by the poor that are practical to subsidize. That would include renewable technologies such as solar panels, which are safer and cleaner than kerosene, as well as particularly appropriate in areas not reached by power lines.[56]

Much more than subsidy reform will ultimately be needed to right what is wrong with unsustainable modern economies. While societies will use subsidies to reward, they will need more fundamentally to use environmental taxes to penalize, and regulations to restrict. Yet as a political proposition, environmentally harmful subsidies have so many strikes against them that reforming them ought to be the easiest step along the path to environmental sustainability. The flaws of these subsidies bear repeating: they hike the cost of government; the resulting higher taxes and prices burden economies; the subsidies do little good even on their own terms; and they degrade the environment, further undermining long-term economic prospects.

Citizens and policymakers determined to forge economies that are just and prosperous for generations to come could do little better than to get out of the business of paying the polluter. If they cannot succeed in this, it is doubtful that they will prevail in the even tougher political fights for more fundamental reforms that lie beyond.

9

Learning from the Ozone Experience

Hilary F. French

On 16 September 1987, negotiators meeting in Montreal finalized a landmark in international environmental diplomacy: the Montreal Protocol on Substances That Deplete the Ozone Layer. The treaty mandated far-reaching restrictions in the use of certain chemicals that damage the ozone layer—the thin, vital veil in the stratosphere 10–50 kilometers above the earth's surface that protects the earth and its inhabitants from harmful ultraviolet (UV) radiation. Scientists projected that without cooperative international action, the ozone layer would be seriously depleted for decades to come. The resulting intense radiation could have grave consequences for human and ecological health—including millions of additional skin cancer cases worldwide, sharply diminished agricultural yields, and extensive damage to aquatic life.[1]

The successful conclusion of the negotiations in Montreal was widely hailed at the time as a historic event, as the protocol was the most ambitious attempt ever to combat environmental degradation on a global scale. Governments from poor counties as well as rich, from the East as well as the West, were involved in the talks. The protocol they agreed on promised to have far-reaching effects for the multibillion-dollar global industry that produced the offending chemicals, as well as for the many businesses and individuals who produced or used products dependent on them. It was signed on the spot by 24 nations and the European Community, and has since been ratified by more than 150 countries.[2]

In the 10 years since that meeting in Montreal, the accord has set in motion myriad actions by national governments, international organizations, scientists, private enterprises, and individual consumers. The results are clear: by 1995, global production of the most significant ozone-depleting substance (ODS)—the chlorine-containing chlorofluorocarbons (CFCs)—was down 76 percent from its peak in 1988. (See Figure 9–1.) The world passed an important milestone at the beginning of 1996, when industrial countries had to stop producing and importing CFCs for domestic use, with the exception of a few "essential uses."[3]

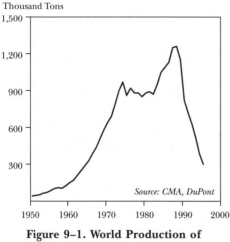

Thousand Tons

Source: CMA, DuPont

Figure 9–1. World Production of Chlorofluorocarbons, 1950–95

But there is a substantial lag between the time when emissions begin to decline and the point at which the ozone layer begins to recover, as it takes years for CFCs and other ozone-depleting compounds to reach the stratosphere, and some last for centuries once there. Current estimates suggest that if all countries comply with the Montreal Protocol, the ozone shield will gradually begin to heal around the end of this decade, with a full recovery expected by about 2045. The world is thus currently suffering through the period in which the ozone layer will likely be most severely damaged. Some of the largest "ozone holes" on record have been experienced above the Antarctic over the last few years as a result, and ozone losses over mid- to high latitudes in both the northern and southern hemispheres have increased rapidly—as have levels of UV radiation over populated and agriculturally abundant corners of the earth such as Canada, Chile, the United Kingdom, and Russia.[4]

Yet it is clear that the Montreal Protocol ushered in a new era of environmental diplomacy. Five years after the negotiations ended, more than 100 heads of state or government convened in Rio de Janeiro for the U.N. Conference on Environment and Development, where they signed treaties on climate change and the loss of biological diversity as well as an ambitious action plan for sustainable development. (See Chapter 1.) Diplomats also finalized a treaty on desertification in 1994 and have initiated discussions on other pressing environmental problems, including the control of persistent organic pollutants.[5]

The tenth anniversary of the Montreal Protocol provides an opportunity to reflect on the lessons of the ozone experience for these various other efforts at international environmental cooperation. On the one hand, the steep decline in CFC production since 1988 offers the first clear example that countries can work together to head off shared threats. Yet today's record levels of exposure to UV radiation are also a sobering reminder that although action eventually was taken, it came too late to avoid serious consequences for human and ecological health.[6]

Although in some ways the ozone story is an inspiration, in other respects it is a cautionary tale. There is much to be learned from both the successes and the stumbling blocks.

THE SCIENCE AND POLICY CONNECTION

Since its beginning, the ozone experience has been characterized by a pathbreaking partnership between scientists and international policymakers. In Montreal, Mostafa Tolba, then Executive Director of the United Nations Environment Programme (UNEP) and a key force in the negotiations, told the assembled delegates that "with this agreement the worlds of science and public affairs have taken a step closer together...a union which must guide the affairs of the world into the next century." As Tolba predicted, the collaboration that was pioneered with the ozone issue has proved to be a warm-up for other challenges such as climate change and biodiversity loss, where this partnership is equally critical but increasingly controversial.[7]

When CFCs were invented in the late twenties, they were viewed as wonder chemicals—nontoxic, nonflammable, noncorrosive, and stable. These properties helped make them popular for use as propellants in aerosol cans, as foam-blowing agents, as solvents, and as coolants for refrigerators and air conditioners. World production doubled roughly every five years through 1970 as a result. Another growth spurt came in the early eighties, as new applications were discovered, including use as a solvent to clean circuit boards and computer chips in California's booming Silicon Valley.[8]

The seeds of the Montreal Protocol were sown in 1974, when chemists Mario Molina and Sherwood Rowland at the University of California at Irvine published a landmark article in *Nature* that hypothesisized that the stability of CFCs, while an asset for industrial applications, might prove deadly for the ozone layer, as it meant that CFCs from ground-based sources might be reaching the stratosphere intact. There, solar radiation could be breaking them apart to free reactive chlorine atoms, thus catalyzing chain reactions that would destroy ozone on a massive scale. Subsequent years proved Molina and Rowland right. In 1995, they received the Nobel Prize in Chemistry (along with Paul Crutzen of Germany's Max Planck Institute) for their work. (In 1970, Crutzen had laid the groundwork for Molina and Rowland by demonstrating that gases from human

activities—namely nitrogen oxides—play a role in destroying ozone.)[9]

Public and media reaction in the seventies sparked the first wave of policy responses to the threat of ozone depletion. By the end of the decade, public pressure led to bans on the use of CFCs for aerosol sprays in Canada, Norway, Sweden, and the United States. Meanwhile, at a UNEP-sponsored meeting in March 1977, 33 national governments and the European Community set in motion a World Plan of Action on the Ozone Layer, which called for international cooperation on research into the causes and effects of ozone depletion. The gathering also led to the creation of a Coordinating Committee on the Ozone Layer to evaluate the science, which included experts from both the industrial and the developing worlds who represented government agencies, the scientific community, industry, and nongovernmental organizations (NGOs). This marked the launch of a unique partnership among these groups that has been a hallmark of the ozone experience ever since.[10]

It is clear that the Montreal Protocol ushered in a new era of environmental diplomacy.

Yet the scientific process was initially slow to yield clear answers. Indeed, models in the early eighties suggested that CFCs would cause less severe ozone depletion than Molina and Rowland had initially hypothesized. Not surprisingly, perhaps, international negotiations toward an ozone treaty during this period produced little in the way of concrete results. Delegates settled in March 1985 for the Vienna Convention for the Protection of the Ozone Layer—a framework document that contained no commitments to control CFCs but that formalized the scientific cooperation and data-reporting provisions already called for under the 1977 World Plan of Action.[11]

Fortunately, the scientific collaboration initiated years earlier began to bear fruit. Robert Watson, then a U.S. National Aeronautics and Space Administration (NASA) scientist, recalls that in the late seventies numerous different agencies were preparing scientific assessments of ozone depletion. "What most people pointed out were the differences between the assessments," Watson told the *New Scientist.* "The differences were more exploited than the similarities....There was a drastic need for an international consensus so there could be no excuse about what the science did or did not say." He travelled the world tirelessly to bring scientists together to produce that consensus, and helped ensure that it was then translated into language policymakers could understand. (In a move that bodes well for the ongoing global warming talks, Watson was elected in September 1996 to chair the Intergovernmental Panel on Climate Change (IPCC).)[12]

Protocol signatories were breaking new ground by deciding to move ahead with international controls on CFCs in the absence of conclusive proof of environmental damage.

Two months after the Vienna agreement was reached, a scientific bombshell provided a much-needed jolt to protocol negotiations just then getting under way. In May 1985, members of the British Antarctica Survey published findings that indicated a 40-percent loss of stratospheric ozone over Antarctica between September and October 1984. Subsequent satellite data confirmed the presence of this ozone "hole"—and found it to cover an area as large as the continental United States.[13]

The findings took the world by surprise: no such precipitous decline had been predicted by any atmospheric models. Indeed, release of the data was delayed because the ozone losses were so large and so unexpected that the scientists involved at first suspected instrument error. When the measurements were finally confirmed, computers translated the data into compelling color images of the hole that appeared on the evening news and transformed the ozone issue from an abstraction into a tangible threat.[14]

In early 1986, Robert Watson's efforts at consensus building paid off when UNEP and the World Meteorological Organization (WMO) released the first comprehensive international scientific assessment on ozone depletion, which concluded that dangerous levels of ozone depletion were likely if CFC production trends continued their steep climb. This new information, combined with the wave of publicity about the ozone hole, helped create the political will needed to reach agreement in Montreal.[15]

Yet when diplomats convened there in September 1987, many gaps remained in scientific understanding of the problem. Uncertainty remained about the role of CFCs in creating the ozone hole over Antarctica. In addition, there were no comprehensive estimates of measured global ozone loss or detectable increases in the UV radiation reaching the earth. The Montreal Protocol signatories were thus breaking new ground by deciding to move ahead with international controls in the absence of conclusive proof of environmental damage. Their actions represented the first significant application of the "precautionary principle"—an emerging tenet of international environmental law that stipulates that lack of complete scientific certainty is insufficient reason to delay an international policy response if such delay might result in serious or irreversible damage.16

Under the terms of the protocol, industrial countries agreed to cut production and use of CFCs in half by 1998, and by 1992 to freeze production and use of halons, a bromine-containing chemical then widely used in fire-fighting. (A bromine atom is about 50 times as efficient as a chlorine atom in destroying ozone, although there is far less of it in the stratosphere.) Countries with a per capita annual CFC consumption below 0.3 kilograms (mainly developing nations) were granted a 10-year extension on the deadlines. In addition, the protocol restricted trade in CFCs and products containing them with countries that were not members of the accord. These provisions were intended to encourage as many countries as possible to join the treaty, and to discourage the creation of "CFC havens" where production would occur for export to treaty members.[17]

In March 1988, a panel of scientists organized by NASA announced that their extensive review of all known global air- and land-based measurements revealed ozone losses two to three times more severe over heavily populated northern latitudes than had been predicted by the models on which the protocol was based. The report also confirmed localized losses as high as 95 percent over Antarctica, and provided persuasive evidence that CFCs were the culprit in causing the seasonal Antarctic "ozone hole." The new information meant that the ozone layer would not recover even if the Montreal Protocol were fully implemented.[18]

The protocol stipulated that the parties to it should convene in 1990 to review whether the accord was adequate, based on reports of panels of experts that assessed relevant scientific, environmental, technical, and economic information. The panels reported that tougher measures were both scientifically urgent and technologically achievable. Fortunately, governments listened. The protocol was strengthened in London in June 1990 to require a full phaseout in industrial countries of both CFCs and halons by 2000. In addition, several previously unregulated ozone-depleting substances were restricted for the first time, including methyl chloroform and carbon tetrachloride. For developing countries, the 10-year grace period now applied to these new requirements.[19]

NASA findings released in April 1991 once again showed depletion proceeding twice as fast as expected over parts of the northern hemisphere—and suggested that 200,000 additional deaths from skin cancer in the United States alone could occur during the next 50 years as a result. Still more alarming news appeared in February 1992, when NASA reported chlorine levels over New England and eastern Canada that were higher than any previously seen over Antarctica.[20]

Once again, new data spurred a call to revise the treaty. As in London, reports of expert panels strengthened the case that further action was needed. In November 1992 in Copenhagen, the phaseout dates for industrial countries were advanced to 1994 for halons and to 1996 for CFCs, methyl chloroform, and carbon tetrachloride. In addition, negotiators took up the question of hydrochlorofluorocarbons (HCFCs), which were being touted by the chemical industry as a substitute for CFCs but which also deplete the ozone layer, though only 2–10 percent as much as CFCs over the long term. Under the Copenhagen agreement, all but 0.5 percent of HCFCs in industrial countries were to be eliminated by 2020, with a complete phaseout scheduled for 2030.[21]

In Copenhagen, limits were placed on methyl bromide for the first time. This chemical is widely used as a pesticide whose fumes rid soil, agricultural commodities, and storage areas of a range of soilborne and airborne pests such as insects, worms, weeds, pathogens, and rodents. However, it also releases bromine to the stratosphere; recent estimates suggest that as much as one third of the Antarctic ozone loss and 5–10 percent of the global total may be caused by bromine. Methyl bromide only lasts for some two years in the atmosphere, so it initially eluded restriction by the Montreal Protocol, which focused on long-term ozone loss. Under the Copenhagen agreement, industrial countries agreed to freeze methyl bromide emissions at 1991 levels beginning in 1995.[22]

The latest round of revisions to the treaty took place in November 1995 in Vienna. Again, this followed new scientific and technical reports linked with the protocol that made the case that further action was not only needed, but achievable. For instance, the 1994 report of the protocol's scientific assessment panel asserted that, among possible further actions, eliminating emissions of methyl bromide would make the largest single contribution to ozone-layer protection. Meanwhile, the methyl bromide technical options committee was reporting that substitutes exist for 90 percent of the uses.[23]

The Vienna meeting responded to this information by strengthening controls on methyl bromide somewhat, although less than many NGO observers had hoped. Methyl bromide use is now to be phased out by 2010 in industrial countries and frozen in developing countries at 1995–98 levels by 2002. The meeting also slightly strengthened HCFC requirements for industrial countries. For developing countries, it imposed a freeze in HCFC consumption after 2015 and a complete phaseout by 2040.[24]

Thus in the 10 years since Montreal, rapidly advancing science and technol-

ogy have contributed to a steady expansion in the requirements of the protocol. So far, each revision that required ratification has eventually been approved by a large number of countries. As of October 1996, 159 countries had ratified the original protocol and 111 had done so for the London amendments, though only 61 had ratified the changes made at Copenhagen.[25]

Meanwhile, those involved with negotiating other international environmental accords are trying to replicate the ways in which evolving scientific and technological information has been brought so successfully to the ozone negotiating table. Intergovernmental panels of scientists have been assembled to study climate change and the loss of biological diversity, and the treaties on both these issues set up groups to channel scientific and technological advice to the negotiators. The experience with ozone has taught the international community that it is important to design advisory bodies so that the chosen experts are independent of their governments, unbiased, and knowledgeable about the issues under consideration. And the process needs to be structured in a way that allows their advice to feed smoothly and constructively into the policymaking process.[26]

INDUSTRY'S RESPONSE

The business community has joined scientists as a constant presence in ozone debates over the years. Though by no means monolithic, as a general rule the position of industry evolved from initial denial of the problem to acceptance and in many cases enthusiasm for developing substitute chemicals and processes for ozone-depleting substances.

The story of industry's involvement in ongoing ozone deliberations is an unusually complex one. Old business sagas—such as competitiveness battles between European, Japanese, and U.S. companies, and delicate relationships between government regulators and the industries they oversee—are suddenly being played out on an entirely new stage: that of international environmental negotiations. Though it first arose with ozone, this same dynamic is now at work in a number of other international negotiations, including those aimed at strengthening treaties on climate change and biological diversity, as well as efforts to restrict traffic in hazardous wastes and banned chemicals and to control persistent organic pollutants.

During the first wave of public concern about ozone depletion in the seventies, chemical companies consistently maintained that the science was not strong enough to justify regulatory action. They did, however, launch research programs that patented possible substitutes. But concern faded in the early eighties in the face of ambiguous scientific findings and the deregulatory zeal of the Reagan administration in the United States. DuPont and other companies later admitted that they abandoned or suspended their research programs into substitutes at that time. In early 1986, the Alliance for Responsible CFC Policy, which represented some 500 CFC producer and user companies in the United States, was still arguing that the science was too uncertain to justify action, and that developing substitutes would be costly. Nonetheless, the group acknowledged later that year that it would be possible to develop substitutes within five years if companies were persuaded that restrictions on CFCs would create a market for them.[27]

Meanwhile, growing public pressure and a lawsuit by the New York–based Natural Resources Defense Council calling on the Environmental Protection Agency (EPA) to take tougher action

meant that the United States was likely to move ahead with unilateral controls if the international process bogged down. U.S. business interests feared this: if there were to be controls on CFCs, they wanted to make sure they applied equally to their competitors elsewhere— something that had not happened when aerosols were controlled in the seventies. They may also have been concerned about possible future lawsuits from skin cancer victims and damage to their public image. In late 1986, the Alliance for Responsible CFC Policy did an abrupt about-face. Concluding that the handwriting was on the wall, the group began to advocate limiting future CFC use.[28]

European industry was slower to come around, partly because of less public attention to the issue in Europe, which made companies there less inclined to view regulation as inevitable. In addition, some apparently believed that research into substitutes was more advanced in the United States, which they feared would put European firms in a vulnerable position in the battle for dominance in CFC substitute markets.[29]

Eventually, however, the European calculus shifted. One impetus may have been some pending U.S. legislation that would have required unilateral action if multilateral talks failed, with the proviso that trade restrictions would be imposed on the imports of countries that were not cooperating. In addition, European companies realized it would be easier for them to implement the production targets being proposed for the Montreal meeting, as governments there had not yet eliminated CFC use in aerosols—a sector with cheap and readily available alternatives. Thus these countries still had a relatively inexpensive step available to help meet the 50-percent reduction target, while the United States did not.[30]

The acquiesence of U.S. and European industry to the protocol was key, as CFC production was then heavily concentrated in these regions. Indeed, by the late eighties, more than 80 percent of world CFC production capacity was concentrated in six U.S. and European chemical companies: DuPont, Atochem, Allied-Signal, Imperial Chemical Industries, Hoechst, and Montefluos. But the industrial interests of other countries were also at stake. The Japanese, in particular, became involved in the negotiations because CFC-113—widely used as a solvent in the electronics industry—was on the table.[31]

After the protocol was finalized, the race began in earnest to develop substitute chemicals and processes. In the United States alone, the annual sales value of CFCs at that time was $750 million, goods and services dependent on the chemicals were worth $28 billion, and end-use equipment and products containing them were worth $135 billion. The Montreal target sent a powerful signal to the market that this would have to change, launching a remarkable period of technological transformation.[32]

One key watershed in this process came in March 1988, when DuPont responded to the release of the protocol's ozone trends panel report with a bold decision: to get out of its $600-million CFC business altogether by shortly after 2000. This private-sector announcement—which went well beyond the stipulations of the protocol—helped redefine the political landscape, putting pressure on government negotiators to strengthen the accord. For those who had pressed DuPont to take decisive action more than a decade earlier, however, the moment was bittersweet.[33]

Though DuPont's belated announcement was in the public interest, it also benefited the company. Besides the desire to protect its image, DuPont hoped that it could profit from developing and marketing substitute chemicals. Its CFC business was becoming steadily less lucrative in any case. DuPont thus accelerated its research programs aimed at developing and patenting alternatives. The company announced in 1992 that it had invested $450 million in developing CFC substitutes since 1986, and that it expected to put $1 billion into this by the end of 1995.[34]

Two types of compounds received the bulk of chemical companies' efforts—HCFCs and hydrofluorocarbons (HFCs). HCFCs were particularly attractive, as they were already being produced on a substantial scale. Unfortunately, both have significant environmental liabilities. As noted earlier, HCFCs are themselves ozone-depleting substances, though significantly less so than CFCs. But HCFCs are far shorter-lived, which means that those emitted today will do most of their damage within the next 10–20 years—precisely the period when the ozone layer is projected to be at its most depleted.[35]

And like CFCs themselves, HCFCs and HFCs are both potent greenhouse gases. For instance, over the 100 years after it is injected into the atmosphere, a ton of CFC-11 will have 4,000 times the global warming effect as the same amount of carbon dioxide (CO_2); a ton of HCFC-22 will have 1,700 times the global warming effect, and a comparable amount of HFC-134a will have 1,300 times the effect. Beyond their contribution to global warming, HCFCs and HFCs share yet another potentially worrisome side effect: recent studies hypothesize that they both will break down in the atmosphere into acids, including trifluoroacetic acid, which falls to earth in precipitation and can accumulate in some areas in concentrations high enough to be toxic to plants.[36]

Parties to the protocol stipulated at the June 1990 London meeting that HCFCs were to be regarded as transitional substitutes only—to be used to buy time while more satisfactory long-term solutions were developed. Yet their use was allowed until well into the next century, in part because the chemical industry argued that they would not invest in manufacturing these substitute chemicals if they were unlikely to recoup their investment costs. Given the urgent need to move away from the far more potent CFCs, governments yielded to this argument.[37]

HFCs were left off the evolving negotiating agenda altogether because they are ozone-benign, despite the fact that they are potent greenhouse gases. In the segmented world of international environmental diplomacy, this was an issue for the climate change talks, which did not even get under way until 1989. The Framework Convention on Climate Change was completed in time for the June 1992 Earth Summit in Rio, but it contained no binding commitments, although negotiations are under way to strengthen it. (See Chapter 1.)

Although the quantities of HFCs being produced are minuscule compared with the amount of CO_2 emitted annually, use of these chemicals has grown rapidly as CFCs are phased out, from less than 200 tons in 1990 to more than 50,000 tons in 1994. According to projections by the IPCC, annual HFC emissions could reach 148,000 tons by 2000 and 1.5 million tons by 2050—roughly equivalent in global warming impact to the current fossil fuel–based carbon emissions of France, Germany, Italy, and the United Kingdom combined. This means that widespread reliance on these substitute chemicals will be solving one environmental problem while contributing to another—something that has happened over and over again as the world has tackled diverse environmental challenges.[38]

Given the substantial limitations of these chemical substitutes, it is fortunate that they are not the only option. The industries that use CFCs discovered that by redesigning manufacturing processes—and sometimes simply by using natural substances such as water—the need to use CFC-like chemicals could be reduced dramatically, and in some cases eliminated altogether. (See Table 9–1.)[39]

Industries that use CFCs discovered that by redesigning manufacturing processes, the need to use CFC-like chemicals could be reduced dramatically.

The electronics industry was at the cutting edge of this trend. AT&T, for instance, cooperated with a small Florida firm to develop a citrus fruit–derived substitute for CFC-113 in cleaning electronic circuit boards, and Hughes Aircraft discovered it could use lemon juice for this same purpose. Breaking with their history of competition, eight U.S.-based multinational companies came together at the instigation of the EPA in 1989 to form the International Cooperative for Ozone Layer Protection, whose mission is to promote the worldwide exchange of information about alternatives to ozone-depleting solvents.[40]

Particularly in this sector, the substitution process often proved to be of economic as well as environmental benefit to the companies involved, resulting in lower costs, simplified manufacturing processes, and improved reliability. The Canadian Mint, for instance, decided in autumn 1995 to switch its coin cleaning from a CFC-based process to an ultrasonic water-based system. The new solution cost only some $700–1,000 annually, while the CFCs had cost some $150,000. The initial investment took just one year to pay for itself.[41]

Other industries also made the switch with relative ease. Foam packaging is a case in point. Even before the protocol

Table 9-1. Substitutes for Ozone-Depleting Substances

Compounds	Applications	Interim Substitutes[1]	Examples of "Not-In-Kind" Substitutes[2]
CFCs	refrigerants	HCFCs, HFCs	Hydrocarbon refrigerants (propane and butane) were introduced in "Greenfreeze" domestic refrigerators by Foron of Germany. The Calor company now makes hydrocarbon refrigerants for commercial refrigeration and air conditioning; these are used in U.K. offices and stores.
	foam insulation	HCFCs, HFCs	The largest foam manufacturer in Canada, Demilec, recently unveiled "Sealection 500," a flexible urethane foam building insulation that is blown with water and is cheaper than its competitors. Some European companies use rigid foam blown with cyclopentane, a hydrocarbon, to insulate refrigerators.
	aerosol propellants	HCFCs, HFCs	Airspray International in the Netherlands makes air-powered spray devices. Systems sold by Blagden Spray in Scandinavia use compressed nitrogen or air. In the United States, hydrocarbon propellants prevail; these low-cost alternatives save U.S. consumers an estimated $165 million each year.
CFCs/ Methyl Chloroform	electronics cleaners/ degreasing solvents	HCFCs, HFC, PFCs	Design changes in the production processes for electronic goods reduced hazardous lead waste and the need to clean circuit boards at Texas Instruments; this saved the company over $300,000 in annual cleaning costs. Water is used for some electronics cleaning. Citric acid solvents are effective degreasers.

was completed, McDonald's found itself facing citizen pressure to stop using packaging made with CFCs. In August 1987, it informed suppliers that they had 18 months to eliminate CFCs from their products. This forced the entire U.S. food-packaging industry to shift out of CFCs in advance of any requirements to do so under the Montreal Protocol. Within 16 months of the announcement, the whole U.S. industry was CFC-free. With the cooperation of the EPA and a number of environmental groups, the U.S. foam packaging industry took the next step, moving beyond the interim HCFCs to completely ozone-safe substitutes. Yet another step came in November 1990, when McDonald's decided to eliminate foam packaging altogether in favor of paper in order to minimize solid waste.[42]

For refrigeration and air conditioning, HCFCs and HFCs were initially used widely as substitutes for CFCs. But

Table 9-1. *(Continued)*

Compounds	Applications	Interim Substitutes[1]	Examples of "Not-In-Kind" Substitutes[2]
Halons	fire extin-guishers	HCFs, PCFs	The Norwegian Fire Research Laboratory, after five years of research, concluded that water is as effective as halons in all instances except small electrical fires. "Inergen," a mixture of argon, nitrogen, and carbon dioxide, is widely used in Europe.
Methyl Bromide	multiuse pesticide (fumigation of soil, commodi-ties, storage areas)	chlorinated pesticides, such as "Telone" and "DD" mixtures	Integrated pest management (IPM), a range of chemical and nonchemical tactics, has completely replaced methyl bromide in some countries. An IPM strategy based on composting replaced methyl bromide for flower production in Colombia and saves growers there about $1,900 per hectare. Carbon dioxide is used to treat stored grain in Indonesia, the Philippines, and Vietnam. In Missouri, Quaker Oats operates a production plant that uses heat to kill pests in the building.

[1] HCFCs are scheduled for eventual phaseout under the Montreal Protocol. HFCs and perfluorocarbons (PFCs) are not scheduled for phaseout, but are labeled as "interim" because they are potent greenhouse gases. Likewise, the pesticides listed as interim are not scheduled for phaseout, but they are carcinogens.
[2]This broad category includes simpler, naturally occurring chemicals as well as design changes that eliminate the need for any chemicals.
SOURCE: Compiled by Worldwatch Institute from sources cited in endnote 39.

nonfluorocarbon substitutes are quickly gaining ground. For instance, ammonia and simple hydrocarbons such as propane and butane have been commercialized for use as refrigerants. Interestingly, the use of these nonfluorocarbon technologies represents a return to coolants used before the development of CFCs. Engineering changes to the appliances have made it possible to use smaller quantities of coolant, thus reducing the risks of flammability and toxicity that prompted the shift to CFCs in the first place.[43]

With the phaseout of methyl bromide shaping up as the next key step in repairing the ozone layer, the search for alternatives to it is beginning to get un-der way in earnest. There is no one chemical that can be substituted for all of this pesticide's many uses, so different strategies will have to be devised for each use. Just as replacing CFCs with HCFCs and other greenhouse gases may solve one problem while contributing to another, relying solely on other toxic chemicals to replace methyl bromide could ultimately endanger human health. Some countries, including the Netherlands and Denmark, have moved away from methyl bromide through heavier reliance on nonchemical pest control methods such as heat treatment and crop rotation.[44]

Meanwhile, the unexpected success of nonfluorocarbon alternatives to CFCs has upset the business plans of DuPont and the other major chemical companies. In 1989, DuPont had estimated that global CFC consumption would be replaced in 2000 by a combination of HCFCs in 30 percent of the cases, by HFCs in 9 percent, by conservation in 29 percent, and by "not-in-kind" (that is, nonfluorocarbon) replacements in 32 percent of uses. By 1992, the projections had changed to 11 percent HCFCs, 15 percent HFCs, 26 percent conservation, and 48 percent not-in-kind.[45]

The chemical industry is thus realizing much lower returns on its investments in substitutes than initially anticipated. This explains its vociferous lobbying against proposals to speed the phaseout of HCFCs. In addition, no doubt worried that HFCs could come under control through the climate treaty, several chemical companies have begun to participate in those negotiations as members of the International Climate Change Partnership, a coalition of companies and trade associations monitoring the climate talks.[46]

Though it may not have helped the chemical industry, for society at large the impressive spurt of technological innovation prompted by the Montreal Protocol is a notable achievement. By 1994, the economic options committee of the protocol's technology and economic assessment panel was able to declare triumphantly that the replacement of ozone-depleting substances had been "more rapid, less expensive, and more innovative" than originally anticipated. As a result, the CFC phaseout in industrial countries passed by on 1 January 1996, without great hardship. It will be worth remembering this as the battles heat up over climate change. The arguments being put forth by some vested industrial interests today sound eerily similar to the dire warnings of economic disruption often voiced in the early days of the ozone debates.[47]

THE NORTH-SOUTH PARTNERSHIP

In addition to involving scientists and industry in new and unique ways, the Montreal Protocol has set new precedents in North-South relations. It was the first international environmental accord to face head-on the difficult equity questions that form an important political backdrop to efforts to set the world on a sustainable course.

When the Montreal Protocol was first negotiated, developing countries used only a small amount of CFCs. Yet their usage of them was projected to grow rapidly in the years ahead as these countries strove to raise living standards by providing refrigerators, air conditioning, and other amenities to their citizens. If these countries did not participate in the accord, growth in developing-world CFC consumption would likely soon swamp any reductions in industrial countries. China and India were of particular concern. Though neither was at the time a significant CFC consumer, together they accounted for nearly 40 percent of the world's population—and both had plans to increase dramatically the production of consumer goods that could contain CFCs. Developing countries were understandably reluctant, however, to accept apparent constraints on development for a problem not of their own making. They are now expressing similar views in the ongoing climate change negotiations.[48]

Besides granting developing nations a 10-year grace period, the original protocol also stipulated that industrial countries should provide funding and technology to help others make the transition. Yet in the days after the accord was finalized, it became increasingly clear that these provisions alone might be insufficient to convince many developing countries to join in the accord. Thus, by the 1990 London meeting, the question of how to ensure the widespread participation of developing countries in the treaty was at the top of the negotiating agenda.[49]

After some tough bargaining, a precedent-setting deal was struck in London. Industrial countries agreed to reimburse developing countries for "all agreed incremental costs" of complying with the protocol—in other words, all additional costs above and beyond any they would expect to incur as they developed their infrastructure and consumer markets in the absence of the accord. Studies conducted by EPA indicated that these costs were relatively low—and paled in comparison with those that a damaged ozone layer would impose. The initial agreement stipulated the creation of a $240-million Interim Multilateral Fund. Key developing countries—including China and India—expressed satisfaction with the outcome, and announced their intention to join in the accord as a result.[50]

The fund was pathbreaking in a number of respects. For one thing, it was created as a joint venture between three U.N. agencies and the World Bank—organizations not accustomed to cooperating. Assisted by a secretariat based in Montreal, the executive committee of the fund was given the task of overseeing the work of the fund's four implementing agencies—UNEP, the United Nations Development Programme, the United Nations Industrial Development Organization, and the World Bank. The method of voting stipulated for the executive committee was also an important innovation. It is a middle ground between the "one-nation, one-vote" system of the United Nations and the "one-dollar, one-vote" procedure of the World Bank. The goal is to reach a consensus. But if this proves impossible, a two-thirds majority vote is required that includes a simple majority of both donor and recipient countries. So far, the executive

committee has never found it necessary to resort to voting, although the possibility that a given matter could be put to a vote undoubtedly influences the bargaining process.[51]

When the Global Environment Facility (GEF) was established in 1991 to finance other investments in developing countries that benefit the global environment, it was modeled in many respects on the ozone fund. Experience with the fund has thus been an important warm-up for the GEF. Though the Multilateral Fund is clearly playing an essential role in helping developing countries move away from reliance on ODSs, it has nonetheless been at the center of a number of controversies that hold lessons for the future.[52]

The fund has so far allocated more than $540 million for nearly 1,300 projects in 99 developing countries. The bulk of the money goes to private enterprises to help them cover the costs of converting their processes or product lines to ozone-benign technologies. Successful completion of the projects is expected to eventually prevent the consumption of more than 75,000 tons a year of ODSs weighted by ozone depletion potential (ODP)—a one-third reduction from developing countries' current annual use of some 230,000 ODP-weighted tons. Yet the implementing agencies have been slow to spend the money that the Executive Committee has approved. Fortunately, this is beginning to change as the fund irons out some of the initial wrinkles in its operations. By the middle of 1996, some 89 projects had been completed that, combined with partially completed projects, will prevent the annual consumption of more than 12,000 ODP-weighted tons. These numbers are expected to rise rapidly in the years ahead.[53]

One of the most difficult issues for the fund is how to fulfill its mandate to underwrite the "agreed incremental costs" of converting to ODS substitutes. This proviso reassured developing countries that they would not have to pay to help solve a problem they did little to create, and it let donor countries view their contributions as a direct subsidization of their own interest in protecting the global commons. The "incremental costs" concept was soon replicated in the Global Environment Facility.[54]

Though at first glance the concept makes sense, implementing projects according to the criterion has been a challenge. A primary problem is that investments that will ultimately save a country money (for example, through using a less expensive, non-CFC-based process to clean electronic circuitry) are ineligible for funding because they are seen as a benefit rather than a cost. Yet these are exactly the kinds of projects the fund would ideally want to encourage. Though these projects could in theory be financed with low-interest loans, the World Bank—the main source for this type of lending—has resisted calls to provide funding for this purpose.[55]

Developing countries are well placed to be at the cutting edge of technological transformation.

Another difficulty is the inherent tension that arises in funding a phaseout at the same time that the 10-year grace period allows consumption to increase. In some cases, donors have been hesitant to provide funds to countries who are also expanding production of ODSs for domestic use and in some cases even for export. And some developing countries have hesitated to move too quickly in phasing out ODSs out of concern that it might jeopardize their funding appli-

cations. In future environmental conventions, it may make sense for funding eligibility to be contingent on good-faith efforts to implement national policies consistent with the treaty's goals.[56]

The need to use funds as effectively as possible is particularly important, given that all promised contributions have not been forthcoming. In 1992, governments agreed to make the Interim Multilateral Fund permanent and in 1993 they replenished it with another $510 million for 1994–96—more than double the previous level. The higher sum reflected the costs to developing countries of meeting additional obligations under the strengthened treaty as well as the growing number of countries that had joined in the accord. But as of October 1996, donor countries were $154 million behind on their promised contributions. Just about half of these funds were owed by countries with economies in transition—that is, those in Eastern Europe and the former Soviet Union. Ironically, these countries are themselves on the receiving end of assistance for ozone depletion projects from the GEF. Nevertheless, this payment record compares favorably with past experience with other environmental trust funds: all told, donor countries have so far contributed 78 percent of the promised funds.[57]

The shortfalls in promised payments have become a political lightning rod in the ongoing ozone negotiations. At the Vienna meeting in 1995, some countries had proposed accelerating the timetables for developing countries further, but this was opposed by others, partially as a result of donor-country unwillingness to pledge more money. Both donor and recipient countries agree that further commitments by developing countries should be matched by promises of new funds. But they disagree on which should come first. In response to developing-country agreement to controls on new chemicals at the Vienna meeting, donor countries agreed to replenish the fund in 1997, though they have yet to decide by exactly how much.[58]

In some cases, governments in developing countries are being pulled away from ODSs by another aspect of the North-South partnership—international trade and investment. The provisions of the protocol that restricted trade in ODSs and in products containing them with countries not party to the treaty have been extremely successful in encouraging widespread participation. Yet they have become controversial in recent years, as international trade experts have questioned whether they are compatible with rules under the General Agreement on Tariffs and Trade, now the World Trade Organization.[59]

As a general matter, export-oriented developing countries tend to be ahead of the phaseout curb, as selling goods in industrial countries requires keeping pace with developments there. China learned this lesson the hard way: it saw its refrigerator exports decline by 58 percent between 1988 and 1991 as demand for CFC-containing refrigerators in industrial countries plummeted. As a consequence, the government moved aggressively to develop ozone-friendly refrigerators, and has said it will phase CFCs out faster than required under the protocol. Similarly, U.S. CFC labelling requirements have prompted Mexico, Thailand, and Turkey to move forward quickly in replacing CFCs.[60]

In addition, many multinational corporations adopt the same practices in their overseas operations that they use at home. In the Philippines, for instance, many foreign-owned electronics manufacturers have already eliminated most uses of ODSs as solvents. Similarly, ODS consumption in Kenya fell by two thirds between 1989 and 1993 due at least in part to changes instituted by investing companies based in industrial countries. By May 1993, more than 60 manufacturers from Canada, Germany, Japan, Sweden, and the United States had ended the use of CFC-113 worldwide.[61]

Yet developing countries are also worried that old CFC-based technologies will be dumped on them as industrial countries complete the phaseout. Already, there are reports of large numbers of secondhand CFC refrigerators being sold in parts of Africa as non-ODS models take off in Europe.[62]

Despite this threat, developing countries are in fact well placed to be at the cutting edge of technological transformation. Rather than being a net cost, in many cases the transition to ozone-benign processes offers substantial economic opportunities. And because the grace period meant that developing countries did not have to rush to replace CFCs, these nations have the advantage of not yet being heavily invested in transitional chemical replacements. It makes more sense to leapfrog directly to the technologies of tomorrow than to invest first in transitional technologies, and then (for much larger populations, and at higher future costs) in the replacements that will ultimately be required.[63]

Fortunately, the ozone experience has spurred an unprecedented level of technology cooperation internationally that will help developing countries make this transition. For instance, the OzonAction program sponsored by UNEP's Industry and Environment Office plays an essential role as a clearinghouse for information about substitute processes and technologies. The private sector is also active; working through the International Cooperative for Ozone Layer Protection, a number of companies have shared important technological innovations free of charge to enterprises in the developing world.[64]

THE RECORD TO DATE

Ten years after the historic Montreal signing ceremony, the response to the protocol around the world has been substantial indeed. (See Table 9–2.)

In the industrial world, many countries have done more than is required by the protocol. As a result, when the official CFC phaseout date arrived in January 1996, most industrial countries

were ready. Several had planned to phase out ozone-depleting substances before they were required to under the protocol. The European Union (EU), for one, completed its move away from CFCs at the end of 1994. The EU has also announced it will phase out HCFCs by 2015—15 years before the protocol requires it to. And the United States is obligated by its Clean Air Act to end the use of methyl bromide by 2001—nine years ahead of current protocol require-

Table 9–2. Use of Chlorofluorocarbons and Halons in Selected Countries, 1986 and 1994[1]

Country or Region	Use		Change
	1986	1994	
	(tons weighted by substance's ozone-depleting potential[2])		(percent[3])
China	46,600	90,900	+ 95
European Comm./Union	343,000	39,700	− 88
Russia[4]	129,000	32,600	− 75
Japan	135,000	19,700	− 85
South Korea	11,500	13,100	+ 15
Mexico	8,930	10,800	+ 21
Brazil	11,300	7,780	− 31
Thailand	4,660	7,230	+ 55
India	2,390	7,000	+193
Argentina	5,500	4,950	− 10
Canada	23,200	4,850	− 79
Malaysia	3,840	4,760	+ 24
Philippines	1,920	4,010	+109
Australia	18,600	3,890	− 79
Venezuela	4,590	3,130	− 32
Indonesia	1,710	2,880	+ 69
South Africa	18,700	2,420	− 87
Poland	10,600	1,680	− 84
Ukraine	1,850	1,530	− 17
United States	364,000	−91	−100

[1]"Use" is production (the amount of a substance produced in a year plus stock at the end of the year minus stock at the beginning of the year) plus imports minus exports minus feedstock use. Thus, if a lot of stockpiled material is used as feedstock to make other chemicals, the consumption number can be negative, as it is for the United States.   [2]Compounds vary in their ability to deplete ozone. These numbers reflect the tonnage of the various CFCs and halons listed in Annex A of the Montreal Protocol (CFC-11, CFC-12, CFC-113, CFC-114, CFC-115, Halon-1211, Halon-1301, and Halon-2402) multiplied by their respective ozone-depleting potentials (ODPs). The ODP value is the ratio of a given compound's ability to deplete ozone compared with the ability of a similar mass of CFC-11.   [3]Percentages may differ from the data due to rounding.   [4]Data are for 1993.

SOURCE: United Nations Environment Programme, "The Reporting of Data by the Parties to the Montreal Protocol on Substances That Deplete the Ozone Layer," Nairobi, 12 September 1996.

ments. A number of other counties, including Denmark, the Netherlands, and Germany, have adopted national rules on methyl bromide that are significantly more stringent than required. Over the years, these kinds of unilateral initiatives have put pressure on the international process, helping to build the political will to toughen the accord in London, Copenhagen, and Vienna.[65]

The protocol granted countries flexibility in designing programs to meet the Montreal targets, and many different approaches have been tried. Considerable effort has gone into designing flexible systems rather than complicated regulations of the command-and-control variety. Such programs have reduced the cost of the CFC phaseout substantially. For instance, several governments—including Belgium, Germany, Mexico, the Netherlands, and Thailand—have successfully forged voluntary pacts with both producers and end-users of ODSs. And a number of countries have used excise taxes on CFCs to help discourage their use. This technique has been adopted in Australia, Denmark, and the United States. In addition, several countries, including New Zealand, Singapore, and the United States, have relied on tradable permit systems to implement their Montreal obligations.[66]

Despite these successes, worrisome stumbling blocks in the protocol's implementation have also emerged. These call into question the assumption of full compliance that lies behind current projections for the ozone layer's recovery. It may also foreshadow difficulties to be faced in translating future ambitious international agreements into action on the ground.

For one thing, the economic and political chaos in the former Soviet Union and in some parts of Eastern Europe has slowed progress in eliminating CFCs. The 9 countries that existed in this part of the world when the protocol was first

signed have since divided into 27—only 21 of which were signatories as of October 1996. In May 1995, Russian Prime Minister Viktor Chernomyrdin informed the Montreal parties that Russia would be unable to meet the January 1996 phaseout target for CFCs. On behalf of Belarus, Bulgaria, Poland, and Ukraine as well as Russia, he requested a four-year extension on the deadline for eliminating CFCs, carbon tetrachloride, and methyl chloroform, and a three-year reprieve for halons, as well as international assistance in meeting the new goals.[67]

The committee on implementation set up under the protocol considered the request later in the year. It recommended against granting a formal extension, as it feared this would create a poor precedent by suggesting that treaty commitments need not be honored. But the committee also advised the parties to the treaty to respond to the situation with cooperation rather than with sanctions so long as the countries involved were making a good-faith effort to remedy the situation. The GEF has since made a $60-million grant to Russia for moving away from ODSs, and the World Bank is spearheading the formation of a multidonor aid program.[68]

The problems in Russia and elsewhere in the region are also contributing to yet another Achilles' heel of the accord: the growth of a black market in smuggled CFCs that threatens to significantly undermine the phaseout in industrial countries. Russia is believed to be a major source of this trade. Other countries on the suspect list include China and India. Estimates of the amount of illegal trade are bound to be uncertain. Nonetheless, hints are available as to its size, including the going legal price for CFCs, which will tend to stagnate if the market is being swamped with illegal imports. The chemical industry—which does not want the market for its substitutes to be undercut by this trade—estimated in late 1995 that as much as a fifth of the CFCs in use worldwide were illegally traded.[69]

The problem first became evident in the United States, where the high price of legal CFCs owing to the excise tax made bootlegged CFCs particularly attractive. In addition, the enormous number of car air conditioners in the United States creates a large demand for CFCs for servicing, as using substitute chemicals requires a costly retrofit. Though it is impossible to know the exact dimensions of this illicit commerce, authorities estimated in April 1995 that illegal CFC traffic through Miami was second only to the drug trade in dollar value. Spurred on by the chemical industry, the U.S. government launched a major crackdown on CFC trafficking in October 1994. The effort has so far led to 18 convictions, the impoundment of more than 450 tons of illegal CFCs, and the receipt of at least $500,000 worth of seized CFCs and cash from criminals trying to buy them from undercover government agents. Recent indications are that smuggling is down as a result.[70]

Black market problems also exist elsewhere. For instance, in Taiwan there have been 16 official seizures of CFCs since production and import became illegal on 1 January 1996. Illegal traffic in ozone-depleting substances is also of growing concern in Europe, which has been slower than the United States to crack down. The chemical industry there is calling for tougher enforcement measures.[71]

Meanwhile, it remains to be seen to what extent rising emissions in developing countries will undermine the accomplishments to date in the industrial world. The protocol requires developing countries to freeze CFC consumption in 1999, and to phase it out altogether by 2010. On the encouraging side, 58 developing countries have stated a commitment to phase out CFCs earlier than required. Five countries—Cameroon, Indonesia, the Philippines, Thailand, and Vietnam—have said they will stop using CFCs by 1998 except for servicing refrigerators and other essential uses, and 21 more claim they will do so by 2001.[72]

Consumption of ODSs is reportedly already falling in a number of developing countries—including Argentina, Brazil, Colombia, Egypt, Ghana, and Venezuela. On the other hand, it continues to rise rapidly in some countries with large populations—and relatively large CFC consumption—including India, China, and the Philippines. Altogether, developing countries' consumption of CFCs and halons increased by about one third from 1986 to 1994, albeit from a small base.[73]

MOVING FORWARD

At a time when global environmental trends appear so daunting, and progress toward reversing them seems so slow (see Chapter 1), it is reassuring to remember that in responding to the threat of ozone depletion, the international community has largely proved itself up to the task. Though the job is by no means complete, without the Montreal Protocol the world would be facing a catastrophic situation indeed. (See Figure 9–2.)[74]

Future historians may well view the signing of the Montreal Protocol in 1987 as a defining moment—a point at which it became clear that the very definition of international security was undergoing fundamental change. In foreign ministries around the world, the focus has shifted in the decade since Montreal away from such cold war concerns as nuclear arms control treaties and toward the burgeoning domain of environmental diplomacy. U.S. Secretary of State

Parts Per Trillion by Volume

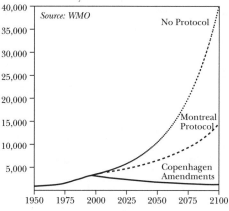

Figure 9–2. Stratospheric Chlorine and Bromine Levels Under Three Scenarios, 1950–2100

Warren Christopher made this new approach official in April 1996 when he announced a far-reaching initiative to integrate environmental concerns into U.S. foreign policy.[75]

In a coincidence of timing, 1997 is not only the tenth anniversary of the Montreal Protocol; it is also the year in which diplomats hope to complete negotiations on a Kyoto Protocol to the climate change convention that it is hoped will accomplish for global warming what the Montreal Protocol did for ozone depletion. In addition, diplomats nearly weekly attend negotiations on issues as diverse as plant genetic resources, the threat to coral reefs, water scarcity, land degradation, and overfishing. As all these crucial efforts continue, it is important to bear in mind some of the overarching lessons of the ozone experience.[76]

For one, the Montreal Protocol pioneered a new relationship between scientists and policymakers. The decision to take precautionary action in Montreal in 1987 in the absence of complete proof of the link between CFCs and ozone depletion was an act of foresight that must be replicated with other issues. It

is worth recalling that several countries went so far as to ban the use of CFCs in aerosols in the mid-seventies, when scientific understanding of ozone depletion was still in its infancy. Few countries have yet taken actions of comparable significance to address climate change, despite the fact that the international consensus on this threat is considerably more advanced now than it was in the seventies on ozone. One lesson from the ozone experience is that the longer we delay action, the greater the potential costs and consequences we can expect down the road.[77]

The gaping hole in the ozone layer over Antarctica also serves as an important reminder that we may be in for some large surprises in the years ahead as the human imprint on the earth grows so large that we are tampering with global ecological systems vital to life itself. Atmospheric scientists believe, for example, that rising concentrations of greenhouse gases could at some point cause a sudden shift in ocean currents and atmospheric flows, disrupting agriculture and threatening many natural ecosystems (see Chapter 5). We are conducting a massive and somewhat reckless experiment the consequences of which are difficult to predict. Notes Nobel-laureate Sherwood Rowland: "One of the strongest warnings from the ozone depletion experience is that the unexpected can work in both directions—some changes will ameliorate the situation, others will make things worse, sometimes much worse."[78]

Beyond the pathbreaking partnerships forged between scientists and policymakers, the experience with reaction to the depleting ozone layer also brought industry into the international environmental orbit on an unprecedented scale. Once the affected businesses overcame their initial resistance, they realized that in many cases the process of phasing out use of ozone-depleting substances offered economic opportunities rather than large costs. This experience demonstrates that binding treaty commitments can spur diverse forms of technological innovation that are impossible to foresee and that make early cost projections a stab in the dark. Yet it is important to bear in mind that technologies seen as solutions to problems may also bring with them important liabilities of their own, as the turn to HCFCs and HFCs has demonstrated.[79]

Binding treaty commitments can spur diverse forms of technological innovation that make early cost projections a stab in the dark.

Meanwhile, once at the negotiating table, industry has decided to stay. Its strong presence is now felt in many different international environmental forums, including those on climate change, biological diversity loss, and the control of persistent organic pollutants.

In the climate change negotiations, a number of U.S.-based industries—such as coal and oil—that are concerned they would suffer under an accord have participated in a group called the Global Climate Coalition that is engaging in unabashedly obstructionist tactics. Others, such as those represented by the International Climate Change Partnership, are more measured in their response. This group is dominated by chemical companies and manufacturers that first joined forces on the ozone issue. Partially because of their experience with ozone depletion, these companies seem to have accepted that stronger international action on climate is inevitable, and are hoping to influence its terms.[80]

Fortunately, there are still other business groups that have staked out positions enthusiastically in favor of a strong

accord. For instance, business councils for sustainable energy have been formed in the last few years in Australia, Europe, and the United States; they represent appliance manufacturers and renewable energy, energy services, cogeneration, and natural gas companies that have calculated that a strong climate treaty would help their bottom lines. The insurance industry has also become a convert to the cause, as it is worried that extreme weather disturbances linked with climate change will translate into steeply rising claims. At the most recent international negotiations on climate, both the U.S.-based Business Council for Sustainable Energy and a group made up of nearly 60 major insurance companies from around the world issued statements supportive of a strong accord.[81]

On the biodiversity issue, some U.S. industries were initially wary of the Convention on Biological Diversity, as they feared its provisions on intellectual property rights might jeopardize their patents. Yet once the treaty was in place, industry soon became a strong supporter of U.S. ratification. Pharmaceutical companies, biotechnology firms, seed companies, and other affected industries want the United States to have a seat at any table where decisions are made that will affect their interests.[82]

Beyond involving industry, responding to the many global environmental challenges the world faces will also require an unprecedented degree of cooperation between the industrial and developing worlds. If developing countries follow the same resource-intensive path that industrial countries did, the consequences for the global environment will be catastrophic. The ozone treaty and its successive amendments represent the most advanced attempt to date to give concrete form to the abstract notion of global partnership advanced at the Rio Earth Summit.

Experience with this partnership offers both reason for hope as well as some cause for concern. On the hopeful side is the ability of the global marketplace to diffuse technological gains worldwide, thus facilitating a widespread sharing of the results of innovation. On the worrisome side, however, bureaucratic bottlenecks have slowed down the global response to the ozone challenge. In addition, the difficulties that donor countries have experienced in raising promised funds suggests that more reliable financing sources need to be identified in the future.

Another important lesson from the ozone experience is how important it is to design treaties so that they can be easily updated to take account of new scientific and technical findings. We have also learned that international institutions make a difference; in this case,

UNEP played an important initiation and leadership role. And the last 10 years have taught us that public concern can indeed translate into action by both industry and government.[83]

Finally, the results since the Montreal Protocol was signed in September 1987 have taught us that individuals matter. Though the accomplishments of the Montreal Protocol could not have occurred without the participation of millions of people all over the world, a handful of tireless individuals confronted the ozone challenge with the fervor of crusaders—scientists, diplomats, NGO activists, business people, legislators, and government officials among them. As we approach the twenty-first century, a new generation of such people faces the task of responding to other daunting environmental challenges that cry out for similar attention—and similar results.[84]

Notes

Chapter 1. The Legacy of Rio

Some of the references in this chapter were obtained on-line from conferences of the Association for Progressive Communications (APC), which in the United States are maintained and archived by the Institute for Global Communications in San Francisco.

1. Population growth is a projection for 1992–97, based on Population Reference Bureau (PRB), "World Population Data Sheet" (wallchart), Washington, D.C., annual; carbon emissions projection is for 1992–97, based on Odil Tunali, "Carbon Emissions Hit All-Time High," in Lester R. Brown, Christopher Flavin, and Hal Kane, *Vital Signs 1996* (New York: W.W. Norton & Company, 1996). Emission figures in this chapter are expressed in tons of carbon, even when the term carbon dioxide is used; as fossil fuels are burned, the carbon in them is combined with oxygen to become carbon dioxide, which has a much greater molecular weight.

2. U.N. Food and Agriculture Organization (FAO), *Forest Resources Assessment 1990: Global Synthesis*, FAO Forestry Paper 124 (Rome: 1995); U.N. Development Programme (UNDP), *Human Development Report 1996* (New York: Oxford University Press, 1996).

3. International Monetary Fund (IMF), *World Economic Outlook* (Washington, D.C.: 1996); environmental effects of trade liberalization from Hans-Peter Martin and Harald Schumann, *The Global Trap: The Assault on Democracy and Prosperity* (Hamburg: Rowohlt Verlag, 1996).

4. United Nations, *Agenda 21: The United Nations Programme of Action From Rio* (New York: U.N. Publications, 1992).

5. Ibid.

6. Hilary F. French, "Hidden Success at Rio," *World Watch*, September/October 1992; Hilary F. French, *Partnership for the Planet: An Environmental Agenda for the United Nations*, Worldwatch Paper 126 (Washington, D.C.: Worldwatch Institute, July 1995).

7. World Resources Institute (WRI), International Institute for Environment and Development, and World Conservation Union–IUCN, *World Directory of Country Environmental Studies* (Washington, D.C.: WRI, 1996); French, *Partnership for the Planet*, op. cit. note 6.

8. "Biotechnology Working Group Outlines Elements for Future Biodiversity Convention Protocol," *International Environment Reporter*, 7 August 1996; fish treaty from "Treaty Ratification, Local Control Efforts on Agenda of Parties to International Accord," *International Environment Reporter*, 26 June 1996; desertification from WRI, United Nations Environment Programme (UNEP), UNDP, and World Bank, *World Resources 1996–97* (New York: Oxford University Press, 1996); "Ban on Waste Exports Outside OECD Pushed Through Basel Treaty Meeting," *International Environment Reporter*, 4 October 1995; "Countries Adopt Program of Action to Curb Marine Contamination from Land," *International Environment Reporter*, 15 November 1995; "Negotiations on Pops Treaty Under Way in Geneva, to Continue in Canberra

in March," *International Environment Reporter,* 21 February 1996.

9. Michael Grubb, *The Earth Summit Agreements: A Guide and Assessment* (London: Earthscan, 1993).

10. Barbara Crossette, "Environment Yielding to Other Worries, U.N. Talks Suggest," *New York Times,* 5 May 1996; United Nations, op. cit. note 4; Organisation for Economic Co-operation and Development (OECD), "Financial Flows to Developing Countries in 1995," news release, Paris, 11 June 1996.

11. Jim Sniffen, UNEP, New York, private communication, 19 August 1996; Rameesh Gampat, UNDP, New York, private communication, 16 August 1996; "Fortune Global 500: The World's Largest Corporations," *Fortune,* 5 August 1996; French, *Partnership for the Planet,* op. cit. note 6; William H. Mansfield, "Remarks at State Department Consultation on Secretary Christopher's Statement and UN Environmental Needs," unpublished, 23 July 1996.

12. Hilary F. French, "Forging a New Global Partnership," in Lester R. Brown et al., *State of the World 1995* (New York: W.W. Norton & Company, 1995).

13. World Bank, *Mainstreaming the Environment* (Washington, D.C.: 1995); Global Environment Facility (GEF) budget data from Anne Bohon, GEF Secretariat, Washington, D.C., private communication, 23 August 1996.

14. World Bank, *Annual Report 1996* (Washington, D.C.: 1996); World Bank, *Making Development Sustainable: The World Bank Group and the Environment* (Washington, D.C.: 1994); WRI, "A New Environmental Sensitivity at the World Bank: Highlights from World Bank President James Wolfensohn's Speech," Washington, D.C., 2 October 1995.

15. Hilary F. French, "The World Bank: Now 50, But How Fit?" *World Watch,* July/ August 1994; Bruce Rich, *Mortgaging the Earth: The World Bank, Environmental Impoverishment, and the Crisis of Development* (Boston, Mass.: Beacon Press, 1994); Nancy Alexander, "Reforming the Management of the World Bank's Loan Portfolio," Bread for the World, Washington, D.C., unpublished, 24 June 1996; Leyla Boulton, "World Bank Admits to Weakness on Environment," *Financial Times,* 4 October 1996.

16. Hal Kane, "Sulfur and Nitrogen Emissions Steady," in Brown, Flavin, and Kane, op. cit. note 1; Odil Tunali, "Lead in Gasoline Slowly Phased Out," in Lester R. Brown, Nicholas Lenssen, and Hal Kane, *Vital Signs 1995* (New York: W.W. Norton & Company, 1995); Anjali Acharya, "CFC Production Drop Continues," in Brown, Flavin, and Kane, op. cit. note 1.

17. Anne E. Platt, *Infecting Ourselves: How Environmental and Social Disruptions Trigger Disease,* Worldwatch Paper 129 (Washington, D.C.: Worldwatch Institute, April 1996); Theo Colborn, Dianne Dumanoski, and John Peterson Myers, *Our Stolen Future* (New York: Dutton, 1996).

18. The data on gross national product (GNP) presented here are based on exchange rate figures, which tend to understate the relative size of developing-country economies. According to figures based on purchasing power parity, for example, China's GNP in 1994 would have been more than three times as large, and only slightly smaller than that of Japan.

19. French, *Partnership for the Planet,* op. cit. note 6.

20. Curtis Moore and Alan Miller, *Green Gold: Japan, Germany, the United States, and the Race for Environmental Technology* (Boston, Mass.: Beacon Press, 1994); Michael Grubb, "Viewpoint: The Berlin Climate Conference; Shifting Alliances Break Political Deadlock," *EC Energy Monthly,* 21 April 1995.

21. Brendan Barrett, *Environmental Policy and Impact Assessment in Japan* (New York:

Routledge, 1991); Miranda Schreurs, "Policy Laggard or Policy Leader? Global Environmental Policy-Making Under the Liberal Democratic Party," *Journal of Pacific Asia*, Vol. 2, 1995.

22. Anjali Acharya, "Plundering the Boreal Forests," *World Watch*, May/June 1995; Mike Moore, "Chernobyl—Ten Years Later," *Bulletin of the Atomic Scientists*, May/June 1996; Duncan Brack, *International Trade and the Montreal Protocol* (London: Earthscan, for the Royal Institute of International Affairs, 1996); Borozin quote from Charles P. Alexander, "Two Years After the Earth Summit It's Time to Take the Pulse of the Planet," *Time*, 7 November 1994.

23. Asian Development Bank, *Climate Change in Asia: The Thematic Overview* (Manila: 1994); effect of rising seas from R.T. Watson, M.C. Zinyowera, and R.H. Moss, eds., *Climate Change 1995: Impacts, Adaptation, and Migration of Climate Change—Scientific-Technical Analysis, Contribution of Working Group II to the Second Assessment Report of the Intergovernmental Panel on Climate Change* (New York: Cambridge University Press, 1996); Rene Bowser et al., *Southern Exposure: Global Climate Change and Developing Countries* (Washington, D.C.: Center for Global Change USA, 1992).

24. PRB, op. cit. note 1; Grubb, op. cit. note 20.

25. "How Poor is China?" *The Economist*, 12–18 October 1996; Lester R. Brown and Christopher Flavin, "China's Challenge to the United States and to the Earth," *World Watch*, September/October 1996; Vaclav Smil, *China's Environmental Crisis* (Armonk, N.Y.: M.E. Sharpe, Inc., 1993); Lester Ross, "The Politics of Environmental Policy in the People's Republic of China," in Uday Desai, ed., *Ecological Policy and Politics in Developing Countries: Economic Growth, Democracy and Environmental Protection* (Albany, N.Y.: State University of New York Press, 1996).

26. J.T. Houghton et al., eds., *Climate Change 1995: The Science of Climate Change, Contribution of Working Group I to the Second Assessment Report of the Intergovernmental Panel on Climate Change* (New York: Cambridge University Press, 1996).

27. Figure 1–1 based on G. Marland, R.J. Andres, and T.A. Boden, "Global, Regional, and National CO_2 Emission Estimates From Fossil Fuel Burning, Cement Production, and Gas Flaring: 1950–1992" (electronic database) (Oak Ridge, Tenn.: Carbon Dioxide Information Analysis Center, Oak Ridge National Laboratory, 1995), and Worldwatch estimates based on ibid. and on British Petroleum (BP), *BP Statistical Review of World Energy* (London: Group Media & Publications, 1995); other emissions from Houghton et al., op. cit. note 26.

28. Marland, Andres, and Boden, op. cit. note 27; Worldwatch estimates based on ibid., on BP, op. cit. note 27, and on PRB, "1995 World Population Data Sheet" (wallchart), Washington, D.C., 1995.

29. United Nations, *United Nations Framework Convention on Climate Change*, Text (Geneva: UNEP/World Meteorological Organization Information Unit on Climate Change, 1992).

30. Chancellor Helmut Kohl, speech to the First Conference of the Parties to the United Nations Framework Convention on Climate Change, Berlin, 5 April 1995; U.S. Climate Action Network and Climate Network Europe, *Independent NGO Evaluations of National Plans for Climate Change Mitigation: OECD Countries, Third Review, January 1995* (Washington, D.C.: U.S. Climate Action Network, 1995); International Energy Agency (IEA), *Climate Change Policy Initiatives, Volume 1: OECD Countries* (Paris: OECD, 1994); emissions from Marland, Andres, and Boden, op. cit. note 27, with Worldwatch estimates based on ibid. and on BP, op. cit. note 27.

31. U.S. Climate Action Network and Climate Network Europe, op. cit. note 30; IEA, op. cit. note 30; Christopher Flavin, "Wind Power Soars," in Brown, Lenssen, and Kane, op. cit. note 16; gasoline tax from IEA, *En-*

ergy Prices and Taxes, First Quarter, 1995 (Paris: OECD, 1995); "Industry Announces Voluntary Strategy to Cut CO_2 Emissions 20 Percent by 2005," *International Environment Reporter,* 3 April 1996; coal subsidy from Nathaniel Nash, "German High Court Bans Energy Subsidy on Utility Bills," *New York Times,* 8 December 1994; "Accord on German Coal Subsidies Highlights Bonn Coalition Rift," *European Energy Report,* 17 March 1995; Wilfrid Bach, "Coal Policy and Climate Protection: Can the Tough German CO_2 Reduction Target Be Met By 2005?" *Energy Policy,* Vol. 23, No. 1, 1995.

32. Marland, Andres, and Boden, op. cit. note 27, with Worldwatch estimates based on ibid. and on BP, op. cit. note 27.

33. President William J. Clinton and Vice President Albert Gore, Jr., *The Climate Change Action Plan* (Washington, D.C.: White House, 1993); U.S. Department of Energy, Energy Information Administration, *Annual Energy Outlook 1996* (Washington, D.C.: 1996); U.S. Climate Action Network and Climate Network Europe, op. cit. note 30.

34. U.S. Climate Action Network and Climate Network Europe, op. cit. note 30; IEA, op. cit. note 30; Dwight Van Winkle, "Japan's CO_2 Emissions Rise Post-2000," APC conference <climate.forum>, 12 June 1995; "Agency Planning More Comprehensive Laws on Global Warming," *Foreign Broadcast Information Service (FBIS) Report,* 27 December 1995; Marland, Andres, and Boden, op. cit. note 27, with Worldwatch estimates based on ibid. and on BP, op. cit. note 27.

35. Marland, Andres, and Boden, op. cit. note 27, with Worldwatch estimates based on ibid. and on BP, op. cit. note 27; Jessica Hamburger, *China's Energy and Environment in the Roaring Nineties: A Policy Primer* (Washington, D.C.: Pacific Northwest Laboratory, 1995).

36. United Nations, op. cit. note 29.

37. IEA, *World Energy Outlook: 1996 Edition* (Paris: OECD, 1996).

38. "Little Progress at Climate Convention Meeting," *Environment Watch: Western Europe,* 15 March 1996; Leyla Boulton, "U.S. Back in Driving Seat on Climate," *Financial Times,* 31 July 1996; Seth S. Dunn, "The Geneva Conference: Implications for U.N. Framework Convention on Climate Change," *International Environment Reporter,* 2 October 1996.

39. Edward O. Wilson, *The Diversity of Life* (New York: W.W. Norton & Company, 1992); John C. Ryan, *Life Support: Conserving Biological Diversity,* Worldwatch Paper 108 (Washington, D.C.: Worldwatch Institute, April 1992); World Conservation Union–IUCN, "Animals in the Red: Mounting Evidence of Jeopardy to World's Species," press release, Washington, D.C., 3 October 1996.

40. "Conservation of Biodiversity," in *China's Agenda 21* (Beijing: China Environmental Science Press, 1994); Smil, op. cit. note 25.

41. Figure 1–2 from World Conservation Monitoring Centre (WCMC), *Global Biodiversity: Status of the Earth's Living Resources* (London: Chapman & Hall, 1992); Kal Raustiala and David G. Victor, "The Future of the Convention on Biological Diversity," *Environment,* May 1996; number of ratifications from "Governments Work Towards Achieving Biodiversity Treaty Goals," press release, UNEP, Montreal, 1 November 1996.

42. Russia's forest area from FAO, op. cit. note 2; China's flowering plants from WCMC, op. cit. note 41.

43. "Statement by the Head of the Brazilian Delegation to the First Session of the Conference of the Parties to the Convention on Biological Diversity, His Excellency Dr. Getulio Lamartine de Paula Fonseca, Deputy-Minister for the Environment and the Amazon Region," Nassau, Bahamas, December 1994.

44. Diana Jean Schemo, "Burning of Amazon Picks Up Pace, With Vast Areas Lost," *New York Times,* 12 September 1996.

45. Government of the Republic of Indonesia, *Country Paper on the Implementation of Biodiversity Management in Indonesia*, submitted to the Second Meeting of the Conference of the Parties to the United Nations Convention on Biological Diversity, Jakarta Indonesia, 6–17 November 1995.

46. Ibid.

47. Ryan, op. cit. note 39; Kathie Durbin, "High Noon in the National Forests," *The Amicus Journal*, Summer 1996.

48. Myers from Anjali Acharya,"The Fate of the Boreal Forests," *World Watch*, May/June 1995.

49. World Wildlife Fund, *Conserving Russia's Biological Diversity* (Washington, D.C.: 1994); biodiversity strategy from Margaret Williams and Eugene Simonov, "Investing in the Future of Russia's Biodiversity: Immediate Action Plan for Russia's Protected Areas," *Russian Conservation News*, May 1995; Vsevolod Stepanitsky, "Russia Adopts New Federal Law on Protected Areas," *Russian Conservation News*, May 1995; Vadim O. Mokievsky, "A New Wildlife Law is Passed in the Russian Federation," *Russian Conservation News*, August 1995.

50. Figure 1–3 from U.N. Population Division, *World Population Prospects: The 1994 Revision* (New York: United Nations, 1995); Carl Haub, PRB, Washington, D.C., private communication, August 8, 1996.

51. C. Alison McIntosh and Jason L. Finkle, "The Cairo Conference on Population and Development: A New Paradigm?" *Population and Development Review*, June 1995; Aaron Sachs, "Population Growth Steady," in Brown, Lenssen, and Kane, op. cit. note 16; Gita Sen, Adrienne Germain, and Lincoln C. Chen, eds., *Population Policies Reconsidered: Health, Empowerment, and Rights* (Boston, Mass.: Harvard School of Public Health, 1994).

52. United Nations Population Fund, *The State of World Population 1995* (New York: 1993); McIntosh and Finkle, op. cit. note 51.

53. U.N. Population Division, op. cit. note 50; U.N. Population Division, *Abortion Policies: A Global Review* (New York: 1995). The total fertility rate is the average number of children that would be born alive to a woman during her lifetime if she were to pass through all her childbearing years. The contraceptive prevalence rate is the percentage of currently married women or women in union of reproductive age (15–49) who are using any form of contraception. The maternal mortality ratio is the number of deaths of women from pregnancy-related causes per 100,000 live births per year, which can be hard to estimate due to misclassifications of death; as a result of a new method developed by Johns Hopkins University, the World Health Organization, and UNICEF, however, these estimates are believed to be much more accurate, and significantly higher than previous estimates.

54. "Indonesia 1994: Results from the Demographic and Health Surveys," *Studies in Family Planning*, March/April 1996.

55. Carolyn Schmidt, "An Analysis of the Fertility Decline in Brazil," Colombia University, New York, 1 May 1996; George Martine, "Brazil's Fertility Decline, 1965–95: A Fresh Look at Key Factors," *Population and Development Review*, March 1996.

56. Fertility rates are estimates from PRB, Washington, D.C., private communication, August 1996; coercive family planning programs from "Family Planning at a Price," *U.S. News and World Report*, 19 September 1994.

57. "Chinese Government White Paper on Family Planning," *Population and Development Review*, June 1996; Sen, Germain, and Chen, op. cit. note 51.

58. Russia's population decline from Toni Nelson, "Russia's Population Sink," *World Watch*, January/February 1996; U.S. population growth from U.N. Population Division, op. cit. note 50; international assistance data from Population Action International, *1995 Annual Report* (Washington, D.C.: 1996).

59. Worldwatch estimate based on current levels of food, steel, wood, and energy consumption per person in the United States, Brazil, Indonesia, and India.

60. Wuppertal Institute study is Ernst U. von Weizsäcker, Amory B. Lovins, and L. Hunter Lovins, "Factor Four: Doubling Wealth—Halving Resource Use," A Report to the Club of Rome, unpublished draft, 1996.

61. Local Agenda 21s from Mary Pattenden, International Council for Local Environmental Initiatives, Toronto, Canada, private communication, 4 October 1996.

62. "Nongovernmental Organizations: A Growing Force in the Developing World," in WRI, *World Resources 1992–93* (New York: Oxford University Press, 1992); Alan B. Durning, *Action at the Grassroots: Fighting Poverty and Environmental Decline*, Worldwatch Paper 88 (Washington, D.C.: Worldwatch Institute, May 1989).

63. Compact fluorescent lamps from Toni Nelson, "Sales of Compact Fluorescents Soar," in Brown, Flavin, and Kane, op. cit. note 1; wind turbines from Christopher Flavin, "Wind Power Growth Accelerates," in ibid.

64. Institute for International Finance from Paul Blustein, "For Developing World, Investments More a Private Matter," *Washington Post*, 25 September 1996; Stephan Schmidheiny and Federico Zorraquín, *Financing Change* (Cambridge, Mass.: The MIT Press, 1996).

65. Hal Kane, "Micro-enterprise," *World Watch*, March/April 1996.

66. Paul Hawken, *The Ecology of Commerce* (New York: HarperCollins, 1993).

67. See Stephan Schmidheiny, with the Business Council for Sustainable Development, *Changing Course* (Cambridge, Mass.: The MIT Press, 1992) (the Council subsequently became the World Business Council for Sustainable Development); UNEP Insurance Initiative, "Position Paper on Climate Change," Geneva, 9 July 1996.

68. For market development of goods without chlorofluorocarbons, see Chapter 9; wind power in India from Flavin, op. cit. note 31.

69. Secretary of State Warren Christopher, "American Diplomacy and the Global Environmental Challenges of the 21st Century," address at Stanford University, Palo Alto, Calif., 9 April 1996.

Chapter 2. Facing the Prospect of Food Scarcity

1 "Grain Prices Continue to Climb; Official Urges Calmer Trading," *New York Times*, 26 April 1996; "Prices for Wheat and Corn Drop on Hopes for Improved Harvests," *New York Times*, 30 April 1996; "Futures Prices," *Wall Street Journal*, various editions.

2. Annual population increase from U.S. Bureau of the Census, as made available in "World Population, Midyear 1950–2050" (electronic database), Economic Research Service (ERS), U.S. Department of Agriculture (USDA), Washington, D.C., updated July 1995; USDA, "Production, Supply, and Distribution" (electronic database), Washington, D.C., February 1996.

3. U.N. Food and Agriculture Organization (FAO), *Yearbook of Fishery Statistics: Catches and Landings* (Rome: various years).

4. James Hansen et al., Goddard Institute for Space Studies Surface Air Temperature Analyses, "Table of Global-Mean Monthly, Annual and Seasonal Land-Ocean Temperature Index, 1950–Present," <http://www.giss.nasa,gov/Data/GISTEMP>, 19 January 1996; USDA, op. cit. note 2.

5. Annual population increase from Bureau of the Census, op. cit. note 2; Asian population from Population Reference Bureau (PRB), "1995 World Population Data Sheet" (wallchart), Washington, D.C., 1995.

6. FAO, op. cit. note 3; annual population increase from Bureau of the Census, op. cit. note 2.

7. FAO, op. cit. note 3; FAO, *FAO Production Yearbooks* (Rome: various years).

8. Figure 2–1 from USDA, "World Grain Database" (unpublished printout), Washington, D.C., 1991, and from USDA, op. cit. note 2; 1996 estimates from USDA, Foreign Agricultural Service (FAS), *Grain: World Markets and Trade*, Washington, D.C., June 1996; Figure 2–2 from USDA (unpublished printout), op. cit. in this note, from USDA, op. cit. note 2, from USDA, "World Agricultural Supply and Demand Estimates," Washington, D.C, January 1996, and from USDA, FAS, *Grain: World Markets and Trade*, Washington, D.C, January 1996.

9. Figure 2–3 from Bureau of the Census, op. cit. note 2, and from USDA, op. cit. note 2.

10. K.F. Isherwood and K.G. Soh, "Short Term Prospects for World Agriculture and Fertilizer Use," presented at 21st Enlarged Council Meeting, International Fertilizer Industry Association, Paris, 15–17 November 1995; USDA, FAS, "World Agricultural Production," Washington, D.C., October 1995; USDA, FAS, *Grain: World Markets and Trade*, Washington, D.C., December 1995; USDA, FAS, *Grain: World Markets and Trade*, Washington, D.C., September 1996.

11. USDA, "World Agricultural Production," Washington, D.C., various issues; USDA, op. cit. note 2; USDA, FAS, *Grain: World Markets and Trade*, Washington, D.C., August 1995; grain price information from International Monetary Fund (IMF), *International Financial Statistics* (Washington, D.C.: various years).

12. FAO, *The State of Food and Agriculture 1995* (Rome: 1995).

13. Gordon Sloggett and Clifford Dickason, *Ground-Water Mining in the United States* (Washington, D.C.: USDA, ERS, 1986);

Vaclav Smil, *China's Environmental Crisis* (Armonk, N.Y.: M.E. Sharpe, 1993); Sandra Postel, *Dividing the Waters: Food Security, Ecosystem Health, and the New Politics of Scarcity*, Worldwatch Paper 132 (Washington, D.C.: Worldwatch Institute, September 1996).

14. USDA, op. cit. note 2.

15. Annual population increase from Bureau of the Census, op. cit. note 2.

16. Bureau of the Census, op. cit. note 2.

17. USDA (unpublished printout), op. cit. note 8; USDA, op. cit. note 2.

18. USDA, ERS, *Agricultural Resources: Cropland, Water and Conservation Situation and Outlook Report*, Washington, D.C., September 1991.

19. "Chinese Roads Paved with Gold," *Financial Times*, 23 November 1994.

20. N. Vasuki Rao, "World's Top Automakers On the Road to India," *Journal of Commerce*, 26 February 1996.

21. FAO, op. cit. note 7; USDA, op. cit. note 2; FAO, op. cit. note 12; USDA (unpublished printout), op. cit. note 8.

22. USDA, op. cit. note 2; Wang Rong, "Food Before Golf on Southern Land," *China Daily*, 25 January 1995.

23. USDA, op. cit. note 2.

24. Ibid.; Bureau of the Census, op. cit. note 2.

25. Isherwood and Soh, op. cit. note 10; USDA, October 1995, op. cit. note 10; USDA, December 1995, op. cit. note 10; USDA, September 1996, op. cit. note 10; USDA, ERS, *Agricultural Resources Inputs: Situation and Outlook Report*, Washington, D.C., October 1993.

26. USDA, op. cit. note 2; USDA (unpublished printout), op. cit. note 8; USDA, January 1996, op. cit. note 8; population from Bureau of the Census, op. cit. note 2.

27. FAO, *FAO Production Yearbook 1993* (Rome: 1994); Bill Quinby, ERS, USDA,

Washington, D.C., private communication, 24 January 1996.

28. Sandra Postel, *Last Oasis: Facing Water Scarcity* (New York: W.W. Norton & Company, 1992); Quinby, op. cit. note 27; Figure 2–4 from FAO, op. cit. note 7.

29. Irrigated area in FAO, op. cit. note 7, with per capita figures derived from Bureau of the Census, op. cit. note 2.

30. FAO, *FAO Production Yearbook 1994* (Rome: 1995).

31. W. Hunter Colby et al., *Agricultural Statistics of the People's Republic of China, 1949–90* (Washington, D.C.: USDA, ERS, 1992).

32. Sloggett and Dickason, op. cit. note 13.

33. USDA, Natural Resources Conservation Service, *Summary Report: 1992 National Resources Inventory*, Washington, D.C., July 1994, rev. January 1995; Sandra Postel, "Forging a Sustainable Water Strategy," in Lester R. Brown et al., *State of the World 1996* (New York: W.W. Norton & Company, 1996).

34. R.P.S. Malik and Paul Faeth, "Rice-Wheat Production in Northwest India," in Paul Faeth, ed., *Agricultural Policy and Sustainability: Case Studies from India, Chile, the Philippines, and the United States* (Washington, D.C.: World Resources Institute, 1993).

35. Professor Chen Yiyu, Chinese Academy of Sciences, Beijing, China, private communication in visit to Worldwatch Institute, 12 March 1996.

36. Ibid.

37. McVean Trading and Investments, Memphis, Tenn., private communication, 29 May 1996.

38. USDA, op. cit. note 33; Postel, op. cit. note 33.

39. John Barham, "Euphrates Power Plant Generates New Tension," *Financial Times*, 15 February 1996; Yuan Shu, "Nations Find Unity in Taming the Mekong," *The WorldPaper*, November 1994.

40. David Seckler, "The New Era of Water Resources Management: From 'Dry' to 'Wet' Water Savings," Consultative Group on International Agricultural Research, Washington, D.C., April 1996.

41. "Justus von Liebig," *Encyclopaedia Britannica* (Cambridge, Mass.: Encyclopaedia Britannica, Inc., 1976); "History of Agriculture," ibid.; Joseph A. Tainter, *The Collapse of Complex Societies* (New York: Cambridge University Press, 1988).

42. Figure 2–5 from FAO, *Fertilizer Yearbooks* (Rome: various years), and from Isherwood and Soh, op. cit. note 10.

43. FAO, op. cit. note 42; Isherwood and Soh, op. cit. note 10.

44. USDA, op. cit. note 25.

45. Figure 2–6 from FAO, op. cit. note 42, from International Fertilizer Industry Association, *Fertilizer Consumption Report* (Paris: 1992), from USDA (unpublished printout), op. cit. note 8, from USDA, op. cit. note 2, and from Bureau of the Census, op, cit. note 2.

46. Figure 2–7 from USDA (unpublished printout), op. cit. note 8, and from USDA, op. cit. note 2; Bureau of the Census, op. cit. note 2.

47. USDA (unpublished printout), op. cit. note 8; USDA, op. cit. note 2; Bureau of the Census, op. cit. note 2.

48. USDA (unpublished printout), op. cit. note 8; USDA, op. cit. note 2.

49. USDA (unpublished printout), op. cit. note 8; USDA, op. cit. note 2.

50. USDA (unpublished printout), op. cit. note 8; USDA, op. cit. note 2.

51. Lester R. Brown, *Tough Choices: Facing the Challenge of Food Scarcity* (New York: W.W. Norton & Company, 1996).

52. USDA, op. cit. note 2.

53. Bureau of the Census, op. cit. note 2.

54. Bureau of the Census, op. cit. note 2; IMF, *World Economic Outlook, October 1995* (Washington, D.C.: 1995).

55. IMF, op. cit. note 54; PRB, op. cit. note 5; USDA, op. cit. note 2.

56. USDA, FAS, *Livestock and Poultry: World Markets and Trade*, Washington, D.C., October 1995; PRB, op. cit. note 5; USDA, FAS, "World Agricultural Production," Washington, D.C., August 1995; USDA, op. cit. note 2.

57. USDA, January 1996, op. cit. note 8.

58. USDA, op. cit. note 2.

59. USDA, December 1995, op. cit. note 10.

60. "Vietnam to Limit Exports of Rice for Four Months," *Journal of Commerce*, 19 May 1995; information on China from Christopher Goldthwaite, FAS, USDA, Washington, D.C., private communication, 25 April 1995; "Wheat Soars to 15-Year High As Europe Puts Tax on Exports," *New York Times*, 8 December 1995; "EU to Conserve Barley by Curbing Exports," *Journal of Commerce*, 12 January 1996.

61. FAO, *Food Outlook*, August/September 1995.

62. Bureau of the Census, op. cit. note 2.

63. Ibid.; USDA, op. cit. note 2.

64. Bureau of the Census, op. cit. note 2.

65. Lester R. Brown, *Who Will Feed China? Wake-Up Call for a Small Planet* (New York: W.W. Norton & Company, 1995).

66. Bureau of the Census, op. cit. note 2.

67. Ibid.; USDA, January 1996, op. cit. note 8.

68. USDA, January 1996, op. cit. note 8; Bureau of the Census, op. cit. note 2.

69. FAO, *World Agriculture: Towards 2010* (New York: John Wiley & Sons, 1995); "Grain Prices Could Double by 2010," *Kyodo News*, 25 December 1995; "Big Rise in Grain Price Predicted," *China Daily*, 26 December 1995.

70. Subsistence-level income from Alan Durning, *How Much is Enough? The Consumer Society and the Future of the Earth* (New York: W.W. Norton & Company, 1992).

71. Unmet need for family planning from U.N. General Assembly, "Draft Programme of Action of the International Conference on Population and Development" (draft), New York, April 1994.

72. Patrick E. Tyler, "China's Transport Gridlock: Cars vs. Mass Transit," *New York Times*, 4 May 1996.

73. Postel, op. cit. note 28.

74. USDA, op. cit. note 2; Bureau of the Census, op. cit. note 2.

Chapter 3. Preserving Global Cropland

1. Clive Ponting, "Historical Perspectives on Sustainable Development," *Environment*, November 1990.

2. Ibid.

3. U.S. Department of Agriculture (USDA), Economic Research Service (ERS), "Production, Supply, and Distribution" (electronic database), Washington, D.C., May 1996.

4. Ibid.

5. Population projection from U.S. Bureau of the Census, as made available in "World Population, Midyear 1950–2050" (electronic database), ERS, USDA, Washington, D.C., updated July 1995; grain self-sufficiency from U.N. Food and Agriculture Organization (FAO), *World Agriculture:*

Towards 2010 (New York: John Wiley & Sons, 1995).

6. Figure 3–1 from USDA, op. cit. note 3; 1996 area estimate from USDA, Foreign Agricultural Service (FAS), *Grain: World Markets and Trade,* Washington, D.C., August 1996. The harvested grain area can be more or less than the actual physical area: a 100-hectare farm that is harvested twice a year is registered as 200 hectares of harvested area, for example, whereas 100 hectares fallowed every other year equals 50 hectares of harvested area.

7. FAO, *FAO Production Yearbook 1958* (Rome: 1959).

8. Carl Zoerb, "The Virgin Land Territory: Plans, Performance, Prospects," in Roy D. Laird, ed., *Soviet Agriculture: The Permanent Crisis* (New York: Praeger, 1965); yield share is a Worldwatch calculation based on data in Lester R. Brown, "Grain Yield Remains Steady," in Lester Brown et al., *Vital Signs 1995* (New York: W.W. Norton & Company, 1995).

9. Grain price decreases (rice, down 16 percent between 1979–81 and 1991–93; wheat, down 17 percent; and corn, down 16 percent) from International Monetary Fund (IMF), *International Financial Statistics Yearbook* (Washington, D.C.: 1994), and from IMF, *International Financial Statistics* (Washington, D.C.: May 1996); grain price increases (wheat, up 34 percent; corn, up 52 percent; and rice, up 32 percent) from first quarter 1995 to first quarter 1996 are from ibid.

10. Yield trends from USDA, op. cit. note 3.

11. In Figure 3–2, grain harvested area from USDA, op. cit. note 3, and population from Bureau of the Census, op. cit. note 5. One hectare is equivalent in area to 1.39 soccer fields.

12. Falling reserves from Lester R. Brown, *Tough Choices: Facing the Challenge of Food Scarcity* (New York: W.W. Norton & Company, 1996); grain consumption from USDA, op. cit. note 3.

13. Bread for the World, *Causes of Hunger: Fifth Annual Report on the State of World Hunger* (Silver Spring, Md.: Bread for the World Institute, 1994).

14. Dipasis Bhadra and Antonio Salazar P. Brandao, "Urbanization, Agricultural Development, and Land Allocation," World Bank Discussion Paper 201, World Bank, Washington, D.C., 1993.

15. Asian growth from IMF, *World Economic Outlook May 1996* (Washington, D.C.: 1996).

16. USDA estimate from Scott Thompson, "The Evolving Grain Markets in Southeast Asia," in USDA, FAS, *Grain: World Markets and Trade,* Washington, D.C., June 1995; Tommy Firman and Ida Ayu Indira Dharmapatni, "The Challenges to Sustainable Development in Jakarta Metropolitan Region," *Habitat International,* Vol. 18, No. 3, 1994.

17. George P. Brown, "Arable Land Loss in Rural China," in *Asian Survey,* October 1995. Arable land in China is officially listed as 96 million hectares, but this is widely acknowledged to be understated. Estimates of actual cropped area range from 123 million to as high as 150 million hectares. Following the work of Vaclav Smil, cropland area is assumed here to be 130 million hectares; see Vaclav Smil, "Environmental Problems in China: Estimates of Economic Costs," East-West Center, Honolulu, April 1996.

18. Brown, op. cit. note 17; potential expansion from Smil, op. cit. note 17.

19. USDA, Natural Resources Conservation Service, *Summary Report: 1992 National Resources Inventory,* Washington, D.C., July 1994, rev. January 1995; American Farmland Trust (AFT), "Farming on the Edge," Washington, D.C., June 1994; USDA, "U.S. Agricultural Exports and Imports," *Agricultural Outlook,* May 1996.

20. AFT, "Alternatives for Future Urban Growth in California's Central Valley: The Bottom Line for Agriculture and Taxpayers," Washington, D.C., October 1995; California

loss estimate from State of California, Department of Conservation, *Farmland Conversion Report* (Sacramento: various years); Los Angeles County from Valerie Berton, "Harvest or Homes? AFT Research Highlights Need to Protect Ag as Central Valley Grows," *American Farmland,* Fall 1995.

21. China from Odil Tunali, "A Billion Cars: The Road Ahead," *World Watch,* January/February 1996; Vietnam from Jeremy Grant, "Vietnam Trebles Car Import Quota," *Financial Times,* 12 January 1996; other Asian countries from Odil Tunali, "Auto Production Rises Again," in Lester R. Brown, Christopher Flavin, and Hal Kane, *Vital Signs 1996* (New York: W.W. Norton & Company, 1996).

22. Road estimates based on International Road Federation, *World Road Statistics 1989–1993* (Washington, D.C.: 1994), and on American Automobile Manufacturers Association, *World Motor Vehicle Data,* 1995 ed. (Detroit, Mich: 1995).

23. James Fahn, "Fore!" *The Nation,* 14 January 1994; Anita Pleumarom, "Course and Effect," *The Ecologist,* May/June 1992.

24. South Korea and Japan from Philip Shenon, "FORE! Golf in Asia Hits Environmental Rough," *New York Times,* 22 October 1994.

25. Analysis modeled on that found in Pierre Crosson and Jock Anderson, "Resources and Global Food Prospects: Supply and Demand for Cereals to 2030," World Bank Technical Paper Number 184, World Bank, Washington, D.C., 1992. Land use patterns vary greatly from city to city; the 0.05 hectare estimate is at best very rough.

26. United Nations, *World Demographic Estimates and Projections, 1950–2025* (New York: 1988).

27. Ashali Varma, "Target: 600 New Cities by the Year 2010," *The Earth Times,* 15–30 April 1996; population increase from Bureau of the Census, op. cit. note 5.

28. Worldwatch estimate, based on State of California, op. cit. note 20, and on USDA, *Summary Report,* op. cit. note 19.

29. Ponting, op. cit. note 1.

30. United Nations study is L.R. Oldeman et al., "World Map of the Status of Human-Induced Soil Degradation: An Explanatory Note," 2nd ed., International Soil Reference and Information Centre and United Nations Environment Programme, Wageningen, Netherlands, and Nairobi, 1991; Anthony Young, *Land Degradation in South Asia: Its Severity, Causes, and Effects upon the People,* World Soil Resources Reports 78 (Rome: FAO, 1994).

31. Strong and extreme degradation from L.R. Oldeman, International Soil Reference and Information Centre, Wageningen, Netherlands, private communication, 21 September 1995; production capacity of lost area is a Worldwatch calculation that assumes a modest yield of 3 tons per hectare, and that 1 ton will feed three people; degradation today from Sara J. Scherr and Satya Yadav, "Land Degradation in the Developing World: Implications for Food, Agriculture, and the Environment to 2020," Food, Agriculture, and the Environment Discussion Paper 14, International Food Policy Research Institute (IFPRI), Washington, D.C., May 1996.

32. Worldwatch calculation based on a methodology suggested in Pierre Crosson, "Soil Erosion and Its On-Farm Productivity Consequences: What Do We Know?" Discussion Paper 95–29, Resources for the Future, Washington, D.C., June 1995, and on Oldeman, op. cit. note 31.

33. Oldeman et al., op. cit. note 30; net and gross erosion from Crosson, op. cit. note 32.

34. Oldeman et al., op. cit. note 30.

35. Figure of 160 million hectares from Per Pinstrup Andersen and Rajul Pandya-Lorch, "Alleviating Poverty, Intensifying Agriculture, and Effectively Managing Natural Resources," Food, Agriculture, and the Envi-

ronment Discussion Paper 1, IFPRI, Washington, D.C., 1994; Maria Concepcion Cruz et al., "Population Growth, Poverty, and Environmental Stress: Frontier Migration in the Philippines and Costa Rica," World Resources Institute, Washington, D.C., 1992.

36. Miguel A. Altieri, *Agroecology: The Scientific Basis of Alternative Agriculture* (Boulder, Colo.: Westview Special Studies in Agriculture, Science, and Policy); Africa and Southeast Asia from Joy Tivy, *Agricultural Ecology* (Essex, U.K.: Longman Scientific and Technical, 1990).

37. "Low-potential" lands from Andersen and Pandya-Lorch, op. cit. note 35; shifting cultivation from N.C. Brady, "Making Agriculture a Sustainable Industry," in Clive A. Edwards et al., *Sustainable Agricultural Systems* (Ankeny, Iowa: Soil and Water Conservation Society, 1990).

38. Sandra Postel, "Forging a Sustainable Water Strategy," in Lester R. Brown et al., *State of the World 1996* (New York: W.W. Norton & Company, 1996); Central Asia yields from FAO, *State of Food and Agriculture 1995* (Rome: 1995).

39. Worldwatch calculation based on land loss data in Oldeman et al., op. cit. note 30.

40. Japan, South Korea, and Taiwan from USDA, op. cit. note 3.

41. Calculations based on area and import data in USDA, op. cit. note 3, and on population data in Bureau of the Census, op. cit. note 5.

42. Calculations based on area and import data in USDA, op. cit. note 3, and on population data in Bureau of the Census, op. cit. note 5.

43. USDA, op. cit. note 3.

44. Ibid.

45. Irrigated share from FAO, *FAO Production Yearbook 1994* (Rome: 1995).

46. USDA, FAS, *Grain: World Markets and Trade,* Washington, D.C., September 1996.

47. Ibid.

48. Ibid.

49. Projection made using population data from Bureau of the Census, op. cit. note 5; figure of 5–8 percent is a Worldwatch estimate, see Gary Gardner, *Shrinking Fields: Cropland Loss in a World of Eight Billion,* Worldwatch Paper 131 (Washington, D.C.: Worldwatch Institute, July 1996).

50. Contracting Kazak area from USDA, op. cit note 3, and from FAO, op. cit. note 38.

51. Conservation Reserve Program (CRP) area from USDA, *Summary Report,* op. cit. note 19; Everglades from John H. Cushman, "Clinton Backing Vast Effort to Restore Florida Swamps," *New York Times,* 18 February 1996, and from Elizabeth Levitan Spaid and Kirk Nielsen, "Florida Cane Farmers Sour on Everglades Restoration," *Christian Science Monitor,* 21 February 1996.

52. Brown, op. cit. note 17.

53. European set-aside grain area of approximately 4 million hectares calculated from data in USDA, FAS, *Grain: World Markets and Trade,* Washington, D.C., June 1996. In the United States, roughly half the CRP land is classified as "highly erodible cultivated cropland." This chapter assumes that the rest, some 7 million hectares, can be cultivated sustainably using careful practices. See USDA, Soil Conservation Service, "1992 National Resources Inventory—Highlights," information sheet, Washington, D.C., July 13, 1994. The U.S. General Accounting Office (GAO) estimates that buffer strips covering 2.5 million hectares—one sixth the size of the current CRP land—could provide a minimum level of environmental protection, which would release a greater amount of CRP land for farming. It acknowledges, however, that environmental goals such as wildlife protection would not be met through a buffer strip program. See GAO, "Conservation Reserve Program: Alternatives are Available for Managing Environmentally Sensitive Cropland," Report

to the Committee on Agriculture, Nutrition, and Forestry, U.S. Senate, Washington, D.C., February 1995.

54. FAO, op. cit. note 5.

55. Nigel Smith, *Rainforest Corridors: The TransAmazon Colonization Scheme* (Berkeley: University of California Press, 1982); Douglas Ian Stewart, *After the Trees: Living on the Transamazon Highway* (Austin: University of Texas Press, 1994); Bruce Babbitt, "Amazon Grace," *The New Republic,* 25 June 1990.

56. Virginia H. Dale et al., "Emissions of Greenhouse Gases from Tropical Deforestation and Subsequent Uses of the Land," in National Research Council, *Sustainable Agriculture and the Environment in the Humid Tropics* (Washington, D.C.: National Academy of Sciences, 1993).

57. FAO, op. cit. note 5. Note that the FAO estimates that what is available is 93 million hectares of physical area, which has more than one crop per year.

58. FAO, "Report on the 1980 World Census of Agriculture," *Census Bulletin No. 22,* Rome, April 1986.

59. Population projection from Bureau of the Census, op. cit. note 5.

60. FAO, op. cit. note 5.

61. USDA, Soil Conservation Service, op. cit. note 53.

62. Conservation tillage use from Conservation Technology Information Center, "1994 National Crop Residue Management Survey, Executive Summary," West Lafayette, Ind., 1994; reduction in erosion from USDA, *Summary Report,* op. cit. note 19.

63. U.K. policy from William Howarth and Christopher P. Rodgers, eds., *Agriculture, Conservation and Land Use* (Cardiff: University of Wales Press, 1993); Norway from Organisation for Economic Co-operation and Development, "Policies Affecting Farmland Mobility," Paris, 1996; other European policies from Margaret Rosso Grossman and Wim Brussaard, eds., *Agrarian Land Law in the Western World* (Wallingford, U.K.: CAB International, 1992).

64. Howarth and Rodgers, op. cit. note 63.

65. AFT, op. cit. note 20.

66. Charles Beretz, AFT, Washington, D.C., private communication, 13 June 1996, and Jennifer Dempsey, AFT, Northampton, Mass., private communication, 12 June 1996.

67. Shim Jae Hoon, Robert Delfs, and Julian Baum, "Seeds of Despair," *Far Eastern Economic Review,* 4 March 1993.

68. Share of grain to livestock from Lester R. Brown, "Worldwide Feedgrain Use Drops," in Brown, Flavin, and Kane, op. cit. note 21; per capita grain consumption from USDA, op. cit. note 3, and from Bureau of the Census, op. cit. note 5.

Chapter 4. Preventing Chronic Disease in Developing Countries

1. Diet changes and less exercise from Ad Hoc Committee on Health Research Relating to Future Intervention Options, *Investing in Health Research and Development* (Geneva: World Health Organization (WHO), 1996); Islamic countries from "Alcohol," in National Research Council (NRC), *Diet and Health: Implications for Reducing Chronic Disease Risk* (Washington, D.C.: National Academy Press, 1989).

2. Shanghai County from Kenneth Stanley, "Control of Tobacco Production and Use," in Dean T. Jamison et al., eds., *Disease Control Priorities in Developing Countries* (Washington, D.C.: World Bank, 1993); see also John Maurice, "Development Kills," *World Press Review,* August 1990; cardiovascular disease as leading killer in China from Ian Darnton-Hill, "Non-communicable Diseases: No Longer Just Diseases of Affluence," *World Health,* November 1989.

3. Harvard School of Public Health (HSPH), World Bank, and WHO, "Summary: Global Burden of Disease and Injury Series," in Christopher J.L. Murray and Alan D. Lopez, eds., *The Global Burden of Disease* (Cambridge, Mass.: Harvard University Press, 1996).

4. Howard Barnum and E. Robert Greenberg, "Cancers," in Jamison et al., op. cit. note 2; 58 percent from Report of the Director-General, *State of World Health* (Geneva: WHO, 1995); doubling of cancer cases from Paolo Boffetta and D. Maxwell Parkin, "Cancer in Developing Countries," *CA: A Cancer Journal for Clinicians*, March/April 1994; increase in cancer incidence from Ad Hoc Committee, op. cit. note 1.

5. Figure of 60 percent from John Maurice, "Cancer Will 'Overwhelm' the Third World," *New Scientist*, 14 December 1991; David McNamee, "Bid to Tackle Oncology in Developing World," *The Lancet*, 14 October 1995; U.S. costs from Elizabeth Frazão, "The American Diet: Health and Economic Consequences," Agriculture Information Bulletin No. 711, Economic Research Service (ERS), U.S. Department of Agriculture (USDA), Washington, D.C., February 1995.

6. Deforestation from Simon Chapman et al., "All Africa Conference on Tobacco Control," *British Medical Journal*, 15 January 1994.

7. Avoidable deaths from Frazão, op. cit. note 5.

8. Genetics and environmental exposure from Samuel S. Epstein and Joel B. Swartz, "Fallacies of Lifestyle Cancer Theories," *Nature*, 15 January 1981; environmental exposures from Ann Misch, "Assessing Environmental Health Risks," in Lester R. Brown et al., *State of the World 1994* (New York: W.W. Norton & Company, 1994).

9. WHO, "Diet, Nutrition and the Prevention of Chronic Diseases," WHO Technical Report Series No. 797, Geneva, 1990.

10. Atherosclerosis from Michael S. Brown and Joseph L. Goldstein, "Heart Attacks: Gone With the Century?" *Science,* 3 May 1996; blood cholesterol from Walter C. Willett, "Diet and Health: What Should We Eat?" *Science*, 22 April 1994; see also NRC, op. cit. note 1.

11. Marian Burros, "Tough New Warning on Diet Is Issued by Cancer Society," *New York Times*, 17 September 1996.

12. Frazão, op. cit. note 5.

13. Figure 4–1 from USDA, "Production, Supply, and Distribution" (electronic database), Washington, D.C., May 1996, and from U.S. Bureau of the Census projections, as made available in "World Population, Midyear 1950–2050" (electronic database), ERS, USDA, Washington, D.C., updated July 1995. Note that data measure the amount of food available not the actual consumption levels; they therefore tend to overestimate consumption of fat and meat. For example, it is difficult to measure how much fat is cut off meat before cooking. Dietary oil consumption data are from the food use category in database.

14. Shifts in types of oils from José A. Gutiérrez Fuentes, "What Food for the Heart?" *World Health Forum*, Vol. 17, No. 2, 1996; ratio of oils is Worldwatch estimate based on oil consumption data from USDA, op. cit. note 13, and from Bureau of the Census, op. cit. note 13. "Good" oils include soy, sunflower, and olive, while palm oil falls in the "bad" category.

15. Health effects from Fuentes, op. cit. note 14; rates of coronary heart disease from Willett, op. cit. note 10.

16. Fat hidden in the diet from NRC, op. cit. note 1; estimate of more than two thirds from Hans Diehl, "Reversing Coronary Heart Disease," in N.J. Temple and D.P. Burkitt, eds., *Western Diseases: Their Dietary Prevention and Reversibility* (Totowa, N.J.: Humana Press, 1994).

17. Meat consumption data from USDA, op. cit. note 13, and from Bureau of the Census, op. cit. note 13.

18. Quadrupled demand for meat from USDA, op. cit. note 13, and from Bureau of the Census op. cit. note 13; "China's Palate Grows Keen for Meat, Fish," *Journal of Commerce*, 30 April 1996. For further discussion, see Lester R. Brown, *Who Will Feed China?: Wake-Up Call for a Small Planet* (New York: W.W. Norton & Company, 1995).

19. Elite and urban populations from United Nations, Administrative Committee on Coordination, SubCommittee on Nutrition (ACC/SCN), "Non-Communicable Chronic Diseases," in ACC/SCN and International Food Policy Research Institute, eds., *Second Report of the World Nutrition Situation 1992* (Washington, D.C.: 1992); urban areas in Africa from WHO, op. cit. note 9.

20. Michael Gurney and Jonathan Gorstein, "The Global Prevalence of Obesity: An Initial Overview of Available Data," *World Health Statistics Quarterly*, Vol. 41, No. 3/4, 1988; Bangkok from L. Mo-suwan, C. Junjana, and A. Puetpaiboon, "Increasing Obesity in School Children in a Transitional Society and the Effect of the Weight Control Program," *Southeast Asian Journal of Tropical Medicine and Public Health*, September 1993; heart disease from F.C.H. Bijnen, C.J. Caspersen, and W.L. Mosterd, "Physical Inactivity as a Risk Factor for Coronary Heart Disease: A WHO and International Society and Federation of Cardiology Position Statement," *Bulletin of the World Health Organization*, Vol. 72, No. 1, 1994.

21. Incidence of stroke and data on urban and rural Chinese from J. Richard Bumgarner, "China: Long-Term Issues and Options in the Health Transition," World Bank, Washington, D.C., October 1992; 1990 data from C.J.L. Murray and A.D. Lopez, "Global and Regional Cause-of-Death Patterns in 1990," *Bulletin of the World Health Organization*, Vol. 72, No. 3, 1994; People's Republic of China–United States Cardiovascular and Cardiopulmonary Epidemiology Research Group, "An Epidemiological Study of Cardiovascular and Cardiopulmonary Disease Risk Factors in Four Populations in the People's Republic of China: Baseline Report From the P.R.C.–U.S.A. Collaborative Study," *Circulation* (American Heart Association, Dallas, Tex.), March 1992.

22. John Briscoe, "Brazil: The New Challenge of Adult Health," World Bank, Washington, D.C., August 1990.

23. Cardiovascular diseases in developing countries from Christopher J.L. Murray and Alan D. Lopez, "Global Patterns of Cause of Death and Burden of Disease in 1990, with Projections to 2020," in Ad Hoc Committee, op. cit. note 1; increase in stroke mortality from Aulikki Nissinen et al., "Hypertension in Developing Countries," *World Health Statistics Quarterly*, Vol. 41, No. 3/4, 1988; Finnish men from Per Thorvaldsen et al., "Stroke Incidence, Case Fatality, and Mortality in the WHO Monitoring Trends and Determinants in Cardiovascular Disease (MONICA) Project," *Stroke* (American Heart Association, Dallas, Tex.), March 1995.

24. NRC, op. cit. note 1.

25. T. Colin Campbell and Junshi Chen, "Diet and Chronic Degenerative Diseases: A Summary of Results from an Ecologic Study in Rural China," in Temple and Burkitt, op. cit. note 16.

26. John Schwartz, "Research Salutes Healthy Diet of Modern Greeks," *Washington Post*, 1 December 1995.

27. Jeremiah Stamler, "Assessing Diets to Improve World Health: Nutritional Research on Disease Causation in Populations," *American Journal of Clinical Nutrition*, Vol. 59, Supplement, 1994; fast food and advertising from "Western Health Perils for Poor Nations' Young," *New York Times*, 24 September 1995.

28. Alcoholics in Saudi Arabia and Bahrain from NRC, op. cit. note 1.

29. Ethanol information from NRC, op. cit. note 1.

30. Health effects from NRC, op. cit. note 1; liver cirrhosis from Anne Cronin, "The Tipplers and the Temperate: Drinking Around the World," *New York Times*, 1 January 1995.

31. Threshold of 30 percent from NRC, op. cit. note 1; risks outweighing benefits from Dr. Derek Yach, Chief, Policy Advisory Coordinating Team, Division of Development of Policy, Programme, and Evaluation, WHO, Geneva, private communication, 8 October 1996, and from HSPH, World Bank, and WHO, op. cit. note 3.

32. Worldwatch estimates based on percent of alcohol-related deaths from James A. Cercone, "Alcohol-Related Problems as an Obstacle to the Development of Human Capital: Issues and Policy Options," Technical Paper Number 219, World Bank, Washington, D.C., 1994; estimate of four out of five from World Bank, *World Development Report 1993* (New York: Oxford University Press, 1993); mortality data from liver cirrhosis from Ad Hoc Committee, op. cit. note 1, given as 1990 data; all other mortality data are for 1993 from Report of the Director-General, op. cit. note 4.

33. Estimates of 5 and 37 percent are based on Cercone, op. cit. note 32; Papua New Guinea from World Bank, op. cit. note 32; South Africa from Ad Hoc Committee Report, op. cit. note 1.

34. Russian data from Sonni Efron, "A Country Besieged By the Bottle," *Los Angeles Times*, 12 November 1995; homicides in Mexico from Cercone, op. cit. note 32, citing M. Medina-Mora et al., "Epidemiologic Status of Drug Abuse in Mexico," *Bulletin of the Pan American Health Organization*, Vol. 24, No. 1, 1990.

35. HSPH, World Bank, and WHO, op. cit. note 3.

36. Loss of earning potential from Ad Hoc Committee, op. cit. note 1; Dorothy P. Rice, "The Economic Cost of Alcohol Abuse and Alcohol Dependence: 1990," *Alcohol Health and Research World*, Vol. 17, No. 1, 1993; National Institute on Alcohol Abuse and Alcoholism, "Estimating the Economic Cost of Alcohol Abuse," *Alcohol Alert*, January 1991.

37. Burkina Faso from Lori Heise, "Trouble Brewing: Alcohol in the Third World," *World Watch*, July/August 1991; South Africa data from "Health and Other Consequences of Alcohol Consumption," in C. Parry and A. Bennetts, "Alcohol Policy and Public Health in South Africa," unpublished manuscript from Charles Parry, Senior Specialist Scientist, Medical Research Council, Tygerberg, South Africa, private communication, 10 October 1996, citing M. Strydom et al., "Home Violence: Some Data from the National Trauma Research Programme," *MRC Trauma Review*, Vol. 2, No. 3, 1994.

38. Consumption and production data from Cercone, op. cit. note 32, citing The Brewers Society, *Statistical Handbook: A Compilation of Drinks Industry Statistics*, 1991; total beer consumed in China and projected beer production from Brown, op. cit. note 18.

39. Underestimation figure from Cercone, op. cit. note 32; African villages from Marja-Liisa Swantz, "Alcohol Research in Developing Societies from the Point of View of Development Studies," in Johanna Maula, Maaria Lindblad, and Christoffer Tigerstedt, eds., *Alcohol in Developing Countries*, Proceedings from a meeting in Oslo, Norway, August 7–9, 1988, Publication No. 18 (Helsinki: Nordic Council for Alcohol and Drug Research, 1990).

40. Heise, op. cit. note 37.

41. Drinking-age laws and advertising from Cercone, op. cit. note 32.

42. Cercone, op. cit. note 32.

43. John F. Burns, "Indian State's Alcohol Ban Pleases Women, Annoys Men," *New York Times*, 18 August 1996.

44. Ad Hoc Committee Report, op. cit. note 1; effects of beer tax from Cercone, op. cit. note 32, citing Charles Phelps, "Deaths and Taxes: An Opportunity for Substitution," *Journal of Health Economics*, 1988.

45. Dominance of tobacco-induced illness from HSPH, World Bank, and WHO, op. cit. note 3; increase in manufactured cigarettes from WHO, Tobacco or Health Program, "The Tobacco Epidemic: A Global Public Health Emergency," in *Tobacco Alert: Special Issue*, World No-Tobacco Day, 1996.

46. Relation of tons of tobacco to deaths produced from Ad Hoc Committee, op. cit. note 1; sustainable development from "Bellagio Statement on Tobacco and Sustainable Development," *Canadian Medical Association Journal*, 15 October 1995.

47. WHO, Tobacco or Health Program, "Tobacco: The Twentieth-Century Epidemic," *Tobacco Alert: Special Issue*, World No-Tobacco Day, in "Sports and the Arts Without Tobacco: Play It Tobacco Free!" Advisory Kit, 1996.

48. Derek Yach, "All Africa Conference on Tobacco and Health: Tobacco Is a Threat to Sustainable and Equitable Development," *Women's Health News* (Women's Health Project, Johannesburg, South Africa), February 1996.

49. WHO, op. cit. note 45.

50. Peto from "Fatal Fags," *Down to Earth*, 15 January 1995; see also HSPH, World Bank, and WHO, op. cit. note 3.

51. World Bank, op. cit. note 32; HSPH, World Bank, and WHO, op. cit. note 3.

52. Nicotine and number of other chemical compounds from American Cancer Society, Inc. (ACS), *Cancer Facts & Figures—1996* (Atlanta, Ga.: 1996); carcinogen from David Stout, "Direct Link Found Between Smoking and Lung Cancer: First Cellular Evidence," *New York Times*, 18 October 1996; bronchitis and second-hand smoke risk from Stanley, op. cit. note 2.

53. Characteristics of nicotine from Office on Smoking and Health, National Center for Chronic Disease Prevention and Health Promotion, Centers for Disease Control and Prevention, Public Health Service, *Preventing Tobacco Use Among Young People: A Report of the Surgeon General* (Washington, D.C.: U.S. Department of Health and Human Services, 1994).

54. ACS, "The Most Often Asked Questions About Smoking, Tobacco, and Health and...The Answers" (pamphlet), Atlanta, Ga., 1982; Office on Smoking and Health, op. cit. note 53.

55. "Fatal Fags," op. cit. note 50.

56. Estimate for 1993 from D.M. Parkin et al., "At Least One in Seven Cases of Cancer Is Caused By Smoking, Global Estimates for 1985," *International Journal of Cancer* (International Union Against Cancer, Lyons, France), Vol. 59, 1994; lung cancer projections from HSPH, World Bank, and WHO, op. cit. note 3.

57. Smoking in developing countries from WHO, op. cit. note 47; marketing from Ron Scherer, "Worldwide Trend: Tobacco Use Grows," *Christian Science Monitor*, 17 July 1996; targeting women from Anna Quindlen, "The Smoke Bomb," *New York Times*, 15 January 1994.

58. "Latin American Women Smokers: Dangerous Habits," *Women's Health Journal* (Isis International, Quezon City, Philippines), April 1994.

59. "South Korea: Survey Claims 30 Percent of Koreans Suffer from 'Chronic Disease'," *Foreign Broadcasting Information Service (FBIS)*, 2 April 1996, citing Hong Son-hui,

Korea Times, 9 March 1996; Bao-Ping Zhu et al., "Cigarette Smoking and Its Risk Factors among Elementary School Students in Beijing," *American Journal of Public Health*, March 1996.

60. Peer pressure from Zhu et al., op. cit. note 59; Chinese children's prospects from Patrick E. Tyler, "In Heavy Smoking, Grim Portent for China," *New York Times*, 16 March 1996, and from Steven Mufson, "China's Cancer Rate Increasing Rapidly," *Washington Post*, 18 October 1995; David Greising, "Two Tales of Smoke, Death and Deceit," *Business Week*, 6 May 1996.

61. Percent of family income from Stanley, op. cit. note 2; Malawi and Zimbabwe from Chapman et al., op. cit. note 6; FAO, "Tobacco: Supply, Demand and Trade Projections, 1995 and 2000," Economic and Social Development Paper 86, Rome, 1990.

62. Tony Walker, "Chinese Smoking Curbs Fail to Break the Habit," *Financial Times*, 15 May 1996. For further discussion, see FAO, "The Economic Significance of Tobacco," Economic and Social Development Paper 85, Rome, 1989.

63. ACS, op. cit. note 52.

64. Michael Specter, "Yeltsin Bans Tobacco and Alcohol Advertising," *New York Times*, 22 February 1995; China from Scherer, op. cit. note 57.

65. Effect of ban from John P. Pierce, "Progress and Problems in International Public Health Efforts to Reduce Tobacco Usage," *Annual Review of Public Health*, Vol 12, 1991; countries with bans and France from WHO, op. cit. note 45.

66. Aggressive stop smoking programs from J. Richard Bumgarner and Frank E. Speizer, "Chronic Obstructive Pulmonary Disease," in Jamison et al., op. cit. note 2; cigarette taxes from Hal Kane, "Putting Out Cigarettes," *World Watch*, September/October 1992, and from Hal Kane, "Cigarette Taxes Show Ups and Downs," in Lester R. Brown,

Nicholas Lenssen, and Hal Kane, *Vital Signs 1995* (New York: W.W. Norton & Company, 1995); Finland, Nepal, Portugal, and Romania from WHO, op. cit. note 45.

67. Teens' sensitivity to price from Kane, "Putting Out Cigarettes," op. cit. note 66, and from Yereth Rosen, "Alaska Mulls Huge Tax to Cut Teen Smoking," *Christian Science Monitor*, 10 May 1996.

68. Feachem quote from Nalia Sattar, "HIV: The Poverty Virus Coming Soon to a Family Near You," *HIMAL South Asia*, May 1996.

69. Overall points on importance of prevention from INTERHEALTH Steering Committee, "Demonstration Projects for the Integrated Prevention and Control of Noncommunicable Diseases (INTERHEALTH Programme): Epidemiological Background and Rationale," *World Health Statistics Quarterly*, Vol. 44, No. 2, 1991; "Mission Statement," Mothers Against Drunk Driving, Irving, Tex., undated.

70. McNamee, op. cit. note 5.

71. Vladimir Kebza and Rudolf Poledne, "Smoking Cessation Models Bring Results in The Czech Republic," *Central European Health and Environment Monitor*, Fall/Winter 1995.

72. Briscoe, op. cit. note 22.

73. Cost of hypertensive medication from Nissinen et al., op. cit. note 23; prevention from Richard Peto, "Statistics of Chronic Disease Control," *Nature*, 16 April 1992.

74. Drop in coronary heart disease in industrial countries from WHO, *World Health Statistics Annual* (Geneva: 1987); decline in United States from Fuentes, op. cit. note 14; low-fat milk and leaner meat from NRC, op. cit. note 1; average U.S. fat consumption from Hans Diehl, "Reversing Coronary Heart Disease," in Temple and Burkitt, op. cit. note 16.

75. World Bank, op. cit. note 32.

76. Chapman et al., op. cit. note 6.

Chapter 5. Tracking the Ecology of Climate Change

1. T.Y. Canby, "El Niño's Ill Wind," *National Geographic*, February 1984; Graeme O'Neill, "Better Warnings a Boon for the Forest," *Ecos*, Winter 1995; R.T. Barber and J.E. Kogelschatz, "Nutrients and Productivity During the 1982/83 El Niño," in Peter W. Glynn, ed., *Global Ecological Consequences of the 1982–83 El Niño-Southern Oscillation* (Amsterdam: Elsevier Publications, 1989); Mark Leighton and Nengah Wirawan, "Catastrophic Drought and Fire in Borneo Tropical Rain Forest Associated with the 1982–1983 El Niño-Southern Oscillation Event," in G.T. Prance, ed., *Tropical Rain Forests and the World Atmosphere* (Boulder, Colo.: Westview Press, 1986); D.C. Duffy, "Seabirds and the 1982–1984 El Niño-Southern Oscillation," in Glynn, op. cit. this note; Peter W. Glynn, "Coral Mortality and Disturbances to Tropical Reefs in the Tropical Eastern Pacific," in Glynn, op. cit. this note.

2. Results of the computer analysis from Kevin Trenberth and Timothy Hoar, "The 1990–1995 El Niño Southern Oscillation Event: Longest on Record," *Geophysical Research Letters*, January 1996.

3. "WMO Reports 1995 Warmest Year Since 1861, Even Factoring in Extreme Climate Anomalies," *International Environment Reporter*, 1 May 1996; Figure 5–1 from James Hansen and Reto Ruedy, "Global Average Temperature," Goddard Institute for Space Studies, <http://www.giss.nasa.gov/data/gistemp/index.html>, updated 21 October 1996; George M. Woodwell, "Biotic Feedbacks from the Warming of the Earth," in George M. Woodwell and Fred T. Mackenzie, eds., *Biotic Feedbacks in the Global Climatic System: Will the Warming Feed the Warming?* (New York: Oxford University Press, 1995).

4. See, for example, B.D. Santer et al., "A Search for Human Influences on the Thermal Structure of the Atmosphere," *Nature*, 4 July 1996.

5. J.T. Houghton et al., eds., *Climate Change 1995: The Science of Climate Change, Contribution of Working Group I to the Second Assessment Report of the Intergovernmental Panel on Climate Change* (New York: Cambridge University Press, 1996); Thomas J. Crowley, "Remembrance of Things Past: Greeenhouse Lessons from the Geologic Record," *Consequences*, Vol. 2, No. 1, 1996; hippopotamuses from Eric Barron, "Climate Sensitivity: A Perspective from Paleoclimate Model Applications," lecture at the U.S. Global Change Research Program, Washington, D.C., July 17, 1996.

6. W. Dansgaard, J.W.C. White, and S.J. Johnsen, "The Abrupt Termination of the Younger Dryas Climatic Event," *Nature*, 15 June 1989; R.B. Alley et al., "Abrupt Increase in Greenland Snow Accumulation at the End of the Younger Dryas Event," *Nature*, 8 April 1993; Stefan Rahmstorf, "Bifurcations of the Atlantic Thermohaline Circulation in Response to Changes in the Hydrological Cycle," *Nature*, 9 November 1995; Konrad A. Hughen et al., "Rapid Climate Changes in the Tropical Atlantic Region During the Last Deglaciation," *Nature*, 7 March 1996.

7. "Technical Summary," in Houghton et al., op. cit. note 5; Robert T. Watson et al., "Technical Summary: Impacts, Adaptations, and Mitigation Options," in Robert T. Watson et al., eds., *Climate Change 1995: Impacts, Adaptations and Mitigation of Climate Change: Scientific-Technical Analyses: Contribution of Working Group II to the Second Assessment Report of the Intergovernmental Panel on Climate Change* (New York: Cambridge University Press, 1996).

8. F.I. Woodward, *Climate and Plant Distribution* (Cambridge: Cambridge University Press, 1987); for the argument that warmer temperatures are basically "good" for plants, see, for example, "Global Climate Research: Informing the Decision Process," *EPRI Journal*, November/December 1995.

9. Michael L. Rosenzweig, *Species Diversity in Space and Time* (Cambridge: Cambridge University Press, 1995); Michael Allaby, ed.,

The Oxford Dictionary of Natural History (Oxford: Oxford University Press, 1985).

10. J. Porter, "The Effects of Climate Change on the Agricultural Environment for Crop Insect Pests with Particular Reference to the European Corn Borer and Grain Maize," in Richard Harrington and Nigel E. Stork, eds., *Insects in a Changing Environment* (London: Academic Press, 1995); William B. Showers, "Diversity and Variation of European Corn Borer Populations," in Ke Chung Kim and Bruce A. McPheron, eds., *Evolution of Insect Pests: Patterns of Variation* (New York: John Wiley and Sons, 1993).

11. Woodwell, op. cit. note 3; Werner A. Kurz et al., "Global Climate Change: Disturbance Regimes and Biospheric Feedbacks of Temperate and Boreal Forests," in Woodwell and Mackenzie, op. cit. note 3; R.A. Fleming and W.J.A. Volney, "Effects of Climate Change on Insect Defoliator Population Processes in Canada's Boreal Forest: Some Plausible Scenarios," *Water, Air, and Soil Pollution*, Vol. 82, pp. 445–54, 1995.

12. Fish from Jerry F. Franklin et al., "Effects of Global Climatic Change on Forests in Northwestern North America," in Robert L. Peters and Thomas E. Lovejoy, eds., *Global Warming and Biological Diversity* (New Haven, Conn.: Yale University Press, 1992); Jonathan A. Patz et al., "Global Climate Change and Emerging Infectious Diseases," *Journal of the American Medical Association*, 17 January 1996.

13. William DeBenedetto, "Sun Stroke? Pacific Coast Salmon Face Menace of Global Warming," *Journal of Commerce*, 3 January 1996; for the general point on aquatic food webs, see S.A. Murawski, "Climate Change and Marine Fish Distributions: Forecasting from Historical Analogy," *Transactions of the American Fisheries Society*, September 1993.

14. Nigel Arnell et al., "Hydrology and Freshwater Ecology," in Watson et al., op. cit. note 7; G. Carleton Ray, "Effects of Global Warming on the Biodiversity of Coastal-Ma-

rine Zones," in Peters and Lovejoy, op. cit. note 12; Fredric J. Janzen, "Climate Change and Temperature-Dependent Sex Determination in Reptiles," *Proceedings of the National Academy of Science USA*, August 1994; "Global Warming Spells Danger for Turtles," *Oryx*, January 1995.

15. Arnell et al., op. cit. note 14; A. Kattenberg et al., "Climate Models—Projections of Future Climate," in Houghton et al., op. cit. note 5.

16. Fred Pearce, "Deserts on Our Doorstep," *New Scientist*, 6 July 1996.

17. Budworm from Fleming and Volney, op. cit. note 11; fungi from A.D.M. Rayner, "Fungi, a Vital Component of Ecosystem Function in Woodland," in D. Allsopp, R.R. Colwell, and D.L. Hawksworth, eds., *Microbial Diversity and Ecosystem Function* (Wallingford, U.K.: CAB International and U.N. Environment Programme (UNEP), 1995).

18. Peter Bullock et al., "Land Degradation and Desertification," in Watson et al., op. cit. note 7; Ian R. Noble et al., "Deserts in a Changing Climate: Impacts," in ibid.; Pearce, op. cit. note 16.

19. N. LeRoy Poff and J. David Allan, "Functional Organization of Stream Fish Assemblages in Relations to Hydrological Variability," *Ecology*, March 1995.

20. Gary S. Hartshorn, "Possible Effects of Global Warming on the Biological Diversity in Tropical Forests," in Peters and Lovejoy, op. cit. note 12; J. Alan Pounds and Martha L. Crump, "Amphibian Declines and Climate Distrubance: The Case of the Golden Toad and the Harlequin Frog," *Conservation Biology*, March 1994.

21. R.A. Warrick et al., "Changes in Sea Level," in Houghton et al., op. cit. note 5; "British Scientists Report Ice Shelves Breaking Off as Result of Global Warming," *International Environment Reporter*, 7 February 1996; D.G. Vaughan and C.S.M. Doake, "Recent

Atmospheric Warming and Retreat of Ice Shelves on the Antarctic Peninsula," *Nature*, 25 January 1996; Kathy Sawyer, "Satellite Data Flaw Inflated Rise in Seas' Surface Levels," *Washington Post*, 27 July 1996.

22. Luitzen Bijlsma, "Coastal Zones and Small Islands," in Watson et al., op. cit. note 7; R. Scott Warren and William A. Niering, "Vegetation Change on a Northeast Tidal Marsh: Interaction of Sea-Level Rise and Marsh Accretion," *Ecology*, January 1993; John W. Day, Jr. et al., "Impacts of Sea-Level Rise on Deltas in the Gulf of Mexico and Mediterranean: The Importance of Pulsing Events to Sustainability," *Estuaries*, December 1995.

23. Joanna C. Ellison, "Climate Change and Sea Level Rise Impacts on Mangrove Ecosystems," in John Pernetta et al., eds., *Impacts of Climate Change on Ecosystems and Species: Marine and Coastal Ecosystems* (Gland, Switzerland: World Conservation Union–IUCN, 1994); John Pernetta, *Mangrove Forests, Climate Change and Sea Level Rise: Hydrological Influences on Community Structure and Survival, with Examples from the Indo-West Pacific* (Gland, Switzerland: IUCN, 1993); blocking of coastal wetland migration from Bijlsma, op. cit. note 22.

24. Storm trends from N. Nicholls et al., "Observed Climate Variability and Change," in Houghton et al., op. cit. note 5, and from Christopher Flavin and Odil Tunali, *Climate of Hope: New Strategies for Stabilizing the World's Atmosphere*, Worldwatch Paper 130 (Washington, D.C.: Worldwatch Institute, June 1996); hurricane estimate from ibid.; storm damage to tropical forests from Sean T. O'Brien, Bruce P. Hayden, and Herman H. Shugart, "Global Climatic Change, Hurricanes, and a Tropical Forest," *Climatic Change*, November 1992.

25. Experiment in North Carolina from Robert C. Cowen, "Excess CO_2 May Bring Abundance of Weeds," *Christian Science Monitor*, 12 December 1995, and from Richard Monastersky, "Pine Forest Thrives on High-CO_2 Diet," *Science News*, 12 August 1995; doubled-carbon dioxide (CO_2) scenario from "Technical Summary," op. cit. note 7.

26. Range of plant responses to CO_2 fertilization from J.M. Melillo et al., "Terrestrial Biotic Responses to Environmental Change and Feedbacks to Climate," in Houghton et al., op. cit. note 5, and from Leon Hartwell Allen, Jr. and Jeffrey S. Amthor, "Plant Physiological Responses to Elevated CO_2, Temperature, Air Pollution, and UV-B Radiation," in Woodwell and Mackenzie, op. cit. note 3.

27. C. Körner, "CO_2 Fertilisation: The Great Uncertainty in Future Vegetation Development," in A.M. Solomon and H.H. Shugart, Jr., eds., *Vegetation Dynamics and Global Change* (New York: Chapman and Hall, 1993).

28. F. Miglietta et al., "Preliminary Studies of the Long-Term CO_2 Response of Mediterranean Vegetation Around Natural CO_2 Vents," in J.M. Moreno and W.C. Oechel, eds., *Global Change and Mediterranean-Type Ecosystems* (New York: Springer Verlag, 1995); wood cores from R.J. Luxmoore, S.D. Wullschleger, and P.J. Hanson, "Forest Responses to CO_2 Enrichment and Climate Warming," *Water, Air, and Soil Pollution*, Vol. 70, pp. 309–23, 1993, and from Gordon C. Jacoby and Rosanne D. D'Arrigo, "Indicators of Climatic and Biospheric Change: Evidence from Tree Rings," in Woodwell and Mackenzie, op. cit. note 3.

29. Michael Smith, "Sneezing While the Earth Warms," *New Scientist*, 24 August 1996.

30. A.D. Watt et al., "The Impact of Elevated Atmospheric CO_2 on Insect Herbivores," in Harrington and Stork, op. cit. note 10; Nancy E. Stamp and Yuelong Yang, "Response of Insect Herbivores to Multiple Allelochemicals Under Different Thermal Regimes," *Ecology*, June 1996.

31. For a skeptical view of the importance of CO_2 fertilization on insect feeding, see Fleming and Volney, op. cit. note 11.

32. Claude Lavoie and Serge Payette, "Recent Fluctuations of the Lichen-Spruce Forest Limit in Subarctic Québec," *Journal of Ecology*, Vol. 82, pp. 725–34, 1994; Julian M. Szeicz and Glen M. Macdonald, "Recent White Spruce Dynamics at the Subarctic Al-

pine Treeline of North-Western Canada,"
Journal of Ecology, pp. 873–85, Vol. 83, 1995;
Jacoby and D'Arrigo, op. cit. note 28; Charles
Petit, "New Hints of Global Warming," *San
Francisco Chronicle*, 17 April 1995.

33. Miko U.F. Kirschbaum et al., "Climate
Change Impacts on Forests," in Watson et
al., op. cit. note 7; Melillo et al., op. cit. note
26; E.C. Pielou, *After the Ice Age: The Return of
Life to Glaciated North America* (Chicago: University of Chicago Press, 1991).

34. Kirschbaum et al., op. cit. note 33;
Melillo et al., op. cit. note 26; extent of possible reduction of the boreal forests from
Kevin Jardine, "Finger on the Carbon Pulse:
Climate Change and the Boreal Forests," *The
Ecologist*, November/December 1994.

35. R.M.M. Crawford and R.J. Abbott,
"Pre-adaptation of Arctic Plants to Climate
Change," *Botanica Acta*, Vol. 107, pp. 217–78,
1994; F. Stuart Chapin, III et al., "Responses
of Arctic Tundra to Experimental and Observed Changes in Climate," *Ecology*, April
1995; Scandinavian plants from Jarle I.
Holten, "Potential Effects of Climate Change
on Distribution of Plant Species, with Emphasis on Norway," in J.K. Holten, G. Paulsen,
and W.C. Oechel, eds., *Impacts of Climatic
Change on Natural Ecosystems, with Emphasis on
Boreal and Arctic/Alpine Areas* (Trondheim:
Norwegian Institute for Nature Research and
the Directorate for Nature Management,
1993); caribou example from H. Henttonen,
"Climate Change and the Ecology of Alpine
Mammals," in A. Guisan et al., eds., *Potential
Ecological Impacts of Climate Change in the Alps
and Fennoscandian Mountains* (Geneva: Botanical Conservatory and Garden, 1995).

36. Chris Bright, "Understanding the
Threat of Bioinvasions," in Lester R. Brown
et al., *State of the World 1996* (New York: W.W.
Norton & Company, 1996).

37. Graeme O'Neill, "Getting the Jump on
Pests," *Ecos*, Winter 1995; R.W. Sutherst, "The
Potential Advance of Pests in Natural Ecosystems Under Climate Change: Implications for
Planning and Management," in John Pernetta
et al., eds., *Impacts of Climate Change on Ecosystems and Species: Terrestrial Ecosystems* (Gland,
Switzerland: IUCN, 1995); Quentin C.B.
Cronk and Janice L. Fuller, *Plant Invaders:
The Threat to Natural Ecosystems* (London:
Chapman and Hall, 1995).

38. Carla M. D'Antonio and Peter M.
Vitousek, "Biological Invasions by Exotic
Grasses, the Grass/Fire Cycle, and Global
Change," *Annual Review of Ecology and Systematics*, 1992; Robert Devine, "The Cheatgrass
Problem," *Atlantic*, May 1993; Barbara Allen-
Diaz, "Rangelands in a Changing Climate:
Impacts, Adaptations, and Mitigation," in
Watson et al., op. cit. note 7.

39. Estimate of one third reported in William K. Stevens, "Scientists Say Earth's Warming Could Set Off Wide Disruptions," *New
York Times*, 18 September 1995.

40. Butterfly from Camille Parmesan, "Climate and Species' Range," *Nature*, 29 August
1996; mosquito from Ross Gelbspan, "The
Heat Is On," *Harper's Magazine*, December
1995.

41. Franklin et al., op. cit. note 12; Faith
Thompson Campbell and Scott E.
Schlarbaum, *Fading Forests: North American
Trees and the Threat of Exotic Pests* (New York:
Natural Resources Defense Council, 1994);
budworm outbreak from Fleming and Volney,
op. cit. note 11.

42. R.W. Sutherst, G.F. Maywald, and D.B.
Skarratt, "Predicting Insect Distributions in
a Changed Climate," in Harrington and
Stork, op. cit. note 10; John H. Lawton, "The
Response of Insects to Environmental
Change," in ibid.

43. Robert W. Sutherst, Robert B. Floyd,
and Gunter F. Maywald, "The Potential Geographical Distribution of the Cane Toad, *Bufo
marinus* L. in Australia," *Conservation Biology*,
December 1995; R.J. Williams et al.,
"Australia's Wet-Dry Tropics: Identifying the
Sensitive Zones," in Pernetta et al., op. cit.
note 37; Sutherst, op. cit. note 37.

44. Spread of aquatic exotics from Venugopalan Ittekkot et al., "Oceans," in Watson et al., op. cit. note 7, and from Aaron Rosenfield and Roger Mann, eds., *Dispersal of Living Organisms Into Aquatic Ecosystems* (College Park, Md.: Maryland Sea Grant College, 1992); for tilapia, see, for example, Walter R. Courtenay, Jr., "Biological Pollution Through Fish Introductions," in Bill N. McKnight, ed., *Biological Pollution: The Control and Impact of Invasive Exotic Species* (Indianapolis: Indiana Academy of Science, 1993); mollusk from Flavin and Tunali, op. cit. note 24.

45. F.D. Podger, "Bioclimatic Analysis of the Distribution of Damage to Native Plants in Tasmania by *Phytophthora cinnamomi*," *Australian Journal of Ecology*, Vol. 15, 1990.

46. R. Harrington, J.S. Bale, and G.M. Tatchell, "Aphids in a Changing Climate," in Harrington and Stork, op. cit. note 10.

47. Andrew Dobson and Robin Carper, "Global Warming and Potential Changes in Host-Parasite and Disease-Vector Relationships," in Peters and Lovejoy, op. cit. note 12; J. Lines, "The Effects of Climatic and Land-Use Changes on Insect Vectors of Human Disease," in Harrington and Stork, op. cit. note 10; dengue fever mechanism from Patz et al., op. cit. note 12.

48. "Springtime for Scientists in Georgia," *The Economist*, 25 February 1995; David J. Thomson, "The Seasons, Global Temperature, and Precession," *Science*, 7 April 1995.

49. Ray T. Oglesby and Charles R. Smith, "Climate Change in the Northeast," in Edward T. LaRoe et al., eds., *Our Living Resources: A Report to the Nation on the Distribution, Abundance, and Health of U.S. Plants, Animals, and Ecosystems* (Washington, D.C.: U.S. Department of the Interior, National Biological Service, 1995); Edward T. LaRoe and Donald H. Rusch, "Changes in Nesting Behavior of Arctic Geese," in ibid.

50. Robert L. Peters, "Conservation of Biological Diversity in the Face of Climate Change," in Peters and Lovejoy, op. cit. note 12; Martin J. Lechowicz, "Seasonality of Flowering and Fruiting in Temperate Forest Trees," *Canadian Journal of Botany*, Vol. 73, pp. 175–82, 1995.

51. John Harte, Margaret Torn, and Deborah Jensen, "The Nature and Consequences of Indirect Linkages Between Climate Change and Biological Diversity," in Peters and Lovejoy, op. cit. note 12.

52. Thomas P. Quinn and Dean J. Adams, "Environmental Changes Affecting the Migratory Timing of American Shad and Sockeye Salmon," *Ecology*, June 1996.

53. J.P. Myers and Robert T. Lester, "Double Jeopardy for Migrating Animals: Multiple Hits and Resource Asynchrony," in Peters and Lovejoy, op. cit. note 12; Adam Markham, "Interrupted Flight: Climate Change Impacts and Bird Migration," WWF Climate Change Campaign, World Wide Fund for Nature (WWF) International, Washington, D.C., October 1996.

54. A.G. Gatehouse and X.-X. Zhang, "Migratory Potential in Insects: Variation in an Uncertain Environment," in V.A. Drake and A.G. Gatehouse, eds., *Insect Migration: Tracking Resources Through Space and Time* (Cambridge: Cambridge University Press, 1995); K. Wilson, "Insect Migration in Heterogenious Environments," in ibid.

55. Norman Myers, "Environmental Unknowns," *Science*, 21 July 1995.

56. David W. Schindler et al., "Consequences of Climate Warming and Lake Acidification for UV-B Penetration in North American Boreal Lakes," *Nature*, 22 February 1996; Fred Pearce, "Canadian Lakes Suffer Triple Blow," *New Scientist*, 24 February 1996.

57. Schindler et al., op. cit. note 56.

58. Ibid.

59. Ibid.

60. Ultraviolet exposure trends from J.R. Herman et al., "UV-B Increases (1979–1992) From Decreases in Total Ozone," *Geophysical Research Letters*, 1 August 1996, and from Fred Pearce, "Big Freeze Digs a Deeper Hole in Ozone Layer," *New Scientist*, 16 March 1996; acidification in Eurasian boreal lakes from Dag O. Hessen and Richard F. Wright, "Climatic Effects on Fresh Water: Nutrient Loading, Eutrophication and Acidification," in Holten, Paulsen, and Oechel, op. cit. note 35.

61. S.B. McLaughlin and D.J. Downing, "Interactive Effects of Ambient Ozone and Climate Measured on Growth of Mature Forest Trees," *Nature*, 16 March 1995; possible problem in Britain from J.L. Innes, "Climatic Sensitivity of Temperate Forests," *Environmental Pollution*, Vol. 83, 1994.

62. Air pollution as a catalyst for disease and pest outbreaks from V.C. Brown, "Insect Herbivores and Gaseous Air Pollutants—Current Knowledge and Predictions," in Harrington and Stork, op. cit. note 10, and from William J. Manning and Andreas V. Tiedemann, "Climate Change: Potential Effects of Increased Atmospheric Carbon Dioxide (CO_2), Ozone (O_3), and Ultraviolet-B (UV-B) Radiation on Plant Diseases," *Environmental Pollution*, Vol. 88, 1995; metals and acid rain from James E. Gawel et al., "Role for Heavy Metals in Forest Decline Indicated by Phytochelatin Measurements," *Nature*, 2 May 1996, and from G.E. Likens, C.T. Driscoll, and D.C. Buso, "Long-Term Effects of Acid Rain: Response and Recovery of a Forest Ecosystem," *Science*, 12 April 1996.

63. Importance of the reef biome from Norman Myers, "Synergisms: Joint Effects of Climate Change and Other Forms of Habitat Destruction," in Peters and Lovejoy, op. cit. note 12; widespread coral die-off and possible extinctions from Pierre Lasserre, "The Role of Biodiversity in Marine Ecosystems," in O.T. Solbrig, H.M. van Emden, and P.G.W.J. van Oordt, eds., *Biodiversity and Global Change* (Paris: International Union of Biological Sciences, 1992; reprint, Wallingford,

U.K.: CAB International, 1994), and from Bijlsma, op. cit. note 22; warming of sea surface temperatures from ibid. and from Ittekkot et al., op. cit. note 44, from which the quote is taken.

64. Coral predators from Bijlsma, op. cit. note 22, and from Ian Anderson, "Return of the Coral Eaters," *New Scientist*, 3 February 1996; overfishing from Clive R. Wilkinson and Robert W. Buddemeier, "Global Climate Change and Coral Reefs: Implications for People and Reefs," Report of the UNEP-IOC-ASPEI-IUCN Global Task Team on the Implications of Climate Change on Coral Reefs, 1994.

65. Wilkinson and Buddemeier, op. cit. note 64; S.V. Smith and R.W. Buddemeier, "Global Change and Coral Reef Ecosystems," *Annual Review of Ecology and Systematics*, 1992.

66. U.S. spending on natural areas from J.A. McNeely, J. Harrison, and P. Dingwall, eds., *Protecting Nature: Regional Reviews of Protected Areas* (Gland, Switzerland: IUCN, 1994); carbon emissions from Flavin and Tunali, op. cit. note 24; U.S. cutbacks in renewable energy from Joseph J. Romm and Charles B. Curtis, "Mideast Oil Forever?" *Atlantic*, April 1996, and from Gary Lee, "Government Researchers Fear Budget Cuts Will Cool Solar Energy Work," *Washington Post*, 25 September 1996.

67. For an applied discussion of some land management issues, see Larry D. Harris and Wendell P. Cropper, Jr., "Between the Devil and the Deep Blue Sea: Implications of Climate Change for Florida's Fauna," in Peters and Lovejoy, op. cit. note 12.

68. Control strategies for exotic plants from Cronk and Fuller, op. cit. note 37; hand pollination of rare Hawaiian plants from Brien Meilleur, executive director, Center for Plant Conservation, St. Louis, Mo., private communication, 24 October 1996.

69. "U.S. Initiative on Joint Implementation: First Round Projects Announcement Ceremony," press release, Washington, D.C., 6 February 1995.

70. Emissions reduction goals from United Nations, *United Nations Framework Convention on Climate Change, Text* (Geneva: UNEP/World Meteorological Organization Information Unit on Climate Change, 1992).

71. Markham, op. cit. note 53; Adam Markham, *Climate Change and Biodiversity Conservation* (Gland, Switzerland: WWF International, 1995); Fred Pearce, *Explaining Climate Change: A WWF Overview of the New Science* (Washington, D.C.: WWF, 1996); size of the insurance industry from Christopher Flavin, "Storm Warnings: Climate Change Hits the Insurance Industry," *World Watch*, November/December 1994.

72. Business Council for Sustainable Energy from Seth S. Dunn, "The Geneva Conference: Implications for U.N. Framework Convention on Climate Change," *International Environment Reporter*, 2 October 1996.

73. Christopher Flavin, "Power Shock: The Next Energy Revolution," *World Watch*, January/February 1996; Christopher Flavin and Nicholas Lenssen, *Power Surge: Guide to the Coming Energy Revolution* (New York: W.W. Norton & Company, 1994).

Chapter 6. Valuing Nature's Services

1. Rudolf S. de Groot, "Environmental Functions and the Economic Value of Natural Ecosystems," in AnnMari Jansson et al., eds., *Investing in Natural Capital: The Ecological Economics Approach to Sustainability* (Washington, D.C.: Island Press, 1994); Paul Ehrlich and Anne Ehrlich, "The Value of Biodiversity," *Ambio*, May 1992.

2. Stuart L. Pimm et al., "The Future of Biodiversity," *Science*, July 21, 1995.

3. Global trade in rattan data from Jenne H. De Beer and Melanie J. McDermott, *The Economic Value of Non-timber Forest Products in Southeast Asia* (Amsterdam: Netherlands Committee for IUCN, 1989); data on the fish industry from U.S. Environmental Protection Agency, *Liquid Assets: A Summertime Perspective on the Importance of Clean Water to the Nation's Economy* (Washington, D.C.: 1996), and from "Wetlands: Values and Trends," Issue Brief 4, Natural Resources Conservation Service, U.S. Department of Agriculture, Washington, D.C., November 1995.

4. Historic information on the production of modern crop varieties from U.N. Food and Agriculture Organization (FAO), "The State of the World's Plant Genetic Resources for Food and Agriculture," Background Documentation Prepared for the International Technical Conference on Plant Genetic Resources, Rome, 1996; contribution of landraces from Cary Fowler and Pat Mooney, *Shattering: Food, Politics, and the Loss of Genetic Diversity* (Tuscon: University of Arizona Press, 1990); wild wheat example from C. Perrings, co-ordinator, "Economic Values of Biodiversity," in V.H. Heywood, exec. ed., *Global Biodiversity Assessment* (Cambridge: Cambridge University Press, for United Nations Environment Programme (UNEP), 1995); origins of crops from Robert and Christine Prescott-Allen, *Genes from the Wild: Using Wild Genetic Resources for Food and Raw Materials* (London: Earthscan, 1983).

5. Importance of traditional medicine from World Resources Institute (WRI), The World Conservation Union–IUCN, and UNEP, *Global Biodiversity Strategy* (Washington, D.C.: WRI, 1992); Katrina Brown, "Medicinal Plants, Indigenous Medicine and Conservation of Biodiversity in Ghana," in T.M. Swanson, ed., *Intellectual Property and Biodiversity Conservation* (Cambridge: Cambridge University Press, 1995); prescriptions derived from plants from Ara DerMarderosian, "The 1990's: The Status of Pharmacognosy in the United States," in Shigeaki Baba, Olayiwola Akerele, and Yuji Kawaguchi, eds., *Natural Resources and Human Health—Plants of Medicinal and Nutritional Value* (Amsterdam: Elsevier, 1992), and from Norman R. Farnsworth, "Screening Plants for

New Medicines," in E.O. Wilson and Francis M. Peters, eds., *Biodiversity* (Washington, D.C.: National Academy Press, 1988); John W. Gruber and Ara DerMarderosian, "Back to the Future: Traditional Medicines Revisited, the Use of Plants in Medicines," *Laboratory Medicine*, February 1996; $40 billion from Mohan Munasinghe, "Biodiversity Protection Policy: Environmental Valuation and Distributional Issues," *Ambio*, May 1992.

6. Microorganisms from WRI, IUCN, and UNEP, op. cit. note 5; taxol from K.C. Nicolaou, Rodney K. Guy, and Pierre Potier, "Taxoids: New Weapons against Cancer," *Scientific American*, June 1996; snakes from J.R. Callahan, "Vanishing Biodiversity," *Environmental Health Perspectives*, April 1996.

7. R.R. Colwell, "Biodiversity and Marine Biotechnology: A New Partnership of Academia, Government and Industry," in F. di Castri and T. Younes, eds., *Biodiversity, Science and Development: Towards a New Partnership* (Wallingford, U.K.: CAB International, 1996); C. Juma and J. Mugabe, "Biodiversity Prospecting: Opportunities and Challenges for African Countries," in ibid.; Walter Reid, et al., *Biodiversity Prospecting: Using Genetic Resources for Sustainable Development* (Washington, D.C.: WRI, 1993); shark example from N.K. Hunton, "All-natural AIDS Protection?" *Technology Review*, August/September 1996, and from Gregory Beck and Gail Habicht, "Immunity and the Invertebrates," *Scientific American*, November 1996; scientist quoted in Gina Kolata, "Deadly Snails Take Pinpoint Aim with Diverse Toxins," *New York Times*, 6 August 1996.

8. Data on flowering plant species from Farnsworth, op. cit. note 5; calculations of lost pharmaceutical value based on David W. Pearce and Dominic Moran, *The Economic Value of Biological Diversity* (London: Earthscan, 1994).

9. Pearce and Moran, op. cit. note 8; Kanchan Chopra, "The Value of Non-timber Forest Products: An Estimation for Tropical Deciduous Forests in India," *Economic Botany*, Vol. 47, No. 3, 1993; Ricardo Godoy, Ruben Lubowski, and Anil Markandya, "A Method for the Economic Valuation of Non-Timber Tropical Forest Products," *Economic Botany*, Vol. 47, No. 3, 1993; Julia Falconer, *The Major Significance of 'Minor' Forest Products: The Local Use and Value of Forests in the West African Humid Forest Zone* (Rome: FAO, 1990); H.J. Ruitenbeek, *Mangrove Management: An Economic Analysis of Management Options with a Focus on Bintuni Bay, Irian Jaya*, Environmental Reports No. 8 (Gabriola Island, B.C., Canada: Environmental Management Project, 1992).

10. Employment data from Ravinder Kaur, "Women in Forestry in India," in Background Paper for World Bank Women and Development in India review (Washington, D.C.: World Bank, 1990); value of trade in non-timber forest products (NTFPs) from T. Panayotou and P. Ashton, *Not by Timber Alone: Economics and Ecology for Sustaining Tropical Forests* (Washington, D.C.: Island Press, 1992).

11. Carol Ireson, "Women's Forest Work in Laos," *Society and Natural Resources*, Vol. 4, 1991; Ghana example in Florence Addo et al., "The Economic Contribution of Women and Protected Areas: Ghana and the Bushmeat Trade," presented at the IV World Parks Congress on National Parks and Protected Areas, Caracas, Venezuela, 10–21 February 1992; Falconer, op. cit. note 9.

12. Belize example from Panayotou and Ashton, op. cit. note 10; Nigeria example from Derek Eaton, International Institute for Environment and Development, London, private communication, 5 August 1996; wild mushroom example from mushroom collector, Darlington, Wash., private communication, August 1995; Falconer, op. cit. note 9.

13. Women in the NTFP economy from Kaur, op. cit. note 10, from D.D. Tewari, "Developing and Sustaining Non-timber Forest Products: Policy Issues and Concerns with Special Reference to India," *Journal of World*

Forest Resource Management, Vol. 7, pp. 151–78, 1994, and from Jeffrey Campbell, *Case Studies in Forest-Based Small Scale Enterprises* (Bangkok: FAO, 1991); rubber tappers from Susanna Hecht, "Sustainable Extraction in Amazonia," in Lea M. Borkenhagen and Janet N. Abramovitz, eds., *Proceedings of the International Conference on Women and Biodiversity* (Washington, D.C.: Committee on Women and Biodiversity and WRI, 1993); India example from Kaur, op. cit. note 10; quote from Madhav Gadgil, "Biodiversity and India's Degraded Lands," *Ambio*, May 1993.

14. Market value of shrimp aquaculture and loss of coastal ecosystems from Solon Barraclough and Andrea Finger-Stich, "Some Ecological and Social Implications of Commercial Shrimp Farming in Asia," Discussion Paper 74, United Nations Research Institute for Social Development, Geneva, March 1996; "footprint" from Carl Folke and Nils Kautsky, "The Ecological Footprint Concept for Sustainable Seafood Production," Beijer Discussion Paper No. 72 (Stockholm: Beijer International Institue of Ecological Economics, 1996), and from Jonas Larsson, Carl Folke, and Nils Kautsky, "Ecological Limitations and Appropriation of Ecosystem Support by Shrimp Farming in Colombia," *Environmental Management*, Vol. 18, No. 5, 1994.

15. Income from J. Honculada Primavera, "Intensive Prawn Farming in the Phillipines: Ecological, Social, and Economic Implications," *Ambio*, February 1991; Malcolm C. Beveridge, Lindsay G. Ross, and Liam A. Kelly, "Aquaculture and Biodiversity," *Ambio*, December 1994; Barraclough and Finger-Stich, op. cit. note 14; Christopher F. Knud-Hansen, "Shrimp Mariculture: Environmental Impacts and Regulations with a Focus on Thailand," *Colorado Journal of International Environmental Law and Policy*, Vol. 6, pp. 183–99, 1995; and Larsson, Folke, and Kautsky, op. cit. note 14.

16. Barraclough and Finger-Stich, op. cite note 14.

17. Quote in Stephen Buchmann and Gary Paul Nabhan, "The Pollination Crisis," *The Sciences*, July/August 1996; see also S. Buchmann and G. Nabhan, *The Forgotten Pollinators* (Washington, D.C.: Island Press, 1996).

18. Buchmann and Nabhan, *The Forgotten Pollinators*, op. cit. note 17.

19. Mrill Ingram, Gary P. Nabhan, and Stephen Buchmann, "Ten Essential Reasons to Protect the Birds and the Bees," Forgotten Pollinators Campaign, Arizona-Sonora Desert Museum, Tuscon, Ariz., 1996; Gary Nabhan, "Pollinator Redbook, Vol. One: Global List of Threatened Vertebrate Wildlife Species Serving As Pollinators for Crops and Wild Plants," Forgotten Pollinators Campaign, Arizona-Sonoma Desert Museum, Tucson, Ariz., 1996; Jonathan Baillie and Brian Groombridge, eds., *1996 IUCN–World Conservation Union Red List of Threatened Animals* (Cambridge: IUCN Publications Service Unit, 1996).

20. Ingram, Nabhan, and Buchmann, op. cit. note 19; Buchmann and Nabhan, *The Forgotten Pollinators*, op. cit. note 17.

21. Data on honeybee loss from Gary Nabham, quoted in "Growers Bee-moan Shortage of Pollinators," *Science News*, 29 June 1996; threats to pollinators from Ingram, Nabhan, and Buchmann, op. cit. note 19, and from Buchmann and Nabhan, *The Forgotten Pollinators*, op. cit. note 17.

22. D. Pimental et al., "Environmental and Economic Costs of Pesticide Use," *Bioscience*, November 1992; Ingram, Nabhan, and Buchmann, op. cit. note 19.

23. Buchmann and Nabhan, *The Forgotten Pollinators*, op. cit. note 17.

24. C.M. Peters, *Sustainable Harvest of Non-Timber Plant Resources in Tropical Moist Forest: An Ecological Primer* (Washington, D.C.: Biodiversity Support Program of World Wildlife Fund (WWF), The Nature Conservancy (TNC), and WRI, 1994).

25. Buchmann and Nabhan, *The Forgotten Pollinators*, op. cit. note 17.

26. Information on long-nosed bats from Buchmann and Nabhan, *The Forgotten Pollinators*, op. cit. note 17; data on percent of bats threatened with extinction from Baillie and Groombridge, op. cit. note 19.

27. Leaf-eating insects from Robert Marquis and Christopher Whelan, "Insectivorous Birds Increase Growth of White Oak Through Consumption of Leaf-Chewing Insects," *Ecology*, Vol. 75, No. 7, 1994; amount of insects eaten by bats from David Holstrom, "They're Bats, They're Back—This Time with Better PR," *Christian Science Monitor*, 16 July 1996.

28. Data on pesticide imports from "U.K. Report Finds 'Balanced' Viewpoint on Compatibility of Trade, Environment," *International Environment Reporter*, 10 July 1996; decline of frog species from Howard Youth, "Amphibian Populations Take a Dive," in Lester R. Brown, Nicholas Lenssen, and Hal Kane, *Vital Signs 1995* (New York: W.W. Norton & Company, 1995).

29. David Pimentel et al., "Environmental and Economic Costs of Soil Erosion and Conservation Benefits," *Science*, 24 February 1995; William J. Broad, "Bugs Shape Landscape, Make Gold," *New York Times*, 15 October 1996; James K. Fredrickson and Tullis C. Onstott, "Microbes Deep Inside the Earth," *Scientific American*, October 1996.

30. Ingram, Nabhan, and Buchmann, op. cit. note 19.

31. Perrings, op. cit. note 4.

32. Donald Hey and Nancy Phillipi, "Commentary Flood Reduction through Wetland Restoration: The Upper Mississippi River Basin as a Case History," *Restoration Ecology*, March 1995.

33. J.M. Hefner et al., *Southwest Wetlands: Status and Trends, Mid-1970s to Mid-1980s* (Atlanta, Ga.: U.S. Department of the Interior (DOI), Fish and Wildlife Service (FWS), 1994).

34. Rivers running dry from Sandra Postel, *Dividing the Waters: Food Security, Ecosystem Health, and the New Politics of Scarcity*, Worldwatch Paper 132 (Washington, D.C.: Worldwatch Institute, September 1996); groundwater reservoirs from David Stanners and Philippe Bourdeau, eds., *Europe's Environment: The Dobris Assessment* (London: Earthscan, 1995).

35. Malaysia example from Pearce and Moran, op. cit. note 8; New York City watershed example from Andrew Revkin, "Agreement on Watershed Plan is Praised," *New York Times*, 11 September 1996, and from Eric Goldstein and Mark Izeman, "The New York City Watershed Agreement: An Appraisal," *Environmental Law in New York*, July 1996.

36. Pimentel et al., op. cit. note 29.

37. Ibid.

38. Dr. Joann Burkholder, North Carolina State University Professor of Aquatic Biology, Remarks at Restore America's Estuaries Briefing, Washington, D.C., 18 September 1996.

39. The role of wetlands from de Groot, op. cit. note 1; wetland values from Ing-Marie Gren, "The Value of Investing in Wetlands for Nitrogen Abatement," *European Review of Agricultural Economics*, Vol. 22, pp. 157–72, 1995, from Ing-Marie Gren, "Costs and Benefits of Restoring Wetlands: Two Swedish Case Studies," *Ecological Engineering*, Vol. 4, pp. 153–62, 1995, from Carl Folke, Monica Hammer, and AnnMari Jansson, "Life Support Value of Ecosystems: A Case Study of the Baltic Region," *Ecological Economics*, Vol. 3, pp. 123–37, 1991, and from Barraclough and Finger-Stich, op. cit. note 14; wetland losses from Michael Moser, Crawford Prentice, and Scott Frazier, *A Global Overview of Wetland Loss and Degradation*, prepared for the Conference of the Parties to the Ramsar Convention, Wetlands International, Slimbridge, U.K., March 1996, and from T.E. Dahl, *Wetland Losses in the United States 1780's to 1980's* (Washington, D.C.: DOI, FWS, 1990).

40. Taylor DeLaney, "Downstream Flood Attenuation and Water Quality as a Result of Constructed Wetlands," *Journal of Soil and Water Conservation*, September-December 1995.

41. Ibid.; Mississippi Basin example from Hey and Philippi, op. cit. note 32.

42. E.B. Barbier, W.M. Adams, and K. Kimmage, "An Economic Valuation of Wetland Benefits," in G.E. Hollis, W.M. Adams, and M. Aminu-Kano, eds., *The Hadejia-Nguru Wetlands: Environment, Economy, and Sustainable Development of a Sahelian Floodplain Wetland* (Gland, Switzerland: IUCN, 1993); David Thomas, "Artisanal Fishing and Environmental Change in a Nigerian Floodplain Wetland," *Environmental Conservation*, Summer 1995; population estimate from "Hadejia-Nguru Wetlands Conservation Project Information Leaflet No. 1," Kano, Nigeria. undated.

43. Barbier, Adams, and Kimmage, op. cit. note 42.

44. C.S. Holling et al., "Biodiversity in the Functioning of Ecosystems: An Ecological Synthesis," in C. Perrings et al., eds., *Biodiversity Loss: Ecological and Economic Issues* (Cambridge: Cambridge University Press, 1995).

45. H.A. Mooney et al., co-ordinators, "Biodiversity and Ecosystem Functioning: Basic Principles," in Heywood, op. cit. note 4; Ehrlich and Ehrlich, op. cit. note 1.

46. Basis of world's food supply from Robert Prescott-Allen and Christine Prescott-Allen, "How Many Plants Feed the World?" *Conservation Biology*, Vol. 4, No. 4, 1990; data on U.S. crop varieties from FAO, op. cit. note 4.

47. Indonesia from WRI, IUCN, and UNEP, op. cit. note 5; Soviet Union from FAO, op. cit. note 4.

48. FAO, op. cit. note 4.

49. China data from FAO, op. cit. note 4; Ministry of Population and Environment, *National Strategy for the Management of*

Biodiversity (Jakarta: Government of Indonesia, 1989); U.S. data from Fowler and Mooney, op. cit. note 4; FAO, *Report of the International Technical Conference on Plant Genetic Resources: Leipzig, Germany, June 17–23 1996* (Rome: 1996).

50. William Broad, "A Spate of Red Tides Menaces Coastal Seas," *New York Times*, 27 August 1996; coastal threats from Dirk Bryant et al., "Coastlines at Risk: An Index of Potential Development-Related Threats to Coastal Ecosystems," WRI Indicator Brief, Washington, D.C., 1995.

51. Christopher Flavin, "Insurance Industry Reels," in Lester R. Brown, Christopher Flavin, and Hal Kane, *Vital Signs 1996* (New York: W.W. Norton & Company, 1996).

52. Information on water recycling from Ehrlich and Ehrlich, op. cit. note 1; desertification from Fred Pearce, "Deserts on Our Doorstep," *New Scientist*, 6 July 1996.

53. Neil Adger, "Approaches to Vulnerability to Climate Change," Working Paper GEC 96–05, Center for Social and Economic Research on the Global Environment (CSERGE), London, 1996; Nguyen Hoang Tri et al. "The Role of Natural Resource Management in Mitigating Climate Impacts: Mangrove Restoration in Vietnam," Working Paper GEC 96–06, CSERGE, London, 1996; carbon sequestration from Neil Adger et al., "Total Economic Value of Mexican Forests," *Ambio*, August 1995, from Jan Bojo, "Economic Valuation of Indigenous Woodlands in Zimbabwe," in P. Bradley and K. McNamara, eds., *Living with Trees: A Future for Social Forestry in Zimbabwe* (Washington, D.C.: World Bank, 1993), from Katrina Brown and David W. Pearce, "The Economic Value of Non-marketed Benefits of Tropical Forests: Carbon Storage," in J. Weiss, ed., *The Economics of Project Appraisal and the Environment* (London: Edward Elgar, 1994), from David Pearce, "Deforesting the Amazon: Toward an Economic Solution," *Ecodecision*, First Quarter 1991, and from Pearce and Moran, op. cit. note 8.

54. Robert Costanza, Stephen Farber, and Judith Maxwell, "Valuation and Management of Wetland Ecosystems," *Ecological Economics*, Vol. 1, pp. 335–61, 1989.

55. Herman E. Daly and John B. Cobb, Jr., *For the Common Good* (Boston: Beacon Press, 1989); Clifford Cobb, Ted Halstead, and Jonathan Rowe, "Redefining Progress: The Genuine Progress Indicator, Summary of Data and Methodology," Redefining Progress, San Francisco, Calif., 1995; Robert Repetto et al., *Wasting Assets: Natural Resources in the National Income Accounts* (Washington, D.C.: WRI, 1989).

56. Ritu Kumar and Carlos Young, "Economic Policies for Sustainable Water Use in Thailand," Working Paper Series No. 4, Programme of Collaborative Research in the Economics of Environment and Development, London, undated; Janet N. Abramovitz, *Imperiled Waters, Impoverished Future: The Decline of Freshwater Ecosystems*, Worldwatch Paper 128 (Washington, D.C.: Worldwatch Institute, March 1996); population affected from "New Mekong River Basin Agreement Will Spur Hydro Development, Groups Charge," *International Environmental Reporter*, 19 April 1995.

57. Perrings, op. cit. note 4; Biodiversity Support Program, *African Biodiversity: Foundation for the Future* (Washington, D.C.: Biodiversity Support Program of WWF, TNC, and WRI, 1993).

58. Cobb, Halstead, and Rowe, op. cit. note 55.

59. Daly and Cobb, op. cit. note 55; Figure 6–1 from Cobb, Halstead, and Rowe, op. cit. note 55.

60. Robert Costanza, Herman Daly, and Joy Bartholomew, "Goals, Agenda, and Policy Recommendations for Ecological Economics," in Robert Costanza, ed., *Ecological Economics* (New York: Columbia University Press, 1991); Edward Barbier, Joanne Burgess, and Carl Folke, *Paradise Lost? The Ecological Economics of Biodiversity* (London: Earthscan, 1994); Jansson et al., op. cit. note 1.

61. Daly and Cobb, op., cit. note 55; water subsidies from Postel, op. cit. note 34.

62. De Groot, op. cit. note 1.

63. Ruitenbeek, op. cit. note 9; H.J. Ruitenbeek of H.J. Ruitenbeek Resource Consulting Limited, Gabriola Island, B.C., Canada, private communication, 5 August 1996.

64. Jaime Echeverria, Vice-President, Tropical Science Center, Costa Rica, private communication, 5 August 1996.

65. "Governments Work Towards Achieving Biodiversity Treaty Goals," press release, UNEP, Montreal, 1 November 1996; "Strategic Plan 1997–2002, Adopted by the 6th Conference of the Contracting Parties, Brisbane, Australia, 19–27 March 1996," Convention on Wetlands Secretariat, Gland, Switzerland, April 1996.

Chapter 7. Transforming Security

Some of the references in this chapter were obtained on-line from conferences of the Association for Progressive Communications (APC), which in the United States are maintained and archived by the Institute for Global Communications in San Francisco.

1. Donatella Lorch, "Rwandan Refugees Describe Horrors After a Bloody Trek," *New York Times*, 3 May 1994; Raymond Bonner, "Rwandans in Death Squad Say Choice Was Kill or Die," *New York Times*, 14 August 1994; Milton Leitenberg, "Anatomy of a Massacre" (op-ed), *New York Times*, 31 July 1994.

2. Human Rights Watch, *Slaughter Among Neighbors: The Political Origins of Communal Violence* (New Haven, Conn.: Yale University Press, 1995).

3. Valerie Percival and Thomas Homer-Dixon, "Environmental Scarcity and Violent

Conflict: The Case of Rwanda," The Project on Environment, Population, and Security, American Association for the Advancement of Science and University of Toronto, June 1995.

4. The meaning of the term "human security" is discussed at length in U.N. Development Programme (UNDP), *Human Development Report 1994* (New York: Oxford University Press, 1994).

5. Child soldiers from UNICEF, *The State of the World's Children 1996* (New York: Oxford University Press, 1996); share of civilian victims from Ruth Leger Sivard, *World Military and Social Expenditures 1989* (Washington, D.C.: World Priorities, 1989), and from Ernie Regehr, "A Pattern of War," *Ploughshares Monitor*, December 1991.

6. Dan Smith, *War, Peace and Third World Development*, Human Development Report Office, Occasional Papers No. 16, UNDP, New York, 1993; Michael T. Klare, "The Global Trade in Light Weapons and the International System in the Post–Cold War Era," in Jeffrey Boutwell, Michael T. Klare, and Laura W. Reed, eds., *Lethal Commerce: The Global Trade in Small Arms and Light Weapons* (Cambridge, Mass.: American Academy of Arts and Sciences, 1995); Christopher Louise, *The Social Impacts of Light Weapons Availability and Proliferation*, Discussion Paper No. 59, U.N. Research Institute for Social Development, Geneva, March 1995.

7. See, for example, Gerald B. Helman and Steven R. Ratner, "Saving Failed States," *Foreign Policy*, Winter 1992–93.

8. James N. Rosenau, "New Dimensions of Security: The Interaction of Globalizing and Localizing Dynamics," *Security Dialogue*, September 1994.

9. Samuel P. Huntington, "The Clash of Civilizations?" *Foreign Affairs*, Summer 1993. For a lucid critique, see Richard E. Rubenstein and Jarle Crocker, "Challenging Huntington," *Foreign Policy*, Fall 1994.

10. Half of all countries experiencing ethnic strife from UNDP, op. cit. note 4; other data from Ted Robert Gurr, *Minorities at Risk: A Global View of Ethnopolitical Conflicts* (Washington, D.C.: U.S. Institute for Peace Press, 1993).

11. Erskine Childers, "UN Mechanisms and Capacities for Intervention," in Elizabeth G. Ferris, ed., *The Challenge to Intervene: A New Role for the United Nations?* Conference Report 2 (Uppsala, Sweden: Life and Peace Institute, 1992); Human Rights Watch, op. cit. note 2.

12. Ted Robert Gurr, "Third World Minorities at Risk Since 1945," Background Paper on the Conference on Conflict Resolution in the Post–Cold War Third World, U.S. Institute of Peace, Washington, D.C., 3–5 October 1990.

13. Stefan Klötzli, "The Water and Soil Crisis in Central Asia—A Source for Future Conflicts?" Occasional Paper No. 11, Environment and Conflicts Project (ENCOP), Bern, Switzerland, May 1994; Sandra Postel, "Where Have All the Rivers Gone?" *World Watch*, May/June 1995.

14. Desertification is defined by UNEP as "land degradation in arid, semi-arid, and dry subhumid areas resulting mainly from adverse human impacts"; Günther Bächler, "Desertification and Conflict: The Marginalization of Poverty and of Environmental Conflicts," Occasional Paper No. 10, ENCOP, Bern, Switzerland, March 1994; percentage of degraded agricultural land from L.R. Oldeman, International Soil Reference and Information Centre, Wageningen, Netherlands, private communication with Gary Gardner, Worldwatch Institute, Washington, D.C., 21 September 1995.

15. L.R. Oldeman, International Soil Reference and Information Centre, Wageningen, Netherlands, private communication with Gary Gardner, Worldwatch Institute, Washington, D.C., 12 April 1996; crisis areas from Astri Suhrke, "Pressure Points: Environmen-

tal Degradation, Migration and Conflict," in Occasional Paper No. 3, Project on Environmental Change and Acute Conflict, American Academy of Arts and Sciences and University of Toronto, March 1993; Mexico from Norman Myers, *Ultimate Security: The Environmental Basis of Political Stability* (New York: W.W. Norton & Company, 1993).

16. "Shifted cultivators" and Mexico from Myers, op. cit. note 15; Rwanda from Percival and Homer-Dixon, op. cit. note 3; Rwandan yields and grain production from U.S. Department of Agriculture, Economic Research Service, "Production, Supply, and Distribution" (electronic database), Washington, D.C., November 1995.

17. Sandra Postel, *Last Oasis: Facing Water Scarcity* (New York: W.W. Norton & Company, 1992).

18. Ibid.; Sandra Postel, "Forging a Sustainable Water Strategy," in Lester R. Brown et al., *State of the World 1996* (New York: W.W. Norton & Company, 1996).

19. Postel, op. cit. note 17.

20. "Coastal Zones and Small Islands" (Chapter 9), in Robert T. Watson, Marufu C. Zinyowera, and Richard H. Moss, eds., *Climate Change 1995: Impacts, Adaptations and Mitigation of Climate Change: Scientific-Technical Analyses* (Cambridge: Cambridge University Press, for the Intergovernmental Panel on Climate Change, 1996); Bangladesh from M. Abdul Hafiz and Nahid Islam, "Environmental Degradation and Intra/Interstate Conflicts in Bangladesh," Occasional Paper No. 6, ENCOP, Bern, Switzerland, May 1993.

21. William K. Stevens, "Scientists Say Earth's Warming Could Set Off Wide Disruptions," *New York Times*, 18 September 1995.

22. Myers, op. cit. note 15; "Coastal Zones and Small Islands," op. cit. note 20.

23. Thomas F. Homer-Dixon, "Environmental Scarcities and Violent Conflict: Evidence from Cases," *International Security*,

Summer 1994; Myers, op. cit. note 15.

24. Calvin Sims, "Workers Bitter at Pay and Privatization Tie Up Bolivian Capital," *New York Times*, 28 March 1996.

25. Nathaniel C. Nash, "Latin Economic Speedup Leaves Poor in the Dust," *New York Times*, 7 September 1994; U.N. Economic Commission for Latin America and the Caribbean, *Social Panorama of Latin America 1994* (Santiago, Chile: 1994); "Mexico and Latin America: Poverty and Integration," *NAFTA and Inter-American Trade Monitor* (Institute for Agriculture and Trade Policy), December 1995.

26. Growing inequality in Latin American countries from International Labour Organisation (ILO), *World Labour Report 1993* (Geneva: 1993).

27. Global ratio from UNDP, op. cit. note 4; United Kingdom from U.N. Research Institute for Social Development, *States of Disarray: The Social Effects of Globalization* (Geneva: 1995); U.S. from David Dembo and Ward Morehouse, *The Underbelly of the U.S. Economy* (New York: Apex Press, 1995).

28. UNDP, *Human Development Report 1991* (New York: Oxford University Press, 1991).

29. Brazil from Myriam Vander Stichele, "Trade Liberalization—The Other Side of the Coin," *Development + Cooperation*, January/February 1996; South Africa from Reinhold Meyer, "Waiting for the Fruits of Change. South Africa's Difficult Road to Equality," *Development + Cooperation*, July/August 1996; Sudan from John Prendergast, "Greenwars in Sudan," *Center Focus*, July 1992.

30. Peter Uvin, "Tragedy in Rwanda: The Political Ecology of Conflict," *Environment*, April 1996; Alan B. Durning, *Poverty and the Environment: Reversing the Downward Spiral*, Worldwatch Paper 92 (Washington, D.C.: Worldwatch Institute, November 1989).

31. African disinvestment from ILO, op. cit. note 26.

32. Anthony de Palma, "In Mexico, Hunger for Poor and Middle-Class Hardship," *New York Times*, 15 January 1995; Carlos Heredia and Mary Purcell, "Structural Adjustment in Mexico: The Root of the Crisis," in the APC electronic conference igc:econ.saps on 7 March 1995.

33. Lack of credit access from Philip Howard and Thomas Homer-Dixon, "Environmental Scarcity and Violent Conflict: The Case of Chiapas, Mexico," The Project on Environment, Population, and Security, American Association for the Advancement of Science and University of Toronto, January 1996.

34. Ray Marshall, "The Global Jobs Crisis," *Foreign Policy*, Fall 1995; Richard J. Barnet, "Lords of the Global Economy," *The Nation*, 19 December 1994.

35. Youth unemployment from ILO, *World Labour Report 1995* (Geneva: 1995); projected growth of global labor force from Hal Kane, *The Hour of Departure: Forces That Create Refugees and Migrants*, Worldwatch Paper 125 (Washington, D.C.: Worldwatch Institute, June 1995); developing countries' annual job creation needs from United Nations, *World Social Situation in the 1990s* (New York: United Nations, 1994); possible reactions from U.N. Department of Public Information, "The Faces of Poverty," factsheet, March 1996, and from Peter Gizewski and Thomas Homer-Dixon, "Urban Growth and Violence: Will the Future Resemble the Past?" The Project on Environment, Population, and Security, American Association for the Advancement of Science and University of Toronto, 1995.

36. Human Rights Watch, op. cit. note 2; Howard Adelman and Astri Suhrke, "Feilschen während Ruanda brennt," *Der Überblick*, March 1996.

37. U.N. High Commissioner for Refugees (UNHCR), *The State of the World's Refugees 1995* (New York: Oxford University Press, 1995); Kane, op. cit. note 35; Hal Kane, "Refugees on the Rise Again," in Lester R. Brown, Christopher Flavin, and Hal Kane,

Vital Signs 1996 (New York: W.W. Norton & Company, 1996).

38. UNHCR, op. cit. note 37; U.S. Committee for Refugees, *World Refugee Survey 1995* (Washington, D.C.: 1995).

39. UNHCR, op. cit. note 37; Kane, op. cit. note 35.

40. Kane, op. cit. note 35.

41. Jodi L. Jacobson, *Environmental Refugees: A Yardstick of Habitability*, Worldwatch Paper 86 (Washington, D.C.: Worldwatch Institute, November 1988); Myers, op. cit. note 15.

42. Volker Böge, "Bougainville: A 'Classical' Environmental Conflict?" Occasional Paper No. 3, ENCOP, Bern, Switzerland, October 1992.

43. Peter B. Okoh, "Schutzpatronin der Ölkonzerne," *Der Überblick*, March 1994; Steve Kretzmann, "Nigeria's 'Drilling Fields': Shell Oil's Role in Repression," *Multinational Monitor*, January/February 1995; Geraldine Brooks, "Shell's Nigerian Fields Produce Few Benefits for Region's Villagers," *Wall Street Journal*, 6 May 1994; Howard F. French, "Nigeria Executes Critic of Regime; Nations Protest," *New York Times*, 11 November 1995.

44. Volker Böge, "Das Sardar-Sarovar-Projekt an der Narmada in Indien—Gegenstand ökologischen Konflikts," Occasional Paper No. 8, ENCOP, Bern, Switzerland, June 1993; "Water in South Asia: Narmada River Fact Sheet," Southern Asian Institute, Columbia University, New York, revised version, May 1995; Narmada Bachao Andolan, "The Narmada Struggle: International Campaign After the World Bank Pullout," in the APC electronic conference igc:dev.worldbank on 6 October 1995.

45. Mohamed Suliman, "Civil War in Sudan: The Impact of Ecological Degradation," Occasional Paper No. 4, ENCOP, Bern, Switzerland, December 1992.

46. Recent confrontations from Diana Jean Schemo, "Brazilian Squatters Fall in

Deadly Police Raid," *New York Times*, 19 September 1995, and from Diana Jean Schemo, "Violence Growing in Battle Over Brazilian Land," *New York Times*, 21 April 1996; acceleration of land occupations from James Petras, "Landless Movement in Brazil," *Z Magazine*, June 1996; Movimiento data from "Brazil: Agrarian Reform Proposed to End Violence," in *NAFTA & Inter-American Trade Monitor* (Institute for Agriculture and Trade Policy), 3 November 1995, in the APC electronic conference igc:trade.news on 3 November 1995.

47. Howard and Homer-Dixon, op. cit. note 33; Tom Barry, *Zapata's Revenge: Free Trade and the Farm Crisis in Mexico* (Boston, Mass.: South End Press, 1995).

48. George A. Collier with Elizabeth Lowery Quaratiello, *Basta! Land and the Zapatista Rebellion in Chiapas* (Oakland, Calif.: Food First Books, Institute for Food and Development Policy, 1994); decline of Lacandón tree cover from Barry, op. cit. note 47; border visibility from space from "The Mexican Rebels' Impoverished Home," *New York Times*, 9 January 1994.

49. Collier, op. cit. note 48; Barry, op. cit. note 47.

50. Hilary F. French, "Environmental Treaties Grow in Number," in Lester R. Brown, Nicholas Lenssen, and Hal Kane, *Vital Signs 1995* (New York: W.W. Norton & Company, 1995); Hilary F. French, "Forging a New Global Partnership," in Lester R. Brown et al., *State of the World 1995* (New York: W.W. Norton & Company, 1995); Jens Mertens and Peter Mucke, "Special Session of the UN General Assembly 1997: Core Issues," as posted by NGO Forum on Environment and Development in the APC electronic conference igc:un.csd.general on 11 May 1996; Peter H. Sand, "International Cooperation: The Environmental Experience," in Jessica Tuchman Mathews, ed., *Preserving the Global Environment: The Challenge of Shared Leadership* (New York: W.W. Norton & Company,

1991); Andrew Jordan, "Financing the UNCED Agenda: The Controversy over Additionality," *Environment*, April 1994.

51. United Nations, "Report of the World Summit for Social Development (Copenhagen, 6–12 March 1995)," New York, 19 April 1995.

52. African debt servicing from Bread for the World, "Easing Africa's Debt Burden," in the APC electronic conference igc:africa.news on 6 March 1996; multilateral creditors from Rose Umoren, "World Bank/IMF Meet Leaves Poor Countries Hanging," Inter Press Service, 23 April 1996, as posted in the APC electronic conference igc:africa.news on 30 April 1996, and from Paul Lewis, "I.M.F. May Sell Gold to Cut Debt of Poor Lands," *New York Times*, 30 August 1996.

53. Durning, op. cit. note 30.

54. Hal Kane, "Microenterprise," *World Watch*, March/April 1996.

55. Durning, op. cit. note 30; Edward A. Gargan, "'People's Banks Help Rescue Poor Indonesians," *New York Times*, 18 February 1996; number of people served by microcredit institutions from Patrick E. Tyler, "Star at Conference on Women: Banker Who Lends to the Poor," *New York Times*, 14 September 1995.

56. Kane, op. cit. note 54.

57. For endorsement of this point, see the "We Believe Statement" in President's Council on Sustainable Development, *Sustainable America* (Washington, D.C.: U.S. Government Printing Office, 1996).

58. Commission on Global Governance, *Our Global Neighborhood* (New York: Oxford University Press, 1995).

59. Larry Diamond, *Promoting Democracy in the 1990s: Actors and Instruments, Issues and Imperatives* (New York: Carnegie Corporation of New York, 1995).

60. For details, see Michael Renner, *Fighting for Survival: Environmental Decline, Social*

Conflict, and the New Age of Insecurity (New York: W.W. Norton & Company, 1996).

61. Military expenditures from Bonn International Center for Conversion, *Conversion Survey 1996: Global Disarmament, Demilitarization and Demobilization* (New York: Oxford University Press, 1996); for a discussion of mechanisms to shift resources from military budgets to other priorities, see Michael Renner, *Budgeting for Disarmament: The Costs of War and Peace*, Worldwatch Paper 122 (Washington, D.C.: Worldwatch Institute, November 1995).

62. UNDP, op. cit. note 4.

63. World Bank, *World Debt Tables 1994–95*, Vol. 1 (Washington, D.C.: 1994).

64. Hilary F. French, "Private Finance Flows to Third World," in Brown, Flavin, and Kane, op. cit. note 37.

Chapter 8. Reforming Subsidies

Some of the references in this chapter were obtained on-line from conferences of the Association for Progressive Communications (APC), which in the United States are maintained and archived by the Institute for Global Communications in San Francisco.

1. U.S. Congress, Committee on Natural Resources, Subcommittee on Oversight and Investigations, "Taking from the Taxpayer: Public Subsidies for Natural Resource Development," Majority Staff Report, Washington, D.C., 1994; a few hundred square meters is the area over which a thousand cubic meters of water would be needed over the life cycle of a single crop, based on Peter H. Gleick, ed., *Water in Crisis: A Guide to the World's Fresh Water Resources* (New York: Oxford University Press, 1993).

2. Charles Victor Barber, Nels C. Johnson, and Emmy Hafild, *Breaking the Logjam: Obstacles to Forest Policy Reform in Indonesia and the United States* (Washington, D.C.:

World Resources Institute (WRI), 1994); on the effects of counting natural resource depletion in Indonesia's gross domestic product, see Robert Repetto et al., *Wasting Assets: Natural Resources in the National Income Accounts* (Washington, D.C.: WRI, 1989).

3. Figure of $500 billion is a Worldwatch estimate, based on sources cited later in text. Figure of $7.5 trillion is a Worldwatch estimate, based on International Monetary Fund (IMF), *Government Finance Statistics Yearbook 1994* (Washington, D.C.: 1994), on IMF, *World Economic Outlook—October 1994* (Washington, D.C.: 1994), on Organisation for Economic Co-operation and Development (OECD), *Revenue Statistics of OECD Member Countries 1960–1994* (Paris: 1995), on World Bank, "World Data 1994: World Bank Indicators on CD-ROM" (electronic database), Washington, D.C., 1994, and on Thomas Sterner, "Environmental Tax Reform: Theory, Industrialized Country Experience, and Relevance in LDCs," Unit for Environmental Economics, Department of Economics, Gothenburg University, Gothenburg, Sweden, 1994. It excludes local and regional government revenue in developing countries, but includes nontax revenue there. For an analysis of the economic burden of taxation, see Dale W. Jorgenson and Yun Kun-Young, "The Excess Burden of Taxation in the U.S.," Discussion Paper No. 1528, Harvard Institute for Economic Research, Harvard University, Cambridge, Mass., 1990, as cited in Roger C. Dower and Mary Beth Zimmerman, *The Right Climate for Carbon Taxes: Creating Economic Incentives to Protect the Atmosphere* (Washington, D.C.: WRI, 1992).

4. Douglas Koplow, *Federal Energy Subsidies: Energy, Environmental, and Fiscal Impacts* (Washington, D.C.: Alliance to Save Energy, 1993).

5. "Quest for 'Green Gold' Fells One of Earth's Oldest Rain Forests," Associated Press, 7 May 1996.

6. For a broad conservative attack on subsidies, see, for example, Stephen Moore and

Dean Stansel, "Ending Corporate Welfare As We Know It," Policy Analysis No. 225, Cato Institute, Washington, D.C., 1995; on the precedence of other societal values over economic efficiency, see Mark Sagoff, *The Economy of the Earth: Philosophy, Law, and the Environment* (Cambridge: Cambridge University Press, 1988).

7.   Kenneth E. Boulding, *Environmental Quality in a Growing Economy* (Baltimore, Md.: Johns Hopkins University Press, 1966), excerpted as Kenneth E. Boulding, "The Economics of the Coming Spaceship Earth," in Herman E. Daly and Kenneth N. Townsend, eds., *Valuing the Earth: Economics, Ecology, Ethics* (Cambridge, Mass.: The MIT Press, 1993).

8.   Figure of 400 million hectares from Charles F. Wilkinson, *Crossing the Next Meridian: Land, Water, and the Future of the West* (Washington, D.C.: Island Press, 1992); Juri Peepre, Canadian Parks and Wilderness Society, White Horse, Yukon, Canada, private communication, 24 June 1996; Thomas J. Hilliard, "Golden Patents, Empty Pockets: A 19th Century Law Gives Miners Billions, the Public Pennies," Mineral Policy Center, Washington, D.C., 1994; U.S. Office of Management and Budget, *Budget of the United States Government, Fiscal Year 1997* (Washington, D.C.: U.S. Government Printing Office (GPO), 1996).

9.   U.S. grazing subsidies from U.S. Congress, op. cit. note 1; British Columbian grazing subsidies from Peepre, op. cit. note 8, and from John C. Ryan, "Hazardous Handouts: Taxpayer Subsidies to Environmental Degradation," NEW Report No. 2, Northwest Environment Watch (NEW), Seattle, Wash., 1995.

10.   Randal O'Toole, "Timber Sale Subsidies, But Who Gets Them?" *Different Drummer* (Thoreau Institute, Oak Grove, Ore.), Spring 1995; Tongass from U.S. Congress, op. cit. note 1; Andrew K. Dragun, "The Subsidization of Logging in Victoria," unpublished, LaTrobe University, Melbourne, 1995.

11.   Wilkinson, op. cit. note 8; Betty Ballantine and Ian Ballantine, eds., *The Native Americans: An Illustrated History* (Atlanta, Ga.: Turner Publishing, 1993); Barber, Johnson, and Hafild, op. cit. note 2; Australia from Alan Thein Durning and Holly B. Brough, "Reforming the Livestock Economy," in Lester R. Brown et al., *State of the World 1992* (New York: W.W. Norton & Company, 1992); American West from William E. Riebsame, "Ending the Range Wars?" *Environment*, May 1996.

12.   "Fastest growing" from Riebsame, op. cit. note 11; John C. Ryan and Aaron M. Best, "NEW Indicator: Northwest Employment Depends Less on Timber and Mining," press release, NEW, Seattle, Wash., 30 November 1994; poll data based on a sample of 1,000 adults in September 1995 by Yankelovich Partners, Inc., Norwalk, Conn., from Kate Stewart, Belden & Russonello, Washington, D.C., private communication and printout, 10 September 1996.

13.   Theodore Panayotou and Peter S. Ashton, *Not By Timber Alone: Economics and Ecology for Sustaining Tropical Forests* (Washington, D.C.: Island Press, 1992); copper figure based on *ICSG Copper Bulletin* (International Copper Study Group, Lisbon), May 1996, and on Daniel Edelstein, U.S. Geological Survey, Reston, Va., private communication and printout, 7 July 1996; oil figure based on United Nations (UN), *World Energy Supplies* (New York: various years), on UN, *Yearbook of World Energy Statistics* (New York: 1983), on UN, *Energy Statistics Yearbook* (New York: various years), and on British Petroleum (BP), *BP Statistical Review of World Energy* (London: Group Media & Publications, 1996); wood figure based on U.N. Food and Agriculture Organization (FAO), *Forest Products Yearbook* (Rome: various years), and on Crissis Vici, FAO, Rome, private communication, 20 August 1996.

14.   Jeffrey D. Sachs and Andrew M. Warner, "Natural Resource Abundance and Economic Growth," Development Discussion

Paper No. 517a, Harvard Institute for International Development, Cambridge, Mass., October 1995.

15. Edward A. Gargan, "Family Ties That Bind Growth: Corruption Is But One Obstacle to Indonesia's Future," *New York Times*, 9 April 1996; Barber, Johnson, and Hafild, op. cit. note 2; Robert Repetto, *The Forest for the Trees? Government Policies and the Misuse of Forest Resources* (Washington, D.C.: WRI, 1988).

16. Botswana from Durning and Brough, op. cit. note 11; Brazil and Côte d'Ivoire from Repetto, op. cit. note 15; Greenpeace International, "Logging In Solomon Islands Takes Its Toll," Greenpeace Briefing, Rome, undated, APC conference <rainfor.general>, 12 December 1995.

17. Oil reserves from BP, op. cit. note 13; size of European subsidies from OECD, *Agricultural Policies, Markets and Trade in OECD Countries* (Paris: 1996).

18. Coal policies from OECD, International Energy Agency (IEA), *Energy Policies of IEA Countries* (Paris: various years), and from Evsey Gurvich et al., "Impact of Russian Energy Subsidies on Green-house Gas Emissions," preliminary draft report to OECD Environment Directorate, Paris, 1995.

19. Increasing farm concentration from U.S. Bureau of the Census, *Historical Statistics of the United States: Colonial Times to 1970* (Washington, D.C.: GPO, 1975), and from U.S. Bureau of the Census, *Statistical Abstract of the United States 1994* (Washington, D.C.: 1994; subsidy distribution from Paul Faeth, *Growing Green: Enhancing the Economic and Environmental Performance of U.S. Agriculture* (Washington, D.C.: WRI, 1995).

20. Réda Soufi and Mark Tuddenham, "The Reform of European Union Common Agricultural Policy," in Robert Gale and Stephan Barg, eds., *Green Budget Reform: An International Casebook of Leading Practices* (London: Earthscan, 1995); grain use percentages are computed relative to the sum of produc-

tion and stock drawdowns for 1995 and are from U.S. Department of Agriculture (USDA), "Production, Supply, and Distribution" (electronic database) (Washington, D.C.: 1996).

21. OECD, op. cit. note 17. Figures exclude Turkey.

22. Rory McLeod, "Market Access Issues for the New Zealand Seafood Trade," New Zealand Fishing Industry Board, Wellington, 1996; $54 billion from FAO, *Marine Fisheries and the Law of the Sea: A Decade of Change*, FAO Fisheries Circular No. 853 (Rome: 1993); oceanic fish catch from "World Fishery Production as of 31 October 1996," from Maurizio Perotti, Fishery Information, Data, and Statistics Unit, FAO, Rome, private communication, 8 November 1996; Peter Weber, "Protecting Oceanic Fisheries and Jobs," in Lester R. Brown et al., *State of the World 1995* (New York: W.W. Norton & Company, 1995).

23. On the competitive advantages of large companies, see John Kenneth Galbraith, *Economics and the Public Purpose* (Boston: Houghton Mifflin, 1973).

24. Barber, Johnson, and Hafild, op. cit. note 2.

25. Tax breaks from U.S. Congress, op. cit. note 1; market share from U.S. Department of Energy (DOE), Energy Information Administration (EIA), *Monthly Energy Review—August 1996* (Washington, D.C.: GPO, 1996).

26. Figure 8–1 and data in text are based on OECD, IEA, *Coal Prospects and Policies in IEA Countries, 1987 Review* (Paris: 1988), on OECD, op. cit. note 18, and on OECD, IEA, *Coal Information* (Paris: various years), with costs converted using a 1995 exchange rate.

27. C. Ford Runge, "The Environmental Impacts of Agricultural and Forest Subsidies," in OECD, *Subsidies and Environment: Exploring the Linkages* (Paris: 1996).

28. Bjorn Larsen and Anwar Shah, "World Fossil Fuel Subsidies and Global Carbon

Emissions," background paper for *World Development Report 1992*, World Bank, Washington, D.C., 1992; figure of 15 based on U.N. Development Programme, *Human Development Report 1994* (New York: Oxford University Press, 1994).

29. Relationship between income and expenditures on energy in Indonesia and other developing countries from Christine Kerr and Leslie Citroen, "Household Expenditures on Infrastructure Services," background paper for *World Development Report 1994*, World Bank, Washington, D.C., undated; for relationship in United States, see James Poterba, "Tax Policy to Combat Global Warming: On Designing a Carbon Tax," in Rudiger Dornbusch and James Poterba, eds., *Global Warming: Economic Policy Responses* (Cambridge, Mass.: The MIT Press, 1991); for relationship in Western Europe, see Mark Pearson, "Equity Issues and Carbon Taxes," in OECD, *Climate Change: Designing a Practical Tax System* (Paris: 1993).

30. Bjorn Larsen and Anwar Shah, "Global Climate Change, Energy Subsidies and National Carbon Taxes," in Lans Bovenberg and Sijbren Cnossen, eds., *Public Economics and the Environment in an Imperfect World* (Boston: Kluwer Academic Press, 1995); energy waste from U.S. Congress, Office of Technology Assessment, *Energy Efficiency Technologies for Central and Eastern Europe* (Washington, D.C.: GPO, 1993); subsidy developments from Gurvich et al, op. cit. note 18.

31. Larsen and Shah, op. cit. note 30; World Bank, Energy Development Division, *Review of Electricity Tariffs in Developing Countries During the 1980s*, Industry and Energy Department Working Paper, Energy Series Paper No. 32 (Washington, D.C.: 1990); Gregory K. Ingraham and Marianne Fay, "Valuing Infrastructure Stocks and Gains from Improved Performance," background paper for *World Development Report 1994*, World Bank, 1994.

32. Giancarlo Tosato, "Environmental Implications of Support to the Electric Sector

in Italy: A Case Study," preliminary draft report to OECD Environment Directorate, Paris, 1995, cited in Laurie Michaelis, "The Environmental Implications of Energy and Transport Subsidies," in OECD, op. cit. note 27; tax breaks from Koplow, op. cit. note 4; loss on power sales from DOE, EIA, *Federal Energy Subsidies: Direct and Indirect Interventions in Energy Markets* (Washington, D.C.: GPO, 1992).

33. U.S. Congress, op. cit. note 1; Tim Fisher, Australian Conservation Foundation, Fitzroy, Victoria, Australia, private communication, 8 July 1996; Sergei Bobyliev and Bo Libert, "Prospects for Agricultural and Environmental Policy Integration in Russia," in OECD, *Agriculture and the Environment in the Transition to a Market Economy* (Paris: 1994); figure of $13 billion from Ingraham and Fay, op. cit. note 31.

34. U.S. Congress, op. cit. note 1.

35. Sandra Postel, *Last Oasis: Facing Water Scarcity* (New York: W.W. Norton & Company, 1992); Bobyliev and Libert, op. cit. note 33.

36. Subsidy distribution from World Bank, *World Development Report 1994* (New York: Oxford University Press, 1994).

37. Access to clean water and electricity from ibid.; Kerr and Citroen, op. cit. note 29.

38. A.C. Pigou, *The Economics of Welfare* (New York: AMS Press, 1978); R.H. Coase, "The Problem of Social Cost," *Journal of Law and Economics*, October 1960.

39. Frank Muller, "Tax Credits and the Development of Renewable Energy in California," in Gale and Barg, op. cit. note 20.

40. Edward C. Wolf, "Raising Agricultural Productivity," in Lester R. Brown et al., *State of the World 1987* (New York: W.W. Norton & Company, 1987); continuing fertilizer subsidies from Sanjeev Gupta, Kenneth Miranda, and Ian Parry, "Public Expenditure Policy and the Environment: A Review and Synthesis," IMF Working Paper, IMF, Washington,

D.C., 1993; continuing pesticide subsidies from Jumanah Farah, "Pesticide Policies in Developing Countries: Do They Encourage Excessive Use?" World Bank Discussion Paper 238, World Bank, Washington, D.C., 1994.

41. Howard Geller and Scott McGaraghan, "Successful Government-Industry Partnership: The U.S. Department of Energy's Role in Advancing Energy-Efficient Technologies," American Council for an Energy-Efficient Economy, Washington, D.C., 1996.

42. Ibid.

43. R&D spending levels from OECD, op. cit. note 18; energy use growth statistics from ibid., and from BP, op. cit. note 13, with wind growth statistics from Paul Gipe, Paul Gipe & Associates, Tehachapi, Calif., private communication, 4 September 1996, and solar growth statistics from Bill Murray, Strategies Unlimited, Mountain View, Calif., private communication, 10 September 1996. Growth figure for solar cells is based on domestic sales of solar cells, not on electricity generated.

44. Keith Kozloff and Olatokumbo Shobowale, *Rethinking Development Assistance for Renewable Electricity* (Washington, D.C.: WRI, 1994).

45. Ibid.; Christopher Flavin and Nicholas Lenssen, *Power Surge: Guide to the Coming Energy Revolution* (New York: W.W. Norton & Company, 1994).

46. Christina Olivecrona, "Wind Energy in Denmark," in Gale and Barg, op. cit. note 20.

47. Kozloff and Shobowale, op. cit. note 44; Neelam Mathews, "Dynamic Market Rapidly Unfolds," *Windpower Monthly*, September 1994; Neelam Mathews, "Tax Credits Just a Catalyst," *Windpower Monthly*, July 1995; Christopher Flavin, "Wind Power Growth Accelerates," in Lester R. Brown, Christopher Flavin, and Hal Kane, *Vital Signs 1996* (New York: W.W. Norton & Company, 1996).

48. Brazil from Lester R. Brown, Christopher Flavin, and Sandra Postel, *Saving the Planet: How To Shape an Environmentally Sustainable Global Economy* (New York: W.W. Norton & Company, 1991); Ed Piasecki, Mineral Policy Center, Washington, D.C., private communication, 4 October 1996; Farah, op. cit. note 40; OECD, *Agricultural Policies, Markets, and Trade in the Central and Eastern European Countries, the New Independent States, and China* (Paris: 1995); Gurvich et al., op. cit. note 18; FAO, *Fertilizer Yearbook* (Rome: 1996); BP, op. cit. note 13.

49. OECD, op. cit. note 18; environmental side effects of imported coal from Ronald P. Steenblik and Panos Coroyannikis, "Reform of Coal Policies in Western and Central Europe: Implications for the Environment," *Energy Policy*, Vol. 23, No. 6, 1995.

50. Production drop from OECD, op. cit. note 18; David Waddington and David Parry, "Coal Policy in Britain: Economic Reality or Political Vendetta?" in Chas Critcher, Klaus Schubert, and David Waddington, eds., *Regeneration of the Coalfield Areas: Anglo-German Perspectives* (London: Pinter, 1995).

51. Waddington and Parry, op. cit. note 50.

52. Soufi and Tuddenham, op. cit. note 20; Robert Greene, "President Signs Farm Legislation," *Philadelphia Inquirer*, 5 April 1996.

53. Brian Chamberlin, *Farming and Subsidies: Debunking the Myths* (Pukekohe, New Zealand: Euroa Farms, 1996).

54. Indonesia from Einar Hope and Balbir Singh, *Energy Price Increases in Developing Countries: Case Studies of Colombia, Ghana, Indonesia, Malaysia, Turkey, and Zimbabwe*, Policy Research Working Paper 1442 (Washington, D.C.: World Bank, 1995), and from Kerr and Citroen, op. cit. note 29.

55. Targeting techniques from Margaret E. Grosh, "Toward Quantifying the Trade-off: Administrative Costs and Incidence in Targeted Programs in Latin America," in Domi-

nique van de Walle and Kimberly Nead, eds., *Public Spending and the Poor: Theory and Evidence* (Baltimore, Md.: Johns Hopkins University Press, for the World Bank, 1995); kerosene stamps from Rhamesh Bhatia, "Energy Pricing in Developing Countries: Role of Prices in Investment Allocation and Consumer Choices," in Corazón Morales Siddayao, ed., *Criteria for Energy Pricing Policy* (London: Graham & Trotman, Ltd., 1985); Jamshid Heidarian and Gary Wu, *Power Sector Statistics for Developing Countries, 1987–1991* (Washington, D.C.: World Bank, 1994).

56. U.S. government support from Koplow, op. cit. note 4.

Chapter 9. Learning from the Ozone Experience

1. Richard Elliot Benedick, *Ozone Diplomacy* (Cambridge, Mass.: Harvard University Press, 1991); United Nations Environment Programme (UNEP), *Environmental Effects of Ozone Depletion: 1994 Assessment* (Nairobi: 1994).

2. Benedick, op. cit. note 1; 159 ratifications from Gilbert Bankobeza, Secretariat for the Vienna Convention and the Montreal Protocol, UNEP, Nairobi, private communication, 8 November 1996.

3. Figure 9–1 is Worldwatch estimates, based on data for 1950–59 from Fluorocarbon Program Panel, "Production, Sales, and Calculated Release of CFC-11 and CFC-12," Chemical Manufacturers Association, Washington, D.C., December 1990, and on data for 1960–95 from, most recently, Sharon Getamal, DuPont, Wilmington, Del., private communication, 15 February 1996; January 1996 deadline from Elizabeth Cook, "Marking a Milestone in Ozone Protection: Learning from the CFC Phase-Out," World Resources Institute (WRI), Washington, D.C., January 1996, and from U.S. Environmental Protection Agency (EPA), "Ozone Layer

Awareness Week, September 16–23, 1995," Washington, D.C., July 1995.

4. World Meteorological Organization (WMO), *Scientific Assessment of Ozone Depletion: 1994* (Geneva: 1995); WMO, "Stronger Ozone Decline Continues," press release, 12 March 1996; "Antarctic Ozone Hole Appears Headed for Record-Setting Season," *Washington Post*, 1 November 1996; J.R. Herman et al., "UV-B Increases (1979–1992) from Decreases in Total Ozone," *Geophysical Research Letters*, 1 August 1996.

5. Michael Grubb et al., *The Earth Summit Agreements: A Guide and Assessment* (London: Earthscan, 1993); "More Than 100 Countries Agree On International Desertification Treaty," *International Environment Reporter*, 29 June 1994; "Proposal on POPs, NO_x, Heavy Metals to be Considered by UNEP at January Meeting," *International Environment Reporter*, 4 September 1996.

6. UNEP, op. cit. note 1; Herman et al., op. cit. note 4.

7. Tolba quote from Benedick, op. cit. note 1.

8. Edward A. Parson, "Protecting the Ozone Layer," in Peter M. Haas, Robert O. Keohane, and Marc A. Levy, *Institutions for the Earth* (Cambridge, Mass.: The MIT Press, 1993); Douglas G. Cogan, *Stones in a Glass House: CFCs and Ozone Depletion* (Washington, D.C.: Investor Responsibility Research Center, 1988).

9. Benedick, op. cit. note 1; Mario J. Molina and F. Sherwood Rowland, "Stratospheric Sink for Chlorofluoromethanes: Chlorine Atom-Catalysed Destruction of Ozone," *Nature*, 28 June 1974; "Ozone Layer Chemists Represent Nobel 'First,'" *Nature*, 19 October 1995.

10. Parson, op. cit. note 8; Madhava Sarma, Executive Secretary, Secretariat for the Vienna Convention and the Montreal Protocol, UNEP, Nairobi, private communication, 7 November 1996.

11. Parson, op. cit. note 8.

12. Debora MacKenzie, "How to Use Science and Influence People," *New Scientist*, 29 April 1989; "Next Intergovernmental Panel Chair Urges More Research by Developing Nations," *International Environment Reporter*, 18 September 1996.

13. J.C. Farman, B.G. Gardiner, and J.D. Shanklin, "Large Losses of Total Ozone in Antarctica Reveal Seasonal ClO_x/NO_x Interaction," *Nature*, 16 May 1985; Parson, op. cit. note 8.

14. Paul Brodeur, "The Annals of Chemistry," *The New Yorker*, 9 June 1986; Cogan, op. cit. note 8.

15. Benedick, op. cit. note 1; Peter M. Morrisette, "The Evolution of Policy Responses to Stratospheric Ozone Depletion," *Natural Resources Journal*, Summer 1989.

16. Benedick, op. cit. note 1; James Cameron and Juli Abouchar, "The Status of the Precautionary Principle in International Law," in David Freestone and Ellen Hey, eds., *The Precautionary Principle and International Law: The Challenge of Implementation* (The Hague: Kluwer Law International, 1996).

17. "Montreal Protocol on Substances That Deplete the Ozone Layer," in Lakshman D. Guruswamy, Sir Geoffrey W. R. Palmer, and Burns H. Weston, eds., *International Environmental Law and World Order*, Supplement of Basic Documents (St. Paul, Minn.: West Publishing Co., 1994); bromine point from WMO, *Scientific Assessment*, op. cit. note 4; Duncan Brack, *International Trade and the Montreal Protocol* (London: Earthscan, for the Royal Institute of International Affairs, 1996). The protocol's trade provisions also foresaw restricting trade in products made using chlorofluorocarbons, although in 1993 the parties decided for the time being that this was not feasible.

18. Parson, op. cit. note 8; Cogan, op. cit. note 8; Benedick, op. cit. note 1.

19. Article 6, "Montreal Protocol," op. cit. note 17; Edward A. Parson and Owen Greene, "The Complex Chemistry of the International Ozone Agreements," *Environment*, March 1995.

20. William K. Stevens, "Ozone Loss Over the U.S. is Found to be Twice as Bad as Predicted," *New York Times*, 5 April 1991; National Aeronautics and Space Administration, "Scientists Say 'Arctic Ozone Hole' Increasingly Likely," press release, Washington, D.C., 3 February 1992.

21. Parson and Greene, op. cit. note 19; ozone-depleting potential of HCFCs from WMO, *Scientific Assessment*, op. cit. note 4.

22. WMO, *Scientific Assessment*, op. cit. note 4; A.D. Anbar and Y.L. Yung, "Methyl Bromide: Ocean Sources, Ocean Sinks and Climate Sensitivity," *Global Biogeochemical Cycles*, March 1996; Parson and Greene, op. cit. note 19.

23. WMO, *Scientific Assessment* op. cit. note 4; UNEP, *1994 Report of the Methyl Bromide Technical Options Committee for the 1995 Assessment of the Montreal Protocol on Substances That Deplete the Ozone Layer* (Nairobi: 1994).

24. "Parties to Montreal Protocol Agree to Phase Out Methyl Bromide by 2010," *International Environment Reporter*, 13 December 1995.

25. Under protocol rules, the phaseout schedule for an already controlled chemical can be changed by the parties by a mere "adjustment" to the protocol, bypassing the need for ratification by national parliaments. Adding a new chemical to the list of controlled substances does require a formal amendment, however, which needs to be ratified, per Donald M. Goldberg, "Procedures for Adopting and Amending Conventions and Protocols" (draft), Center for International Environmental Law–U.S., Washington, D.C., unpublished, undated; ratification information from Bankobeza, op. cit. note 2.

26. Lee A. Kimball, *Treaty Implementation: Scientific and Technical Advice Enters a New Stage*

(Washington, D.C.: American Society of International Law, 1996); Submission of the Technology and Economic Assessment Panel of the Montreal Protocol, presented by Co-chairs Stephen O. Andersen, Suely Carvalho, and Lambert Kuijpers, August 1995; Melissa Taylor, Office of the U.S. Global Change Research Program, Washington, D.C., private communication, 17 September 1996.

27. Stephen O. Andersen, EPA, Washington, D.C., private communication, 16 October 1996; Parson, op. cit. note 8; Benedick, op. cit. note 1.

28. Benedick, op. cit. note 1; Ian H. Rowlands, *The Politics of Global Atmospheric Change* (Manchester, U.K.: Manchester University Press, 1995).

29. Rowlands, op. cit. note 28; Benedick, op. cit. note 1.

30. Rowlands, op. cit. note 28.

31. Ibid.

32. Estimates from Alliance for Responsible CFC Policy, cited in Cynthia Pollock Shea, *Protecting Life on Earth: Steps to Save the Ozone Layer*, Worldwatch Paper 87 (Washington, D.C.: Worldwatch Institute, December 1988); Benedick, op. cit. note 1.

33. Forest Reinhardt, "DuPont Freon Products Division (A)," Harvard Business School case study, Cambridge, Mass., 28 March 1995; Cogan, op. cit. note 8.

34. Reinhardt, op. cit. note 33; Bronwen Maddox, "Industry Heated over CFC Ban," *Financial Times*, 25 November 1992.

35. Curtis A. Moore, "Industry Responses to the Montreal Protocol," *Ambio*, October 1990; WMO, *Scientific Assessment*, op. cit. note 4; Arjun Makhijani and Kevin Gurney, *Mending the Ozone Hole: Science, Technology, and Policy* (Cambridge, Mass.: The MIT Press, 1995).

36. Intergovernmental Panel on Climate Change (IPCC), *Climate Change 1994: Radiative Forcing of Climate Change and an Evalua-*

tion of the IPCC IS92 Emission Scenarios (Cambridge: Cambridge University Press, 1994); Steven E. Schwarzbach, "CFC Alternatives Under a Cloud," *Nature*, 27 July 1995; T.K. Tromp et al., "Potential Accumulation of a CFC-Replacement Degradation Product in Seasonal Wetlands," *Nature*, 27 July 1995.

37. Benedick, op. cit. note 1.

38. Alternative Fluorocarbons Environmental Acceptability Study, *Production, Sales and Atmospheric Release of Fluorocarbons through 1994* (Washington, D.C.: 1995); IPCC, *Climate Change: The IPCC Response Strategies* (Washington, D.C.: Island Press, 1991); carbon emissions from Christopher Flavin and Odil Tunali, *Climate of Hope: News Strategies for Stabilizing the World's Atmosphere*, Worldwatch Paper 130 (Washington, D.C.: Worldwatch Institute, June 1996).

39. UNEP, *1994 Report of the Economic Options Committee for the 1995 Assessment of the Montreal Protocol on Substances That Deplete the Ozone Layer* (Nairobi: 1994); Table 9–1 is based on the following: UNEP, *1994 Report of the Technology and Economics Assessment Panel for the 1995 Assessment of the Montreal Protocol on Substances That Deplete the Ozone Layer* (Nairobi: 1994); Greenpeace International, *No Excuses* (The Hague: 1995); Ed Ayres and Hilary French, "The Refrigerator Revolution," *World Watch*, September/October 1996; Calor Gas Refrigeration, *Calor Gas News* (Slough, U.K.) Winter 1995; "Ozone-Friendly Spray Foam Introduced," *Global Environmental Change Report*, 26 July 1996; Peter Mapleston, "Appliance OEMs Gain Wider PUR Foaming Options, *Modern Plastics*, March 1996; "Changing Climate for Spray Packaging," *Manufacturing Chemist*, March 1996; "Early Phaseout of Aerosol CFCs Largely Unheralded," *Ozone Depletion Network Online Today* (Environmental Information Network, Inc.), 5 February 1996; Don Hinrichsen, "Fixing the Ozone Hole is a Work in Progress," *Amicus Journal*, Fall 1996; Rob Edwards, "Firefighters Abandon Halons for Water," *New Scientist*, 20 July 1996; Patric McCon, "Replacements for Halogenated Fire Extinguishing

Agents in Fixed Systems: Where We Stand," *Professional Safety*, April 1996; UNEP, op. cit. note 23; Melanie Miller, ed., *The Technical and Economic Feasibility of Replacing Methyl Bromide in Developing Countries: Case Studies in Zimbabwe, Thailand and Chile* (Washington, D.C.: Friends of the Earth, 1996); Dan Strub, ed., *Into the Sunlight: Exposing Methyl Bromide's Threat to the Ozone Layer* (Washington, D.C.: Friends of the Earth, 1992).

40. Benedick, op. cit. note 1; Curtis Moore and Alan Miller, *Green Gold* (Boston, Mass.: Beacon Press, 1994); Hinrichsen, op. cit. note 39; International Cooperative for Ozone Layer Protection (ICOLP), "The International Cooperative for Ozone Layer Protection (ICOLP), 1990–1995, A New Spirit of Industry and Government Cooperation," Washington, D.C., June 1995. The founding members of ICOLP were AT&T, Boeing, Digital, Ford, General Electric, Honeywell, Motorola, Nortel, and Texas Instruments.

41. UNEP, *1994 Report of the Economic Options Committee*, op. cit. note 39; Brack, op. cit. note 17.

42. Elizabeth Cook, "Wrapping it Up," in Elizabeth Cook, ed., *Ozone Protection in the United States: Elements of Success* (Washington, D.C.: WRI, 1996).

43. UNEP, *1994 Report of the Technology and Economics Assessment Panel*, op. cit. note 39; UNEP, Industry and Environment Office, "Non-Fluorocarbon Alternatives for Refrigeration and Air Conditioning," *OzonAction Special Supplement No. 2* (UNEP, Paris), September 1994.

44. Miller, op. cit. note 39; UNEP, op. cit. note 23.

45. "Not-in-Kind ODS Alternatives: How Big a Role Will They Play?," *Global Environmental Change Report*, 24 June 1993; Elizabeth Cook, "Overview," in Cook, op. cit. note 42.

46. Brack, op. cit. note 17; David Rotman, "Dawn of the Post-CFC Era," *Chemical Week*, 17 January 1996; Jenny Luesby, "Hoechst Pulls out of CFC Substitutes," *Financial Times*, 6 June 1996; David Stirpe and Kevin Faye, Alliance for Responsible Atmospheric Policy, Memo to Alliance Members, "Results of Vienna Montreal Protocol Meeting," Arlington, Va., 29 December 1995; David Stirpe, Alliance for Responsible Atmospheric Policy, Memo to Alliance Members, "Montreal Protocol Working Group Meeting—August 26–29, 1996," Washington, D.C., 3 September 1996; International Climate Change Partnership, "ICCP Supports U.S. Call for Long-Term Focus on Climate Change Issue," press release, 17 July 1996; W. Ross Stevens III, DuPont, Wilmington, Del., private communication, 31 July 1996.

47. UNEP, *1994 Report of the Economic Options Committee*, op. cit. note 39; Pamela S. Zurer, "As CFC Ban Quietly Comes Into Force, Attention Turns To Other Concerns," *Chemical & Engineering News*, 4 December 1995; Cook, op. cit. note 3; Global Climate Coalition, "U.S. Business Faults Clinton Administration Climate Change Policy, Foresees Significant Negative Job, Trade, Economic Impacts," press release, Washington, D.C., 17 July 1996; Brodeur, op. cit. note 14.

48. Benedick, op. cit. note 1; Armin Rosencranz and Reina Milligan, "CFC Abatement: The Needs of Developing Countries," *Ambio*, October 1990; Peter Otinda, Climate Network Africa, "Negotiate but...No Solution Without Equity Consideration," *Eco* (NGO newsletter), Second Conference of the Parties, Geneva, 8 July 1996.

49. Benedick, op. cit. note 1.

50. Richard J. Smith, chief U.S. negotiator for the London Amendments, "The Ozone Layer and Beyond—Towards a Global Environmental Diplomacy," remarks to the American Chemical Society, Washington, D.C., 24 August 1994; Benedick, op. cit. note 1.

51. Benedick, op. cit. note 1; Multilateral Fund for the Implementation of the Montreal Protocol, "Working Together to Protect the Ozone Layer," brochure, Montreal, undated;

"London Amendments to the Montreal Protocol on Substances that Deplete the Ozone Layer with Annexes (1990)," in Guruswamy, Palmer, and Weston, op. cit. note 17.

52. The Global Environment Facility (GEF) is also a joint initiative of the World Bank and U.N. agencies; since its replenishment in 1993, the GEF's voting mechanism has been somewhat similar to the ozone model, per GEF brochure, Washington, D.C., December 1991; GEF, "Instrument for the Establishment of the Restructured Global Environment Facility," Report of the GEF Participants Meeting, Geneva, Switzerland, 14–16 March 1994; Elizabeth R. DeSombre and Joanne Kauffman, "The Montreal Protocol Multilateral Fund: Partial Success Story," in Robert O. Keohane and Marc A. Levy, eds., *Institutions for Environmental Aid* (Cambridge, Mass.: The MIT Press, 1996); COWIconsult, "Study on the Financial Mechanism of the Montreal Protocol," Draft Final Report, UNEP, Nairobi, March 1995.

53. Executive Committee of the Multilateral Fund, "Funds Allocated by Country and Sector" (electronic database), Montreal, October 1996; Executive Committee of the Multilateral Fund, "Total ODS to be Phased Out by Country and Sector (ODP Tonnes)" (electronic database), Montreal, October 1996; UNEP, "The Reporting of Data by the Parties to the Montreal Protocol on Substances That Deplete the Ozone Layer," 12 September 1996; COWIconsult, op. cit. note 52; Executive Committee of the Multilateral Fund, "Consolidated Progress Report," Montreal, 24 September 1996; Tony Hetherington, Deputy Chief Officer, Secretariat for the Multilateral Fund for the Implementation of the Montreal Protocol, Montreal, private communication, 22 October 1996. Different CFCs and halons vary in their ability to deplete ozone; the ODP value is the ratio of a given compound's ability to deplete ozone compared with the ability of a similar mass of CFC-11.

54. DeSombre and Kauffman, op. cit. note 52; COWIconsult, op. cit. note 52; Smith, op. cit. note 50; Amanda Wolf with David Reed, *Incremental Cost Analysis in Addressing Global Environmental Problems* (Washington, D.C.: World Wide Fund for Nature–International, 1994).

55. Caroline Mason, "Evaluation of Incremental Cost Methodologies for Phasing Out Ozone-Depleting Substances: Case Studies of India, Turkey, Jordan, and Zimbabwe," in Kenneth King and Mohan Munasinghe, eds., *Ozone Layer Protection: Country Incremental Costs* (Washington, D.C.: GEF and World Bank, 1995); COWIconsult, op. cit. note 52.

56. Elizabeth R. DeSombre, Colby College, "Compliance Implications of the Multilateral Fund," presented at the International Conference on Ozone Protection Technologies, Washington, D.C., 21–23 October 1996; Owen Greene, "The Montreal Protocol: Implementation and Development in 1995," in J. Poole and R. Guthrie, eds., *Verification 1996: Arms Control, Environment, and Peacekeeping* (Boulder, Colo.: Westview Press, 1996); Alan Miller, Renewable Energy Policy Project, University of Maryland, College Park, Md., private communication, 24 October 1996.

57. Rowlands, op. cit. note 28; UNEP, Executive Committee of the Multilateral Fund, "Report of the Twentieth Meeting of the Executive Committee of the Multilateral Fund for the Implementation of the Montreal Protocol," Montreal, 18 October 1996; UNEP, "Report of the Seventh Meeting of the Parties to the Montreal Protocol on Substances That Deplete the Ozone Layer," Vienna, 5–7 December 1995.

58. Greene, op. cit. note 56; "Working Group Agrees to Propose $436.5 Million Budget for Developing Countries," *International Environment Reporter*, 4 September 1996.

59. Brack, op. cit. note 17.

60. UNEP, *1994 Report of the Economic Options Committee*, op. cit. note 39.

61. COWIconsult, op. cit. note 52; UNEP, *1994 Report of the Economic Options Committee*, op. cit. note 39.

62. Brack, op. cit. note 17; Multilateral Fund Secretariat, "Country Programme Summary Sheets," Montreal, October 1996.

63. Guy D. Phillips, "CFCs in the Developing Nations: A Major Economic Development Opportunity. Will the Institutions Help or Hinder?" *Ambio*, October 1990.

64. UNEP, Industry and Environment Office, "The OzonAction Programme: An Overview," <http://www.unepie.org/ozat/ozatfly.html>, viewed 7 November 1996; Stephen O. Andersen, EPA, remarks at Summit on Protection of the World's Climate, Washington, D.C., 5 September 1996; ICOLP, op. cit. note 40.

65. Parson and Greene, op. cit. note 19; Zurer, op. cit. note 47; Greene, op. cit. note 56; Brack, op. cit. note 17; "Vienna Plus Ten," *OzonAction* (UNEP, Paris), special supplement, November 1995; Marnie Stetson, "Relief for the Ozone Layer?" *World Watch*, July/August 1992; J. Raloff, "U.N. to Oversee Methyl Bromide Phaseout," *Science News*, 16 December 1995; Maria Nolan, Department of the Environment, London, U.K., "International Update on Methyl Bromide," remarks at the International Conference on Ozone Protection Technologies, Washington, D.C., 21–23 October 1996.

66. UNEP, *1994 Report of the Economic Options Committee*, op. cit. note 39; Organisation for Economic Co-operation and Development, *Environmental Taxes in OECD Countries* (Paris: 1995); Andrew Hoerner, "Taxing Pollution," and David Lee, "Trading Pollution," in Cook op. cit. note 42.

67. Brack, op. cit. note 17; UNEP, Industry and Environment Office, *Ozone Action*, various issues; Bankobeza, op. cit. note 2; Greene, op. cit. note 56.

68. Brack, op. cit. note 17; Greene, op. cit. note 56; "Financing May Accelerate Russian CFC Phaseout," *Global Environmental Change Report*, 10 May 1996.

69. Jim Vallette, "Deadly Complacency: US CFC Production, the Black Market, and Ozone Depletion," Ozone Action, Washington, D.C., September 1995; Brack, op. cit. note 17; "CFC Smuggling Highlighted at Environmental Crime Seminar," *Global Environmental Change Report*, 25 October 1996; "Chemical Production: Holed Up," *The Economist*, 9 December 1995.

70. Brack, op. cit. note 17; Julie Edelson Halpert, "Freon Smugglers Find Big Market," *New York Times*, 30 April 1995; Tom Watts-Fitzgerald, U.S. Department of Justice, Miami, Fla., "Illegal Trade: Enforcement and Prosecution," remarks at the International Conference on Ozone Protection Technologies, Washington, D.C., 21–23 October 1996; Luesby, op. cit. note 46; Tom Watts-Fitzgerald, U.S. Department of Justice, Miami, Fla., private communication, 5 November 1996.

71. Johnsee Lee, Industrial Technology Research Institute, Hsinchu, Taiwan, remarks at the International Conference on Ozone Protection Technologies, Washington, D.C., 21–23 October 1996; Brack, op. cit. note 17; "Europeans Calling for CFC Trade Ban," *Chemical Marketing Reporter*, 23 September 1996.

72. UNEP, Industry and Environment Office, "OzonAction Information Clearinghouse Database," <http://www.epa.gov/docs/ozone/intpol/oaic.html>, viewed 7 November 1996; Multilateral Fund Secretariat, op. cit. note 62.

73. UNEP, op. cit. note 53.

74. Figure 9–2 from WMO, *Scientific Assessment*, op. cit. note 4.

75. Steven Greenhouse, "The Greening of U.S. Diplomacy: Focus on Ecology," *New York Times*, 9 October 1995; Secretary of State Warren Christopher, "American Diplomacy and the Global Environmental Challenges of the 21st Century," address at Stanford University, Palo Alto, Calif., 9 April 1996.

76. Seth S. Dunn, "The Geneva Conference: Implications for U.N. Framework Convention on Climate Change," *International*

Environment Reporter, 2 October 1996; "Calendar of Selected Sustainable Development Meetings," *Earth Negotiations Bulletin* (International Institute for Sustainable Development, Winnipeg, Man., Canada), issued periodically.

77. Michael Prather et al., "The Ozone Layer: The Road Not Taken," *Nature*, 13 June 1996; F. Sherwood Rowland, University of California Irvine, comments prepared for the Round-Table Discussion on Global Climate Change, Washington, D.C., 11 June 1996; J.T. Houghton et al., eds., *Climate Change 1995: The Science of Climate Change, Contribution of Working Group I to the Second Assessment Report of the Intergovernmental Panel on Climate Change* (New York: Cambridge University Press, 1996); Stephen O. Andersen and Alan Miller, "Ozone Layer: The Road Not Taken" (letter to the editor), *Nature*, 1 August 1996.

78. Wallace S. Broecker, "Chaotic Climate," *Scientific American*, November 1995; Houghton et al., op. cit. note 77; Rowland, op. cit. note 77.

79. Elizabeth Cook and Alan Miller, "Framing Policies to Reduce Greenhouse Gas Emissions and Promote Technological Innovation: Lessons from Other Environmental Challenges," presented to Climate Change Analysis Workshop, Springfield, Va., 6–7 June 1996; James Wei, Dean, School of Engineering and Applied Science, Princeton University, "Source Control Technology: CFCs," in *Global Environmental Accords: Implications for Technology, Industry and International Relations*, Symposium Proceedings, Massachusetts Institute of Technology, Cambridge, Mass., 24–25 September 1992.

80. Global Climate Coalition, op. cit. note 47; "Moderate Climate Change Industry Coalition Sees Growing Support," *Inside EPA*, 13 September 1996.

81. Flavin and Tunali, op. cit. note 38; Business Council for Sustainable Energy, "Business Leaders Support U.S. Statement at Climate Negotiations," press release, Washington, D.C., 17 July 1996; UNEP, "Insurers Call for Cuts in Greenhouse Gas Emissions," Geneva/New York, press release, July 1996.

82. See, for example, P. Roy Vagelos, Chairman and Chief Executive Officer, Merck & Co., Inc., letter to Senator Claiborne Pell, 23 March 1994, Richard D. Godown, Senior Vice-President, Biotechnology Industry Association, letter to Senator Claiborne Pell, 21 June 1994, David R. Lambert, Executive Vice President, American Seed Trade Association, Inc., letter to Senator Claiborne Pell, 14 April 1994, and Dwayne Andreas, President and Chief Executive Officer, Archer Daniels Midland Company, letter to Colleagues, Senators, and Congressmen, 11 August 1994, all in "U.S. Ratification of the Convention on Biological Diversity, Comprehensive Packet of Relevant Documents," Bionet, Washington, D.C., undated.

83. David Leonard Downie, "UNEP and the Montreal Protocol," in Robert Bartlett, ed., *International Organizations and Environmental Policy* (Westport, Conn.: Greenwood Press, 1995); Elizabeth Cook, "Global Environmental Advocacy: Citizen Activism in Protecting the Ozone Layer," *Ambio*, October 1990.

84. Rowlands, op. cit. note 28; Andersen, op. cit. note 64.

Index

Now you can import
all the tables
and graphs from
State of the World 1997
and all other Worldwatch
publications into your
spreadsheet program,
presentation software,
and word processor
with the...

1997 WORLDWATCH DATABASE DISK

The Worldwatch Database Disk gives you current data from all Worldwatch publications, including the *State of the World* and *Vital Signs* annual book series, *World Watch* magazine, Worldwatch Papers, and Environmental Alert series books.

The disk covers trends from mid-century onward...much not readily available from other sources. All data are sourced, and are accurate, comprehensive, and up-to-date. Researchers, professors, reporters, and policy analysts use the disk to ..

- Design graphs to illustrate newspaper stories and policy reports
- Prepare overhead projections on trends for policy briefings, board meetings, and corporate presentations
- Create specific "what if?" scenarios for energy, population, or grain supply
- Overlay one trend onto another, to see how they relate
- Track long-term trends and discern new ones

Order the 1997 Worldwatch Database Disk for just $89 plus $4 shipping and handling. To order by credit card (Mastercard, Visa or American Express), call 1-800-555-2028, or fax to (202) 296-7365. Our e-mail address is wwpub@worldwatch.org. You can also order by sending your check or credit card information to:

Worldwatch Institute
1776 Massachusetts Ave., N.W.
Washington, DC 20036